Donated to

Visual Art Degree
Sherkin Island

Czech Cubism

Architecture, Furniture, and Decorative Arts

1910–1925

Czech Cubism

Architecture, Furniture, and Decorative Arts 1910–1925

Edited by
Alexander von Vegesack
With texts by
Milena B. Lamarová
Vladimír Šlapeta
Petr Wittlich
Jiří Šetlík
Josef Kroutvor
Olga Herbenová
François Burkhardt
Alessandro Mendini

Laurence King
Vitra Design Museum

Published in 1992 by Laurence King Publishing

A catalogue record for this book is available from the British Library

ISBN 1 85669 030 x

Printed and bound in Canada

Design and production
Stefanie Lew
Kevin C. Lippert
Translation from the Czech
Michal Schonberg
Editor
Käthe Roth
Editorial Assistant
Marie-Josée Arcand, CCA
Copy editor
Edward Tingley
Publications Manager
Christine Dufresne, CCA

Special thanks to
Tim Fast, Antje Fritsch, Clare Jacobson, Wolf-Dieter Thiem, Erika Updike, Ann C. Urban, and Lisa Wolf

The exhibition on which this book is based was prepared by the Museum of Decorative Arts, Prague, in collaboration with the National Technical Museum, Prague, and Vitra Design Museum, Weil am Rhein, Germany.

The exhibition was realised under the patronage of Václav Havel, President, Czechoslovak Federal Republic, and Richard von Weizsäcker, President, German Federal Republic.

Acknowledgments
The following individuals and institutions assisted with the demanding preparations of the exhibition:
Dr. Kateřina Dostálová, Museum of Decorative Arts, Prague
Dr. Karel Holešovský, Moravian Gallery, Brno
Dr. Daniela Karasová, Museum of Decorative Arts, Prague
Stanislava Korcová, Prague
Dr. Dagmar Koudelková, Moravian Gallery, Brno
Dr. Hana Lendrová, Regional Museum, Hradec Králové
Dr. Eliska Lysková, Moravian Gallery, Brno
Angelo Raguza, Rome
Jitka Rottová, Prague
Adriena Skálová, painter, member of the Academy
Zdeněk Svoboda, C.Sc., Prague
Dr. Věra Vokáčová, Museum of Decorative Arts, Prague
Dr. Mimi Wilms, Stedelijk Hoger Instituut Voor Visuelle Kommunikatieen, Amsterdam
The Embassy of the German Federal Republic in Prague
The organizers of the exhibition wish to express their gratitude for the help and cooperation provided by the above.

Contents

Foreword

About eighty years ago, in 1911, progressive young Czech architects, painters, sculptors, and theoreticians founded the Group of Plastic Artists, and just a year later they exhibited their work at the Municipal Hall in Prague. The following year, they participated in an exhibition in Munich, and in 1914 they were represented at the exhibition of the German Werkbund in Cologne. In a speech he made at the time, V. V. Štech, the Group's theoretician, identified the entry of Czech modern art into the European context as the result of a national culture created over the previous hundred years. He said that Prague had played a decisive role in the process, since it was the only centre and the only point of departure of Czech cultural activity; it thus was part of the spirit of Europe.

After the disruptions of wars and postwar events, the "return to Europe" is very real for Czechs today—not only in terms of culture, not only in Prague, but throughout the nation. The exhibition *Czech Cubism: Architecture and Design, 1910–1925* is one step in this direction: through it we are repaying a debt we owe not only to ourselves, but also to Europe, which is why it was conceived as a travelling exhibition. It is also significant that the last venture of this kind, which uncovered the phenomenon of Czech cubism, took place in Paris in 1966—that is, at a time of political relaxation. Cubist interior work was for the first time extensively incorporated into the 1969 exhibition *Czech Cubism* in Prague. At the very beginning of the years of normalization, the Museum of Decorative Arts managed to include in its exhibition schedule *Czech Cubist Interior*, representing a summation of the museum's specialized activity, but above all, of its collecting efforts. As early as 1951, the director of the museum, E. Poche, had purchased the first cubist furniture, a group by Josef Gočár. To Olga Herbenová (d. 1990), Milena Lamarová, and the other curators of the museum goes the credit for the systematic searching out, acquisition, and restoration of objects, resulting in the creation of the museum's largest and most complete collection. In the eighties, despite definite interest from abroad, it was not possible to exhibit the hitherto unknown material in Europe, although in 1984 the exhibition travelled to Japan.

Since the cubist collection of the Museum of Decorative Arts is linked with the portfolio of architectural drawings deposited at the National Technical Museum, this exhibition of Czech cubism includes the full breadth of its unique three-dimensional aspect—furniture, pictorial documentation, and architecture. The thoroughness of the exhibition was helped in no small measure by the co-operation and interest displayed by the Vitra Design Museum, whose director, Alexander von Vegesack, immediately understood the unusual nature and complexity of the Czech cubist phenomenon and its relationship to modern culture and design.

We hope that the unique contribution of Czech cubism from the early twentieth century will, at the century's end—thanks to this exhibition—reintroduce Czech culture into Europe.

Dr. Helena Koenigsmarková
Assistant Director, Museum of Decorative Arts, Prague

Foreword

More than eighty years ago, when the National Technical Museum at the Schwarzenberg Palace in Prague's Hradčany Castle first opened its collections to the public, visitors could view a large model of the St. Vít cathedral. The establishment of an architectural archive thus became part of the museum's birthright. The archive later evolved into a department of architecture and construction which documents the history of these fields, especially from the nineteenth and the first half of the twentieth centuries. In addition to its large archive, the museum owns an important collection of architectural models, and its technical library, with its wealth of literature on architecture and urbanism, has become essential to scientific research.

The cultural politics of recent years did not favour modern art or avant-garde architecture. Although the times of paying tribute to historicism – the traditionally oriented architecture of the fifties – are long gone, information on and exhibitions of Czech avant-garde work are still inaccessible or nonexistent, both abroad and at home. Architectural cubism is a specific aspect of the avant-garde: in the global context it was the only building style which, in the years 1910–1914 (that is, until the beginning of the First World War) and 1918–1924 (in the form of rondo-cubism) evolved in both theoretical and practical terms. This exhibition is therefore the first large, conceptually thorough presentation of Czech cubist architecture and design in relation to its time.

When we speak of Czech cubist architecture and design, it is clear that the principal task of preparing and realizing an appropriate exhibition rested with the Museum of Decorative Arts and the National Technical Museum, both in Prague, for these institutions have the most extensive collections and the most knowledgeable staff. (There is also a historical tradition of mutual co-operation: in 1940, during the Second World War, when the National Technical Museum did not have its own building, the Museum of Decorative Arts staged an exhibition called *Toward New Architecture* from the former's collection, dealing with buildings from the years 1918–1940). Another significant factor is the fact that the same circle of designers is involved in both parts of the exhibition. The names Josef Gočár, Pavel Janák, Vlastislav Hofman, Josef Chochol, and Otakar Novotný (other architects, even Jan Kotěra, were, of course, also influenced by cubism) are found on architectural documentation, as well as on furniture creations and designs. This attests to the fact that Czech cubism penetrated into all areas of the arts – the applied arts and architecture as well as fine art; it actually created a style, an aesthetic, and a life style.

This exhibition has an important mission: to remind the Czech public of the refinement of its past culture. It also serves as an invitation to foreigners to visit Prague, since the city, with its centuries of harmoniously blended architecture, richly deserves its label "the Jewel of Europe." A walking tour of the city should also include cubist architecture: Chochol's buildings below Vyšehrad, Gočár's At the Black Mother of God building, the cubist street lamp on Jungmann Square. We hope that this exhibition will serve as a guide.

Ivo Janoušek, Dip. Eng., C.Sc.
Director, National Technical Museum, Prague

Preface

Three decisive influences affected my work on the exhibition *Czech Cubism: Architecture and Design, 1910–1925.* The first was the deconstructivist architecture of our museum, designed by Frank O. Gehry; the second was an earlier project realized in co-operation with the Czechoslovak museums; and the third consisted of the friendly and collegial relations that developed during the collaboration with the Museum of Decorative Arts in Prague, and especially my respect for the admirable work of the curator Milena Lamarová.

If I had been an art historian I most certainly would have at some point come across the unique national phenomenon of Czech cubism. But I am not an art historian, and so my primary tool was not books and documents, but rather my enthusiasm about the artists and their works, which strengthened my resolve to document the unique collection in Prague's Museum of Decorative Arts and the broad range of architectural drawings and designs at the National Technical Museum in Prague.

Still, without the friendly relationships that were established, we would not have had a strong enough motivation to overcome the complications stemming from the current political transition. Nor would we have established such a lively approach to our theme, which I hope will be reflected in the exhibition.

I also consider the fact that the presidents of our two countries, Václav Havel and Richard von Weizsäcker, are patrons of the exhibition to be a confirmation of our renewed acquaintance and an appeal for more intensive exchanges.

Alexander von Vegesack
Director, Vitra Design Museum, Weil am Rhein

Otakar Novotný, teachers' housing, 1919, detail

On Cubism
Texts and Reflections

Texts and Contexts, 1910–1914

Milena Lamarová

In the period just before the First World War, the atmosphere in Europe was charged, filled with manifestos, programmes, and fantasies, most of them by artists trying to reformulate positions, means, and objectives. As if foreshadowing the coming catastrophic war, there was a feverish search for a model that would express the spiritual foundation of the person in a world increasingly dominated by industry and technology, in which new structural relationships of matter, energy, and space-time were being discovered.

Out of the ruins of the Secession flowed avant-garde European thought from north to south and from west to east, accompanied by anxiety, aggressiveness, protests, and declarations. Its legacy was provocation, cynicism, farce, and mystification: works which continue to excite us, although they have supposedly all been definitively analyzed, categorized, described, and evaluated.

No longer was the avant-garde concerned with only figurative art: it critiqued culture, protested against society. It was concerned with the articulation of a truthful image of the world. It was concerned with life. The spiritual and cultural unity of the nineteenth century had expired; there was nothing left to do but revolt and organize the resistance movement.

This may also explain why the avant-gardes integrated literature, architecture, applied arts, theatre, and dance. The artists themselves became theoreticians and critics. Beyond intellectualization, the gates into the realms of fantasy, utopia, and the world of visions were wide open. On club stages, in groups, newspapers, and magazines, cultural and creative efforts became institutionalized.

The avant-gardes of the first decade of the twentieth century had a very plastic topography. They did, however, have a common thematic denominator: in general, they were directed toward abstract expression. At the same time, they were revising the geometry of space in order to reach an understanding of its composition. In his 1913 essay "Les Peintres cubistes," Apollinaire wrote, "Geometry is for the plastic arts what grammar is for the art of writing. . . . The painters were quite naturally, as if by intuition, drawn toward dealing with possible measures of space, which in the language of modern studios are commonly and concisely referred to as the fourth dimension. . . . It is space as such, the dimension of infinity; it is this which gives plasticity to objects."[1]

Between 1909 and 1912, the Italian futurists published three seminal manifestos. The conclusion of the *Manifesto of the Futurist Painters* contains, among other things, a revolt against the tyranny of the words "harmony" and "taste," praise for every form of originality, regardless of how crazy or forced it might be, and expression and celebration of present-day life, ceaselessly and violently restructured by victorious science. The *Technical Manifesto of Futurist Painting* states, "For us the gesture will no longer be a captured moment of general dynamism; it will simply be immortalized dynamic feeling." The proclamation declares, " . . . motion and light destroy the substantiality of objects."[2] In Kasimir Malevich's *Manifesto of Suprematism*, published in 1915 in Petrograd, is a passage which extends in a broader sense to the problems of applied art. Malevich writes, "The sensations of running, standing, and sitting are first of all plastic sensations, which give impetus to the creation of appropriate 'utilitarian objects' and determine their material appearance. A table, a bed, and a chair are not utilitarian objects, but forms of a creative sensation. Thus the common conviction that all objects of daily use are the result of practical considerations is based on false assumptions. We have countless opportunities to prove to ourselves that we are never able to recognize the real practical value of things, and we will never manage to construct a truly practical and utilitarian object."[3]

In this context, two noteworthy influences came from northern Europe; as they spread through central Europe they left the same kind of impression as does a photographic negative: an imprint, but of a particular silhouette and hue. The first was the Edvard Munch exhibition, which in the Prague of 1905 caused a cultural explosion, and was greeted as a revelation. Munch's expressionist language aroused an ardent response among Czech artists. The second flowed from the views of German and Viennese modernists, who drew from the reformist tendencies of the Arts and Crafts movement. The German attitude, represented especially by the Werkbund, was directed not toward revolutionary destructiveness, but toward resolution of the relationship between art and production, a goal agreed on by such diverse personalities as Henry van de Velde, Hermann Muthesius, and Richard Riemerschmid, despite Adolf Loos's ironic commentaries.[4]

The German Werkbund (1907) set as its goal "the ennoblement of the artistic crafts, with the co-operation of art, industry, and crafts, through education, promotion, and responsible attitudes toward appropriate issues." Otto Wagner wrote, "Doubtless it may—indeed, must—reach the point that nothing visible to the eye can be created without the blessing of art,"[5] at the very same time as Jan Kotera, in Prague, and Walter Gropius, Richard Riemerschmid, and August Endell, in Germany, were designing the interiors of railway cars, and Peter Behrens was becoming the prototype of the modern industrial designer (his collaboration with AEG Berlin began in 1907).

The 1914 exhibition of the Werkbund in Cologne reflected the uncertainty of a Europe vacillating between the avant-gardes, the crafts, industrial design, and commerce. The interiors by Prague cubist architects drew considerable attention; the exhibition also included Bruno Taut's glass house, and among the other participants were Olbrich, Obrist, van de Velde, Pankok, Behrens, Endell, Gropius, Paul, and Riemerschmid.

Subsequent avant-gardes were aware of all the contradictory realities, but especially of the frustrating relationship between art, production, and commerce. In 1918 appeared the first *Manifesto of De Stijl*, the first *DADA Manifesto*, and Ozenfant and Jeanneret's *Manifesto of Purism*. But times had changed. The bitterness of the First World War had altered everything; the "imperial climate" described by Josef Kroutvor in his study *Fenomén 1910* (Phenomenon 1910) would never return. And yet cubism remained, recognized not as a style or a dogma, but as the point of departure for the modern perception of the world.

If we read even a fragmentary selection of the theoretical texts written between 1910 and 1914 by Prague architects, we recognize the reality, the thoroughness—indeed, the stubbornness—with which they, along with other European avant-gardists, pursued a subjective sense of life.

Notes

1. G. Apollinaire, "Les Peintres cubistes" (Paris, 1913), quoted in M. de Micheli, *Umělecké avantgardy dvacátého století* (Prague, 1964).
2. Italian futurism was known in Prague. Prampolini designed the set for the Teatro Sinttetico Futurista at the Švanda Theatre in Prague in 1921.
3. Quoted in M. de Micheli, *Umělecké avantgardy dvacátého století* (Prague, 1964).
4. See the essay "Přebyteční" (The Superfluous), quoted in Burkhardt, 1980, p. 104.
5. In Otto Wagner, *Moderne Architektur* (Vienna, 1914), p. 96.

Pavel Janák

"Od moderní architektury k architektuře" (From Modern Architecture to Architecture)

Styl, vol. 2 (1910), pp. 105–109

J. Gočár, house in Libodřice, 1912–1913, detail

Modern architects therefore behaved very materialistically, wanting to base their creations on construction and materials, because the expression of construction and the animation of materials comprise a materialistically narrowed principle; whenever it has appeared in history, it has always appeared at the beginning of new movements, and has always been soon abandoned—in favour of going beyond, toward the architectural form of the whole. The growth of architecture as a responsive, formative, and spiritual creation corresponds with the silencing of the material and construction elements and their subordination to the artistic intention. Even the modern architectural conception of the individualization of material—that is, the extraction of artistic form from the natural and physical properties of material—we find to be materialistic and directionless, and to result in the subordination of the architect's free creativity to the interpretation of material; it is advice and interdiction, which must necessarily result in a condition of flattening and monotony in modern architecture.

. . . We set our abstract thoughts and forms above the individual properties of materials. Not only do we respect, but we count on the strength and bearing properties of materials, which we expose, for the sake of the idea, to certain stresses and tensions.

. . . Finally, we also have more certain ideas for poetry in architecture, through which we elevate poetry from its subordinate position in Wagner's motto. If we have a criticism of modern architecture, it is that until now it contained much poetry in the sense that could be expressed by the term "poetry in architecture," but not enough architectural beauty.

Evolution very soon saw through the absurdity of this kind of appended poetry—which is why it was discarded, and things remained as before—the technical, naked skeleton.

. . . Until now modern architecture understood only—and historically it was the correct evolution—the problems of practical need; it barely understood at all the problem of space or the problem of matter and form. Modern architecture did not recognize these problems, and it was not sufficiently theoretical: this will be its future field of activity, if it is to be architecture.

It is possible to predict the future direction of architecture: creativity, in which artistic thought and abstraction will take over leadership from practicality, which cedes its place. It will advance in its pursuit of plastic form, and in the plastic realization of architectural concepts.

"Užitečnost uměleckého průmyslu" (The Usefulness of Artistic Industry)

Umělecký měsíčník, vol. 1 (1911–1912), pp. 147–149

The seminal reason for the birth of the nineteenth-century industrial arts is therefore not internal and artistic in the sense of art growing a new branch. It has more of a socio-cultural character: ideas and reforms in living, brought about by the democratization of education and by humanitarianism, were added to newly instituted protective and altruistic social benefits. There is no mistake here: tasteful living is more a demand, a prescription, a guide, a notion of cultural hygiene than a shift in nineteenth-century art; it is more a requirement for sustenance of life than the result of art.

Our interest in the industrial arts goes even further in the following sense: the plastic aspect of objects is more important to us than the utilitarian and motive aspect. To be perfectly clear: the shifting of interest to the plastic side does not mean negation of purpose, nor does it mean an effort to create useless things. Instead, it indicates that artistic interest has grown to the point that we no longer simply want to serve the industrial arts and create, out of a sense of duty, lamps, jewels, and inkwells, because that is what life demands. The minor arts grow in complementarity and conjunction with the rest of art because of our own inner need to create, not just for the good of society and out of necessity. In the past, art was used to create pillows, jewels, and so on; now it expresses itself in cups, trays, and so on. It is incumbent upon artists, who are led by conscious will toward form, to express as broadly as possible the newfound feelings of forms and relationships, to try them out in a number of realities and in all variations, in order to ensure their value and veracity. And production in a single material alone does not suffice: if form is to be a significant part of stylistic composition, it must be purified to the point of abstraction—that is, to its ultimate essence, which is valid in all materials (wood, glass, stone, etc.). It must be able to resist and conquer formally all of these materials without exception. This is how creativity in the minor arts comes to the aid of architecture: it does the preliminary work of architecture and complements its experiences.

In this regard, painters and sculptors will have the freedom of endeavour: they will create forms according to imagination, not market demand, as is the case with the industrial arts; as they do with paintings and sculptures, purchasers will choose this work primarily for its creative side.

"Hranol a pyramida" (The Prism and the Pyramid)

Umělecký měsíčník, vol. 1 (1911–1912), pp. 162–170

All shapes that occur in inanimate nature and are geometrically complex evolved with the collaboration of a third force. The oblique fall of rain is caused by the additional element of wind; similarly, snowdrifts, washouts, ravines, caves, sink-holes, and volcanoes are, in general, either positively or negatively created forms made out of inanimate matter by another invading force, which deforms it and diverts it from the natural form in which it was deposited. Crystallization offers the most beautiful example: here the invading force (crystallization) is so great in comparison to the weight that we can almost say that the weight of matter has no effect on crystallization; the force of crystallization itself seems to be some sort of a weight forcefully concentrated within matter; it is so powerful that it transforms itself, under all circumstances, into a concentrated, self-contained world.

. . . If, then, the vertical and horizontal bi-plane is the shape of rest and of the separated equilibrium of matter, the creation of obliquely shaped forms was preceded by more dramatic events and complex unions involving multiple forces.

The following conclusion can be drawn from all of this concerning the means of artistic creation: if inanimate matter is to be plastically overcome—that is, animated—so that something may happen within it, this must happen through the system of the third plane, which joins the natural bi-plane.

A beautiful parallel between the means of human activity and the means of artistic creation offers itself here: wedges, arrows, posts, knives, levers, all of which overcome matter physically, are generally oblique planes.

. . . In comparison to natural building, architecture is a superior activity. Generally, it combines two activities: technical, prismatic bi-planar construction and the abstract reconstitution of matter in a tri-planar system, be it oblique or curvilinear. The more dominant of the architectural impulses also creates the building's overall character.

. . . Baroque, as we know, augmented and affixed, intensified the expression of all shapes by further addition and agglomeration of matter: the pedestals and capitals of pillars, the architraves, and the cornices are more acutely profiled and extended farther out both as individual elements and as a whole; the slabs of architraves and the cornices are bevelled, and there are conically narrowed pilasters, consoles, and buttresses. Besides this means of intensifying expression of the original form as such, the Baroque discovered another way to reach abstraction, arising gradually and logically from this intensification: the rotation and movement of entire forms from their original, calm, antique position into planes standing obliquely and dramatically against the heart of the building. The pillars and posts in portals and the towers in the facades of churches are built obliquely against the diagonal, as if the matter of the building had come to life and erupted outward or withdrawn inward, moving all of the formerly flat composition of the architecture. In principle, the most abstract idea and opportunity is to allow a living, shaping force to remodel entire facades by lifting and by pressure, directed outward and inward to the foundation of the building.

. . . If Baroque abstraction consists of the strengthening and animation of matter and the moving of masses, then the principle of the northern style of architecture is quite the opposite: it overcomes the tranquillity and material quality of matter by delving into it, and by reducing matter in the direction of the third oblique plane.

"O nábytku a jiném" (Of Furniture and Other Matters)

Umělecký měsíčník, vol. 2 (1912–1913), pp. 21–29

There always were and always will be, side by side, cauldrons and goblets, rubber coats and vestments, granaries and great halls . . .

. . . The world is arranged in such a way that the human being draws upon, and always will, two separate spheres: the physical and the spiritual; as a result, technology and art are two independent, separate activities, which are, and will always be, simultaneously next to and independent of each other. A person is active in both spheres. Architecture and the industrial arts are therefore not a higher level of the technological. Technology is not directed by or subordinated to art.

It can no longer be claimed that all human activities should be ennobled by art, and it is no longer permissible to use one to fight against the other (by using technology—engineering projects, industry—against art, or by using art against technology). Art in particular should not be given the role of refining or tempering the world; it is a self-determined activity with no obligations outside of itself. Therefore: no more making life aesthetic—instead, life and art! Thus, furniture which used to be, is, and, by certain standards, always will be suited for merely practical—that is, non-artistic—human applications, nonetheless becomes the subject of art in other, higher states of spiritual life. This is because, although it appears to be inanimate matter, the mind demands that it be spatially oriented. It is the everlasting quest of the spirit to possess matter from all sides—by means of science to discover its measure, physical properties, chemistry, and so on. Our hearts demand that we explain its origin, reasons, and place in the universe through philosophy, and possess it emotionally by lending it form.

Pavel Janák, page from journal, 1912

. . . In every place where the spirit was thus active, the surface was changed, moved, as if in all its folds and waves it consisted of a mixture of matter, within, and of space, without. It should be pointed out that anything box-like in an apartment now gives us the feeling that it deprives space of air, that it devours space; works of art, even if they are of similar size, give satisfaction, though they take up the same amount of space. In compensation for the room they occupy, their animated surface seems to reflect space.

. . . Now, the new trend, guided by its primary concern with form, pays hardly any attention to all of this. We do not see the materials, we see in all of them only matter. We can say of the world of forms that for the time being the concern is generally with plastic ideas, and it is irrelevant in what material they are realized, be it rare or the most common. The monochromatic is welcomed, as is simple colour; materials that are coloured in this fashion are preferred because plastic relationships can interact more purely in them. Another characteristic of the new furniture is its unity; it looks as if it is made from one piece. The earlier period of applied art prided itself on its emphasis on construction, on how the furniture was built in terms of craftsmanship. It also emphasized externally the individual parts that make up the structure. Today, when what is valid is the attitude of spirit toward matter, and when the latter is turned toward the former according to its ideas and images, matter is rendered entirely secondary and subordinate to the members and elements of which the actual structure is built. We always think of the material whole, a whole in which the elements and the limbs (i.e., legs, posts, braces) lose their individuality and become nothing more than articulated matter in a particular place.

And so the ideational structure of the piece rises above its matter. It might be expressed, for instance, only in the edges, instead of in its earlier complete substantiality, and the external surfaces generally remain on the object to mark the path from reality to image.

"Obnova průčelí" (Renewal of the Facade)

Umělecký měsíčník, vol. 2 (1912–1913), pp. 85–93

If imagination and artistic depiction comprise some sort of a logical, contemporary, and sensitively created system of assembly and confrontation, in which objects and forms are brought into relationships or contrasts, they can do so only in relation to a common, all-encompassing base, which, for cubic purposes, is the picture plane. If I want to compare things which are generally separated, and to depict their relationship, I do so by considering and depicting them side by side, and at the same time by endowing them with all the properties that characterize their commonality.

The visual point of view thus created in architecture has a specific and characteristic entity: the facade. The spirit of the styles that issue from this point of view focus interest and energy particularly toward facades. All the other walls of the cube and the building are, of course, neglected, as if the entire content of the building were drawn into the facade and the gable. Nevertheless, if the side walls are plastically modelled, this is done through the spatial modelling of the plane, so that on the surface the cube appears to consist of two planes.

. . . So far, we know only that to make a space cubic, three-dimensional, is not, in our opinion, the creation of space, because it is no more than reality; creating the means to extract more than was here before—that is, creating volume and space—is achieved, above all, by spatial modelling of the surface areas; that is, we are leaning toward the expression of matter not centrally, but frontally.

Josef Chochol

"K funkci architektonického článku"
(On the Function of the Architectural Detail)

Styl 5 (1913), pp. 93–94

True art never seeks to ingratiate itself, to curry favour in exchange for the attention given to it; it knows no considerations besides its own laws, and lives its own life of imagination, even under circumstances of complete misunderstanding. Art simply does not have the need to please, and discounts the superficial motives that determine it. It discards all of this, along with the appropriate systems of decorative details and elements, regardless of how self-important or strict these claim to be. This is why, today, we have lost interest in minor architectural detail, and why we do not believe in it. We are enthusiastic about total form, felt and presented with excitement, form that is all-encompassing and has a total and instant effect. We do not want to taste, bite by bite, the separate parts of an object broken up by an overabundance of elements, and we do not need the unnecessary, obsolete systematic separation of forms into "fields of view," artificially outlined in dead planes to please the eye. We first and always demand and need the fresh excitement of new artistic intensities, springing from the tumultuous and glowing mass of contemporary life.

The decomposition into elements that we have in mind developed especially in the styles born of the Southern European psyche: it is found in the Greek styles, and in antiquity in general. As they were established far too rationally, they lack the elements of emotion, fantasy, and excitement that are related to our own Northern character. The separation into elements always gives the sense of assembly, of rational and painstaking construction, as opposed to the sense of ceaseless growth and movement with which we would be more comfortable.

We do not wish to disrupt that rare, clean, smooth effect of a modern creation—austere as well as fantastic—by unbearable impediments of multitudes of indifferent little ornaments and details. Just as modern technical means enable us to glance quickly across a landscape and gain an extraordinarily concentrated and synthetic sense of it, we also try to reach the sense of this speed, even instantaneity, in a synthetically rendered work.

Today's hurried character is in no way inclined toward the prolonged feasting of the eye on sweet and interesting surfaces, broken up by additions: it is not attracted by the selection of specific small particles on the surface, the elevation of individual points, or lines in front of or behind the surface, arranged into motifs lifelessly bound together ornamentally and pictorially, according to, for instance, the arrangement of water molecules shrunken radially on the freezing surface of a window pane. This ornamental predisposition, always suited to effeminate and formalistic personalities, does not fit today's trend toward masculinity, which gravitates toward the unusual and suggestive roughness of seeming vulgarity and always spontaneously favours the grandiose, effective simplicity of the inner concentration of matter, rather than exterior flatteries and superficial "charm." The mannered, ornamentalized interior architecture of a work might be conceivable today only in the sense that we see it very clearly in a certain phase of the Gothic, in which technology and fantasy work together. But while we have much sympathy for the Gothic sentiment, Gothic and its stylistic consequences are nonetheless, like antiquity, a finished chapter.

Josef Gočár, staircase of house on Tychon Street, 1913

Vlastislav Hofman

"Nový princip v architektuře" (The New Principle in Architecture)

Styl, vol. 5 (1913), pp. 13–24

We know the art of the primitive nations, the manifestation of a youthful, thirsty organism, strong and simple expression; although we can to a certain extent formally analyze it, we cannot know the reasons for its formal organization, as we do not have the perceptual ability of that period.

. . . New art uses the most conspicuous and expressive means, which are also formally the most abstract (effort toward simple expression). It does not merely create abstractions, it does not merely process moods, but rather it converts ideas from reality into artistic reality.

. . . Modern architecture does not require surface forms, which is why we dislike contaminating form with detail. The basic form is that which evolved from the inherent potential of matter (notion of the movement of matter); this potential is caused by the vision of a space and its interior.

Architecture organizes technical expression by rhythmic form, thereby creating its own original principal relationships of spaces. These are the property of art, they belong to the principles of architecture, and are exempt from the most recent scientific consequences of technology.

. . .The principle of "space in matter" seems to dispense entirely with the need for decoration.

Václav Vilém Štech

"České cesty k modernímu interiéru" (Czech Paths Toward a Modern Interior)

Written in 1914 for the Werkbund exhibition in Cologne; published in 1915 in the book *Čechische Bestrebungen um ein modernes Interieur*

. . . In our country—and this is symptomatic of the uncertainty of the times—the young architects first moved toward primitivism; they sought in the old art of the thirteenth and fourteenth centuries analogies to what they themselves were trying to achieve, which was as clean and naked a form as possible. Not until architects purged their practices of all capricious moments—that is, of the period's purely decorative quality—could they dare to bring their own work toward further practical and theoretical results. Of considerable influence was the similar, parallel work of the young generation of painters, who at that particular time were setting aside optical and modal impressionism and undertaking a critical revision of the fundamental principles of their art. The colour analysis and blotchy shapelessness of earlier art were being converted by the painters into concentrated and defined form, and naturalistic impressionism was replaced by compositional work. Architects were then able to cut into the stillness of the block by plastic treatment, reach deeper into its physical organism, and interfere with the natural ordering of its parts. They united elements, destroyed their autonomy, and subordinated to formal ideas the tectonic functions of the post, the pillar, the cornice, and the roof. Against construction, purpose, and material, they placed the idea of form; they entered into an active relationship with matter, and set it in motion. Motion was perceived as a spiritual activity which transformed matter: it was the assertion of creative will against mere existence, a more profound appropriation of the inorganic world and its conquest through expression. Architects now penetrated matter.

Earlier they had stopped at its frontiers, at the surface, much like painters, who were simultaneously building a new space for themselves. Architects were discovering the force of the third dimension, achieved through motion. The old frontiers of matter were broken and the block was animated first by compromises, for instance by an indication of plasticity; then it was deliberately and systematically interrupted by oblique planes, as the sensuous and graphic means of expressing creative activity.

. . . Furniture was treated like architecture. Each piece was a separate organism, related to others by virtue of growing under the same principles, in the same style—not by mere planar and decorative adaptation—into a tonally unified interior. The architects Gočár and Janák dared to go to the very limits of statics, creating in small objects—vases and so on—the fulcrum and balance, shaping planes into sharp profiles and deep incisions, bringing their art, through practice and conviction, toward the principles of the Gothic and the Baroque. They sympathized with the *Sturm und Drang* romanticism and emotional harmony of the second Rococo period.

. . . Simultaneously with painting, which arrived at the new conception of space in a plane by the shifting of axes, the changing of perspectives, and the planar transformation of depth relationships, architecture also changed the factual movement of matter through oblique plane into ideal movement, compacted into surface. In free architecture this meant the recovery of the facade as the unidirectional culmination of the sum of all spaces and their mutual relationship, and the movement of all creative forces active within the interior of the building. In furniture the inner growth of organisms was concentrated on the surface; these then seemed to solidify within the object, and the depth of motion was broken into planar elements.

. . . Only from such unified feeling can new space grow. It seems that we are concerned only with form, which is always personal and individual, but this is completely congruent with our direction. Contrary to theories (those formulated by Semper or Schmarsow), architecture does not begin with ornament, or with space: at the beginning of all creation is form. It is the expression of creative will, the sign erected by people against nature, albeit in accordance with its laws.

Josef Chochol, triplex below Vyšehrad, 1912–1913, detail of facade

The Road to Cubism

Petr Wittlich

In discussing why cubism achieved such remarkable heights in Bohemia, to the point of being considered the representative style of the modern era, not only in painting and sculpture but also in architecture and the applied arts, we must consider both the concrete relationships between artists and a number of more general circumstances. In the years preceding the First World War, cubism was in a sense the culmination of efforts by Czech artists to meet the standards of foreign art and to prove the worth of the national cultural endeavour by actively participating in the creation of contemporary European cultural values. This initiative grew out of the earlier discovery by Czech painters of what was beyond their cultural horizon—in particular, the phenomenon of French modern painting.

In the 1880s, young Czech artists, dissatisfied with the poor standard at the Prague Academy of Painting, departed en masse for Munich. The most assertive among them, including Alfons Mucha and František Kupka, finally headed for Paris and managed to prove themselves even there. Famous for its belles lettres and poetry, Paris was known as the "City of Light," and French cultural primacy yielded a plentiful harvest of literary and artistic discoveries; the city had a bewitching effect on Czechs well into the twentieth century.

A significant event in this context was the Paris World Exhibition of 1900, where the Czechs discovered the work of Auguste Rodin at his pavilion on Place d'Alma. So intense was their interest that in Prague two years later they organized a large one-man exhibition of Rodin's work, which had a very deep influence not only on sculptors, but on all plastic artists. Rodin's great artistic authority paved the way for spontaneity of expression and creative hyperbole, which in Czech art had been strongly suppressed, to be accepted as modern values. Without Rodin's strong example, Czech cubism could not have manifested such creative plasticity, usually attributed to the lesser influence of the indigenous Baroque tradition.

In painting, Czech progress toward modernism was at first much less clear. Miloš Jiránek, an ardent spokesman for the generation of painters of the fin de siècle, was confused by the centennial exhibition accompanying the Paris World Exhibition and sought sanctuary in the Louvre. The exhibition of French painting mounted in Prague in the same year as Rodin's showed mostly intimists, whose work was in a style fashionable in the 1890s. A profound change in attitude came only after the reevaluation of impressionism, and especially of post-impressionism, that accompanied the next large exhibition, in 1907; the main attraction this time was Gauguin. The sharp impact of the 1905 exhibition of works by Edvard Munch, featuring his "bleeding colours," fundamentally polarized Czech art criticism. After these events, there was an avalanche of actions by Czech painters.

Theory and art criticism played a significant role in the process of opening up to the issues of modern art. Critics felt an urgent need to replace "capricious" evaluation of works of art with a view that would take into account the internal relationships of individual artistic operations in a logical order and as a developmental inevitability. The earliest groundwork for modernism in the Czech milieu was laid by the response to Julius Meier-Graefe's book *Developmental History of Modern Art*, and especially to his controversial works on Böcklin, in which he attempted to do away with many current idols.

Jiránek tried to apply modernism to Czech art in an important lecture given in 1909. In it he ventured some ruthless criticism, concluding,

> Our art is characterized precisely by incompleteness, artistic irresponsibility, immaturity, and inconclusiveness. We had a number of talented people, but few artists—that is, responsible people—who

would complete a work that was desired and intended. Every one of those whom I will mention made beautiful things which will last, but if you examine them closely, you will see that they are more or less happy accidents, where the motif and the positive side of the artist's talent came together. His inadequacies did not emerge, they remained hidden. You will not find here the firmly connected logical evolution that distinguishes French art.[1]

Undoubtedly these unpleasant words hit their mark, especially among those in the younger generation who were about to enter the Czech art scene. It was bound to make them critical of their older colleagues; ironically, it provoked rejection of Jiránek's own impressionistic painting style.

The painters who formed the core of the new generation met at the Academy of Plastic Arts in the studios of Professors Thiele and Bukovac. Although the rehabilitation of late academism has recently renewed interest in Bukovac's photographic illusionism, with its symbolic content, the young artists of the early twentieth century took an altogether different route. After Munch and Van Gogh they discovered Gauguin, although they were more interested in the monism that had started with impressionism. Instead of visual "painterliness," they sought unity of the painting in a deeper, more expressive sense.

In 1907 money was found to mount the first exhibition of the Group of Eight. Those exhibiting were both Czech and German: Otokar Kubín, Antonín Procházka, Bohumil Kubišta, Emil Filla, Bedřich Feigl, Max Horb, Willy Nowak, and Emil Pittermann, the last behind a curtain. The only positive evaluation of the exhibition was written by the author Max Brod.

The second exhibition of the Group of Eight took place in 1908 in the renowned Topic Salon. Horb, who had died, and Kubín, who was not in Prague, were replaced by new members Vincenc Beneš and Linka Procházková-Scheithauerová. This exhibition was reviewed by the art critics, but again the reception was generally negative. To older critics, such as Arnošt Procházka, the founder of the decadent-symbolist *Modern Review*, or K. B. Mádl, who favoured intimism and impressionism and who, until the scandal around the Munch exhibition, had supported new art, the works of the young painters seemed to be nothing more than willfulness and the pursuit of "ingenious" innovation. Even younger critics, such as the Čapek brothers, were not particularly enthusiastic. The Čapek brothers' review, while acknowledging the existence of "synthetic art," made the same objection as the others did to the young artists' work since the advent of cubism: this art could not be rejected out of hand, because its intentions were serious and because it was "an enclave of French artistic culture in our country," but the new synthesists were, "rather than painters, speakers painting psychological tracts, a world of empty inanimate shadows, forms without matter or shape, a world of mere parables, and of non-corporeal life."[2]

Josef Čapek himself soon became an avant-garde painter, but his critique of the 1908 exhibition of the Group of Eight shows how complicated it was in Prague to change contemporary views of modern art. As late as 1912, on the occasion of the first exhibition of the Group of Plastic Artists, which featured cubist works, the important Czech critic F. X. Šalda declared that his sympathies for the young artists had fallen substantially. Although he had in fact personally supported and encouraged them, and had been convinced of the serious nature of their effort, he now wrote, "The gentlemen present formulas and schematics, not works of art, not declarations and expressions of personalities and the richness of their lives. It is possible that this will feed the artist of future ages, but abstraction so radically offered has no magic for me other than a cold and unengaged amazement at a bizarre hypothesis."[3]

Regardless of their opinions, the critics in general agreed in pointing out the unusual conceptualism, which became the main axis of the new avant-garde aesthetics. The unyielding, stubborn attitude of the young generation on this issue was also the principal source of conflicts with the older generation of painters. In 1909, an opportunity still existed to draw the young heretics into Mánes, the leading association of the Secessionist plastic artists. Among the artists included in its twenty-ninth exhibition were Filla, Beneš, and Václav Špála; they became members of the association at the invitation of the most progressive members of the Mánes executive, the architect Kotěra and the painters Preisler and Jiránek, who were aware of the need to recruit young talent for the association and of the changes to which the plastic arts were being rapidly subjected in the first decade of this century.

In 1909, the Mánes Association mounted an exhibition of works by the sculptor E. A. Bourdelle. In his lecture, given in Prague in conjunction with the exhibition, Bourdelle clearly rejected the romantic, "illegitimate" modelling of his teacher Rodin—though he did praise Rodin's muse on Whistler's tomb—and he emphatically called for an "architecturally" built form. Response to Bourdelle's Prague visit can be assessed from its immediate effect on the city's sculptors, some of whom knew Bourdelle personally from Rodin's studio. In the fall of that year, the very young Otto Gutfreund began attending Bourdelle's school in Paris. He noted in his diary, "Bourdelle . . . crowds figures into one plane, gives all of them the same plasticity. . . . But they also have their light effects, which he achieves by exaggerating some of the depth details. By doing so, he undulates, breaks up the plane into small refracting and colliding surfaces—it gives a very moving impression."[4] Gutfreund's first cubo-expressionist sculptures followed soon after.

It is quite apparent from the above excerpt that the Czech artists' interest in the new constructive quality of plastic form was not purely rational. The entire Czech modern movement was strongly influenced by the monistic conception of new art as new style. Šalda expressed it convincingly as early as 1903: "From derivative shapes, built up by fantasy or convention, we return to shapes which are *basic, simple, and useful*, from deceptions and subterfuges to honesty and strength, from fake decorations to structure and framework, from the secondary to the principal and primal. All of the artists are liberating themselves from their isolation of substantive enclosure, and they feel with ever-increasing intensity that their foundation and root is *ornamental and symbolic*, and their purpose is to work toward decorating life, to work on the whole, and to serve it: *style* as the highest cultural value, the unity of art and life, becomes the object of our aspirations."[5]

The question arises whether this programme was really synthetic, as Šalda desired, or, rather, syncretic. Synthesis was an oft-used word in Czech thought on art, especially in the first five years of the century, as can be seen in the Čapek brothers' assessment of the Group of Eight's second exhibition. Synthesis was a highly optimistic term, signifying the victorious fusion of art and life. As the creator of a new decorative style, Gauguin was recognized as the model of such a synthesis: "This great, beautiful goal—the creation of a new decorative art, an art of great, legitimate beauty and purity—rises ever more clearly on the horizon of contemporary painting: all roads lead toward it," Salda proclaimed in 1907.[6]

In 1909, shortly after Bourdelle's exhibition, Émile Bernard's work was shown at the Mánes Association pavilion; Bernard was hailed as a friend of Gauguin, indeed as his successor. However, the young painters were completely disappointed with this exhibition. Their views were expressed by Kubišta, who, after some difficulties, published his review in *Volné směry*: "The composition with regard to intellectual content lacks any symbolic property or effect on the viewer's psyche; it is utterly objective, unpainterly, unplastic, and works through a notional symbolism which is abstract and unartistic; it stops at the point of visual excitation by arabesque, without eliciting a deeper impression through intuition—in fact, it stands in opposition to feeling. . . . The colour composition achieves the beauty of colourized kerchiefs and rugs, the colour is always local, lacking any plastic or spatial ability; at best, it balances and complements the total pictorial melody."[7] To the young painters, this review brought the ideal of the "new decorative art" to a quick end; mere decorativism became one of the mortal sins of modern painting.

Another such sin was naturalism. It should be noted that what was being attacked was not so much the sharp illusionism of the end of the nineteenth century, but rather the derivative of impressionism, which meshed well with the period decorative tendencies in Czech art, especially in the area of "mood" landscape painting. The revulsion of the young members of the avant-garde against what was, in their opinion, totally superficial art, went so deep that it ended up in a court of law.[8]

Filla's essay "On the Virtues of Neo-primitivism" became a sort of summation and manifesto for the young artists, who were trying to sail between the Scylla of decorativism and the Charybdis of naturalism. The essay appeared in *Volné směry*, where Filla worked as editor, with illustrations by Picasso. It caused such a storm of revulsion that, after a sharp exchange of views, fifteen young painters, architects, and theoreticians resigned from Mánes and established their own Group of Plastic Artists. This secession, in 1911, completed the evolution started in the 1880s, which, in three generational waves, culminated in a form of institutionalized radical avant-garde. The Group of Plastic Artists immediately started to publish its own journal, *Umělecký měsíčník* (The Arts Monthly); although it underwent changes in personnel and departures, it was the focus of radical ideology until the beginning of the First World War.

The establishment of its own institutional base was closely connected with the very rapid ideological crystallization of the creative and intellectual profile of the young artists. In 1910, Filla's infamous article proclaimed primitivism as a powerful contemporary movement, which one-sidedly and deliberately limited the painter's interest in revival of the plastic form. But even this new form must, in Filla's opinion, be extracted from a new understanding of nature: "To see nature *en gros* means the transformation of a multitude of forms and the complexity of shapes to a very limited number of original shapes, and consists of a method of simplifying and reducing multineity into unity."[9] Filla felt that the goal of neo-primitivism was not adherence to dogmatic prescription or stereotype, or the "devaluation" of reality: rather, it was a preparatory phase "headed toward the final ideal of all art, stylistic classicism."[10]

For Filla and his colleagues, André Derain's painting *Bathing* became an example of such modern primitivism. They managed to place it at the head of the selection for the exhibition of contemporary French painters called Les Indépendants organized by Mánes in the spring of 1910. The fauvists were the most strongly represented at the exhibition. On the basis of their work, the young theoretician Antonín Matějček, in the introduction to the exhibition catalogue, proclaimed that expressionism, "in opposition to analytical impressionism, brings the synthesis of new expression, leading to symbols describing more accurately and in greater depth the emotional content of the times."[11]

Derain's canvas remained in Prague thanks to a subscription raised in cafés. It documents the crossroads at which the young Czech avant-garde artists found themselves. The painting's theme and the elementarization of figures into simple linear signs made it a "primitivist" re-working of Cézanne's *Bathing*. In the

André Derain, *Bathing*, 1908–1909, oil on canvas, 180 x 230 cm, National Gallery, Prague

reduction of colours to a grey, brown, and green toning of shape, it came close to the reduced colour scale of analytic cubism. However, the figures in motion are consistent, more stylized than deformed, and they fill the surface of the painting essentially in a decorative manner. Derain's primitivism was already directed toward classicism.

It seems that this particular conglomeration of different developmental phases, which at first glance may have seemed monolithic, called for a competition between ideals, spurring Czech artists to refine their new style and orientation. Thus, it is not surprising that a number of individual approaches sprang up which continued with the tradition of a figurative imagery, yet pushed to the farthest limits of tenability.

In 1910, Filla, who was chiefly responsible for obtaining Derain's canvas, painted *Autumn*, in which, in contrast to the Frenchman's linear elegance, the figures are expressively outlined. Though the colour is also reduced to the dominant blue and purple, it is doubtless emotionally more engaged. Derain's unifying decorativeness was retained more in Vincenc Beneš's *Idyl*, also painted in 1910, although the volumes of figures were proto-cubistically faceted. Also interesting was Kubišta's reaction, expressed in the 1911 paintings *Spring (Women Bathing)* and *Men Bathing*. Kubišta, who painstakingly planned his compositions and, in contrast to his more intuitive colleagues, constructed them with the aid of the golden section and triangular grids, imbued these paintings with lessons from

Emil Filla, *Autumn*, 1910, oil on canvas, 116 x 150 cm, National Gallery, Prague

Bohumil Kubišta, *Spring (Women Bathing)*, 1911, oil on canvas, 127 x 160 cm, National Gallery, Prague

Poussin, the Japanese, Antiquity, and El Greco. The result may seem somewhat heavy-handed, but the disparity is overcome by Kubišta's determination to achieve expression, and by an unusual austerity of colour. Kubišta's paintings were a clear signal of the Czech artists' dissatisfaction with Derain's neo-primitivism. Their objection was soon formulated by Kubišta: "Logically and intellectually understood form is not adequately filled with a content of ideas. This process of gradual filling must come through evolution."[12]

According to this statement, the Rubicon of modern painting was to be crossed by the gradual maturation of new content. But it is obvious that the process was accelerated by the break between the generations in 1911, leading to the establishment of the independent Group of Plastic Artists, which enabled a clear differentiation of opinions. It suffices to compare two paintings, both from 1912, and both titled *Bathing*. The painting by Jan Preisler, the best painter of the generation of

Jan Preisler, *Bathing*, 1912, oil on canvas, 90 x 76.5 cm, Gallery of Western Bohemia, Plzen

Emil Filla, *Bathing*, 1912, oil on canvas, 125 x 83.5 cm, National Gallery, Prague

the nineties, while influenced by Cézanne, respects even in the spatial composition of the figures the entire decorative surface, and presents a harmony of figures and landscape. In the painting by Filla, the focus is created by two analytically decomposed figures, connected according to the compositional principle of a rotating crystal with an inert centre.[13] Rising up in the background are the diagonal forms of a city.

But it was not just a matter of a break with the older generation: that now seemed to be clear and complete. The young generation's declaration of independence was followed by great euphoria. It also immediately resulted in two large collective exhibitions by the Group in Prague in 1912, which in turn led to a quick expansion into the surrounding Central European milieu.[14] This was, however, followed by a much more troublesome, and ultimately just as acrimonious, split within the young generation.

In their great thirst for true modernism, some Czech painters became acquainted with cubism as early as 1910; however, it was some time before they came to terms with the principles of cubist aesthetics. This first period of contacts with cubism, which extended into 1912, is termed cubo-expressionism. Characteristic of the style are the 1911 works by the sculptor Otto Gutfreund. Even their titles, such as *Anxiety*, *Hamlet*, *Don Quixote*, indicate that the artist's interest was not just formalistic. Other artists also used literary themes: Filla used Salome as a subject, and Procházka used Prometheus. Obviously, the young Czech artists did not perceive their activity as the negation of tradition, but as its radical renewal. The Group's magazine, *Umělecký měsíčník*, was filled with essays on the Gothic, the Renaissance, and the Baroque. Gutfreund's cubo-expressionism was the direct descendant of Czech radical Baroque, of Donatello's original interpretation of the spatial conception (as compared to the spatially passive Maillol), and had a concrete connection to Daumier (whose *Ratapoil* Gutfreund admired) and Rodin. From there Gutfreund moved to physiognomical symbolism, the conviction that every emotional movement finds a natural resonance in body motion. But he did not convey strong emotion through external sensualism, turning rather to the psyche for its origins, where he found the only requirement for plastic imagination: the abstract geometric plane. He wrote about this in his interesting 1912 essay "Plane and Space," and in his notes: "The sculptor transposes a vision which is planar into space. . . . The real space into which the sculptor transposes his planar visions is in turn constituted of planes; the final effect is once again planar observation."[15] The plane, bearer of the artist's vision, asserts itself on the figurative object, which it deconstructs, or rather reconstructs and thus turns into a sculpture: "As the abstract vision of the sculptor acquires solid form, it must help itself by forms already existing in reality. The only form which we can construct is geometric, so that the final creation is a composite of these two: the geometric body as the residue of an abstract vision and real form."[16]

Otto Gutfreund, *Anxiety*, 1911, plaster, h. 148 cm, National Gallery, Prague

Well expressed in Gutfreund is the common rational foundation that led Czech artists toward cubism. It was a fundamental turn from an external model to an internal one, in which, through a zone of emotional movement, radiated "a shining crystal of transcendental form"—the actual core of art—as Kubišta later said.

In his deliberations, Kubišta does not doubt that modern art has its own matter, which is quite different than it was when art and the world view were dominated by religion. The responsibility of the modern artist was to penetrate to this matter (which is why Kubišta named his concept penetrism), to the living creative sense of the modern era; along the way, it was also possible to achieve a new sense of style. The search for a new style was ubiquitous in the Czech modern movement; this is why the architects and designers became so heavily involved in it. Kubišta also realized that several styles may evolve at any one time, depending on how the three basic premises of stylistic expression are created and combined: first, the rationally, geometrically, and symbolically created "transcendental form," expressing humanity's intellectual relationship with infinity; second, creative will, which itself determines the basic elements of transcendental form and binds the visions induced by them; and finally, emotionally induced mental feelings, which regulate transcendental form dynamically. Every combination of these three stylistic premises is an expression of its time: "And this realization is important especially for our own time, which does not have a united collective mind, or will, or mental feelings, and which shall be ruled by chaos for as long as it takes for these to become concentrated."[17]

This conclusion of Kubišta's 1911 essay amply illustrates how the cloven hoof of substantialism protrudes even from this sympathetically pluralistic theory.

Antonín Procházka, *Girl with a Peach*, 1912, oil on canvas, 35 x 30 cm, National Gallery, Prague

(Kubišta did not join the Group; later, in a letter to the painter Jan Zrzavý, he explicitly rejected the hegemony of cubism.) The particular problem of stylistic "concentration" then became very significant for the future development of the Czech avant-garde.

The offensive within the Group of Plastic Artists was started by the section that was completely oriented toward the very heart of Parisian cubism, constituted by the work of Picasso and Braque. A significant role was played by the theoretician and art historian Vincenc Kramář, who, through Kahnweiler, had been buying works by these artists since 1911, amassing a remarkable collection which directly stimulated the Czech artists. Thanks to his contacts, these paintings also appeared in substantial numbers at the Group's exhibitions. (The Third Prague Exhibition, in May of 1913, had nine Picassos, eleven Braques, five Derains, and two works by Gris.)

The example of the Parisian protagonists of cubism attracted particularly Filla and Gutfreund, and to a lesser extent also Beneš and Procházka. One major effect of this was that they abandoned the cubo-expressionistic psychologism and the original symbolist and existential themes, and concentrated to a greater extent on plastic problems. Their return to analytic and, occasionally, hermetic cubism could be characterized as a sort of lesson in ideological catharsis. However, their output quickly moved into the sphere of analytic cubism and toward a new object-oriented grasp of painting. They were less concerned with the problems of collage,

Otto Gutfreund, *Cubist Bust (Man's Head)*, 1913, bronze, h. 60 cm, National Gallery, Prague

Emil Filla, *Smoker*, 1913–1914, oil on canvas, 45 x 30 cm, National Gallery, Prague

a medium that at first was actually imitated by painterly means. Filla and Gutfreund went furthest in understanding the pictorial and plastic space as the stage of creative events, carried out by realities and material elements of new logograms. Filla rehabilitated colour in this context, giving the universe of his forms an increasingly lyrical and intimate feeling. Gutfreund constructed and coupled volumes and surface planes, which in the wooden sculptures he made during the war brought him almost to the boundary of concrete art.

Soon, however, opposition arose against the so-called orthodox section of the Group. By the end of 1912, the painters Čapek, Špála, and L. Šíma, the designer Brunner, and the architects Hofman and Chochol had left the Group as the result of a difference of opinions. Čapek became the leader of the opposition; early in 1914 he organized, in collaboration with the French poet Mercereau, the

Václav Špála, *Three Washerwomen*, 1913, oil on canvas, 72 x 81.5 cm, National Gallery, Prague

exhibition called "Modern Art," using the premises of the Mánes Association. This became the pretext for an incongruously sharp and personal confrontation between the two wings of the generation. Čapek's approach was quite incorrectly branded futurism (Marcousis, Gleizes, Metzinger, and Lhote were indeed represented at the exhibition, but so were Delaunay, Dufy, Mondrian, Brancusi, Archipenko, and others) and was condemned by the believers for destroying the quality of modern art.

What was actually involved was a conflict between the "pluralistic" and "concentrated" interpretations of modern style and a differentiation growing out of what had originally been a common cubo-expressionistic point of departure. It has been already well determined by M. Lamač that for Čapek and Špála (and also for the late symbolist J. Zrzavý), the contact with cubism meant acquisition of the ability to elementarize the figure in signal terms in the spirit of neo-primitivism in such a way that, after a certain progression toward more informal themes, a new typization of the figure could occur, encompassing the contemporary urban (for Čapek) and rural (for Špála) environments.[18] This typization proved to be very useful in 1920, when modern art had to react to a substantially changed social and ideological situation, and to address it in terms of the continuity of modern art.

The above-mentioned artists became the principal movers in the group called Tvrdošíjní (The Stiffnecked). They were the only ones who took on the task and were able to complete it at that time.

The polarization of the generational efforts illustrates how cubism helped the Czech artists on their journey toward their own modern style. Its results helped to obscure somewhat the point of the generational encounter which, possibly, was the most interesting part of the movement. This is not adequately understood by foreign authors, who measure Czech cubism against contemporary Parisian cubism, discounting the value of Czech cubo-expressionism, which cannot be seen simply as a passing phase. A certain cruel yet sublime heroism was aptly expressed by Kubišta in his *St. Sebastian* (1912), which also serves as the ideal self-portrait and symbol of the modern artist. Although Kubišta is considered to be a typical Czech artist, Thomas Mann wrote at the time in *Death in Venice*, "A new type of hero, who returns in various individual personifications, whom this author took to liking, was soon described by a keen analyst as being a conception of 'intellectual and youthful manliness, who, proudly ashamed, clenches his teeth and stands calmly, while swords and spears pierce his body.' . . . This was beautiful, brilliant, and precise, despite its seemingly all-too-passive cast, for a firm attitude toward fate and grace in suffering do not imply simply passive acceptance. It is an active performance, a positive triumph, and the figure of Sebastian is the most beautiful symbol. If not of art as such, then certainly of the art in question."

Bohumil Kubišta, *St. Sebastian*, 1912, oil on canvas, 98 x 74.5 cm, National Gallery, Prague

Notes

1. M. Jiránek, "O českém malířství moderním" (About Czech Modern Painting), *Volné směry* 13 (1909): 199–210, 251–263.
2. K. Čapek and J. Čapek, "Syntéza a výstava Osmi" (Synthesis and the Exhibition of the Eight), *Snaha*, 21 July 1908.
3. F. X. Šalda, "Umělecká výstava v Obecním domě u Prašné brány" (The Art Exhibition at the Municipal Hall near Prašná brána), *Novina* 5 (1912): 247–248.
4. O. Gutfreund, "Diary," entry from 5 December 1909. In Otto Gutfreund, *Zázemí tvorby* (The Hinterland of Creativity), Vol. 1, ed. J. Šetlík (Prague, 1989), p. 18.
5. F. X. Šalda, "Etika dnešní obrody aplikovaného umění" (The Ethics of Today's Renaissance of Applied Art), *Volné směry* 7 (1903): 137.
6. F. X. Šalda, "Impresionism: jeho rozvoj, rezultáty i dědicové" (Impressionism: Its Development, Results and Inheritors), *Pokroková revue* 4 (1907): 70, 159.
7. B. Kubišta, "Émile Bernard," *Volné směry* 13 (1909): 80.
8. In 1911, when the generational struggles intensified, the Topic Salon exhibited the notorious painting called *Boronali*, completed by a donkey. The picture had caused a scandal earlier at the Salon Les Indépendants in Paris. Kubišta wrote maliciously that the picture reminded him of sketches by some of the Prague "mood" painters, a comment for which he was attacked with a whip in public by the painter Ullmann.
9. E. Filla, "O ctnosti novoprimitivismu" (On the Virtues of Neo-primitivism), *Volné směry* 15 (1911): 69–70.
10. Ibid.
11. Catalogue for the 31st Exhibition of S. V. U. Mánes, *Les Indépendants*, February–March 1910.
12. B. Kubišta, "Nicolas Poussin," *Volné směry* 16 (1912): 201.
13. M. Lamač, *Osma a Skupina výtvarných umělců, 1907–1917* (The Eight and the Group of Plastic Artists, 1907–1917) (Prague, 1988), p. 270.
14. The Group of Plastic Artists had strong contacts with Die Brücke. The second Prague exhibition, in 1912, included some twenty works by Heckel, Kirchner, Müller, and Schmidt-Rottluff. Czech artists often exhibited in Germany, for instance, at the exhibition of the Sonderbund in Cologne (May–September, 1912), quite frequently at the Goltz Salon of New Art, and at the New Secession in Berlin. Later they settled at H. Walden's Berlin gallery Der Sturm; Walden mounted a separate exhibition of the Group's artists, Beneš, Filla, Gutfreund, Janák, and Gočár, in October of 1913. Beneš, Filla, Gutfreund, Kubín, and Procházka also participated in the First German Autumn Salon, organized by Walden the same year in Berlin.
15. Gutfreund's theoretical statements have been collected in Otto Gutfreund, *Zázemí tvorby.*
16. Ibid.
17. B. Kubišta, *Předpoklady slohu* (The Presuppositions of Style) (Prague, 1947).
18 M. Lamač, op. cit., pp. 432–463

Josef Čapek, *Head*, 1914, oil on canvas, 46.5 x 37 cm, National Gallery, Prague

Cubism in Architecture

Vladimír Šlapeta

At the end of the first decade of the twentieth century, Czech architecture experienced a profound change. On the one hand, the founder of modern Czech architecture, Jan Kotěra, was designing buildings of rationalistic spirit, including his own villa, the house of the publisher Jan Laichter in Prague, and particularly the municipal museum in Hradec Králové; on the other hand, the new generation of Kotěra's students and collaborators, born around 1880, was beginning to assert itself. These architects, including Josef Gočár, Josef Chochol, and Pavel Janák, emerged on the scene with a new programme.

In 1898, at the age of twenty-seven, Kotěra was appointed professor at the Prague School of Decorative Arts; as he was also the chairman of the Mánes Association of Plastic Artists, he was destined to become the leading spirit of his generation. He called for Czechoslovakia to "open the windows into Europe" and to "catch up to and outdistance Europe,"[1] in order to liberate Czech plastic arts from its dependence on Vienna. Kotěra's programme was founded on the Semperian-Wagnerian branch of modern architecture. He maintained that "the creation of space and construction, not shape and decoration, must be the purpose of the new movement," and that "any movement whose point of departure is not in purpose, construction, and place, but arises from form, is utopian."[2] His turn-of the-century programme was inspired by sources from England and Holland and by the early work of Frank Lloyd Wright; he then developed a personal rationalistic style which established him, by the end of the decade, as a leading personality in European architecture. But not even Kotěra's strong example could prevent the young generation from using different points of departure.

At the beginning of 1908, Kotěra's studio was occupied by collaborators of far greater importance than ever before or after: Gočár, who had been working in Prague since 1905, was joined by Janák, who had been at Otto Wagner's specialized school at the Academy in Vienna. Both are mentioned as co-architects of the Pavilion of Commerce, which Kotěra designed for the Prague Jubilee Exhibition in 1908.[3] The facade of this building, which contrasts the symmetrical gable of the

Jan Kotěra, collaboration with Josef Gočár and Pavel Janák, Pavilion of Commerce at the Jubilee Exhibition, 1908, Prague

Pavel Janák, sketch of pavilion, 1908

main facade against lateral wings, flanked by Jan Štursa's massive sculptures, gives an indication of the thematic sphere being discussed by the young architects, which they were about to promulgate. In contrast to sober rationalism, they were concerned with the problems of matter and spirit, and of the spiritual enrichment of architecture through plastic forms.

Also in 1908, the Association of Architects of the Mánes Group was founded. The executive, composed of, among others, Janák, Otakar Novotný, and Gočár,[4] marked the imminent arrival of the young generation. With Zdeněk Wirth as editor, the Association started to publish a new magazine, *Styl*, for "architecture, the applied arts, and urbanism." In the second issue, Janák published an article about Otto Wagner,[5] in which he pointed out the importance of his teacher to modern architecture—not so much in Wagner's teaching, based on the motto "function, construction, poetry,"[6] but because in his finest works he managed to overcome the causal links between function, construction, and form. Janák wrote,

> The spirit of the new style is already defined, and the road to its plastic means by penetration to the very nature of matter is clear: it includes geometric forms, prismatic and cubic, the most intrinsic essentials of all forms, purged of everything secondary; their natural constructive arrangements are the new compositional principles, with the function of decoration transposed to only accentuating, which, like framing or underscoring, lacks all independent form. This is the state of Wagner's art today. It offers positive proof of his efforts toward art with timeless and permanent values. It is a natural, manly statement against all creative weakness and ailments, as seems to be the ideal of the time. It stands against sentimentality, emphasis on colour, picturesqueness, intimacy, and capriciousness. None of these have anything to do with the healthy, strong nature of the modern individual, or with his resultant effort not to succumb, and to persist through his personality under all circumstances.[7]

Gočár's design for the Barrow of White Mountain, done in collaboration with the sculptor Stanislav Sucharda, was used to introduce the first volume of the magazine *Styl*, and illustrated the young generation's move toward the absolute, basic forms of prism and pyramid.[8] These tendencies are also visible in Janák's studies for the proposed solution for the entrance to the Letná Plain via a tunnel,[9] and, in the same location, the monument to Tyrš and Fügner, the leaders of the

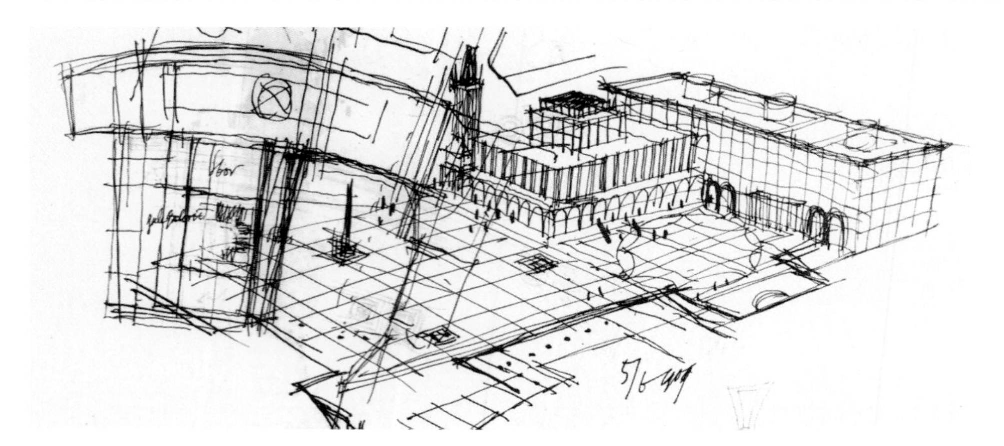

Pavel Janák, sketch for competition design for the Old Town City Hall, Prague, 1909

Sokol Athletic Union.[10] The stepped-pyramid motif appeared in Janák's studies for the third competition for the Old Town Hall in Prague in 1909,[11] and especially in the monumental design by Gočár, which shocked the public.[12]

Janák and Gočár also found a willingness to embrace the large architectural form in Josip Plečnik, whom they met through Kotěra, and whose works they regularly published in *Styl.* Some of Plečnik's designs—for instance, the 1905 facade of the Stollwerk factory in Vienna, or the 1907 study for the interior of a chapel[13]—used oblique and slanting surfaces and formations, and garnered a strong response from Prague architects. In 1909, Josef Chochol returned from Wagner's school and joined Janák and Gočár, as did Vlastislav Hofman, who was first noticed at the exhibition of the Club of Architecture Students of the Czech Technical University in 1908.[14]

Other sources of inspiration for the new wave of architecture were also surfacing: cultural events in Prague, including the Edvard Munch exhibition in 1905; the Group of Eight's first exhibition in 1907; the Group's second exhibition in 1908; the French sculptor Bourdelle's exhibition the following year; and the exhibition of the Parisian group Les Indépendants in 1910. In Paris, proponents of analytic cubism, such as painters Pablo Picasso and Georges Braque, broke the surface of the painting into a three-dimensional vista; this movement encouraged

Josip Plečnik, design for facade of the Stollwerk factory, Vienna, 1905

Josef Gočár, exhibition design for the Old Town City Hall, Prague, 1909

the Prague architects to transpose comparable experiments into space. The lively exchanges with German expressionists also had an effect, especially those with the group Die Brücke (whose membership included the Czech painter Bohumil Kubišta, a friend of Otto Müller), and with the theoretician Julius Meier-Graefe, who visited Prague several times. Strongly felt as well were the effects of German aesthetics, especially Theodor Lipps and Wilhelm Worringer's "theory of empathy" and the works of Adolf von Hildebrand,[15] which were translated into Czech and critiqued by Janák and Chochol. Finally, a major inspiration was found in Czech historical architecture: the late-Gothic diamond vaults of southern Bohemia and southern Moravia, which anticipated the cubistic morphology, and the sporadic early-eighteenth-century work of Giovanni Santini-Aichel, conceived in the spirit of the Baroque Gothic. Especially important were Santini-Aichel's 1722 cemetery and burial chapel at St. Jan Nepomucenus in Žďár nad Sázavou, with its strong plastic and expressive ambitions. Zdeněk Wirth, an art historian and friend of the Mánes Group of Architects, wrote his dissertation on the Czech Baroque Gothic in 1908.[16]

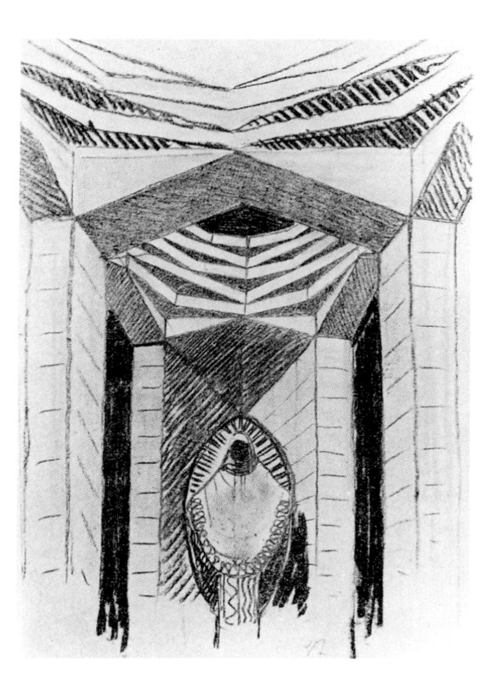

Josip Plečnik, sketch of interior of a chapel, 1907

Respect for domestic traditions probably provided a historical context for the architects of this generation, and enabled cubist architecture and the Gothic and Baroque buildings to coexist harmoniously in the *genus loci* of the historic centres of Czech towns. This is aptly documented by Janák and Hofman's design for preserving and adding a superstructure to the Braun house in Prague in 1910.[17]

In July of 1910, Janák critiqued Wagner's teaching in his programmatic essay "From Modern Architecture to Architecture."[18] Janák's premise was that a change in architecture was on the way. Until that time, modern architecture had had more of a purifying, social, and practical character rather than being concerned with plasticity; thus, Janák proposed that the third point of Wagner's doctrine be reevaluated and elevated to become the primary purpose of architectural creation, as had been the case with historical architectures. According to Janák, modern architecture knew "only the problems of practical need; it barely understood at all the problem of space or the problem of matter and form. Modern architecture did not recognize these problems, and it was not sufficiently theoretical";[18] it was specifically in theory that he saw its future application. From this perspective, he noted

Vlastislav Hofman, design for addition to the Braun house, Prague, 1910

that Plečnik's artistic approach to architecture is vindicated. Janák concluded, "It is possible to predict the future direction of architecture: creativity, in which artistic thought and abstraction will take over leadership from practicality, which cedes its place. Architecture will advance in its pursuit of plastic form, and in plastic realization of architectural concepts. This coincides with the development of matured creative energy, which is now strengthened and is able to penetrate deeper into architectural problems. It will go deeper into substance, to draw from it form."[18]

This anticipated development was fast approaching. At the end of February of the following year, the art historian V. V. Štech, who was on a study trip in Berlin, received travel money and a telegram from Gočár, telling him to return immediately to Prague to deal with problems that the young generation of the Mánes Association of Plastic Artists was having at the editorial offices of *Volné směry.*[19] The cause of the conflict was a protest by the printer Grégr at the Mánes general meeting against Emil Filla's article "Neo-primitivism," illustrated by Picasso, publication of which caused a mass withdrawal of subscribers. When Grégr's position was supported by the association's chairman, Kotěra, the entire young generation decided to secede from Mánes.[20] That summer, the breakaway group founded a new association called the Group of Plastic Artists, and in the fall they started to publish their own magazine, *Umělecký měsíčník* (The Arts Monthly). Josef Čapek returned from Paris and became its editor. The centre of the theoretical debate on the meaning of new architecture thus shifted from *Styl* to *Umělecký měsíčník,* which soon became the platform of Prague cubism.

We can assess the breadth of the polarity of the debate from two lectures which took place in Prague at the beginning of 1911. On 17 March, Adolf Loos spoke on "Ornament and Crime" at the German Technical University, when he introduced the Czech public to his theory that in the area of construction, only the monument and the gravestone belong in the sphere of art. Also in March, Janák spoke in the context of the cycle of lectures of the Association of Architecture Students at the Czech Technical University. In contrast to Loos, and in the spirit of his own critique of Wagner, he spoke against the notion that architecture should serve only a social purpose and the needs of the present: "To proceed from the purpose to the planning of the whole, to the selection of construction and materials, will of course suffice completely for good contracting, but architecture requires more. Architecture is an art, whose justification is an inner need—emotion. Indeed, not even contemporary architecture reduces itself merely to purpose, material, and construction, but creates above these elements abstract forms."[21] A tendency toward abstraction, animation, and idealism thereafter characterized the manifestos and articles published in *Umělecký měsíčník.*

Janák was the leading theoretician of the group. In the article "Against Mood in Architecture" (1911–1912),[22] he identified mood, sentimentality, and intimacy as a sickness in architecture, distracting attention from the objective reality that "architecture concerns the substance of space and its creative laws."[22] His theoretical efforts culminated in the essay "The Prism and the Pyramid,"[23] in which he differentiated between two families of European architecture—the southern, Antique, and the northern, Christian—both of which affected the evolution of Czech architecture. According to Janák, southern architecture consists of the natural way of building. The building elements of architrave and pillar maintain their character, and one is placed on the other according to the natural law of gravity. In contrast, northern architecture proceeds "from the everyday earthly building to a supernatural beauty," to the overcoming of substance by spirit and abstraction. Architecture up to the present time Janák assigned to the materialistic southern style, and he criticized its avoidance of the supra-material and spiritual form. He

Group of Plastic Artists in Prague, New Year's Eve, 1911 (standing left to right: Vincenc Beneš, Otto Gutfreund, Josef Čapek, Josef Chochol, Karel Čapek; middle row, left to right: Josef Gočár, Vilém Dvořák, Vlastislav Hofman, Pavel Janák; front row, left to right: František Langer, Jan Thon, Emil Filla)

discussed the laws of inorganic nature, in which geometrically more complex shapes are created with the collaboration of a third force, as in crystallization. If the vertical and horizontal planes are the form of rest and equilibrium for matter, then oblique shapes are caused by dramatic events and by a more complex concentration of forces. It thus follows that if inanimate matter is to be plastically re-created and animated so that something might change within it, this must occur through intervention of a third plane, which joins the natural bi-plane. Therefore, Janák proposed re-creation of the substantiality of the matter of the prism through the use of oblique planes. The object created by the action of oblique planes is the pyramid—the noblest shape of spiritually abstracted matter. "In comparison to natural building, architecture is a superior activity. Generally, it combines two activities: technical, prismatic bi-planar construction and the abstract reconstitution of matter in a tri-planar system, be it oblique or curvilinear. The more dominant of the architectural impulses also creates the building's overall character." Janák reflected on these theoretical considerations in many studies; he did not restrict himself to the cubistic forming of planes and the study of inanimate crystals, he also studied the application of organic and natural shapes for the modelling of facades and cornices.

cat. no. 53

cat. nos. 57–62

"Everything that was new," wrote Jan Sokol, "was thought up by Janák, but realized by Gočár."[24] Indeed, at the same time as Janák was publishing his most important essays on the cubist theory of architecture, Gočár was realizing buildings, excelling in stylistic self-assurance and noblesse, and establishing his international reputation. The U černé Matky Boží (At the Black Mother of God) building, in Prague's Old Town, fitted in an exemplary way into its historical surroundings; like a *Gesamtkunstwerk*, it was completed, to its last craftsman-like

cat. no. 8a

Josef Gočár, design for a garden pavilion, Krucemburk, 1913

detail, with a coherent intention. Gočár's sanatorium at the Bohdaneč spa was conceived in a grandiose, energetic horizontal layout, and articulated in an elegant cubist grammar.

Like Gočár in U černé Matky Boži, Janák was confronted with projects in an historical context: first, the competition design for the town hall at Havlíčkův Brod (formerly known as Německý Brod), where he had to work within a Gothic idiom, and then in the reconstruction of the house of Dr. Fára in Pelhřimov, where his style evolved from a Gothic inspiration into a very remarkable transposition of Baroque Gothic.

cat. no. 68

cat. no. 18a–c

The third of the quartet of eminent architects of the Prague cubist group, Chochol—possibly influenced by Loos's lectures—wrote about the function of ornament and architectural detail.

> At the moment, when we want to be left alone to create, everything old actually becomes alien to us, and only that which dictates the inner arrangement—the architecture of the object and its interior organization—demands with redoubled force to exist. The parts that appear to be ornamental are, in our case, always in the same measure, or even more so, necessary in the total organism of the work. So necessary, in fact, that under no circumstances is it possible subsequently to tear them out of the whole. . . . We want to replace the ornamental quality with an intellectualized vitality of form; at least as much as we reject in decoration and ornament, we try to achieve through the force of a concentrated and complete effect, marked by a taste for mathematical exactness, rugged curtness, and hearty roughness. We prefer this to the erstwhile stiffness of scented, fallow dandyisms and perversities, as well as to the petit-bourgeois naïveté, that feigns jollity. . . . Standing at the threshold of the newly developing world of artistic forms, we replace the former decorative detailing with the fuller and more concentrated expression of the three-dimensional evolving matter.[25]

Josef Chochol best illustrated this opinion in the construction of three apartment houses in Prague below Vyšehrad in which the cubist segmenting of surfaces becomes an organic part of the whole.

The youngest member of the group, Vlastislav Hofman, tried to introduce into cubist architecture psychological and kinetic moments based on the study not only

Josef Chochol, design for a factory, 1912

of Europe's architectural heritage, but also of Oriental traditions, especially Indian architecture, which he studied with the author Karel Čapek.[26] Hofman assumed that the person's mental state is determined by inner movement, and that to conquer matter means to impart to it one's own spiritual movement. This occurred whenever styles arose or grew side by side with or independently of one another, as happened in Egypt, the Orient, India, the Gothic, and the Baroque, as opposed to the classicist principle or times of decadence. Creativity in architecture therefore means putting matter into motion; its goal is the form that, while still, captures this motion. Such a principle presupposes "the thinning and reduction of the matter to its property of strength, in order to achieve operative effect, a sense of ease, and the possibility of abstracting the material into formal motion. Form overpowers matter and does not strive to affect through the quantum of material; it creates a plastic element, achieved by intellect."[27] Hofman considered the move-

Vlastislav Hofman, design for a cemetery, Prague–Ďáblice, 1912

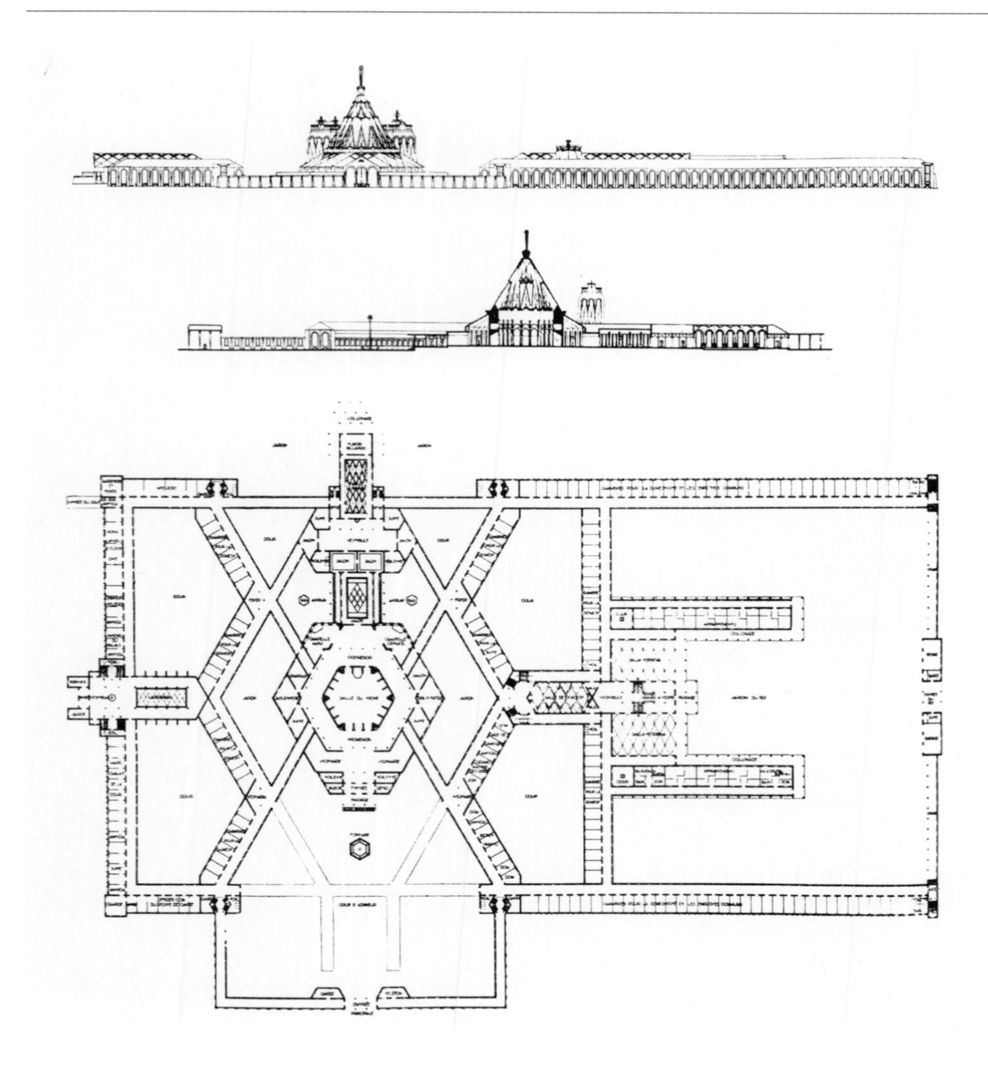

Otakar Novotný, competition designs for royal palace, Sofia, 1912

ment of matter not only in terms of cubist forms, but also through curves; this lent his designs and studies a new dynamic element, in contrast to the strict static character of Chochol's buildings.

The end of 1912 brought a change in the perspective of the cubist group. Otakar Novotný became the editor of *Styl*. Unlike his contemporaries Gočár, Chochol, and Janák, he was a proponent of Kotěra's rationalism and remained loyal to the Mánes Association. Nevertheless, he now opened the magazine to cubist statements. Although originally he had maintained a certain distance from this movement, he now tried for the first time to come to terms with it. This is evident in his design for the royal palace in Sofia: the rhomboidal plan culminates in a cubist pyramidal element in the centre. Other architects also aligned themselves with cubism, including Vladimír Fultner, Petr Kropáček, and the builder Matěj Blecha, in whose office the gifted architect Emil Králíček worked.[28]

Vladimír Fultner, study for villa, 1912

The most important event of 1913 was the competition for a monument to the fifteenth-century Czech warrior-hero Jan Žižka at Vítkov Hill in Prague, which offered the architects and sculptors of the cubist generation an opportunity to express themselves in a new style on a task of monumental scale. In a number of the designs it is possible to discern the strong influence of Janák's article "The Prism and the Pyramid." The pyramid was chosen as the basic design element by Gočár; Otto Gutfreund contributed the relief articulation to the design. Gutfreund also collaborated with Janák on the latter's design for the monument, which was composed of a cluster of crystals growing out of the basic volume of a truncated pyramid. Ladislav Machoň and the sculptor Jaroslav Horejc also used a

cat. no. 69a–c

Petr Kropáček, competition design for a savings bank, Pardubice, 1913

Petr Kropáček, competition design for a savings bank, Pardubice, 1913, detail of gable

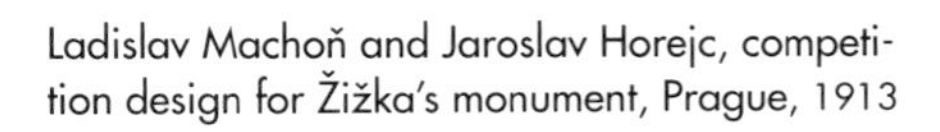

Ladislav Machoň and Jaroslav Horejc, competition design for Žižka's monument, Prague, 1913

Vlastislav Hofman and L. Beneš, competition design for Žižka's monument, Prague, 1913

cubistic truncated pyramid, with edges accented by monumental figurative sculptures. The sculptor Jan Štursa, with Kotěra, designed a massive equestrian sculpture of Žižka with an expressively conceived entourage of warriors by his side. Vladimír Fultner, with the sculptor Ladislav Kofránek, proposed the monument as a solitary figurative statue of Žižka on a cubistically conceived pedestal. The young Bedřich Feuerstein, at the time still a student at the Prague Technical University, produced his first significant work for the competition: an almost intimate design, consisting of an equestrian statue of Žižka on a cubist pedestal, situated on an oval plateau embraced by symmetrical oval flights of stairs. One of the most interesting designs was submitted by Hofman. His solution divided the monument into an entrance area with a graduated and inclined observation terrace oriented toward Prague, and the actual mausoleum building treated in an expressive cubist interpretation.[29]

cat. no. 80a–b

cat. no. 42

Another competition, announced soon after and influenced by the Vítkov competition, was for Rieger's barrow at Kozákov. Hofman once again used the idea of the graduated observation terrace; Feuerstein, having learned from the earlier competition, used a grand scale and a convincing three-pronged crystal-like composition, for which he won second prize.[30] At the time, Hofman was also interested in

cat. no. 43a–d

Vlastislav Hofman, design for Palacký Square, Prague, 1913

large urbanistic projects in Prague, and he proposed a cubist solution for the area of the Palacký bridge near the Emaus Monastery, and the development of Letná.

In 1913, the Group of Plastic Artists' international relations broadened considerably. In January, Herwarth Walden promoted *Umělecký měsíčník*, along with other avant-garde journals, in his magazine *Der Sturm*. In September, he dedicated the eighteenth exhibition at his gallery[31] to the work of Prague cubist painters, sculptors, and architects. He also organized their participation at the first German Autumn Salon;[32] subsequently, he frequently published in *Der Sturm* works by Emil Filla, Josef and Karel Čapek, Vincenc Beneš, and Vlastislav Hofman, which doubtless boosted their self-esteem and spurred them to intensify their efforts to succeed in Europe.[33] Soon they had an appropriate opportunity to do so.

When word reached Prague of the upcoming Werkbund exhibition in Cologne, architects, designers, and entrepreneurs established the Association of Czech Accomplishment, as a parallel to the German and Austrian Werkbunds.[34] The purpose of this was to enable Czech artists to appear as a separate group in the Austrian Pavilion, which was designed by Josef Hoffmann in total spiritual antithesis to Prague cubism. Thanks to interventions by Kotěra, the effort succeeded, and the Association of Czech Accomplishment was given four rooms in the Austrian Pavilion for its own presentation. The installation was the first executed cubist work by Novotný. The Czech artists' exhibition provoked much interest, especially among foreign visitors, and even the otherwise skeptical critic Walter Curt Behrendt wrote that "it might be possible to get the juices flowing and to speed up the pulse of the German industrial arts, if the Slavic nations can pass their excess energy on to the non-Slavic industrial arts. The tempestuous exhibition of the Association of Czech Accomplishment shows that a powerful fermentation is taking place."[35] The Werkbund exhibition closed sooner than planned due to the outbreak of the First World War, and so the success received no response at home or abroad. It also marked the end of the prewar cubist period.

Pavel Janák, study for a facade, 1913

As the ties with Germany were very intense, it is worthwhile to examine the similarities and differences between the architects of the Prague cubist group and their Berlin expressionist colleagues. First of all, the Czech architects were able to actually build a number of projects at the time, while in Berlin expressionism in architecture was only just being conceived by Paul Scheerbart, Bruno Taut, and Adolf Behne, all of whom were part of the circle around Walden's magazine *Der Sturm*. Much like Janák, Taut dismissed utilitarian and social demands and emphasized purely artistic ambitions.[36] The Berlin expressionists were also inspired by the spiritual quality of the Gothic and by the beauty of the crystal. However, whereas the Prague architects called for the conquest of matter by spirit, the superiority of depersonalized principles and laws, abstraction over naturalism, causality, and sentimentality, the Berlin theoreticians placed the person at the centre of all efforts.[37] Behne declared that the epoch of comprehension of the world through physical and chemical means, which led to materialism, would now be replaced by biological understanding. He saw this as the direct route to idealism and wrote, "Idealism in modern art is cubism."[38] The Germans' greater emphasis on individuality also led to a greater interest in the interior, in the understanding of architecture "from the inside to the outside," while Prague was still dominated by the outer wrapping, the external appearance of architectural matter: the concern with control over matter was greater than that with control of the interior space. Out of the German movement came Paul Scheerbart's attempt at greater transparency, and the introduction of glass architecture:

If we want to further elevate our culture, then we are compelled to transform our architecture. And this will be possible only if we remove the *Geschlossene* [sense of being enclosed] from the spaces in

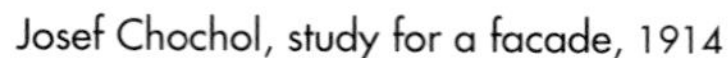

Josef Chochol, study for a facade, 1914

Josef Chochol, design for a corner building, 1914

which we live. We can do this, however, only through the introduction of glass architecture which admits sunlight, moonlight, and starlight into rooms not merely through a few windows, but rather directly, through as many walls as possible being completely glazed in coloured glass. The new environment that we will thereby create must bring us a new culture.[39]

Pavel Janák, sketch, 1916

In 1914, there was a difference of opinions among the architects of the Group of Plastic Artists. While Janák and Gočár strove for an ever greater plasticity of the facade, in the sense of Janák's article "The Renewal of the Facade,"[40] Chochol radically reduced his formal repertory and designed totally purged facades, anticipating early postwar purism. During the First World War, Janák sketched a number of monuments and facades in which he tried to develop a national style. Likely inspired by ancient Slavic models, these were to be markedly colourful and plastic. It would be wrong to assume that any of these studies, featuring prismatic treatment of the walls, anticipated neo-plasticism; the principal goal of Dutch neo-plasticism was a spatial continuum of the inner space clearly articulated on the outside, while Janák's effort was restricted to external matter. After the war, when Janák and Gočár became the leading official representatives of Czech architecture, they used these ideas in a number of monumental buildings with rondo-cubistic detail. But the dynamic charge of prewar cubism seemed to disappear under the weight of the plastic and colour decoration. The substance of the classical composition of the buildings for the Legionnaires' Bank and the Riunione adriatica di Sicurtá insurance company seemed lifeless and closer to a Renaissance conception, something from which the cubists had originally tried to distance themselves. Soon after the Czechoslovak Republic was established, Janák summed up what had been achieved and laid out directions for the future journey in his article "A Third of the Way."[41] He identified displacement of the grammar of the old styles the first part of the journey, already completed. The second part he considered to be the search for a new order of architecture, the new "fibres and warps," which had begun with the cubist movement's efforts to dominate matter through spirit. Janák defined as

Pavel Janák, sketch for a pyramidal monument, 1914

Pavel Janák, sketch, 1916

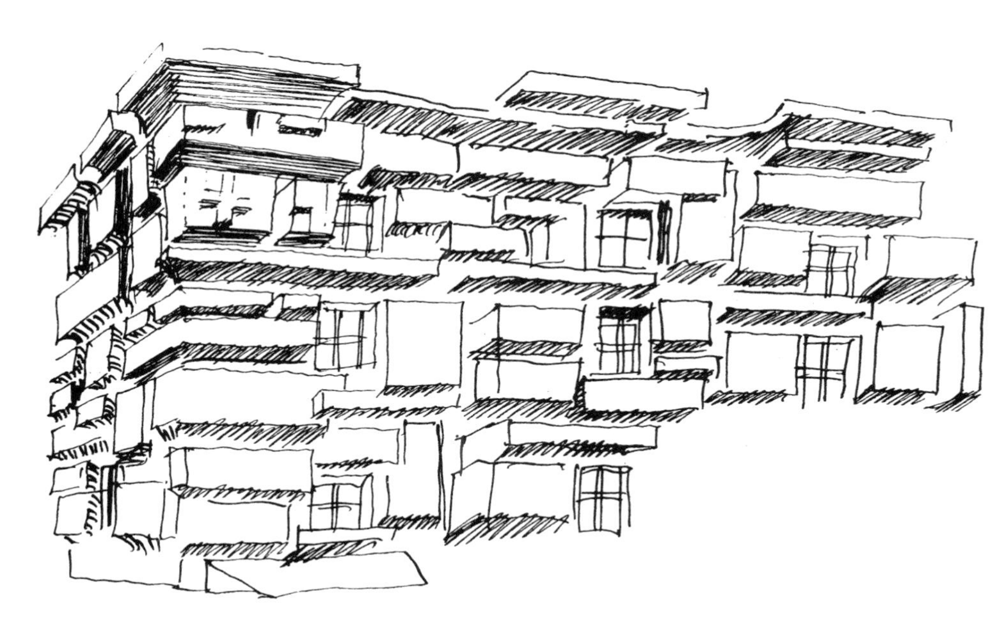

Pavel Janák, sketch from journal, 1917

Josef Gočár, Masaryk Square, Hradec Králové, 1922–1924

the last part of the journey social and utilitarian goals, which were connected with national objectives distinct from the prewar programmes. "While fighting its futile battle of the discovery of matter, our architecture did not dedicate itself to social issues: while it did establish itself firmly on its own, and appropriately started to build from the bottom, it must, if it is to be a national architecture, turn from creating its own order to organizing the purpose of Czech life."

The social idea proposed by Janák was, as usual, most consistently realized by Gočár, for instance in the plan for development of Hradec Králové. Realized in the early thirties, it created an overall unity with a number of charming urban spaces and accents. One of the most impressive—Masaryk Square, with its statue of the president—consummated the development of prewar rondo-cubism as the national style. Behind the Masaryk monument, Gočár created a unifying, almost theatrically effective backdrop of facade gables with high, lively articulated attic storeys.

cat. no. 14a

At the same time, Hofman was trying to incorporate examples of folk Gothic, which would tone down the triangular austerity of the young Czech movement and lead toward a less analytical and more poetic architecture.[42] Hofman's attempts were akin to the experiments of Josef Havlíček and Alois Wachsmann. In 1918, Jirí Kroha was the next to make a significant contribution to cubist architecture. In his first published article, "On Architectural Space and Its Limits,"[43] he emphasized the importance of space, departing from the current line of Czech architecture and bringing to it an unusual dynamic monumentality.

cat. no. 83a–c

cat no. 85

Other architects of Kroha's generation, especially Josef Štěpánek (a student of Plečnik's) and Bohuslav Fuchs, both of whom went through Kotěra's school at the Academy of Plastic Arts, had to come to terms with the heritage of the cubist

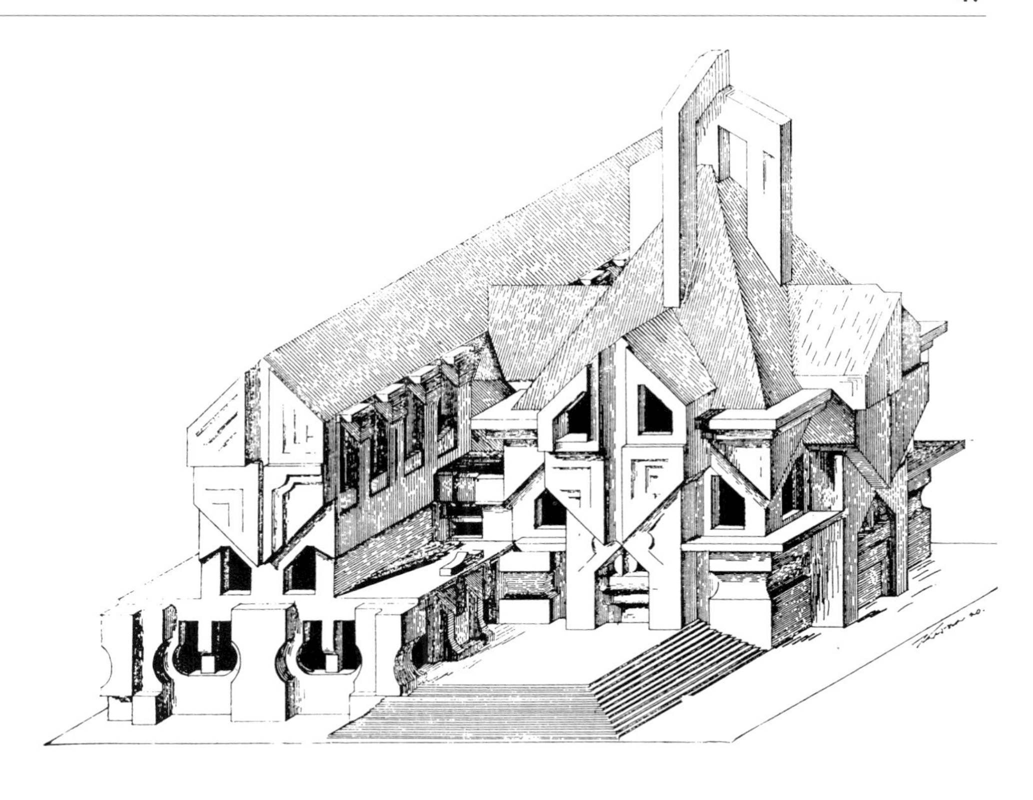

Jiří Kroha, design for a crematorium, 1921

Vlastislav Hofman, study for a monumental building, 1914

Vlastislav Hofman, study for facade, 1914

Vlastislav Hofman, study for garden pavilion, main cornice, 1914

Jiří Kroha, technical school, Mladá Boleslav, 1922–1924

tradition. Besides cubist or rondo-cubist decoration, function, as well as space and its expression, took on greater importance. There was obvious influence from the Berlin architects of the Die gläserne Kette group,[44] and from the works of Erich Mendelsohn, whom these architects knew. An example is the comparison of two designs for the hydro-electric power station at Háj near Mohelnice. Janák's design is similar, in its formal aspects, to his crematorium in Pardubice: interest in the decorative treatment takes precedence over expression of the functional content, resulting in a static, frozen impression. On the other hand, the realized design was by Štěpánek and Fuchs, who also used rondo-cubist detail but allowed it to grow organically and support the effect of matter, culminating in the arch of the roof, thus dynamically expressing the purpose of the building. Around 1918, Novotný realized two cubist apartment buildings: the teachers' housing co-operative in Prague's Old Town, and the hitherto little-known Domovina co-operative apartment complex in Znojmo;[45] in another teachers' co-operative building at Letná in Prague he experimented with rondo-cubist detail. However, Novotný assessed the evolution of the movement skeptically:

cat. no. 79

cat. no. 6a

"The movement of matter" is a seductive slogan, which discredits present ideas on tectonics; it has no laws of gravity, it makes no distinction between the supporting element and that which is supported; the pillar and architrave are replaced with a jumble of crystals—that is, with multifarious interpenetrations of prisms and pyramids, cylinders and cones, various globes. This elemental force has nothing left in common with symmetry; in fact, an attempt is made to suppress the rhythm, which is the oldest element of architecture and matter. At this moment, and precisely through this attempt, architects discover the danger of formal anarchy in their work. The incongruity of the effort, as concerns real possibilities, is understood; the architect, with his practical spirit, of course understands the danger of his ways and returns to natural tectonics—now, however, enriched by the motility of the new form with its countless possibilities.[46]

Novotný himself returned to rough-brick architecture.

Rudolf Stockar added his name to the roster of cubist architects when he designed the Materna factory in the Prague suburb of Holešovice and a villa in Olomouc; in 1920 he added the development of the narrow depression at Prague's Můstek intersection. Ladislav Machoň also designed some buildings in the rondo-cubist style in the early twenties in Pardubice.

Only Josef Chochol did not return to cubism; he bypassed rondo-cubism altogether. At that time he was already leaning toward purism, or, as in the design for the Czechoslovak Embassy in Belgrade, to austere, purified classicism; he expressed his views laconically in the manifesto *What I Strive For*:

That form should be a truly living being and an individuality clearly determined.
That it should speak in a clear language and be instantly comprehensible.
That it should be the empowered expression of the purpose, whose face it is.
That it should stop precisely at the function of this purpose, and be devoid of anything nonessential.
That its simplicity should spring from the sense of an inner life, rich with complex and exciting activity.
That the classic sophistication of its simplicity should not be criss-crossed with fake scratches and wild paintings like the face of an Iroquois chief.
That its still surfaces should submit to a transcendental and perhaps even mystical idea, and align themselves obediently according to its law.
That it should finally be liberated from all archaic influences, epigonism, and eclecticism, and never be touched by the poisonous stench of the decaying corpses of yesterday's styles.
That it should be the strongest and purest exponent of the modern spiritual movement of the world.[47]

Jaroslav Fragner, design for a villa, 1920

Jaroslav Fragner, design for an apartment building, 1921

The next generation of Czech architects—known as the one "run over by a gun-carriage"—was connected with the Devětsil Artists' Association. It included, among others, Jaroslav Fragner, Evžen Linhart, Vít Obrtel, and Karel Honzík. Their leader was the theoretician Karel Teige, who rejected rondo-cubism, and their patrons were Chochol and Feuerstein. When the magazine *L'esprit nouveau* appeared in Prague, in 1921, this generation found new inspiration in it, eventually resulting in the birth of purism and poetism.

Although some monumental building projects were still being completed in 1923 and 1924, architectural design was headed in another direction. The era of cubism and rondo-cubism, the period of efforts to conquer matter by spirit, was now closed.

"The efforts and struggle for plastic expression and architectural form preoccupied us completely for more than ten years," Janák concludes in his article "Matter or Spirit":

First there were only starts and attempts to make new forms, but new forms came soon after, and finally actual logical aggregates. After solitary shapes and objects emerged, the necessity to penetrate further was revealed to us with ever-increasing urgency. By the same logic which gave rise to shapes, we looked also for principles of spatial composition and construction, in order to build into a style the law of matter which we felt. The creation had its developmental phases, new ideas would come, but all of those phases we experienced truly and passionately, and none can be repealed. Gradually a number of architectural and spatial works were created in our country, to which we can point to show our activity, our vitality: they grew out of our conditions, our soil, and our spirit, through local creative work, which we consciously directed, and tried to predict with complete honesty.[48]

In January of 1925, Le Corbusier lectured for the first time in Prague. He mentioned, among other things, the resistance to modern architecture in France; he then went on to say, "In your country you have a similar experience, as I gather from the massive building of Assyrian character, which I notice across the street." He was referring to Janák's Riunione adriatica di Sicurtá building. Oldrich Stary, the senior editor of the magazine *Stavba*, spoke to Janák after the lecture: "He really let you have it, my friend, didn't he?" Janák calmly responded, "What the gentleman is talking about, we have already finished with."[49]

Evaluation of historical events can be very relative . . .

Notes

1. Otakar Novotný, "Úvod k členské výstavě S.V.U. Mánes" (Introduction to the Members' Exhibition of S.V.U. Mánes), *Volné směry* 29 (1932): 61.
2. Jan Kotěra, "O novém umení" (On New Art), *Volné směry* 4 (1900): 189–195.
3. *Styl* 1 (1908–1909): 164, 171, 172, 177.
4. *Styl* 1 (1908–1909): 161–162.
5. Pavel Janák, "Otto Wagner," *Styl* 1 (1908–1909): 41–48.
6. B.H., "Otto Wagner," *Styl* 3 (1911): 187–188.
7. See note 5.
8. *Styl* 1(1908–1909): 2.
9. *Styl* 2 (1909–1910), "Kronika" (Chronicle), April 1910, p. 77.
10. Olga Herbenová and Vladimir Šlapeta, "Pavel Janák, 1882–1956, architektura a užité umění" (Pavel Janák, 1882–1956, Architecture and Applied Art), Guide to the UPM, NTM, and CFVU Exhibition, Prague, 1982.
11. Olga Herbenová and Vladimir Šlapeta, "Pavel Janák 1882–1956," *Architektur und Kunstgewerbe* (Vienna, Semper-Depot), 1984.
12. *Styl* 2 (1909–1910): 56–59.
13. *Styl* 1 (1908–1909): 132.
14. *Styl* 1 (1908–1909): 72.
15. Wilhelm Worringer, "Architektura a plastika z hlediska vcítění" (Architecture and the Plastic from the Point of View of Empathy), *Styl* 4 (1912): 77–100. Adolf von Hildebrand, "Tesání do kamene" (Carving in Stone), *Volné směry* 13 (1909): 367. Theodor Lipps, "Estetika prostorová" (Spatial Aesthetics), *Styl* 5 (1913): 98–117. Theodor Lipps, "Stylizace" (Stylization), Styl, 5 (1913): 127–137. Pavel Janák reflected on Hildebrand's theories in his journals; see the essay by Olga Herbenová in this catalogue. Both essays by Theodor Lipps were translated by Josef Chochol.
16. Zdeněk Wirth, "Barokní gotika v Čechách v XVIII. a 1. polovici XIX. stoleti" (The Baroque Gothic in Bohemia in the 18th and First Half of the 19th Centuries), *Památky archeologické a mistopisné* 23 (1908): 128.
17. Pavel Janák, "Jak může byt zachován Braunův dům?" (How Can the Braun House Be Preserved?), *Za starou Prahu* 1, no. 8 (1910): 60–61.
18. *Styl* 2 (1909–1910), "Kronika" (Chronicle), July 1910, pp. 105–109.
19. V. V. Štech, *Za plotem domova* (Behind Home's Fence) (Prague: Československý spisovatel, 1970), p. 23.
20. Miroslav Lamač, *Osma a Skupina výtvarných umělců 1907–1917* (The "Eight" and the Group of Plastic Artists 1907–1917) (Prague: Odeon, 1988), p. 177.
21. *Styl* 3 (1911): 121–122.
22. Pavel Janák, "Proti náladě v architektuře" (Against Mood in Architecture), *Umělecký měsíčník* 1, no. 3 (1911–1912): 78–80; no. 4 (1911–1912): 105–107.
23. *Umělecký měsíčník* 1, no. 6 (1911–1912): 162-170.
24. Jan Sokol, "K otevření Janákovy výstavy" (On the Occasion of the Opening of Janák's Exhibition), in Pavel Janák, *Vybrané stati autorovy a příspěvky ze semináře ke stému výročí architektova narození* (The Author's Selected Essays and Contributions to the Seminar Celebrating the Centenary of the Architect's Birth) (Prague: Museum of Decorative Arts, 1985), pp. 89–91.
25. Josef Chochol, "K funkci architektonického článku" (On the Function of the Architectural Detail), *Styl* 5 (1913): 93–94.
26. Karel Čapek and Vlastislav Hofman, "Indická architektura" (Indian Architecture), *Styl* 5 (1913): 55–92.
27. Vlastislav Hofman, "Příspěvek k charakteru moderní architektury" (Contribution to the Character of Modern Architecture), *Umělecký měsíčník* 1, no. 8 (1912): 228–231.
28. Zdeněk Lukeš and Jan Svoboda, "Architekt E. Králíček— zapomenutý zjev ceské secese a kubismu" (The Architect E. Králíček—the Forgotten Figure of Czech Secession and Cubism), *Umení* 32 (1984): 441–449.
29. Otakar Novotný, "Architektura symbolická, pomník a Žižkuv pomník" (Symbolic Architecture, the Monument, and the Monument to Žižka), *Volné směry* 18 (1914), 84–85. Miroslav Lamač, *Osma a Skupina výtvarných umělců* (The "Eight" and the Group of Plastic Artists) (Prague: Odeon, 1988), pp. 415–419.
30. *Volné směry* 18 (1914), insert entitled "Zprávy" (News), vol. 1, no. 5–7.
31. Ständige Ausstellungen der Zeitschrift Der Sturm—Achtzehnte Ausstellung—SKUPINA/Prag. Gemälde/Skulpturen/Architektur. Filla, Beneš, Procházka, Gutfreund, Gočár, Janák. Exhibition, 20 September–1 November 1913.
32. Erster Deutscher Herbstsalon Berlin 1913. Represented were Beneš, Filla, Gočár, Gutfreund, and Janák.
33. *Der Sturm* 3, no. 182–183 (1912–1913): 117, a woodcut by Emil Filla called "Still Life." *Der Sturm*, 4, no. 198–199 (1914): 175, Emil Filla, "Head." *Der Sturm* 5, no. 2 (1914–1915), p. 9, Otakar Kubin, "Drawing"; no. 3, p. 17, Otakar Kubin, "Drawing"; pp. 18–19, Josef Čapek, "Moderne Architektur" (essay); p. 21, Vlastislav Hofman, "Design of Cemetery near Prague 1912"; no. 4, p. 25, Vlastislav Hofman, "Detail of Facade 1914"; no. 6, p. 45, Vlastislav Hofman, "Corner House 1914"; no. 8, p. 62, František Langer, "Die Uhr. Schattenspiel im Zimmer der verstorbenen Frau"; no. 10–11, p. 73, Emil Filla, "Drawing"; no. 13–14, p. 89, Vincenc Beneš, "Linocut"; p. 94, Vlastislav Hofman, "Monumental Building 1914"; no. 19–20, pp. 118–119, Vlastislav Hofman, "Upper Cornice of a Garden Pavilion." *Der Sturm* 6, no. 12 (1915–1916): 5, Josef Čapek, "Linocut."
34. Vladimir Šlapeta, "Svaz českého díla—Der tschechische Werkbund," in Astrid Gmeiner and Gottfried Pirhofer, *Der österreichische Werkbund* (Vienna: Residenz Verlag Salzburg, 1985), pp. 191–207.
35. Quoted in Otakar Novotný, "Počátky Svazu českého díla" (The Beginning of the Association of Czech Accomplishment), *Věci a lidé* 1 (1947): 280–283.
36. Bruno Taut, "Eine Notwendigkeit," *Der Sturm* 4, no. 196–197 (1914): 174.
37. Richard Fuchs, "Die neue Kunstanschauung," *Der Sturm* 1, no. 63 (1910–1911): 502.
38. Adolf Behne, "Biologie und Kubismus," *Der Sturm* 5, no. 11 (1914–1915): 68-71.
39. Paul Scheerbart, "Glasarchitektur," in *Der Sturm. Herwarth Walden und die Europäische Avantgarde Berlin 1912–1922.* Catalogue of an exhibition held at the Nationalgalerie at the Orangerie of the Schlosse Charlottenburg Berlin, 24 September–19 November 1961.
40. Pavel Janák, "Obnova průčelí" (The Renewal of the Facade), *Umělecký měsíčník* 2, (1912–1914): 85–95.
41. Pavel Janák, "V tretine cesty" (A Third of the Way), *Volné směry* 19 (1918): 218–226.
42. Vlastislav Hofman, "O dalším vývoji naší moderní architektury" (Concerning the Future Development of our Modern Architecture), *Volné směry* 19 (1918): 193–206.
43. Jiří Kroha, "O prostoru architektonickém a jeho mezích" (On Architectural Space and Its Limits), *Veraikon* 6 (1920).
44. Personal communication with Bohuslav Fuchs, June, 1971.
45. *Styl* 1, no. 6, tables 84 and 86.
46. Otakar Novotný, "L'architecture et l'art décoratif modernes en Tchécoslovaquie," *L'amour de l'art* 4 (1923): 663–670.
47. *Musaion* 1 (1921): 47.
48. *Styl* 5, no. 10 (1924–1925): 170–174.
49. See note 24.

Cubism in Applied Arts and Design

Milena Lamarová

Josef Gočár, bookcase, 1913

Parting Ways with the Nineteenth Century

When we walk by cubist houses and are affected by their unusually dramatic exterior walls, we must also wonder about their interior space. Do these interiors offer the spatial experience that is indicated by the facade? Once inside, would we encounter sharply fractured walls and angled planes? If we enter, we find in the halls and stairways preserved parts of grilles, iron fittings, door panels, and floor mosaics, occasionally a shaped stuccoed ceiling in the foyer—ornamental signs of a style which did not have enough time to really mature, to be lived, cultivated, and anchored, especially in the interiors.

The floor plans of cubist buildings provide ample evidence that their interiors remained within the conventional scheme of traditional living, be it in villas or apartment buildings—there was no revolutionary concept regarding the interior organization of space as such. Nonetheless, the furniture designed by cubist architects between 1910 and 1914 is impressive for its uncommon expressive strength, which seems to propose a new perception of space—a desire to persuade us of the possibilities of a new choreography of kinetic relationships between person, object, and space.

At the threshold of the twentieth century, scientists had formulated new mathematical and physical laws concerning the structure of space, time, matter, and motion.[1] It was a propitious time to use art as a sounding instrument for the perception of new cognitive, scientific, and technical ideas. Einstein's discovery that the spatio-temporal continuity is interrupted by the movement of matter implied new ways to approach spatial reality in terms of the activation of matter and shape, which would reciprocally affect space. This new spatio-temporal dimension became one of the basic points of departure for theoretical considerations about cubism as the means of "making matter dynamic." The principle of cubist painting, comprising the dynamics of motion and a fragmentary perception of the world, were, after all, in direct contradiction to the Euclidean conception of space filled with forms in constant geometric relationships adopted in the positivistic nineteenth century.

The atmosphere in Prague around 1910 cannot be understood without considering the city's richly structured cultural life, combining Kafkaesque themes of existential anxiety, the sense of an inability to grasp the modern world, the sophistication of the symbolist and expressionist literature of the Czech and Prague German circles (associated with, among others, Kafka, Werfel, Brod, Meyrinck, Jiří Karásek ze Lvovic, Jakub Deml, and Otokar Březina), and an intuition of the impending catastrophic war. Nonetheless, the Czech artistic avant-garde, which was firmly established in 1911 with the foundation of the Group of Plastic Artists, was based on an essentially self-assured and self-realizing optimism. This was the generation that revolted against provincial obtuseness and the post-impressionistic interpretation of the world. For the architects of the cubist group it was also a generational revolt, directed even against their great teachers, Jan Kotěra and Otto Wagner.

The group's basic premise was the Nietzschean conviction that one has the right to see and create according to one's innermost imagination, in keeping with Riegl's formulation of *Kunstwollen* as the real action of an immanent force penetrating and subjugating matter. Another important catalyst was Bergsonian vitalism; its concept of intuitive knowledge as an integration of rational knowledge was promulgated by the poet and critic Richard Weiner: "[Cubism] is, however, less of a common property than anything else, because it demands much intuition and intelligence, but especially because it demands that intuition be consciously subordinated to intelligence. It is not actually a trend—it is a phenomenon."[2]

The cubist generation strengthened and broadened the spiritual ties between art and philosophy, as can be seen in its publications, translations, and diaries.[3] Josef Chochol also defended this linkage in his essay "On the Function of the Architectural Detail": "This is why we have lost interest in minor architectural detail and why we do not believe in it. We are enthusiastic about total form, felt and presented with excitement, form that is all-encompassing and has a total and instant effect. . . . We need the excitement of new artistic intensities, streaming from the tempestuous and fervent substance of contemporary life."[4]

These were signs of the definitive break with naturalism, decorative tendencies, and the ornamentation of historicism and the Secession, which dominated Czech furniture production at that time. The construction boom at the end of the nineteenth century stimulated the routine manufacture of furnishings in the neo-Baroque and neo-Renaissance styles and imitating superficially perceived models from the Secession.

Abandoning ornament was an external factor, but it was nonetheless determining for the development of forms. It had earlier been demanded by Loos, and to a certain extent also by Josef Hoffmann, both of whom were moving toward rationalism in construction, and even toward a complex spatial integration of interior and exterior. In Prague, however, the issue was different: it did not involve ridding form of ornament, but making the shape itself so dynamic that it could autonomously fulfill an ornamental function. Chochol wrote, "We want to replace ornamentalism with an intellectualized vitality of form, and whatever we reject in decoration and ornament, we try to more than make up for by the power of concentrated and total effect. Its signs include a taste of a certain mathematical exactness, unpolished curtness, and hearty roughness, which we prefer to the former starched quality of perfumed, fallow dandyisms and perversions, and the falsely naïve geniality of the petite bourgeoisie."[5]

The new spatio-temporal concept was intuitively accepted by the young architects as a protest against convention, and at the same time as a justification for subjective self-expression and creative exaltation, which by the use of deformed shapes gave new movement, and thus meaning, to space and matter. As well, it signified an escape from Czech provincialism and from obtuse adherence to tradition, in favour of opening up to Europe and the world. The new generation of architects saw as their task the creation of a common modern cultural awareness. National consciousness had outgrown its revivalist diapers: it was no longer a case of Czech against European. Europeanism in Bohemia was an intellectual certitude.

In furniture design, the parting with the Secession was decisive, although the influence of Viennese modernism, Hoffmann, and the Wiener Werkstätte was a pronounced feature of the early pieces, particularly those by Pavel Janák and Otakar Novotný. In the field of glass and ceramics, there was a certain natural affinity for form determined by traditional production relationships. (For instance, the glass for the Wiener Werkstätte was made in Czech factories.) This break with the past was manifested by a rejection not only of its organic ornamentation and decorativeness, but also of its ideology. For the cubist architects, art became an autonomous category, and not just a decoration. It no longer served life, it was

Josef Chochol, apartment building,
Neklan Street, Prague, 1913

Strolling in the Vrtbovská Garden are Z. Foustková-Borovičková (left), V. V. Štech (second from left), Vlastislav Hofman (sitting), the author Langer (next to Hofman), the industrialist Sochor (bottom right), the critic and theoretician Antonín Matějček (top right), and Pavel Janák (top centre)

above all a vehicle for the artist's expression. It was supposed to convey a contemporary world view, but it did not function this way. The idea of the *Gesamtkunstwerk*, embraced by the Secession and consistently nurtured for decades through the efforts of the Arts and Crafts revival movement, disappeared from the horizon. A utilitarian object became, in the eyes of the cubists, a theme for the creation of a discrete work of art, in which functional considerations and ties to production were secondary. The material and the technological process also took a back seat to concentration on shape and its dynamics.

Olga Herbenová made a detailed analysis of the production technology of cubist furniture in her article "Czech Furniture from 1911 to 1915 in the Collection of the Museum of Decorative Arts in Prague." She described the extent to which the designers placed their formal ideas above any practical, realistic conditions of traditional cabinet-making: "The Prague art workshops in which the furniture was built found it very difficult to fulfill the special demands of the designer. . . . The bevelled corners had to be faked; they are hollow, for otherwise the furniture would have been disproportionately heavy. . . . The architect's demands would probably have been better served by a malleable material such as concrete, which Gočár was used to working with . . . he starts neither from construction nor from material. He turns Semper's laws just about inside out."[6] It seems that the syntax of the cubist architects anticipated the modern technologies, which permit "casting from one piece" or "the cutting of matter in depth." Ironically, just like the designers of the Secession, the cubists too would turn back to the crafts.

Josef Gočár, dining table, 1912–1913, shown at the 4th Exhibition of the Group in Prague in 1913

Josef Gočár, interior, 1912, table and armchair shown at the 1st Exhibition of the Group

Pavel Janák, room of the director of the Protective Association of Breweries, 1912–1913, manufactured by PUD

The radical demand for furniture as an art form representing a self-possessed organism charged with new inner energy—this is what Vlastislav Hofman had in mind when he wrote, "Modern spirit does not like naturalism served up plain. Today we require different formal ties, structurally distinct from the ways of the Secession. What we want today is shape purged of the formal surface that was required by realism after the end of the Secession. In contrast to the realistic liveliness of the vegetal form of the Secession, today's look seems to be more compatible with a smooth, machined look and the purity of formal mood. Thus, what occurs in most modern architecture is the impression of a certain dissimilarity with anything found alive in nature—a formal character which might be called the abstraction of appearance."[7] Hofman referred to movement in space, stereometric vision, and intuited relativity between shape, people, and space as a "certain dissimilarity with anything found in nature," which would inevitably lead to a natural consequence—the "abstraction of appearance." It may have been that very abstraction, liberating furniture from the narrative citations of historicism or naturalism, that made of Czech cubist furniture a manifesto of the future. The naturalistic symbols of nature became unnecessary. On the contrary, the centre of interest became a new, artificial "nature" involving a group of abstract crystalline formations organized not in a geometric system but in an inner rhythm, determined by the artist's will to create form.

Cubist furniture is in striking contradiction with its surroundings, as we can see in period photographs: the conventional central placement of the table with chairs around it; a cabinet filled with decorative ceramics, some actually adorned with floral or folk patterns; a table and chairs near a tiled stove, Persian carpets on the floors—these banal environments of the traditional middle-class life style give a somewhat confusing picture of the revolutionary nature of Czech cubist furniture, which we would ideally imagine to be part of an entirely new spatial conception. It was in fact a system of singles, although its components were bound together by the excuse of an order and of a typological purpose. Although Janák allowed that the items should serve some purpose, this furniture was actually an exercise in creation of individual abstract objects that were as complex as sculptures. It was to be another sixty years before Ettore Sottsass exhibited his meditative furniture-objects,

Otakar Novotný, interior for J. Štenc, ca. 1912

placed—unlike the naïve cubist avant-garde ones—in an empty, liberated space. Herbenová wrote of cubist architects, "Their interior was the epilogue of the nineteenth-century culture that they so passionately rejected."

Cubist furniture made for various clients—usually artists or followers of the avant-garde—was designed in terms of conventional typological groups. In its character and conception, it anticipated the emancipation of the piece of furniture as an independent object with the right to be perceived and evaluated autonomously. The functional aspects of living did not concern the cubists. The objective was for the designer's artistic idea to shine through.

The persuasiveness of this notion was so emphatic that, in the case of certain objects, it led not only to formal abstraction but to a semantic shift: an ashtray became minor architecture, a glass cabinet a crystalline formation, a dresser a warped wooden polygon. The designers moved in astatic, shifted planes of form, but also of meaning. They had the ability to create a new "landscape" and to abstract a variety of objects.

What began as simply the subtext to seriously expressed philosophical postulates, in no way programmatically deliberate, engendered the possibility of a new semantic structuring. As Hofman wrote in a 1913 text, "On the Individualizing Form in Architecture," "Every object is part of a new nature without veristic air and raw juice. It is something for its own sake and exists in a self-supporting formal life. The formal interest in the animation of matter is different than it was during the Baroque period, when movement in matter was understood materially. This individualization brushes aside the old logic of buildability and replaces it with its own logic of artistic imagination, ideas about the object . . . it is about as free as painting. . . ."

But the inconclusive and, at the time, unrealized dream of the cubist architects was expressed by Janák in his key article "About Furniture and Other Things."[8] He wrote that while practical requirements should be retained, the higher requirements of proportionality, expression, form, and spatial relationships, according to which furniture and living space became "an expression of spiritual life and spiritual organization," must prevail. This view was the absolute antithesis of what the Czech avant-garde of the twenties began to assert a decade later.

Pavel Janák, commode, 1913

Cubism—Expressionism

In Prague, the year 1912 was unusually rich in cultural activities. Cubism as a new trend had begun to assert itself significantly in Czech art, architecture, and applied arts. The first cubist houses were being built in Prague on Celetná and Tycho de Brahe streets and in Podolí; on the Smetana Embankment, Artěl's display windows featured provocatively shaped cubist ceramics; and through Gočár's and Janák's initiative the Prague Artistic Workshop was founded for the manufacture of furniture and lighting fixtures.[9] Local, thematic, and stylistic integration also began to occur, as "Czech cubism began to actively intervene in the environment in which it was created" (Lamač).

The Group of Plastic Artists organized its first and second exhibitions at the Prague Municipal Hall in 1912. At the first one, Gočár, Janák, Hofman, and Chochol exhibited both designs and furniture. At the second, Gočár, Janák, and Hofman were represented by photographs of furniture, furniture pieces, and designs. Also in 1912, Gočár and Janák exhibited with the Group in Munich.

The surface geometry of cubist painting was the basic point of departure, but transference to a plastic-spatial model for the structural building of shapes was attempted by each architect in his own way. Although they learned a great deal from Otto Gutfreund, who mastered the three-dimensionality of spatial dynamism superbly in his sculptures, they found that the total break-up of the volume of matter and its deconstruction into separate formal data posed certain obstacles when applied to a house or a utilitarian object.

This may be why studies, drawings, and designs form such an important part of the oeuvre of the movement. They exude the spontaneity of the new vision, a determined effort to create a spatial reworking of an intellectually understood cubist principle. The drawings also reveal clearly the extent to which material was a secondary concern. For instance, Hofman's pen studies for seating furniture seem intended to be made in poured concrete. Gočár's sketches for cabinets and sideboards seem amorphous as far as materials are concerned, but also speak of superb architectural discipline. Janák's drawings, especially those from his journals, reveal a feverish study of the most extreme limits of an object's stability, its spatial

Pavel Janák, sketch from journal, 1912

Pavel Janák, design for a writing desk, 1912

dispersion, or even its "absorption." The counterpoint to these drawings is found in some of the designs for actual orders, which seem to be imbued with the drawing skill of the Biedermeier. Thus, visionary fantasies and concern for conventions of living are juxtaposed.

The influence of cubist painting is quickly revealed in a glance at the colour scale of cubist interior furnishings. Wood—very often beech, sometimes pine or walnut—is in brown and black tones, with the least possible surface treatment, so that the structure of the wood does not interfere with the intentions of the shape. The materials used for accessories (opaque glass and marble slabs) are black or white. This is in direct opposition to the sensuality of the Secession's artistic crafts.

The main feature of an early furniture group designed by Janák for Dr. Borovička in 1911–1912 is the contrast of the black and white surfaces on the bookcase and the writing desk. Particularly in the consistently deformed angles of the desk, the white surfaces are laid out in a rhythm suggesting the function of light and shadow in early cubist painting.

Pavel Janák, design for a writing desk, 1911–1912; desk was shown at the 1st Exhibition of the Group

Up to this point, very little attention was paid to upholstery coverings. Leather or dull-coloured fabric was used in Hofman's and Chochol's designs. Stripes were often the pattern of choice, as can be seen in the pictorial documentation. The coverings designed by František Kysela were usually greeted with puzzlement. The stylized vegetal design apparently contradicted the shapes of Gočár's furniture in the pieces designed for the actor Otto Boleška and the historian V. V. Štech. Kysela's natural preference for ornamental decorativism did not seem to agree with the orthodoxy of cubist theories. However, if we look at the rhythmicized, expressionistic compositional arrangement of some of Špála's paintings from 1912 and 1913 (*The Brickworks*, *Women by the Water*, *Three Washerwomen*, and *Rainbow II*), or if we compare Picasso's 1907 paintings of women and viaducts and Braque's 1908 paintings of houses in Estaque with their organic, shattering rhythmization of the landscape, then Kysela's textile designs are not out of context. On the contrary, not only are the sophisticated, stylized leaves and flowers akin to a

Vlastislav Hofman, sketches of table and small tables, 1912

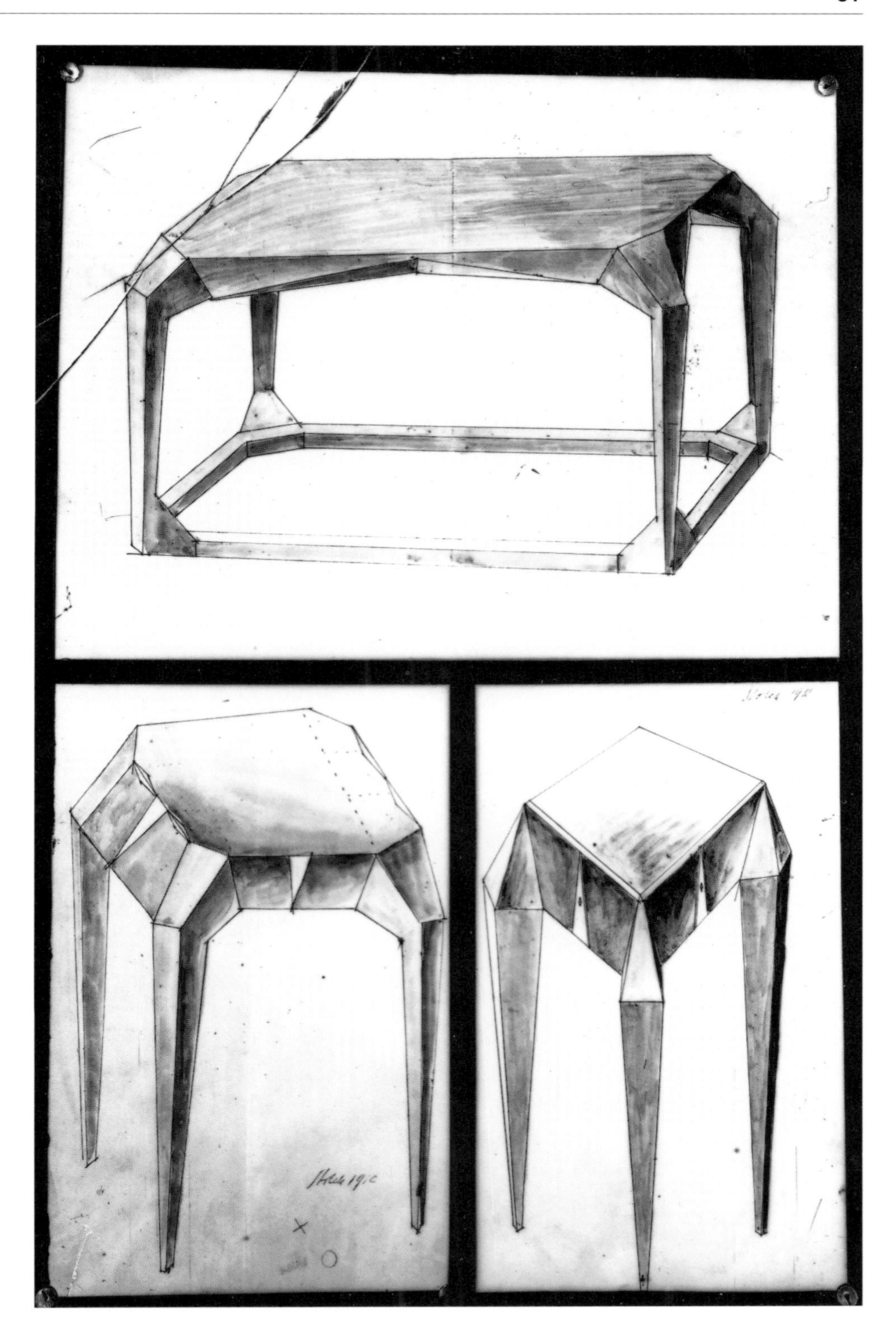

painterly treatment of the natural element—for instance, in Bohumil Kubista's painting *Still Life with a Skull* (1912)—but in application to the dynamic shape of the sofa for Štech they amplify the visual spatial activity of this eccentric object, which thus actually penetrates its surroundings. In the sofa for Boleška, the wooden frame of which firmly outlines the architectural volume of the object, Kysela's ornamentation becomes the transition between stable and rotational percept.

cat. no. 114

cat. no. 109

The effect of cubist painting on furniture should not be overestimated. The meaning of its form lies in the fact that it was created as an independent paraphrase of cubism, with emphasis on theoretical conclusions and not only on visual impressions. The tendency to dramatize the cubist principle often led to the transference of the inner tectonics to the plastic surface contour of a building or object;

Josef Gočár, terrace of spa building in Bohdaneč, 1912

the transference was sometimes concentrated on the ornamental distribution of the structure. From this it was not far to the expressionist gesture, which certainly was not foreign to the Czech *genus loci.* That "Dionysian vertigo" (Pehnt)—dramatic suspense, dissonance, pluralism of forms—was at the same time arbitrarily controlled by the rationalism of architectural design.

A heretical approach to grand stylistic impulses, with a quiet sense of humour underlying an unexpectedly powerful statement, a refined feeling for contradiction and formal multiplicity, reaching all the way to the grotesque, always manifested itself in Bohemia during peripheral periods of stylistic transitions, sometimes in expressions indistinguishable from mannerism. The Czech sensibility absorbed them as uniquely its own in an inimitably idiosyncratic fashion, as it had with the Gothic and the Baroque. The cubist initiative in the first decade of the twentieth century was no longer a slowly developing inspiration, but a real movement within the trenchant Czech culture of around 1910.

In the context of contemporary terminology, Štech identified this work—although with some reservations—as "Czech expressionism"; he found analogous movements in Italy, Hungary, Germany, and Poland. This seems to indicate that the term cubo-expressionism fits a segment of furniture production, especially after 1912. Production reacted to a certain degree to analytic and synthetic cubism, but it also reflected some of the accompanying inspirational sources of the period, such as neo-primitivism and the summary simplicity and compression of the Egyptian pyramids. Karel Čapek and Vlastislav Hofman write, in their essay "On Ancient Indian Architecture," about the "spiritualized abstraction of matter," which corresponds well to cubistic theory.

The influence of neo-primitivism was particularly evident in the work of Chochol and Hofman. The small table, armchair, and sofa designed by Chochol in 1911 for the English Circle in Prague have generously arranged surfaces, based on octagons and hexagons. The armchair and the sofa have closed full backrests and are evocative of a throne or of ancient Egyptian architecture, especially given their original placement, shown in a period photograph of the Prague Municipal Hall. (They were fitted with wheels for easier manipulation.) However, their substantiality and monumentality are only apparent; in reality, this is elegant, restrained furniture.

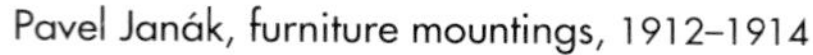

Pavel Janák, furniture mountings, 1912–1914

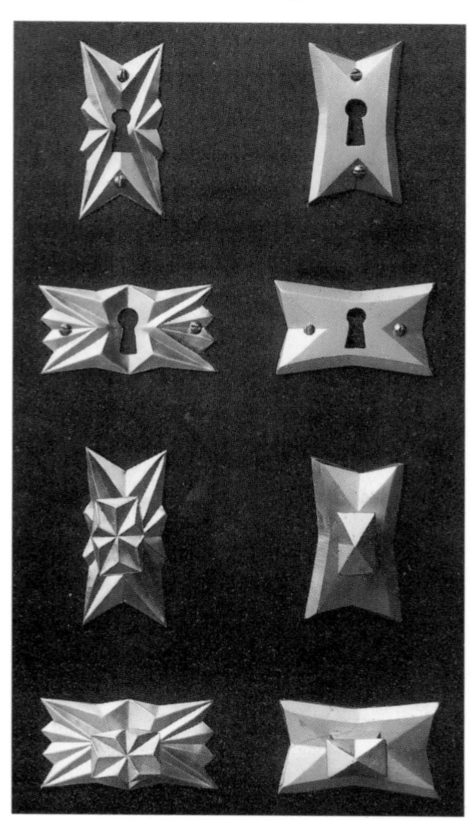

Josef Gočár, bookcase, 1913

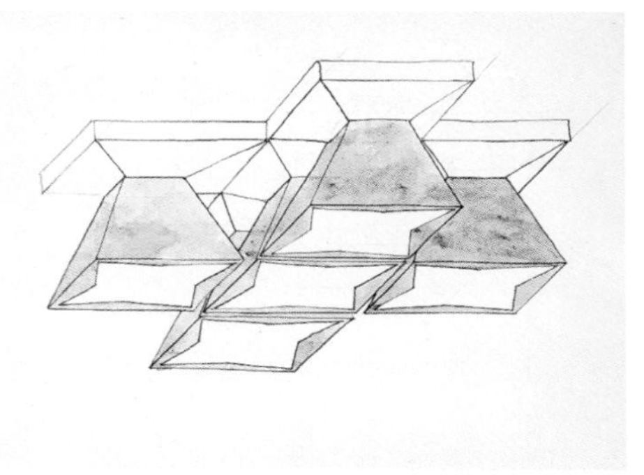

Antonín Procházka, design for a ceiling lighting fixture, 1911–1914

Josef Gočár, interior of spa building, Bohdaneč, 1912

Throughout his short fling with cubism, Chochol revealed an uncommon sensitivity for the organization of the inner tectonics of an object in a restrained form. This restraint was also what led him away from cubism before it reached its culmination. Chochol's early purism (1914) was the logical conclusion of his cubist creative phase, which he worked through with noble assurance.

The almost daily exchanges, joint exhibitions, and collaborations brought the architects into very close personal contact with the painters and sculptors. But problems still had to be solved independently in architecture and in the design of utilitarian objects. The split between analytic and synthetic cubism was not entirely unambiguous.[10] It seems that designers tried to apply various cubist principles to individual furniture types. What they had in common was the great attention that they all paid to the design of writing desks.

There were obvious differences in temperament and method between the two principal designers, Gočár and Janák. Gočár was spontaneous and productive, and did not theorize. His initial work consisted of designs for his own home, of which the most prominent components are two large pieces of furniture—or, rather, monumental architectural structures—a sideboard and a cabinet. Their considerable mass is segmented by a complicated system of prisms; the wedge-shaped frames rest on bevelled polygonal plinths, and the upper parts open out like wings, almost resembling deformed crystalline structures from a paleolithic landscape. These pieces, which were extremely difficult to manufacture, have been exhibited often, and stand up to critical standards applied to sculpture. The total effect is further enhanced by veneer laid diagonally in different directions. To these monuments is added an armoire, less dazzling at first glance, but generously balanced in its proportions and refracted angles.

Josef Gočár, chandelier for a girl's room, 1913

Gočár's robust, occasionally moving statement was developed further in a combined bedroom–study group designed for Boleška in 1913. The unrestrained experimentation he exercised in designing his own living space apparently yielded to the requirements of the client; thus he interpreted the dynamics of matter more in the contour plan than in matter as such. The sharply articulated feet and the consistent rhythm of the recessed flat lines place this furniture within the cubo-

cat. nos. 103–112

Josef Gočár, wall lighting fixture, 1912

cat. nos. 109 and 107

expressionist idiom. The most significant pieces are the sofa and the writing desk: in them, Gočár reached for the expressive linear gesture of jagged cornices, which somewhat resemble the solution for the entrance of the spa building at Bohdaneč. A chandelier and a clock are also part of the set. In its distribution of mutually interpenetrating masses with dramatic angles, the table clock is an autonomous cubist plastic work, a monument reduced in size. The chandelier has expressively bent wings. Its plastic and lighting dynamics are accentuated by rows of glass ornaments, which may be interpreted as a manufacturing tradition of chandeliers or as an inheritance from the Secession, but also as an attempt to deepen the spatial luminous dynamics.

cat. no. 257

cat. no. 256

The design of the interior for Štech was the culmination of Gočár's period of classic cubism. Here, he tried for the last time for the spatial constructive properties of the original cubist principles, provoking Štech's famous pronouncement that "the furniture in question is rather theoretical." In this furniture group, diverse tendencies are demonstrated in the use of different types of wood, but also in the conception. While the writing desk is divided into a discernible composition of sharply articulated masses, the sideboard contains certain elements of transparency, used earlier by Gočár in a bookcase with jagged verticals in a 1912 group. An

cat. no. 118

cat. no. 117

cat. no. 95

Josef Gočár, chandelier, 1913–1914, exhibited at the Werkbund Exhibition at Cologne, 1914

almost bizarre monumental chord is sounded in the backrest of the sofa, with its three sharply cranked apexes and intricately executed upholstery, which follows all the sharp angles of the complicated structure.

cat. no. 114

The sofa was shown in 1914 at the German Werkbund exhibition in the Austrian pavilion, which was designed by Otakar Novotný. This exposition could be termed cubo-expressionist. It contained Gočár's furniture from the years 1912 to 1914, a distinctly monumental chandelier with glass ornaments, and murals and a carpet designed by František Kysela. (Unfortunately, the chandelier and the carpet no longer exist.) In this exhibition interior is clearly seen the penetration of formal progression from spatial cubist deconstructions to expressive linearity, which in its ornamentality alone presages Art Deco. The German critic Peter Jessen assessed this interior in the 1915 yearbook of the German Werkbund: "Beauty is sought here in surfaces and objects through sharp contours and intrepid angles, by the abdication of everything irrational . . . tectonic cubism is born here from thought rather than from feeling . . . the future alone will show us if the full-blooded genius of this new movement will evolve further."[11]

Janák's approach was quite different; he was in fact the leading theoretician of cubism in architecture, and his ideas were reflected in his realized designs. In his article "The Cube and the Pyramid" are stated the principles that are consistently reflected in his executed works.

cat. no. 141

The chair from the furniture group for Dr. Borovička, designed in 1911, is a perfect transposition of Janák's intellectual approach to work. The triangle becomes the principal formal sign, determining the entire contour. Each new perspective on this visually prickly, but in fact comfortable, chair offers animated silhouette views; it moves in space like a sophisticated, fragile bibelot. Janák never underestimated the horizons of views. The bevelled shapes of his chairs' very thin legs contribute to the stereometric perception of the contour as a whole. This approach achieves maximum effect in the dinner table designed for the Jakubec family in 1912. Here, the significant element also involves the counterpoint between the thin legs, which seem to have a screw-like rotation, and a massive top with bevelled veneering. A commode which is part of the same group could be called an actual illustration of Janák's cubist theories. The substance of the commode is distributed into rhythmically faceted sharp angles. The object rests on slanted legs, and its aggressive silhouette protrudes into space in bare surfaces.[12]

cat. no. 145

cat. no. 143

Janák used pyramidal shapes arranged in an agitated spatial rhythm to replace the classic vertical of the right-angled strut. This element occurs in his work very frequently; it would seem that he was concerned with the question of statics theoretically and practically to an almost obsessive degree. This is also evidenced in his journals. (See also O. Herbenová's study.)

Janák's study for a monumental interior (1912) shares characteristics with the design for a conference-room group from 1913 (the furniture is preserved only in period photographs), in which the faceted leg, supporting a polygonal table top,

Pavel Janák, bedroom furniture for Dr. Borovička, 1912

Pavel Janák, dressing table, 1912–1914

the thin legs of the seating furniture with bevelled edges, and the trapezoidal seats and backs in sophisticated complex angles evoke the dynamics of "matter penetrating into space." In Janák's conception, their mutual integration seems to create rotating movement, evoking the feeling of "an eccentric situation of spatial experiencing" (Fry), a certain sense of being drawn into a space in motion, rather than of confinement in a static cube.

Finally, the dressing table designed for a lady's room for the theatre director Vojta Novák is an extremely significant cubo-expressionistic object in terms of spatial dynamics. The mass of the table, with its wing-like break, is surmounted by a three-part mirror, framed in irregular bevelled angles. This arrangement shifts the mass of the object into almost unreal horizons. Its astatic nature breaks with the laws of tectonics, creating tension and dissonance and reflecting an inner contradiction; it also creates a flowing space (*Raumflucht*) in the imagination of the observer, who is thrust into it by the artist's will, as if into the real action of an immanent force.[13]

Both Gočár and Janák were profoundly affected by cubism and by theoretical thinking regarding its influence on perception of the world. While the movement's so-called classic phase, filled with convincing and vital creativity, ended in 1914, they further developed and transformed its message.

Between 1910 and 1914, Vlastislav Hofman was also developing his oeuvre; he did not restrict himself to architecture, furniture, and ceramics, but worked also in the graphic arts, painting, scenography, and writing.[14] Like Chochol, he was strongly influenced by neo-primitivism early in his career. He wrote, "We know the art of the primitive nations, the manifestation of a youthful, thirsty organism, a strong and simple expression. . . . New art uses the most conspicuous and expressive means, thus formally also the most abstract."[15]

cat. nos. 131–132

The pyramidal legs on the furniture designed in 1911–1912, for the sculptor Maratka, were a kind of overture to all of Hofman's future work, including its details and decorations. The broad-minded simplicity, almost austerity, in his furniture anticipated his later scenographic work, in which he reached maximal expressiveness by very simple means. The contours of this furniture are lapidary, as if purged almost to the point of being emblematic.

Hofman was the only designer to contract with small shops in order to realize his designs in more than one sample. In a letter from Artěl to Hofman dated 16 December 1911, there is mention of delivery of the design for a bedroom to the cabinetmaker František Glazar in the district of Královskě Vinohrady in Prague, using Artěl as the agent. Another firm in Vinohrady which carried out Hofman's designs for Artěl was owned by František Červenka. Artěl also arranged the manufacture of glass sets at the Pryl glass factory in Růženín. Published illustrations of liqueur sets and the existing sets show, however, that regardless of how passionately avant-garde Hofman's theories may have been, in traditional materials he held to conventional shapes and geometric design.

Hofman developed dynamic spatial experiments in an absolutely superior manner in architectural drawings, metal, and ceramics. His architectural designs and expressionistically tuned studies (many of which were linocuts) demonstrate not only an awareness of movement, but also an emphasis on rhythm. Hofman's approach in essence confirms the contemporary view of space as a system of tensions with clearly defined distribution, which determines space as a process of extension, and not as a simple summation of impulses.

Motion as a technical discipline was a natural inspiration in contemporary pan-European cultural activity, expressed most significantly in Marinetti's declaration "On the Beauty of Speed" in the *Futurist Manifesto* of 1909. Not all Czech

Opposite page
Pavel Janák, chair, 1911–1912

architects had the same attitude toward Italian futurism; some were rather critical. However, comparison of Czech and Italian dynamism throughout the oeuvre does indicate a clear differentiation between visualized motion in the work of Italian futurists and an animated perception of motion, emanating from the inner tectonics of matter per se, as it was manifested in Bohemia, where the concern was with matter in motion and not with depicted motion. Gutfreund coined the term "latent kinetics," and according to Josef Čapek "dynamism is much more likely a spiritual form of modern life." Later attempts at optical and volume-related "levitations"—for example, G. Balla's study of the Löwenstein house in Düsseldorf in 1912, the experiments concerning a chromatic environment, and later work by Marinetti, van Doesburg, El Lissitzky, designers of De Stijl, and others—were connected to this kinetic sense.

It is no accident that Gutfreund, in his essay "Plane and Space," refers to the movement, technique, and aesthetics of dance. The entire generational group was very keenly aware of the notion of physicality.[16] Movement as an artistic discipline was characteristic of the contemporary intellectual stylistic approach. The new art of dance used as its point of departure ideas similar to those of cubist architecture about the distribution of mass and movement in space. Isadora Duncan disrupted the "segmented system" of classical dance; the Bratislava native Rudolf von Laban worked out a complex methodology, based on German expressionism. The teachings of Jacques Dalcroze influenced Adolphe Appia's creation of rhythmic spaces (1909–1910), in which he wanted to use the expressive element as opposed to the sign. In so doing, he was disrupting the connotative system of contemporary classical choreography in a way similar in essence to the attempts by those practising the avant-garde plastic arts.

Josef Gočár, metal coat-hook, 1912–1914

The conception of space in which symbolically objective perception is transformed to spatially related perception when new expressive methods of visual language are evoked by interventions of physicality—a sort of metaspace—may have been the subconscious desire of the Czech cubist avant-garde. The recent avant-gardes of the seventies, then those of the nineties, have also tried to capture this. The signs of expressionism were very vividly absorbed in Czech cubist work, although it often was a spontaneous way out of an unresolved cubist problem.

Crystal

At the pinnacle of his career, Gočár worked on designs for metal objects, mostly lighting fixtures, but also for more mundane pieces such as coatracks, in which the designer's superior feeling for the lapidary but manifold meaning of form was revealed. For quite a long time, Janák and Hofman designed ceramics for the Artěl Co-operative.

Artěl was founded in 1908 on a principle analogous to that of the Wiener Werkstätte, although it was more modestly conceived. In its programme declaration, Artěl said, "Our association emerged to stand against the factory-made stereotype and surrogate; we want to resurrect the feeling for plastic work and taste in daily life."[17]

Initially, Artěl played a progressive role in the interpretation of art in production, but it was generally seen, especially during the twenties, as the purveyor of antiquated views of "applied arts." By emphasizing traditional crafts and folklore, it supported decorative tendencies in an era that was making different demands.

The collaboration between the cubists and Artěl gave its production a more pronounced character and served as a useful counterweight to its folklorizing tendencies, which were a part of its profile from the beginning. Through their

cat. nos. 214–215

designs, Janák and Hofman influenced some designers who were outside of the cubist circle. Horejc, for instance, created several strongly pure cubist vases. The ceramics for Artěl were manufactured by the firm of Rydl and Thon in Svijany-Podolí.

Even the multi-talented Rudolf Stockar designed jewellery and glass for Artěl. Glass, the traditional Czech material, was rather neglected by the cubist architects; this may have been attributable to its visual and technological exclusivity. The exception is tableware made of diamond-cut glass, designed by Josef Rosipal and Stockar. It is not a perfect fit with the collection of furniture and ceramics, as its surface glitter contradicts the cubist view.

Artěl was known in Vienna, as it participated in the industrial-arts exhibitions in the Österreichisches Museum für Kunst und Industrie (today known as Österreichisches Museum für angewandte Kunst) from 1909 to 1914.[18] On the one hand, designing for Artěl was a kind of supplementary activity which was supposed to characterize the cubist interior; on the other hand, ceramics served in corroborative spatial studies. Janák wrote, "It is therefore necessary to have art, which is led consciously and deliberately toward form, and which will realize and try in a number of realities and in all variations those newly discovered feelings of forms and volumes. . . . Thus, such plastic creativity in the lesser arts stands to help architecture; it reworks it and supplements its experiences. While architecture expresses plastically certain large entities and more complex encounters of forces, the candle holder, the bowl, and the jug offer an opportunity for simple dramatic situations, actions and volumes . . . which generally provide the conditions to realize our cubist notion of matter and the volume of matter."[19]

cat. no. 217

In 1911, Janák designed a ceramic box with a crystal-shaped finial. (It was made as a solitaire, and does not appear to be part of any series.) Its shape

Rudolf Stockar, bedroom, 1913

represents the perfect materialization of Janák's theories, something that was not manifested with the same consistency in any of the furniture pieces. The box, comprising a system of angles, edges, and planes in a complicated composition, too cryptic to be solved by visual examination, aggressively attacks its surroundings. The soft earthenware, with a stained-white crackled glaze and shaky, not quite straight black lines along the edges, multiplies the spatial dynamics of this object, as well as the absolute loss of its original functional connotation.[20]

The crystal, as a formation of the inorganic world, was a frequent means of expression for the cubists, and in some sense perhaps even a mystical symbol of "transcendental stylistic elements," as Bohumil Kubišta described them. The intoxication with the symbolism of the crystal in the twenties constitutes, however, a rather different chapter. The crystalline shapes in Vassili Luckhardt's drawings of cult buildings, Wenzel Hablik's drawings from the Ausstellungsbaute cycle, the work of Bruno Taut and others working in German utopian and expressionistic architecture, and the creations of the Dutch designer Hendrik Theodor Wijdefeld have connections to the ideas and philosophical sources of projects realized by Czech architects a decade earlier. This was another, postwar spirit, as seen in the application of the crystalline form to Ernst Neumann's 1921 design for an automobile body, titled "Diamond Coupe." Nonetheless, Hans Poelzig's opinion that "Form derives from the mystic abyss" echoes Hofman's convictions about form being determined by the spirit and ideas of the time. A parallel view was to reappear in Bohemia in the postwar period, when the work of the cubists was temporarily invaded by a mystical nationalistic symbolistic colouring.

Janák's ceramics from 1911 and 1912 are uniformly concavely or convexly polygonal; with the exception of a group of colourfully painted boxes, the palette is limited to dull white, black, and gold. Linear decoration, even on cannular vases, is frequently an accompanying feature. The influence of Vienna is visible to a certain extent, but in completely new formal connections and functions. The principal purpose of the black-and-white zigzag decoration on the polygonal coffee and tea sets also seems to be to render the structure of the object dynamic. The decorations are in fact an expressive circumscription of the tectonics of matter.[21]

cat. nos. 231–236
cat. nos. 224–225

In some ways, Hofman was more consistent than Janák in his pursuit of the principle of "the breaking of substance," its "trimming" and penetration. This is seen, for instance, in a 1911 vase with pale-yellow glazing and dart-like penetrations of pyramidal formations. A small ashtray from 1912, with a system of oblique surfaces on a square base, is at the same time a reduced architectural model. The same can be said of a tall, monumentalized ashtray from the same year.

cat. no. 199
cat. no. 203
cat. no. 204

Artěl produced a small edition of a remarkable coffee set with triangular bases and sharply angled handles. Part of the series had linear black decoration, including a stylized, simplified sign of a flower. Hofman's robust spirit did not remain within the confines of dogmatic theory, but at the same time he often expressed it with uncommon generosity. One such example among the ceramics is a vase from 1919, in which he once more repeated the monumental architectural form, emphasized here by the red colour.

cat. no. 205
cat. no. 206
cat. no. 212

Decorativism

In 1914, the most intense cubist period came to an end. Chochol began to move toward purism, and soon after toward constructivism; Gočár turned away from sharp angles in favour of curves, and from the austerity of amorphous materials to decorative woods and colours. A year after the exhibition in Cologne, in 1915, he designed furniture with circular shapes and round backs, executed in stunning

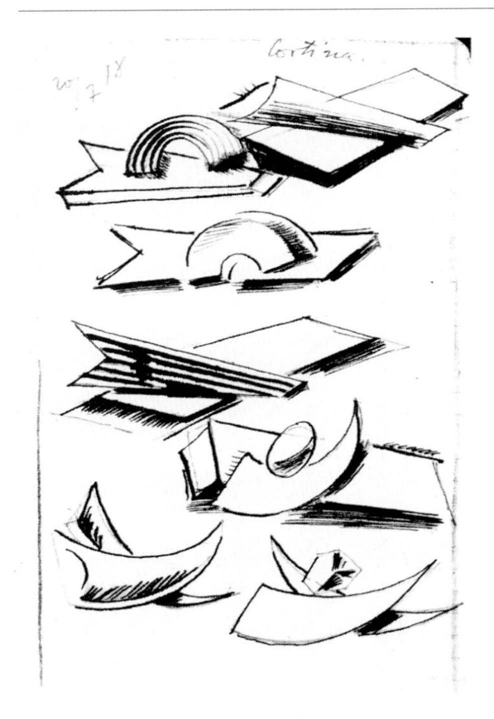

Pavel Janák, page from journal, 1918

imported wood, for the potter Helena Johnová. The appreciation of monumentality remained, but the volumes had become heavy and static.

With the foundation of the Czechoslovak Republic in 1918 emerged the desire to create a "national style." In the initial phases of the search for a national identity, a representation of the state, and their dignified expression, the artistic crafts exploited the conformist tastes of the stabilizing state. "The work ceased to involve discovery and revolt, and became celebration and adornment" (Adlerová). A decorative style was emerging in which efforts to revive the crafts triumphed. It was both the last style of this type and the last time when architecture and the applied arts drew unabashedly from historic memory, which they quoted and transposed with earnest pathos and a deadly serious face. (The irony of postmodernism was yet to come.)

An ornamental system gradually evolved, planar or plastic, which was invaded by motifs from folklore, albeit in a stylized form. Completely new was the use of colour. The national colours, red and blue, became especially prominent, in keeping with the patriotic fervour of the time. In comparison with pre-First World War cubism, the plasticity of form was preserved, but it lost its dramatic, masculine character. Round and undulating shapes were incorporated into the geometric formations, linking them to ancient Slav mythology. To describe this style, the terms "rounded style" and "rondo-cubism" (M. Benešová) were coined. Rondo-cubism was manifested especially in architecture and in representative public projects, while the broader spectrum of work in the applied arts, typography, and posters was not quite as uniformly conformist.

Both of the initiators of cubism, Gočár and Janák, were for a time proponents of the "rounded" national decorativism. They attempted to transpose the plasticity of the facade into a new, softer module, which they also applied to furniture. The route taken through this transitional period by Gočár seems to have been more self-assured and logical than that chosen by Janák. The connection between architectural form and the construction of furniture was so familiar to Gočár that the bookcase he designed for a gentleman's study in the twenties was, in principle, a transposition of the facade of the Legionnaires' Bank in Prague's Na poříčí into a smaller scale. Identical elements of the circle or semi-circle, always differentiated by material or colour, appear also on the 1922 conference-room group with leather upholstery. The furniture for a gentleman's room, with a richly structured writing desk and armchairs with energetic, expressively bent lines, are from the same period.

cat. no. 124

cat. nos. 126–127

cat. nos. 128–130

Josef Gočár, design for small table and armchairs, 1917

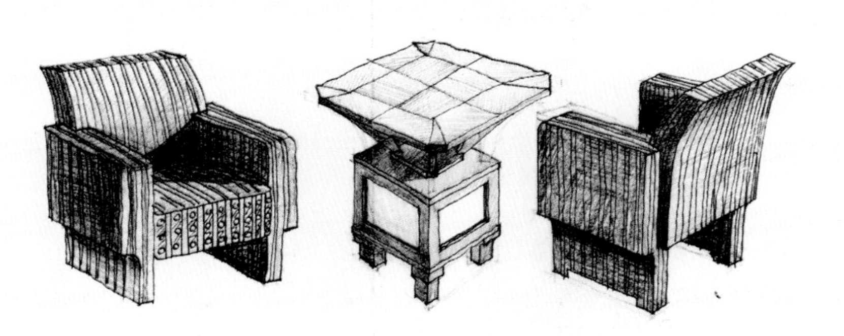

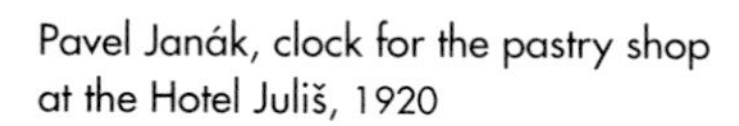

Pavel Janák, clock for the pastry shop at the Hotel Juliš, 1920

Janák seemed to be floundering at the time. He did not avoid either historicizing or folk inspirations. A bizarre reminder of his efforts to create a national style can be seen in the furniture used on the first floor of the chalet in Nové město nad Metují, which corresponds to his architectural design of the 1921 crematorium in Pardubice.

Hofman developed his expressionist statement particularly in scenic design, which allowed for a dramatic dynamization of space that he was unable to realize in architecture. (He collaborated with the pioneer of modern Czech theatre, Karel Hilar.) His multifaceted work of the postwar period included collaborations with Artěl (furniture, glass, ceramics, metal), but also graphic work, illustration, and painting. His furniture for Artěl from the twenties represents in a way a planar transposition of cubo-expressionism into an applied interior, in which his typical signature, with pyramids and triangles creating a perfect stylistic unity, appears repeatedly. Hofman had a restless and dissatisfied spirit, and he never ceased in his conceptual quest. Although he briefly sought inspiration in national mythological symbols, his thinking was wider in range and always gravitated toward the notion of modernity.[22]

It was not just cubist architects who went up the blind alley of decorativism; a whole attitude, represented by institutions such as Artěl and the Union of Czechoslovak Artwork, was burdened by the regressive dream of the "industrial arts," by nationalistic romanticism, and by an inability to embrace the concept of industrial production.[23] In 1921, the confused situation in Czech architecture was ironically mirrored in applied art and design. While the radical avant-garde Devetsil Artists' Association was founded in Prague, United Industrial Art Manufacturers was established in Moravia; under the leadership of its director, Jan Vaněk, plans were made to produce standardized furniture and to collaborate with Le Corbusier. That same year, the First Exhibition of the Union of Czechoslovak Artwork was organized, featuring variations on national decorativism. Some of these were in Art Deco style—for instance, the unusually playful and charming furniture group for a girl's room by Ladislav Machoň. Rudolf Stockar wrote a critical article about kitsch in the exhibition, and the Union's exposition at the Prague Sample Fair was flooded with folklore.[24] The trend of national decorativism ended, in effect, with the participation of Czechoslovakia in the 1925 International Exhibition of Decorative Arts in Paris, where the artistic crafts took precedence in the areas of glass and textiles by introducing into the international Art Deco

Josef Gočár, interior from the Association of Czechoslovak Accomplishment exhibition, 1921

Pavel Janák, gentleman's room in the chateau at Nové Město nad Metují, 1922

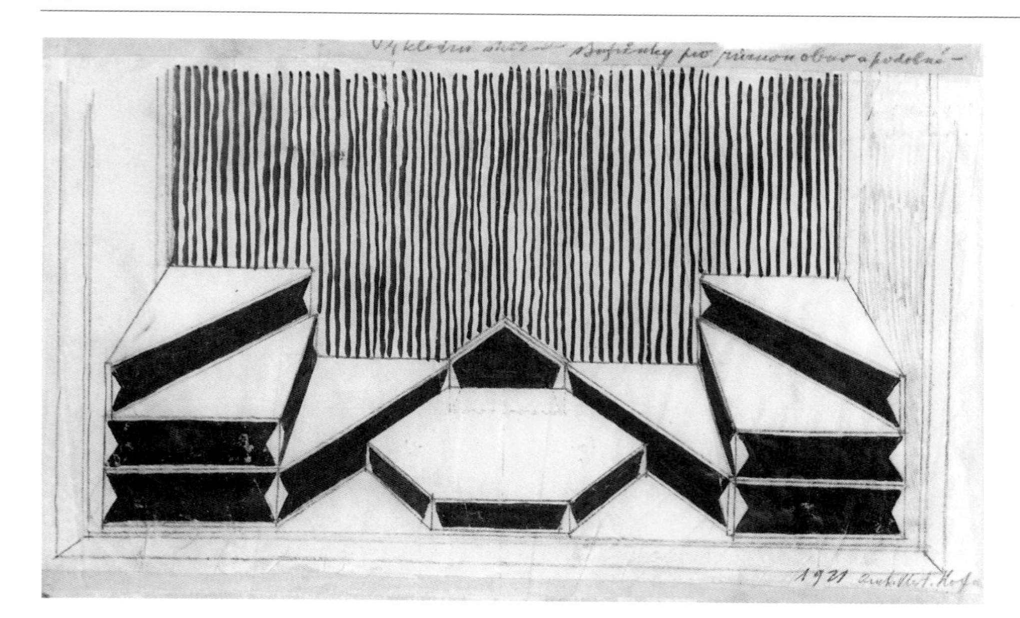

Vlastislav Hofman, design for Artěl store-window display stands, 1921

movement some artistically valuable characteristic elements of the Czech national identity.

The epilogue for and summation of prewar cubism was the furniture group designed in 1922 by Otakar Novotný, one of the founders of modern Czech architecture, a collaborator with the Group, and designer of several cubist exhibitions. The glass-fronted bookcase and the sideboard again display the concave and convex open-work crystalline structure, while the chairs and armchairs possess a cogency and a dynamic reminiscent of the years 1910–1914. This furniture group corresponds, expressively and temporally, with the late-cubist apartment building on Pařížská Street, in which Novotný used expressive details with compositional mastery. They are repeated in the grille-work, entrances, and stairways. Novotný was critical of cubism, and the furniture group mentioned above was in essence contradictory to his nature. However, it appears that he too saw Czech cubism as one of the ways to attain a "national expression."

cat. nos. 178–183

Cubist Interpretations

Even in the twenties, cubism proved to be an important source of inspiration, and was used as a point of departure by avant-garde movements of subsequent generations. The young artists in and around Devětsil, especially Feuerstein and Kroha, were critical of the older generation, but at the same time cubism provided them with instruction and a starting point for work which moved toward neo-plasticism, purism, and eventually constructivism.

One of the most interesting interpreters of late cubism was Jiří Kroha. His 1918 project for the modification of the interior of the Montmartre nightclub—the meeting place of the Prague avant-garde—is a consistent transposition of the plasticity of cubism into a more dynamic phase. This phase of Kroha's work involved an elaboration of Hofman's and Chochol's ideas from the years 1912–1914 and extended spatial dynamics into dynamics of both space and time, implicitly situating the individual within angles that are both delimited and delimiting. Kroha's work was conditioned by a powerful charge of personal dynamism, of spontaneous "personal force," which even bears traces of eroticism.

Kroha's notions on the perception of space were almost cosmically exalted: in his diaries he wrote about the "substantiality of man" and about planetary space. He resurrected the problem of the facade, which had earlier concerned Janák.

Kroha wrote, "The facade is now the result of a relationship between two spaces, whereas earlier it used to be a constructional, artistic membrane, separating substance from space."[25] He also compared the architectural facade to the surface of water. "[The facade] . . . conceals behind itself a substantial liquid space—it is a mirror. . . . The wall—matter—is the interface between the space created by people and space in general; this area is the crystallized content of inner space."

The acuity of Kroha's critical assessment of cubism is attested to by the following observation: "Cubism revealed new properties of matter, liberated creative form, and discovered the texture of expressive form, but it did so on the ruins of historic systems. Cubism did not find the structure—the symbiotic construction." This directly revealed the unfinished legacy of prewar cubism, which Kroha expressed simultaneously in his work: on the one hand there was the cubo-expressionistic Montmartre club; on the other "Prvoplány" (Primary Plans), containing a furniture design, that had emerged a year earlier in 1917.[26] However, until the early twenties, Kroha repeatedly returned, in his studies, to monumentalizations and rambunctious furniture pieces in the destructive cubo-expressionist style, lacking the assuredness of Gočár or Janák. Kroha's neo-plasticism later showed up markedly in his architecture and exhibition designs, as well as in designs for utilitarian objects for Artěl. In this work, he would start from asymmetrical connections between simple geometric forms, sharply accented by colours. It is not known whether any of these were produced. Judging by the drawings, Artěl's profile may have been disrupted by these new, more abstract designs.

cat. no. 172
cat. no. 174

Bedřich Feuerstein, Josef Havlíček, and Jaroslav Fragner also tried to utilize cubism in a neo-plastic transformation in designs for utilitarian objects, but these were only individual attempts and nothing of consequence was produced, since the designers were far more dedicated to architecture. The end of the twenties ushered in Czech functionalism. Cubism was forgotten as a formalistic developmental

Jiří Kroha, competition design for the crematorium in Pardubice, 1919–1920

extemporaneity. In 1927, Karel Teige condemned it as "picturesque and decorative"; in 1958, Novotný called it "a short-lived aesthetic episode."

Not until the end of the sixties did cubism again begin to rise to the awareness of the experts and the public, aided by an exhibition of Czech cubism in Paris in 1966, and another one in Prague in 1969. The first more complete view of Czech cubist furniture and ceramics was offered at the Czech Cubist Interior exhibition mounted at the Museum of Decorative Arts in Prague in 1976.[27]

Czech cubism was virtually unknown abroad; there were only occasional references to it in the specialized literature.[28] Only in the eighties did it enter into the European cultural consciousness, due to specialized exhibitions and a somewhat broader publicity. But even then, during the reevaluation of the movement's theoretical legacy, its interpretation encountered the language barrier and a general lack of knowledge of Czech cultural history.

The Legacy

Although the cubist exhibition at the Werkbund in Cologne in 1914 created considerable interest, there is no knowledge of any direct influence on works abroad. Only later, in the twenties, were there relationships which drew from similar principles, but in a different sense. These include, for instance, the famous jug by Kasimir Malevich from 1920, which was the materialization of the suprematist view: the denial of material signs on an object which is a part of the "immaterial world." There are also the 1924 designs for jugs by deGroot, which are more or less formal studies in construction on the theme of diagonals. The Dutch De Stijl influenced the Moderne Kunst circle, which was founded in 1919 in Belgium by Jozef Peeters with Van Dooren and Jan Cockx. From this group emerged in 1923 the design for a tea table by G. Michielsens with a complicated construction of right-angled and oblique planes. Peeters designed furniture with pyramidal decoration and geometric veneering.

Only in the sixties did Czech cubism reemerge occasionally as a source of inspiration, albeit partial or indirect. It is referred to in Italian design (Sottsass, Mendini), and appears in the work of the American sculptor Scott Burton in the eighties. Czech artists also acknowledge the cubist heritage. Milan Knížák has been creating furniture since the early seventies, as well as clothing and objects, which draw from it. It also became one of the starting points for the members of the Atika group, which was formed in the eighties.

Why has this heritage been so carefully scrutinized in the last twenty years? Its essential features are identical to those of the postmodern movement, above all in the principle of anti-rationalism and the need to be directed toward inner expression, in the individualization of the object in space, and in the transformation of traditional function into a functionality of a higher order that will fulfill more than just mechanical requirements—that will create an independent object with the complexity of a work of art. The cubist morphology offers a wide repertory of abstract expressive terms, which in certain compositions or rhythms acquire the emotive interpretational qualities of music. Finally, cubism is a basic perceptive experience, which leads to more acute spatial thought, to a self-awareness of movement—of actual physical substance as spatio-temporal existence.

The creative act of Czech cubists in the early twentieth century was in fact an experimental gesture, which anticipated a number of further avant-garde movements. It took place in a closed spatio-temporal circle, in the clear-cut sociocultural situation of a small nation, and in modest circumstances without a large audience, but with such intensity and conviction that it managed to reach far into the future—to this very day.

Jiří Kroha, study of spatial dynamics, 1917

Notes

1. Planck's quantum theory of relativity appeared in 1900, the first version of Einstein's theory of relativity in 1905. In 1908, Minkowski geometrically interpreted Einstein's physical findings about the structure of space and time by combining them in four-dimensional space-time. The notion of the fourth dimension is found in the early writings of H. G. Wells (1895), Apollinaire, Gleizes and Metzinger (1912), Larionov (1913), and Malevich (1915).
2. Richard Weiner, *Volné směry* 17 (1913): 29–30.
3. The magazines *Umělecký měsíčník* (Arts Monthly), *Volné směry* (Free Directions), and *Styl* (Style) published topical foreign texts and translations of works by Theodor Lipps, Wilhelm Worringer, and Adolf von Hildebrand. Hildebrand's work *The Problems of Form in the Plastic Arts* was published in Czech in 1913.
4. *Styl* 5 (1913): 93.
5. Ibid.
6. Herbenová also subjects Janák's furniture to a technological critique: "On the other hand, the dining-room table with the polygonal top and a wide hoop has disproportionately thin legs set at such an oblique angle that it almost loses stability. Even more severe construction problems arose, for instance, from the design for a conference table for a set made of polished veneered oak, manufactured around 1912. The realization of the fantastic design by cabinet-making methods proved to be so inadequate that the whole structure, with its angled legs joined by ties, subsequently had to be reinforced with metal pins and plates. From Pavel Janák's self-critical remarks on some of his designs, it is clear that he must have been well aware of the difference between theory and practice." In *Acta UPM C. Commentationes* 8, no.1 (Prague, 1973): 112.
7. Vlastislav Hofman, "O secesi" (On the Secession), *Styl* 5 (1913): 118. This had in fact been noted earlier by V. V. Stech, who wrote that furniture had been constructed just like other architecture, with each piece an independent organism connected to others by virtue of having grown according to the same principles and in the same style. In *Cechische Bestrebungen um das moderne Interieur* (Prague, 1915).
8. *Umělecký měsíčník* 2 (1912–1913): 21–29.
9. The announcement of the founding of the Prague Artistic Workshop (PUD), published in *Umělecký měsíčník* 1, no. 8 (1911), states that "the guiding principle is first and foremost artistic consideration . . . [and that] given certain consideration to utility, the furniture should not just try to satisfy good taste . . . but . . . should be serious art of significant content." Later, PUD management even considered the manufacture of standardized furniture, as we see in J. Gočár's designs from 1912 to 1914.
10. Compare O. Herbenová in the catalogue *Český kubistický interiér* (Czech Cubist Interior), p. 31.
11. In *Jahrbuch des deutschen Werkbundes* (Munich, 1915), p. 10.
12. O. Herbenová assessed this commode as a "reversed paraphrase of the old Baroque commode. The undulating sides and convoluted Baroque silhouette are deformed and broken up by significantly sharp angles; they are almost expressionistically spasmodic." In catalogue *Český kubistický interiér*, p. 35.
13. Compare with Gombrich, *Art and Illusion* (London, 1962), p. 16.
14. Besides his programmatic articles in *Styl* and *Umělecký měsíčník*, Hofman also published in a number of other magazines, among them *Cerven*, *Lípa*, *Zivot*, *Stavba*, *Nové české divadlo*, and *Jeviště*. In 1916, he was awarded a prize for a collection of essays, *Věci v kosmu* (Things in the Cosmos), the manuscript of which has been lost.
15. Vlastislav Hofman, "Nový princip v architektuře" (New Principles in Architecture), *Styl* 5 (1913):13–24.
16. Vlastislav Hofman wrote an article, "Tělesnost tance" (The Corporeality of Dance); Rudolf Stockar translated E. Dalcroze's text "On the Meaning of Rhythmic Exercise," *Styl* 4 (1912); and Pavel Janák also wrote about it in "Šibalství Scapinova" (The Tricks of Scapin) in *Umělecký měsíčník* 2 (1913).
17. The founding members of Artěl were Jaroslav Benda, Vratislav H. Brunner, Pavel Janák, Helena Johnová, Jan Konůpek, Marie Teinitzerová, Otakar Vondráček, and Alois Dyk. In the following years, Artěl co-operated closely with the Group of Plastic Artists. Among the architects and artists who worked regularly with Artěl were Josef Rosipal, Jan Zrzavý, František Kysela, Rudolf Stockar, Jaroslav Horejc, Ladislav Machoň, Bedřich Feuerstein, and Jaromír Krejcar. Artěl's repertory included ceramics, glass, metal objects, toys, furniture, jewellery, textiles, wallpaper, and stencils for house painters. In 1921, Artěl became a public company, and in 1934 it went bankrupt due to the Depression.
18. See Vera Behal, "Artěl—das Atelier für Kunstgewerbe in Prag," in *Zeitschrift für Kunstgeschichte* 50, no. 1 (1987): 116–130.
19. Pavel Janák, "O užitečnosti uměleckého průmyslu" (On the Usefulness of the Artistic Industry), *Umělecký měsíčník* 1 (1911–1912): 148.
20. Compare Miroslav Lamač, *Osma a Skupina výtvarných umělců 1907–1917* (The "Eight" and the Group of Plastic Artists 1907–1917) (Prague, 1988), pp. 250–252. Among other things, Lamač analyzes cubist ceramics in relation to painting and the plastic arts.
21. Waltraud Neuwirth, in *Österreichische Keramik des Jugendstils* (Munich, 1975), published examples of ceramics produced at Artěl, which is well represented in the collection of the Museum für angewandte Kunst in Vienna. Neuwirth mentions the influence of Josef Hoffmann and Kolo Moser, but at the same time she notes the specificity of Artel's production.
22. In a letter to Bohuslav Reynek, Vlastislav Hofman wrote, "During the exhibition, the critics swore at me for not being modern. According to them, it can be argued that model cubism has been completely established in the republic. Of course I broke away from decorative cubism, I am looking for something classical and modern . . . most important is the spiritual side, not the material or prosaic . . ." (Letter in the family archives)
23. The Union of Czech Artwork was founded in 1914, at the instigation of Jan Kotěra. It was revived in 1920 as the Union of Czechoslovak Artwork, when it published its Material Programme of Seventeen Points. Point 1 states, "It is an organization dedicated to plastic work in the spirit of the present day. It also incorporates folkloric plastic efforts." The chairman at the group's foundation was Josef Gočár, the secretary Pavel Janák.
24. The controversial nature of contemporary opinion is demonstrated in the foreword to the catalogue for the First Exhibition of the Union of Czechoslovak Artwork, written by Otakar Novotný: "The exhibition is to remind our manufacturers and industrialists of the artistic industry. It should prove to them again the importance of the spirit in manufacturing. . . . Especially in these new times, the artistic industry is on the ground on which the specific national expression, a form, is resurrected."
25. See Kroha's diary from the year 1919, p. 4. In a private archive.
26. The "Prvoplány" series was created in the years 1917–1920, and is related to the neo-plastic constructivism of Kroha's buildings in Kosmonosy and Mladá Boleslav. They are similar to El Lissitzky's *Prouns* or to Malevich's suprematist *Architectons*, which were created independently of each other. Here, Kroha approaches the analogous tendencies of the Bauhaus and De Stijl. See J. Císařovský, *Jiří Kroha a mezivalečna avantgarda* (Jiří Kroha and the Avant-garde Between the Wars) (Prague, 1967), pp. 11–12.
27. Czech authors who have been working on cubism since the sixties include J. Šetlík, J. Zemina, M. Lamač, M. Pistorius, M. Benešová, J. Císařovský, and O. Herbenová.
28. The first foreign reference to Czech cubism is in an article by F. Czagan, "Kubistische Architektur in Böhmen," in *Werk* 2 (1969): 75, in which the author assesses it as a transition from the Secession to functionalism. It is identified as a secondary stylistic phenomenon within the framework of global cubism by D. Cooper in his book *The Cubist Epoch* (London, 1971). W. Pehnt defines it as a premature attempt at an interesting experiment in *Die Architektur des Expressionismus* (1973).

Cubism and Posters

Josef Kroutvor

Czech cubism was not only an adventure in the conquest of space for painters and sculptors, it was also a search for style and for play among decorative elements. This was true for architecture, furniture, and ceramics, but also for the applied graphic arts, especially poster design. Formally pure and typographically effective statements, with aesthetics completely different from those of the Secession, began to appear on street corners before the First World War. The new style of poster moved away from symbolic pictures in favour of the modern language of simple signs. The typographical posters of Frantisek Kyšela and the perfect works of Jaroslav Benda showed graphic purism, modesty, discipline, and totally original elegance that parted ways with the principle of ornamental decoration and headed in new, constructive artistic directions.

The Secessionist poster was connected with the tradition of painting, but modern poster designers wished to select and use only their own means and to use their innate graphic sense as a point of departure. There was also a certain degree of professionalization in poster production, because the new, modern posters were produced mostly by graphic artists—specialized designers—rather than by painters. Benda's poster "The Old Graphic Masters" is a completely pure graphic work, doubtless influenced by cubism. This poster easily withstands comparison with Czech cubist architecture and furniture, and is a work of equal value.

The period around 1910 was uncommonly inspirational: in Bohemia, the late geometrical Secession, influenced by Vienna, encountered the revolutionary ideas of French cubism. Picasso and Braque exhibited in Prague, where for the first time American songs were heard and the first cars appeared in the streets. Construction of the late-Secession Municipal Hall was still underway, but at the same time monumental modernist palaces and houses were going up. Lithographers were adapting the complex Secessionist style to new conditions; a good example is the poster by Oldřich Koníček for the 1914 members' exhibition of the Mánes Association of Plastic Artists. The composition, using the old symbolism of the eternal tree of life, was overlaid with the pronounced influence of Derain and French cubism. Many cubist-oriented posters from this period were printed on poor-quality pulp paper, a reminder that poverty and lack of resources also attended the birth of modern art. In many ways, this anticipated the postwar use of the poster as a means of mass communication, determined by moment and purpose. In her black-and-white cubo-expressionist poster, Augusta Nekolová-Jarešová gave up colour, but this only enhanced the work's urgent, mysterious message. The mad violinist played on street corners, and war, poverty, hunger, and every human misery followed him into the city.

cat. no. 282

In the prewar years, the Montmartre cabaret on Řetězová Street became the meeting place of writers, actors, painters, and plastic artists; after the war, this tradition was quickly renewed. Some hurried to the Kalich, the favourite pub of the good soldier Švejk, and others to the renowned establishments of the Prague Bohemians. At the Montmartre, both tangos and Apache dances were performed. In the cabaret atmosphere, cubist trends freely mingled with expressionistic ones; this is the inspiration behind Jiří Kroha's unique cubo-expressionist décor. At the back of the hall stood a kind of massive, angular, polygonal alter, at which black masses were said and pamphlets were read from a missal. Kroha also designed the cubo-expressionistic poster featuring a dancing girl whirling in crazy intoxication. His contemporaries reported that the liveliest numbers involved eccentric dances by Emča Revolution, the famous partner of the "furious reporter" Egon Ervín

Josef Čapek, illustration for G. Apollinaire's *La Zone*, 1919

Kisch. This was borne out in the "revolutionary tuning of colours" in Kroha's poster—the use of the red, white, and blue national tricolour in a thoroughly non-traditional manner. The dynamic poster almost reeks of rapacity and instinctive carnality, the modern eroticism of the city linking alcohol and new political passions. Twentieth-century society fundamentally changed the poetics and the aesthetic criteria—the throngs and crowds, the human masses in revolutionary motion, gigantic antique choruses chanting social slogans in the streets. These images were also behind Kroha's next cubo-expressionist poster, for the New Oresteia, a mass scene, shown at the Prague Exhibition in 1923.

Cubism was so deeply rooted and profoundly experienced in Prague that it could cross the threshold of the cabaret and function at one moment as parody and at another as a setting provoking the bourgeoisie. Sometimes it is difficult to distinguish serious meaning from simple paraphrase, caricature, a kind of entertainment. The poems of František Gellner, an existentialist long before existentialism, were recited at the cabaret Červená sedma (The Red Seven) against a backdrop on which was depicted a street whose houses leaned menacingly, smotheringly, over the performer. This motif is encountered frequently in expressionist graphics, but also in literature and poetry. Josef Čapek used it in the poster for the anarchist magazine *Červen*. The cubo-expressionist design of the cabaret stage was done by Jiří Dréman, an actor and designer with the Červená sedma group of performers. Dréman leaves us constantly wondering whether his drawings are paraphrases, or attempts at authentic form. His poster for the appearance of Červená sedma at the Hotel Central shows a cubistically decomposed figure of a man, mercilessly flogging a bourgeois audience with a horsewhip. While it is an interesting poster, something is missing: we sense certain gaps in its avant-garde stylization. An example of true cubist conviction, an artistic credo, and the mastery of cubist form is Čapek's poster for the play *Mrtvá* (The Dead One), also performed at the Červená sedma. Čapek's poster takes us down to the underworld of the modern city, where two men are suffering from an unhappy love whose image hovers above them like pitiless fate. The depicted scene aims for iconic simplicity and synthetic expression through the use of cubist forms; the catastrophic content is, of course, profoundly expressionistic.

cat. no. 278

cat. no. 277

In 1918, the group Tvrdošíjní (The Stiffnecked) had an exhibition in Prague, which was advertised on street corners by an uncompromising poster by Václav Špála. The black rhombus appears to be a primitive symbol, an African mask, but is also an angular, cubist shape with an expressive charge. Špála was captivated by African art at the time, and he and Čapek studied it together. Both transferred symbolic, iconic, and synthetic principles into their work, while at the same time placing the poster within the broader context of modern art. The elementary graphic form of Špála's poster is so highly charged with internal energy that it actually deforms and subordinates the lettering. If we compare Špála's poster—which resembles a scream—with the stateliness of Secessionist posters, we understand not only the extent of the revolutionary changes in artistic depiction, but also the changes in people's perceptions. Špála also created other interesting posters, including one for Artěl in 1921, but he never re-created such spontaneous impact and crystalline concentration.

cat. no. 271

Špála's poster for the Tvrdošíjní was reminiscent of the first manifestos of modern art—in fact, it was a manifesto in itself! Cubism in Špála's œuvre then merged naturally with his work, ceased to be discrete, and became a perfectly natural means of expression. Something similar happened with cubism in general: it entered the mainstream of Czech modern art in the twenties and thirties. All that remains to be said is that Špála is considered to be a typical example of a purely Czech painter; his broader cubo-expressionist point of departure is no longer worrisome.

The Contribution of Otto Gutfreund to the Phenomenon of Czech Cubism

Jiří Šetlík

Cellist, 1912–1913, bronze, h. 47.5 cm, not signed, National Gallery, Prague

The importance of the work of the Czech sculptor Otto Gutfreund has not yet been fully evaluated in the context of the world avant-garde movement. This is especially true of his cubist work (1910–1920). Gutfreund's aesthetic sense was formed in the cultural environment of a Czech Jewish family, and his intellect developed in a Prague which, at the turn of the century, was opening up to the world as a productive centre of literature, theatre, music, architecture, and the plastic arts. Behind the surface perturbation of nationalistic feuds between Czechs and Germans, a unique symbiosis of the Czech, German, and Jewish cultures evolved within this intellectual infrastructure.

Gutfreund graduated from the ceramics school in Bechyne and then studied at the School of Industrial Arts in Prague, but his stay with E. A. Bourdelle on La Grande Chaumière in Paris in 1909 and 1910 was a crucial turning point. In the creative hub of the European art scene, he matured as an artist and as an individual. He was able to immerse himself in the best work of the past and present, at the same time gaining important self-knowledge. When he returned home, he quickly sloughed off his teacher's style of modelling and composition, as he showed in a series of expressionistic sculptures. He also kept an eye on the cubists, especially Picasso, in whom he was most interested. He progressed from analytical to synthetic cubism in his sculptures and drawings and, simultaneously, in his theoretical writings; his work was coloured by his characteristic expressionism, both in his formal development and in his need for content, which he conveyed through his thematic choices.

Gutfreund found admirers only among a small group of supporters. He had few commissions, and he paid for his loyalty to the avant-garde by making a meagre living. The artistic community in which he was recognized and admired consisted of the young generation who had created the Group of Plastic Artists in 1911. The Group brought together painters, graphic and decorative artists, architects, writers, musicians, and critics; Gutfreund was the only sculptor. In fact, it was not his unique choice of profession that gained him respect, but his personality, his tolerance and tactfulness, his strength of character and intelligence, and, above all, his creative authority. His views and his work had a decisive influence on other artists, who depended on his theoretical erudition. (Only a few of Gutfreund's essays appeared in the Group's magazine, *Umělecký měsíčník;* the rest are in the artist's estate.) As the Group's president, he managed to keep it alive even after a number of members left. Finally, he established international contacts for the Group, beginning in Germany in 1913, when members were well received at the Berlin Herbstsalon organized by H. Walden's *Der Sturm.* In April of 1914, Gutfreund went to Paris to work, and to try to promote Czech cubists both there and in other cities. He had high hopes for his collaboration with D. H. Kahnweiler and A. Basler, but these were dashed by the fury of the First World War.

Gutfreund's life now changed radically. He abandoned his work and, in the name of patriotism, volunteered to fight alongside the French. The Czech company was assigned to the Foreign Legion; Gutfreund joined a protest against the conditions within the Legion and was imprisoned in a concentration camp in 1916. He returned briefly to work, creating three sculpture-assemblages, but as a prisoner he could not continue any further. After the war, he abandoned cubism during a brief stay in Paris in 1919–1920. His war experiences, his need to

Study for glass vessels, 1911–1912, india ink, 21 x 17 cm, not signed, private collection

conquer depression resulting from the humiliation he had suffered, and, above all, his sensitive perceptions of a changed world led his artistic interest toward the objective world of ordinary people; even his cubist work was inspired by the quotidian.

In the simplified forms of socially motivated civilism, he sought a poetic interpretation of common reality, as did the "new practicality" movement in another part of the world. Gutfreund returned to exploration of the volume of form, which he enhanced by magical colouring; as well, he applied his earlier use of relief, on which his cubist work was founded, to a new context. His success brought him official commissions, but these seldom coincided with his creative objectives; he was less interested than were his clients in the growing trend toward neo-classicism. He wanted to return to his creative search, and the professorship he obtained at Prague's School of Decorative Arts was intended to help him do so. Other than two realized works—*Great Act* and *Composition with Machine Motif* for the attic of the Škoda Works Palace in Prague (1926–1927)—only some remarkable studies remain from the later phase of his work. They summarize his experiences with cubism and civilism, and show his shift toward form as an abstract sign of sovereign simplicity and plastic cogency. His return to the forefront of European sculpture was cut short by his tragic death.

Study for his father's gravestone, 1913, pencil, 19.8 x 15.8 cm, not signed, private collection

The paradoxes that haunted his life affected evaluation of Gutfreund's œuvre after his death. The works most highly valued in his own country during the inter-war period were his thematic "republican" sculptures. During the Nazi occupation of Czechoslovakia, his work was seen as an example of Jewish *Degenerate Art.* If he was mentioned at all under the totalitarian regime following the Second World War, it was as a lackey of debased Western art and as a fellow traveller from the Masaryk republic. Only since the sixties, through the efforts of younger artists and historians, has he been introduced to the broader public in Czechoslovakia and worldwide. No appropriate place has yet been found for him in the history of the avant-garde.

In order to assess Gutfreund's decisive effect on Czech cubism, especially in architecture and design, it is necessary to take a look at his own production. Upon his untimely death, at the age of thirty-six, his friends unhesitatingly expressed their love and admiration for him. They also acknowledged his moral and artistic influence, without analyzing it in proper detail. More is revealed in the artist's correspondence with friends, in his theoretical articles, and in notes made by his friends (most noteworthy here are passages from Pavel Janák's journal). Most important are comparisons of Gutfreund's cubist morphology, as seen in his sculptures and drawings, with the works of architects – their projects, designs, and realized buildings and utilitarian objects. Gutfreund seemed to be a charismatic figure among Czech cubists, who were drawn to his plastic concepts, backed up by his knowledge of art history, and to his theoretical reflections. He followed new trends in contemporary creativity more for information than inspiration, and filtered his own thoughts through his wide knowledge of scientific literature. He also attracted the attention of his peers with his ability to combine the rational with the emotional in the creative process, while others were still relying on instinct and feeling. His artistic authority made him a natural advisor, as well as a judge and critic of his peers' work; they used his sculptures and drawings, both consciously and unconsciously, as examples of pure cubist morphology.

Gutfreund's cubism comprised a radical reduction of the classical volume of the sculpture to a plane – or, rather, to a system of mutually interconnected planes, plastically modelled. The configuration of the form thus created enabled observation of the object from several angles. The original object, which bound Gutfreund's imagination to the semantically laden content, was transformed into an icon. He came to terms with the specificity of sculpture by respecting its substantive structure and its unavoidable relationship to real space (as distinct from painting, which even in cubism is bound automatically to one plane and to an

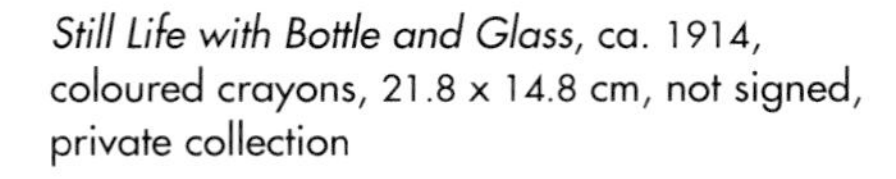

Still Life with Bottle and Glass, ca. 1914, coloured crayons, 21.8 x 14.8 cm, not signed, private collection

evocation of a specific visual illusion). His solution was to reduce volume to plane by emphasizing relief; thus, he interconnected outer and inner spaces by combining edges and curves in the concave and convex parts of the sculpture. He always treated the resulting shape as an organic totality, a unique icon, to be viewed frontally; later, when he explored synthetic cubism, he gradually separated the relief from the underlying surface to integrate the sculpture into its surroundings. He learned much, both formally and in terms of conveying a complex message, from early Gothic reliefs, and created a personal language which resonated in the dramatic nature of his motifs and sought poetry as a state of the spirit in themes of life's simplicity.

Two aspects of Gutfreund's cubist sculpture touch upon architecture and design. The first is his approach to sculpture as construction – a composition of reconstructed and abstracted elements; the other is his view of sculpture as a means of expression and stylistic order. When we compare Gutfreund's output with the studies, projects, and realized buildings, the furniture, and the utilitarian objects by his contemporaries, the architects Pavel Janák, Josef Gočár, and Vlastislav Hofman (and, to some extent, Josef Chochol, the older Jan Kotěra and Otakar Novotný, and later the younger Vladimír Fultner and Bedřich Feuerstein), we recognize a remarkable similarity and interaction in the morphology – which is not to denigrate the inventiveness and initiative of the other artists. Much is revealed in the identification of Czech cubist architecture as "sculptural." In fact, typical of Czech cubism was the conspicuous plasticity of the facade, the ordering of windows, the

Concert (detail of relief), 1912–1913, patina-toned plaster, h. 19.5 cm, not signed, National Gallery, Prague

Reclining Woman (detail), 1913, patina-toned plaster, h. 19.5 cm, not signed, National Gallery, Prague

contrasts of light and shadow and construction details, rather than transformation of the floor plan or distribution of space and matter. Even Gutfreund's own furnishing accessories and furniture, somewhat regrettably, were sculptural rather than functional, as were his tea and coffee sets, vases, clocks, ashtrays, inkwells, and lighting fixtures. Where possible, he used coloured glazing to underscore the dynamics and plastic quality of the forms, in a sort of transformation of the principles of sculptural cubism, in which bent edges and angles give the effect of optical contrasts.

In textile design, book design, and scenography, cubist painting was the initial source. But although there was an evolved and accepted system in painting, this was not the case in sculpture; thus, Gutfreund's pioneering work in three dimensions was reflected in architecture and design, and guided the artists in these disciplines when they broke with the conventions of the past to search for new forms for which utility alone was not sufficient justification. Even among avant-garde designers, these forms contained a revealing decorative order, which tended to substitute for new style. The efforts of the architects and designers to humanize an alienating world and physical environment were somewhat analogous to Gutfreund's attempt to endow sculpture with a spiritual aspect as the fundamental message of new art. They also matched the spirit of the times, which suffered from a lack of firm values.

Janák's Journal 1911–1914

Olga Herbenová

More beautiful than a real castle is a castle built of wind. More beautiful than a palpable tower is a tower that is not possible, conceived in a way that cannot be built and would not stand.

Pavel Janák, entry of 30 July 1912

Pavel Janák's journal, part of his extensive estate deposited in the National Technical Museum in Prague, is one of many documents that complement Janák's early work. Unknown—let alone edited—until now, it seems to be an extremely important piece of evidence in showing how logically and methodically his practice developed, constantly accompanied by theory. The journal offers a more intimate view of Janák's personality, his method, and his extraordinary meticulousness. Janák has been regarded as a realist, but the journal shows that, in his early years, he was a great dreamer. It also shows the balance between the pure plasticity permeating his theory and his great understanding of the client's needs.

The journal is bound in leather, and the author divided it, for greater clarity, into several sections. The first and largest, pages 1–91, contains entries, notes, drawings, sketches, floor plans, and elevations. These are for the most part dated, commencing on 27 November 1911, and concluding on 25 September 1914. The next section, pages 139–160, contains carefully recorded bibliographies of books Janák had read on architecture, philosophy, and art. A third, much smaller, section is set aside for thoughts on Czech architecture and excerpts from literature. These three sections are interconnected: they complement and react to each other. They comprise an extraordinarily important record, indicating how Janák drew ideas from literature, observation, and criticism. For instance, on 11 July 1912, he noted, "Even painting sometimes succumbs to the system of physicality by depicting in reality things which are conceived plastically (for example, Picasso), and by being not sufficiently visual."

The fourth section is reserved for practical matters, such as notes on the kinds of textiles available at the firm of Haas, accounting, a list of competitions in which Janák participated, and so on. Then there is a short list of individuals, including, among others, V. V. Štech, A. Matějček, V. Špála, and L. Šíma, who were probably reading the same books as Janák. Most interesting is the address book, containing the names of many legendary figures from the first quarter of the twentieth century who were instigators of the modern art movements, especially cubism: G. Apollinaire, O. Kokoschka, A. Figdor, H. Kahnweiler, Adolf Loos, F. Feigl, Vincenc Kramář, Sergei Makovskij (the editor of *Apollon* from Petrograd), H. Tietze, H. Walden, W. Uhde, A. Soffici, A. Vollard, H. O. Mietke, F. Langer, V. Nebeský, S. K. Neumann, F. X. Šalda, and others.

The essence of almost all of Janák's significant theoretical articles, which were published in *Umělecký měsíčník* and *Styl* is contained here in original explicit abbreviations. Janák also refers directly to Adolf von Hildebrand and confirms his basic principles; for instance, he finds support for Hildebrand's view that architecture is exclusively an art form in a quote by Leo von Klenzc: "Architecture concerns art, not shelter." Janák also cites Alois Riegel, another of Hildebrand's disciples: "Architecture is the result of goal-oriented artistic will, which prevails in the war with utility, material, and technique; these three factors are oppressive, preventive, and negative—they are no more than working coefficients of the whole product." Janák rejects the more primitive, antique, "naked prismatic system" found throughout architectural history and comes to a realization that the foundation of

Sketch of chairs, 1911

all artistic architecture consists of triangular and pyramidal forms. He explains this discovery in his journal in a critique of an antique temple, which he defines as a prism. "The prism is matter whose circumference only pleases the eye—the moment I begin to think about it, that is the moment I begin to doubt its matter; in one place there might be too much of it and I take some away, I direct it toward an idea, toward God, toward power, or I place it where I think it should be, or where it really is necessary." On the other hand, Janák has a much higher opinion of Egyptian pyramids, Gothic cathedrals, and Renaissance buildings, because they have the dramatic quality of "pyramidally built-up sections." On 19 June 1912, he writes, "Our architecture might be somewhere midway from Italy to the North. Gočár's building might be representative . . ." (It is not clear whether he means the At the Black Mother of God building.)

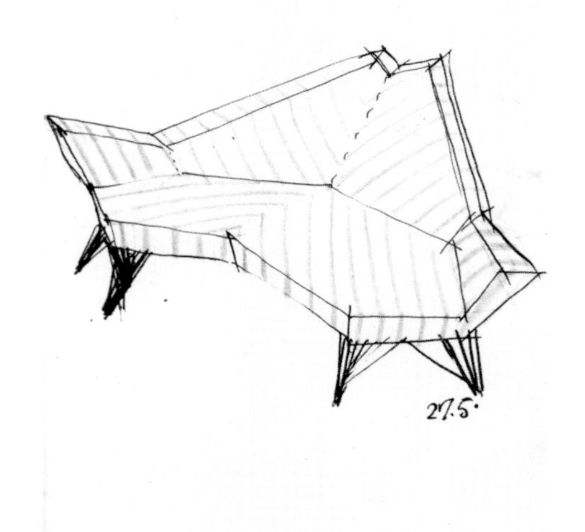

Sketch of sofa, 1911

Following this notion even further, Janák states, "The system of our time is probably different from the old naturalistic system, which always creates things enclosed by curves, erect, stalk-like, vegetal, such as pillars and capitals, where it crystallizes as if the matter were formed, naturally, in three palpable dimensions, in which there is no distinction in the way we see them and how we can confirm them by touch. . . . The new system is more one of relief"—again referring to Hildebrand—"here matter does not change and its substance has no effect on the form, which comes from the outside, from the emotional decisions of the person, and is conveyed visually: matter is deformed, its surface changes (but it does not obtain a new surface—rather, the original surface of the material changes), it loses the qualitative property of the material."

Analogous views can be found in the theory of painting, but they appear most significantly in the writings of the sculptor Otto Gutfreund, Janák's friend and close collaborator. Gutfreund may have understood Hildebrand's theory better than Janák; he applied it in his 1912–1913 article "The Plane and the Space."

Besides general theories on architecture, Janák's journal reveals from the very beginning an interest in furniture (entries from 27 October 1911 to 20 February 1912, and from 4 September 1913 to 9 August 1914). This interest goes through two phases; the second one contains thoughts on furniture which approaches neo-plastic style, while the first one relates to designs and realizations of cubist furniture and is dedicated to basic shapes. In this first phase, Janák notes, "Of the two, we prefer the more contrasting one: we abandon the more balanced for the more effective—the rhomboid rather than the square." At another point he considers "the highest possibilities of the triangle, in two contrasting systems." Elsewhere, he uses his point of view to take issue with Gothic, Romanesque, and folk furniture for being materialistic. He also includes in this category the furniture of Henry van de Velde, who, in Janák's words, "cuts everything out of planks in such a way that it is preserved in size and volume." He writes an extensive criticism of Velde on 20 February 1912, illustrated with drawings. He takes great exception to Velde's "introduction into cubes and formal aggregates of some sort of linear references as to their evolution. He is no longer concerned with the three-dimensional origins; now he is interested in the genesis and context of lines. This is where he falls short of *our position.* It is one-sided. He is probably best at chairs, tables, and walls; bad at armoires and cupboards in general." How we are to understand the term "our position" is explained in the note of 3 November 1911, accompanied by sketches: "I find that (for me) (in the special case of the forming of furniture) there are in total probably three levels: 1) the movement of matter according to planes: matter slides behind plastic planes; 2) reduction of matter into profiles, for instance perpendicular to one another; 3) the replacement of matter by a linear system, which is what we know up to now."

These reflections, and others—for instance, on the irrelevance of construction, on the suppression of elements, on links, and so on—are later developed in the study "On Furniture and Other Things," published in *Umělecký měsíčník* in 1913. In this piece, Janák distinguishes "modern art" (which he dates approximately between 1895 and 1910) and "new art," which follows. New art, which we now identify as cubism, Janák refers to as "the style of our time." To this period belong the notes and sketches from 21 May 1912: he draws a sofa and various details on the basis of the triangle, and beside them he notes, "The triangle relates to rotation and is used to measure architectural time. . . . The triangle, as opposed to the square, carries weight because it relates to architectural imagination and connects with the weight of matter." Janák studies the use of the triangle by Palladio, Vasari, Vitruvius, and other architects. By means of the triangle he measures the quality of architecture of Prague. The entry reads that he follows it "with bated breath as to how it will qualify. It made out well, especially the Týn [cathedral] portal, the Vladislavský Hall, the Wallenstein loggia, the Kinský Palace. So far I have not seen any more."

As far as we can discern from his journal, Janák's working method in the applied arts had a totally programmatic, experimental character. The basic idea is first verbally formulated in the journal, usually accompanied by a small sketch; further progression is generally of a technical nature. The sketch is either reworked in colour or given a firmer contour. The first sketches are usually temperamental, daring, spirited. In one case, Janák sketches the same piece of furniture five times, in another case up to seventy times. The definitive designs, working drawings by nature, are often mounted on cardboard with detailed instructions for cabinetmakers—for instance, "Table with working extensions, please pay attention to that," or "Drawers on the sides, as the future owner is a professor and has many notebooks and papers," or "Careful that the sofa has good dimensions, here it

Drawing from journal, 1916–1917

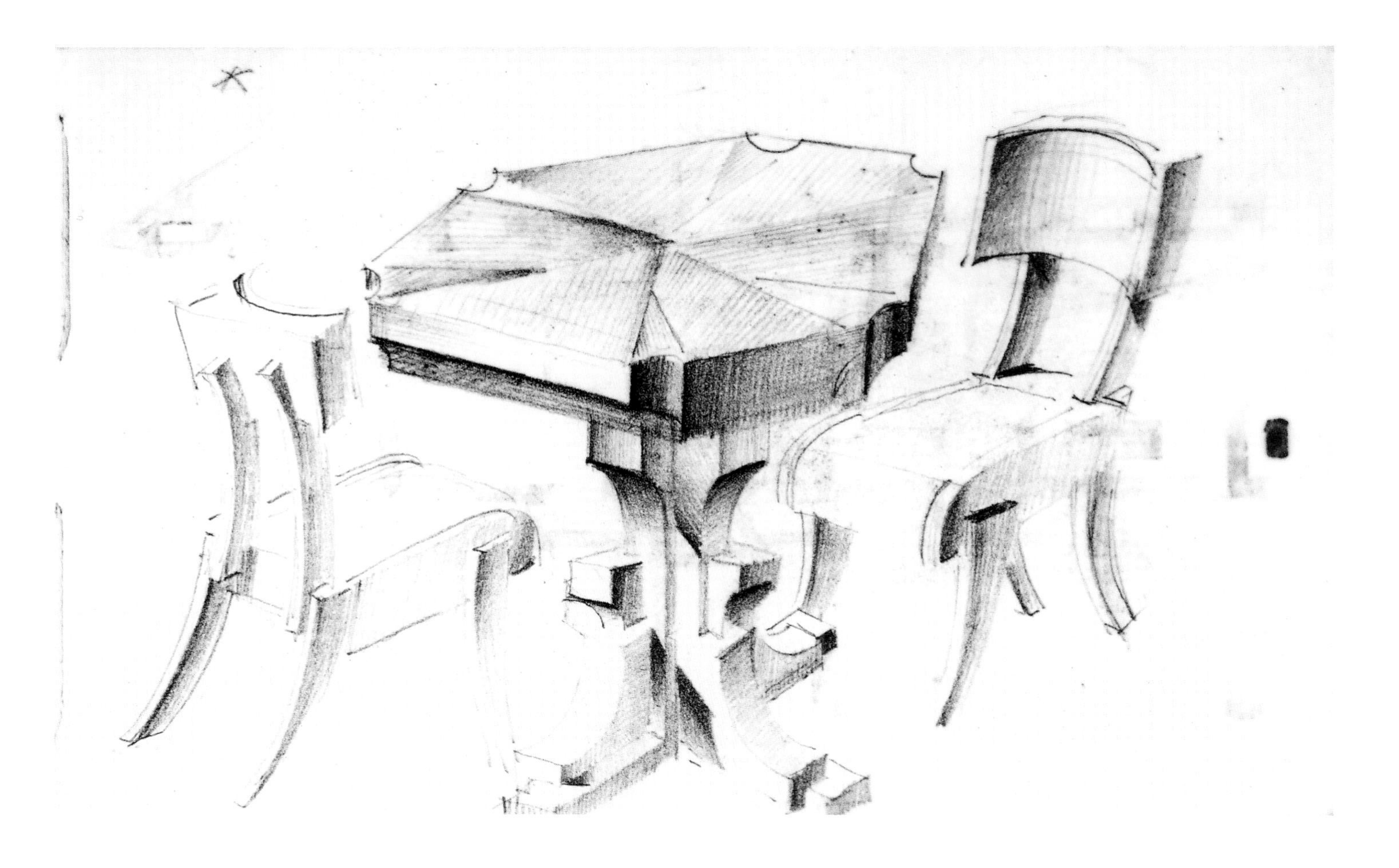

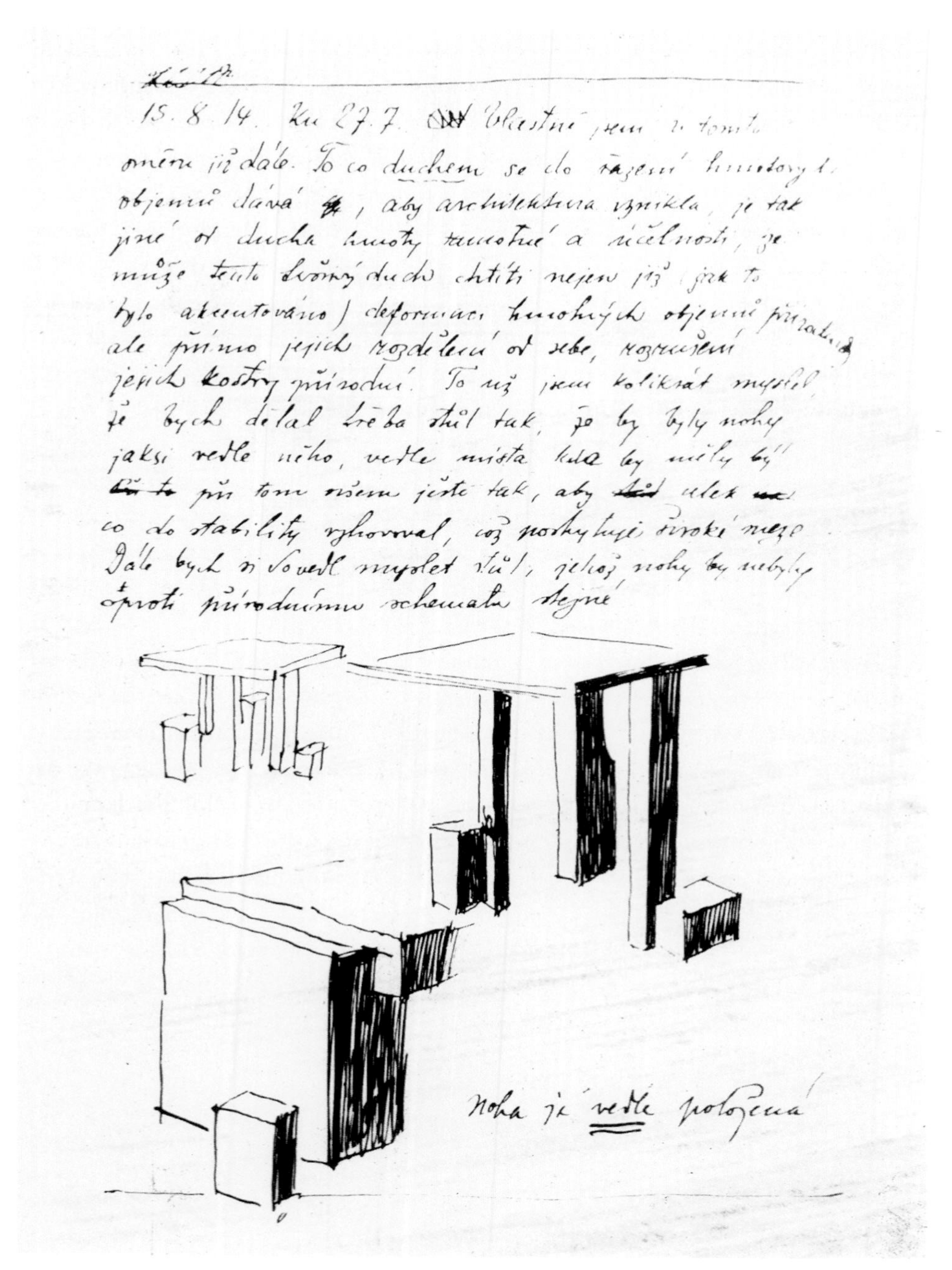

Page from journal, 1914

seems a little long." Many of the early sketches are on sheets torn out of diaries and sketchbooks. They are very interesting, most of them issuing from turn-of-the-century Viennese modernism. This early period marked Janák deeply; not only was it the starting point for his cubism, but he returned to it often in the twenties. In sketches from 1909 on, his Viennese modernist phase clearly recedes and the cubist period begins: rhomboids, triangles, trapezoids, and bent lines appear. At first he applies them only to caning in furniture, backrest panels, and so on. Later they are used, for instance, as the form of a small table and a sofa. Thus, what first emerges are fantasies of futuristic furniture; at the same time Janák sketched his romantic notion of a solitary person's house completely furnished. He realized these ideas and theories in a series of furniture dated between 1911 and 1914.

A completely different and new period, which up to now has never been detected in Janák's work, took over his furniture designs from 1915 on: bent forms are straightened out, the square replaces the triangle and the rhomboid, the concave breaks give way to squared lines. Horizontals and verticals and large fields of contrasting colours, asymmetrically grouped, become the main compositional element. These furniture designs have much more in common with contemporary abstract painting than with cubism. Janák discovered a new harmony through the combination of rectangles, squares, and contrasting colours. His work approached Dutch neo-plasticism, as it was formulated a few years later, in 1918, by the De Stijl movement. Janák expresses his thoughts on the subject in his journal as early as 29 July 1914: "When there is an opening, I think that there must be a form to fit it in this relationship: they are together, but they lie side by side and not on the same axis." On 15 August 1914, he notes, "In fact I have progressed further in this regard. . . . The creative spirit can now take on more than the deformation of natural material volumes (as has been accepted already), but in fact their actual separation from one another, the disruption of their natural structure: I have often thought that I would like to make a table in such a way, that its legs would be somehow next to it, next to the place where they should be. Beside everything else, the whole should satisfy as far as stability is concerned, which allows for broad boundaries. As well, I can imagine a table with legs that are not similar, contrary to the natural scheme." These thoughts are accompanied by pen sketches and coloured designs, none of which were realized. However, some of them provided the inspiration for his work in later decades.

The study and analysis of Janák's unknown journal covering the years 1911 to 1914 has yielded two revelations. First, we can confirm (for instance in the bibliographical notes) current hypotheses concerning the cross-fertilizing influence of certain theoretical writings. By noting how consistently they were applied, we can better explain the programmatic purity, and even the uniqueness, of Czech cubist architecture and plastic work. Second, we can trace the logical progression from Janák's cubist work to his hitherto unknown period of neo-plasticism.

Reprinted from Acta UPM C. Commentationes *19, no. 4 (Prague, 1985).*

Czech Cubism Today

François Burkhardt

The great value of the cubist movement is that it constituted a rupture in the continuity of the figurative tradition. In addition, it had within it all the preconditions for renewal that characterized the first thirty years of the twentieth century in European culture. One of its principal achievements was a new way of subdividing depicted objects by using the planar dimension of geometry to reveal their plastic character. This was the first time since the Renaissance that an artistic movement forsook depiction of objects from a single point of view, to portray them instead via their component parts. Through these new structural properties, a dynamic was created in which a new element, time, gained the same value as height, width, and depth—whence the idea of the fourth dimension. Research was thus concentrated on new measures, a means of extending the area of inquiry, at the very moment when mathematics, physics, and philosophy were confronting the same problems.

Thus, one of the greatest achievements of the Czech cubist movement—and the source of its uniqueness—was its tenacious search for theoretical support and its transposition of the fourth dimension into the fields of architecture and interior design. No other movement has had such a fundamental influence on a new perception of art and space. In its time, Czech cubism alone incorporated in ideas and research the problems of everyday objects. Who could have imagined that cubist research, so closely linked to the modernistic nature of avant-garde movements, would catch a second wind, and in fact assume a leading role in the debate on postmodernist architecture, as we are presently witnessing in the deconstructivist movement? This second wind would be unthinkable without reference to constructivism and cubism.

It was, however, the "postmodernist condition," a kind of transitional phase between modernism and postmodernism, that facilitated the gathering of elements necessary for reevaluation of the Czech cubist movement, emphasizing not simply the renewal of cubism, but also the freedom that postmodernism offers. Beyond stylistic clashes, it has allowed the aggregation of the basic factors necessary for a new creative impetus in our turbulent period of history. Even under these new circumstances, cubism has preserved the inherent principle of its destiny: to be a force of rupture, rigour, and method. To expand its horizons beyond the frontiers of modernism, it has added the emotional dimension, which touches upon the new postmodern sensibility.

Today, Czech cubism retains its validity and its raison d'être, first, through the typically Czech tradition of operating in a specific gnoseological tradition (in the sense of profiting from knowledge of other cultures), integrating and converting "foreign" influences into specifically "regional" ones; second, through the accessibility of its symbolism, which allows for the identification of politics with architecture; and, finally, through its evolution toward expressionism, arising from the cubist concept and providing access to a new deconstructivist aesthetic. It seems to me that these three aspects make the Czech cubist movement of lasting interest and justify its continued existence. They also show that a reevaluation of the historic concept of cubism allows for a re-actualization or elucidation of the conditions that gave rise to it, without which it could not have existed. The modern, linear history of cubism is replaced by a parallel history, assembled from fragments and montages, which will be evaluated according to the circumstances behind the origins of the movement.

Pavel Janák, reconstruction of a Baroque house in Pelhřimov, 1913, detail of gable

Given the political changes of the early nineties, Karel Čapek's statement that it is possible to "draw a line between Western and Eastern Europe, running approximately through the centre of our republic [Czechoslovakia]" is truer than ever. It is impossible not to notice that Central Europe, which became a peripheral region after the Second World War, is once again finding itself at the crossroads of cultural exchange and intermingling. To quote Čapek again, it is "on this small island, where all the great currents of European development cross and occasionally even collide," that a reabsorption and reproposal of the concepts which have traversed this land may occur, with "no other claims except to show . . . some general properties of Czechoslovak art."

Art was always welcomed in Prague, where it was transformed: innovative aspects of other cultures were absorbed and used to create indigenous, distinctive, and surprising works, such as those by Parler, Ried, Dietzenhofer, and Santini-Aichel. The cubists became part of this tradition. An example is the church of St. Barbara in Kutná Hora. Since this remarkable late-Gothic structure took two centuries to build, it could not have a homogeneous look. On the contrary, it illustrates the adaptation of the laws of Gothic construction to local conditions by absorbing foreign construction elements—for instance, the decorations and motifs

Benedikt Ried, church of St. Barbara in Kutná Hora, 1440–1547, vault of the main nave

adopted from a brace of chapels, brought from France by Mathieu of Arras, who worked in Bohemia. The crown of the vault above the nave, with high, monumentally profiled pillars with no capitals, supporting a flat vault segmented by a decorative network of elliptical curves, was a personal interpretation by Benedikt Ried. Together with the unique tent-like roof of the church, they give the building a silhouette unequalled in Bohemia or elsewhere.

A second example is the original and the pilgrimage church in Žďár nad Sázavou by G. B. Santini-Aichel. This exceptional architect managed to interpret the lessons of the Piedmontese and Roman Baroque of Guarini and Borromini: the system of curves; the alternation of concave and convex movements, which, with the protruding edges, give the building an aggressive and dynamic dimension; and the spatial penetrations with an intermittent succession of massive volumes and subtle membranes. The mass of the church is worked in a specific manner. When one enters, one sees a large cupola which overarches the lateral spaces, superimposing on the different elements in such a way that the light sources, always indirect, are never revealed, thus enhancing the plastic effects. A special aspect of the building is the Baroque plan: on each floor is a pentagram (or five-pointed star), to which is added a different geometric form consisting of circles and triangles, grouped around the Gothic system of a pointed arch. Santini-Aichel renounced the language of architectural orders in favour of a space sparse in decoration but resplendent in absolute whiteness. Unlike the Italian or German Baroque masters, he did not emphasize the symbolic message; rather, he used a very modest decorative system. The church, cemetery, and gallery, a sacral complex situated on a hill, foreshadowed, in a general sense, German expressionist architecture.

Giovanni Santini-Aichel, cemetery chapel of St. John Nepomuciensis, Zdár nad Sázavou, 1722

A third example, which very closely touches upon Czech cubism, is late-Gothic diamond vaulting. This Central European specialty saw renewed popularity in the eighteenth century, when it was called ribbed vaulting, and left an extraordinary heritage in southern Bohemia. It was last used in the 1880s. It should not be surprising that Pavel Janák particularly admired the formal aspect of this construction system, as it contained a concept analogous to the one he described in relation to cubist aesthetics in his famous study "The Prism and the Pyramid" (1910). The diamond vaults, with their dominant geometrical arrangement, sharp edges, and oblique, constantly touching lines, bear a formal resemblance to cubist

Church of St. Peter and St. Paul in Soběslav, 1499–1501, detail of diamond vaulting

Josef Chochol, villa in Prague–Podolí, 1913, detail of facade

constructions in their prismatic corpus and crystalline forms, their system of oblique surfaces and bevelled planes.

We must bear in mind the free interpretations of the cubist artists, who juxtaposed very diverse styles and epochs. Thus, the mixture of late Gothic with the Baroque in Bohemia has led historians to coin the term "Baroque Gothic"; at first glance completely contradictory and illogical, it illustrates the eclecticism with which architects approach history: everything is possible, if we free ourselves from oppressive dogmas. This type of historical montage is found in many projects by Janák, whose goal was a sensitive integration of the traditional Baroque facade and the cubist conception. The reconstruction of the Baroque building in the town square at Pelhřimov is a unique example of the successful joining of two styles without interference with the overall urban image.

As for the influence of French cubism on its Czech counterpart, it must be pointed out that research in Prague was fully supported by achievements in Paris: analytical cubism was followed, after a hiatus appropriate for the plastic-arts movement, by synthetic cubism. The Czech preference was to use the research in applied arts and architecture. The only known analogous example in architecture is Raymond Duchamp-Villon's "Cubist house," designed in 1912. It is very likely that ideas were exchanged between the French and the Czechs, possibly through František Kupka, whose studio was near Duchamp-Villon's, or through the magazine *Umělecký měsíčník*, which was available at the cubist galleries; the cubist motif above the entrance portal of Duchamp-Villon's "Cubist house" is very similar to the motifs used by Janák. A more thorough study would be necessary to explain this rapprochement of ideas more completely. I would not rule out the possibility that Czech architects played an important role in the development of the decorative arts, which are suffused with, among other things, cubist elements. A manifest example of the assimilation, transformation, and renewed proposal of a style is Janák's famous double drawing of a cubist gable and an interior ("A Monumental Interior," 1912). Janák emphasized the idea of the gable so forcefully that he converted it completely into a facade: it took on a pyramidal shape and was incorporated into the cubist thematic field.

Clearly, this dialectic, this proposal for transformation, could be recognized only within critical circles which considered this process to be positive. This is why history has long been silent with regard to this movement. It is obvious that postmodern criticism values the kinds of interventions which allow for differentiation and appreciation of individual regional practices, thus enabling an appreciation of the ambivalent and eclectic Czech cultural potential, which nonetheless may be defined within the framework of rational aesthetics. It is in fact this duality of the controllable, rational approach and expressive emotion that made Czech cubism the harbinger of a cultural climate marked by three dominant phenomena: research into the movement of matter according to Albert Einstein's theories of physics; Wilhelm Worringer's principle of abstraction; and the new concept of visual perception flowing from Theodor Lipps's discoveries.

Thus, cubism became an adjunct theory of such scientific disciplines as physics, mathematics, epistemology, and, not least, philosophy. We can speak of simultaneously occurring pragmatic and intuitive research, and of the figurative projection of contemporary science—the first such example in the history of the modern avant-garde movement.

A second point concerns the renaissance of national symbolism and regional aesthetics. In recent years, a lively debate on this theme has developed, contrasting

Pavel Janák, reconstruction of a Baroque house in Pelhřimov, 1913, detail of entrance

Traditional Baroque facades in the town square at Pelhřimov

Raymond Duchamp-Villon, "La maison cubiste," 1912, model

regionalism, as an expression of local cultures, against the centralizing character of internationalistic aesthetics (for instance, "international style" or "good design"). Its sources lie in using connections to local roots as a means of liberation from oppression, whether purely theoretical or even political. Although it could have been expected to have reactionary, nationalistic intentions, in the case of Czech cubism it is precisely this model of critical regionalism that we must turn to in order to arrive at a new evaluation of its regional tradition.

It must be noted that the interest in cultural renewal was directly linked to the process of national liberation that was burgeoning in the countries of the Austro-Hungarian Empire. In Bohemia, Moravia, and Slovakia, there were repeated calls for freedom and independence, which could be silenced only by the imperial authority. These ranged from claims by Bohemia, a country in full-fledged industrial development, through demands for social reforms to deal with the serious emigration problems in the poorest agricultural areas of Moravia, to the struggle for an indigenous language and culture in Slovakia. Alongside the Czech and German bourgeoisie developed an industrial proletariat. The Czechs gradually acquired political experience in Vienna and nurtured an intellectual vitality around their universities, ensuring a fertile climate for the flourishing of a Prague culture which had a wealth of exchanges with, in particular, Germany and France. Close to the hearts of Prague's cultural circles around 1910 was, in addition to an interest in the developing cubist movement, an anti-Austro-Hungarian side, for instance in its references to a more advanced and less conservative nation and the search for an open and free cultural opposition.

Regional feelings were central to the interests of the Czech patriots. The philosopher Paul Ricœur maintains that critical, or prospective, regionalism is based on mutual influence between cultures with strong local roots and universalistic cultures. According to the historian Friedrich Achleitner, this constant dialectic is the inherent point of departure of the cultural renewal of a particular region or place. Achleitner also says that regionalism develops in centralized states, especially in their outlying regions. This reflects precisely the political development of the Czech state up to the creation of its first republic.

In the first years of the new republic, there was a search for a unifying national aesthetic and a corresponding means of artistic expression. The result was a new architecture and style, which were doubtless rooted in the works of Janák and Josef Gočár from 1914 and 1915. This style, with the unfortunate name "rondo-cubism," has nothing in common with cubism in theoretical terms. Its name is derived from the fact that it was developed by leading cubists, who began to use visual plastic elements based not on triangles or hexagons, but on circles, rings, and cylinders. The critic and historian Maria Benešová saw in the movement a continuity with purely decorative intentions: first, cubist forms and ornaments are applied to the facade, then rondo-cubist ones. The idea that cubist architecture is only external was born from this erroneous opinion.

We must also recognize a desire for content in rondo-cubism—for instance, in the unified transmission of elements of folk architecture accumulated in the three provinces which were now united in the new republic. Janák's crematorium in Pardubice is a representative work in this sense: it uses certain signs and techniques to create an unified whole conveyed in an intelligible, non-abstract language, which is less intellectualized than cubism—that is, a transition from the avant-garde approach to the vernacular, which was better understood by the people.

The phases of rondo-cubism clearly document the concerns of its creators with completely different questions: first, the search for elements of sculptural, plastic,

Rose Amada and Luis Domenech, Tapies Foundation, Barcelona, 1990, view of ceiling with lateral natural lighting

Vlastislav Hofman, chair, 1911–1912 (far right)

Adriano and Paolo Suman, chair, 1988 (right)

Pavel Janák, competition design for reconstruction of the town hall at Havlíčkuv Brod (formerly Nemecký Brod), 1913–1914

and abstract transfiguration, carried out in parallel with cubism; then the search for a popular expression of national unity using folk elements; and, finally, projects that are better developed, richer, more monumental and heroic, in which classicizing tendencies are integrated through the enlargement of certain elements to contrast them with the sophisticated and surprising elements of symbolic interpretation. One must note the opulent eclecticism, rich in fantasy and endowed with unusual properties—as, for instance, in Gočár's Legionnaires' Bank.

The opening of contacts abroad, after a period of internal consolidation, gave access to rationalism and international functionalism. The desire for internationalization was the logical result of a national effort to achieve universality as a basic sign of a prosperous country in full industrial development and open to international exchange. Two things fascinate me about the protagonists of Czech modern architecture. On the one hand, they perceived aesthetics as an instrument serving collective expression, conceived by their will to interpret, through architecture, change, progress, freedom, and autonomy—in keeping with the expressive means defined by the period and by their own history. On the other hand, they were excellent architects in the styles of, in turn, the Secession, early modernism, cubism, rondo-cubism, and functionalism; for people like Janák, Gočár, and Novotný, this was a sign not of subordination or weakness, but rather of strength.

Pavel Janák, study of a facade, 1913–1914

It was they who determined the history of these movements, and changed or re-oriented them according to the particular time or region—outside of any academic structure.

There is every hope that this remarkable example of living culture, which was interrupted by the various prohibitions of totalitarian regimes, has regained its freedom of expression and will find in its own tradition the idiom appropriate to its aspirations. Postmodernism, with its return to critical regionalism, may breathe new life into a movement which has earned the historical right to continue.

The interest in the problematic of the cubist movement, its re-actualization, and the aesthetics derived from it fall on fertile ground, especially today—and not by accident. The postmodern movement, which breaks with the rationalistic, realistic, and scientifically verifiable conceptions, makes room for other efforts directed more toward communication. It takes into account diverse sensibilities, sometimes even very marginal ones, in which social and cultural contradictions live side by side without conflict—which, of course, makes a concentration of dominant expressions impossible. It certainly results in a loss of expressive force with regard to communication of content and tends to get lost in the profusion of other expressions. In any case, the movement encourages the liberation of expressions considered peripheral, or even minor, such as, for instance, the cubist movement in architecture.

Although it is based on humanism and on the evolution of industrial society, the technological revolution is bringing a new approach to projects, involving the elimination of interdisciplinary barriers. Design concerns itself with "drawing from the great plankton of technologies, structures, and linguistic and information services" says Andrea Branzi, and "artists stand helpless in the face of this destructive freedom." They would first draw from the past, which is known, and revise that which has already been achieved from new perspectives.

This is how we can explain the remarkable resurgence in production of "neo-cubist" design objects in the last few years, as well as of architectural works from the deconstructivist movement. There are also many examples of a renewal of the methods of cubist composition in interior design. Some of these, such as the "Kandissi" sofa by Alessandro Mendini, are directly linked to designers' personal

Pavel Janák, crematorium in Pardubice, 1921, detail

reflections on cubism in the face of historical material which had previously been beyond their sphere of interest and common knowledge. Other designers, Czechs such as Milan Knižák, found in the connection to the historical cubist movement a new source, affirming their regional identity and their relationship to an avant-garde looking for new recognition. There are even designers who very skillfully create a "revival" inspired by the publication of works on cubist furniture. Teaching methods also seem to be taking into account this rediscovered aesthetic, legitimized by the liberation provided by anti-functionalism. Finally, there are those who, through their own extended search, find themselves in the neighbourhood of a past which has already become part of history.

The works of Zaha Hadid and of the Coop-Himmelblau group give the impression that they want to deform the central perspective and replace it with several simultaneous perspectives, or to try to depict the object in its spatial totality, for example by representing it from the outside and the inside simultaneously, in frontal elevation and in section, which is very reminiscent of cubist depiction. Research is also concentrated on the creation of spatial interpenetrations, on the faceted decomposition of objects, in order to attain the alienation of normal perception, and to exclude all references to the depicted object in order to achieve an allusion to floating planes. In its approach to the object, for instance in composition, this style of architecture and its corresponding "furnishings" recall the works of the Czech cubists.

Through similar efforts to destabilize the laws of statics, the cubists and neo-cubists challenge the laws of construction and matter. Priority is placed on the dynamism of expression, with the aim of transforming the weight and inertia of matter through plastic extension into a vision of lightness, by overturning physical laws and the psychology of perception. The Coop-Himmelblau group attempts a rapprochement with the object through the "psychogram" (a sort of psychological diagram): the artists, in accordance with their feelings and internal rhythms, note down gestures which create spaces, which they try to render constructible in a second phase. They speak of physical communication with space, with the hand as the seismograph of emotion tracing power curves which eventually become construction elements. Analogous to cubist emotions, a psychological approach is

Zaha Hadid, from the catalogue of the exhibition *Deconstructivism* at the Museum of Modern Art, New York

Coop-Himmelblau, *Long, Thin, Yellow Legs of Architecture*, 1988, plastic, Rotterdam

combined with matter, giving the impression of being put in motion by gravitation, and then solidified by a randomly arranged geometry, which determines the feasibility of construction.

In order to fully appreciate the importance of Czech cubism, we must remove all taboos that were unfairly attached to it as the result of a series of unfavourable assessments, which attempted to diminish its influence and reduce it to "one of the decorative trends," or characterize it as an "exercise in facades" which had no impact. This is a serious mistake. The essential message and merits of Czech cubism are threefold: first, drawing from a long history, it revitalized a specific tradition of Czech culture through assimilation, adaptation, and transformation, then launched an original style which contributed new and specific values to the enrichment of great stylistic movements. Second, it defined a theory of the cubist construct, corresponding to advanced scientific research and ideas of the time. Third, it ascribed to architecture the role of mediator of substance, reaching far beyond the boundaries of the usual functions of architecture.

Milan Knížák, cabinet from the Cocub series, 1971, from the exhibition catalogue

Thanks to new social conditions, Czech cubism can today become the model for the renewal of creative practice, especially in those countries which, like Czechoslovakia, have recently recovered their freedom of expression.

Proof

Alessandro Mendini

Ceramic panels, manufactured by Tendenza, 1985

In the early seventies I visited Prague a number of times, and I had an opportunity to see cubist architecture, contemporary furniture designs, and pieces of applied art. I was attracted to the wealth of forms and colours in cubism and to the theme of cosmic decomposition found in certain pictures by Kandinsky, as well as to some of the pointillist works—for instance, those by Signac. Czech cubism seemed to me an exemplary and holistic transference of the cubist principle into the sphere of applied art. To decompose form—or even to negate it—with the use of nervous gestures in order immediately to re-compose it seemed to me an interesting exercise, which I enjoyed applying not only to the creation of new objects, but also to the modification of already existing objects. To this end I sometimes used a method which I later named "Re-design," or sometimes simply "Design." This method was taken up by other designers later on; for me it was often the basic starting point for preparation of my own projects.

At that time I was charmed by a certain Prague cubist upholstered sofa with a wooden frame. There is another version of the same object, where the entire sofa is upholstered. One day, I laid tracing paper over the photograph of the sofa and started to trace its form in pencil—this was how I developed the "Kandissi" sofa. Instead of a symmetrical design, I composed the object asymmetrically; instead of natural wood, I used polychromed and lacquered wood, and the upholstery fabric has a cubist design. To take the process of decomposition further, I designed a "Kandissa" mirror and a "Kandissone" tapestry as complementary objects. At the same time, using similar principles, but with a more literary theme, I designed the "Proust" armchair.

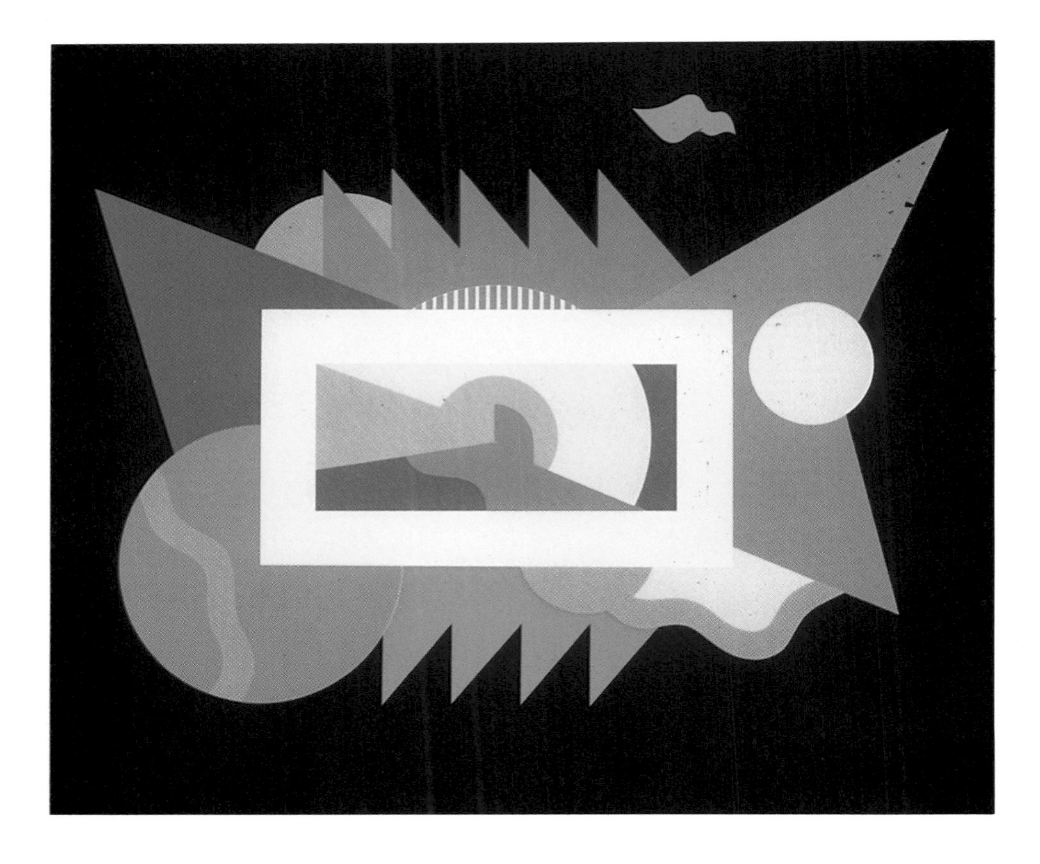

Untitled, paint on canvas, 75 x 90 cm, 1986

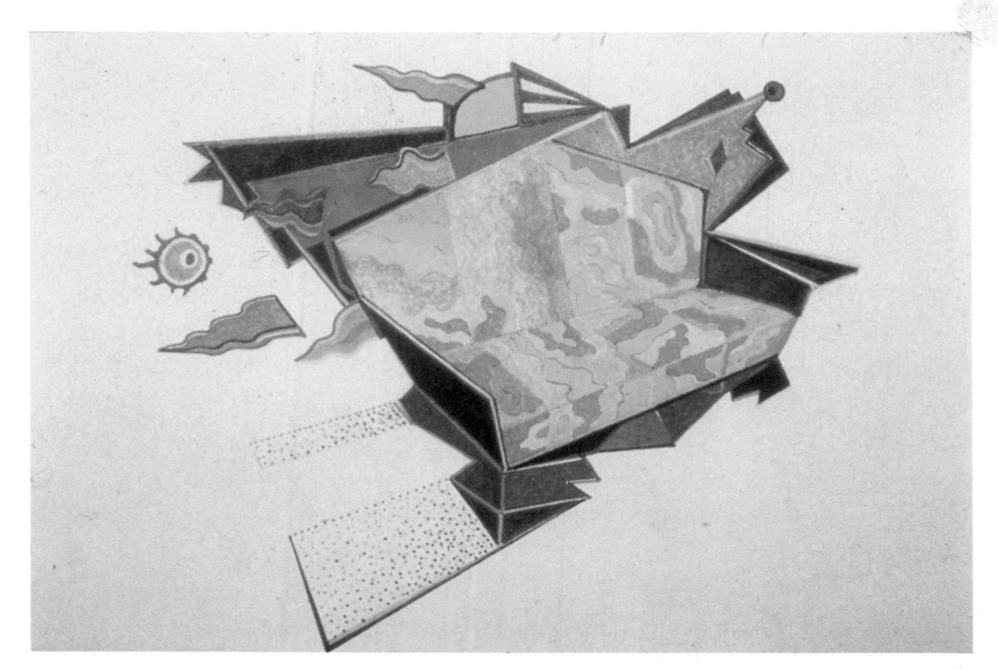

Drawing of "Kandissi" sofa, 1979

"Kandissi" sofa, 1979, Bauhaus 1 collection, Alchimia 1979

Oriented, tempera, 70 x 100 cm, 1984

At this point, Czechoslovak cubism, with its rich fantasy and uncommon originality, became the basis for the neo-modernistic phase of my work, which started with the first two "Alchimia" furniture groups, continued through the development of basic stylistic forms (triangles, arches, amoebas, lightning bolts, and pennants), and culminated in 1984 in the creation of the "Mendinigrafo" graphic system. Even the "Macaratu" armchair and sofa, designed in 1988 for Vitra Edition, is built on these basic forms, in this case blended with memories of a trip to Brazil. Italian futurism, and especially the highly original work of Fortunato Depero, were and are an important part of my heritage. Therefore, I must add that the iconography connected with my eclectic work process is very extensive and also contradictory; it ever-increasingly departs from the realm of the visible and moves toward theoretical and philosophical sources. In any case, I must say, without being able to explain it any further, that I very much admire Prague cubism, and that I owe it much intellectually.

Interior of Kaess-Weiss Gallery, Stuttgart, 1987

Catalogue

Architecture

Matěj Blecha

1.
Lamppost, 1912
Jungmann Square, in front of house no. 14, Prague–Nové Město
Emil Králíček, designer (formerly attributed to Vlastislav Hofman)

Full view, with a gothic portal in background, taken prior to repaving of Jungmann Square

Existing Structures

Catalogue nos. 1–27

2.
Diamant commercial and apartment building, 1912–1913
Spálená Street no. 4/82, Prague–Nové Město

Detail of railing, present condition

Corner view, present condition

Detail of entrance, present condition

Josef Chochol

3.
Villa below Vyšehrad, 1911–1912

Libušina Street no. 3/49, Prague–Vyšehrad

Facade on Libušina Street, present condition

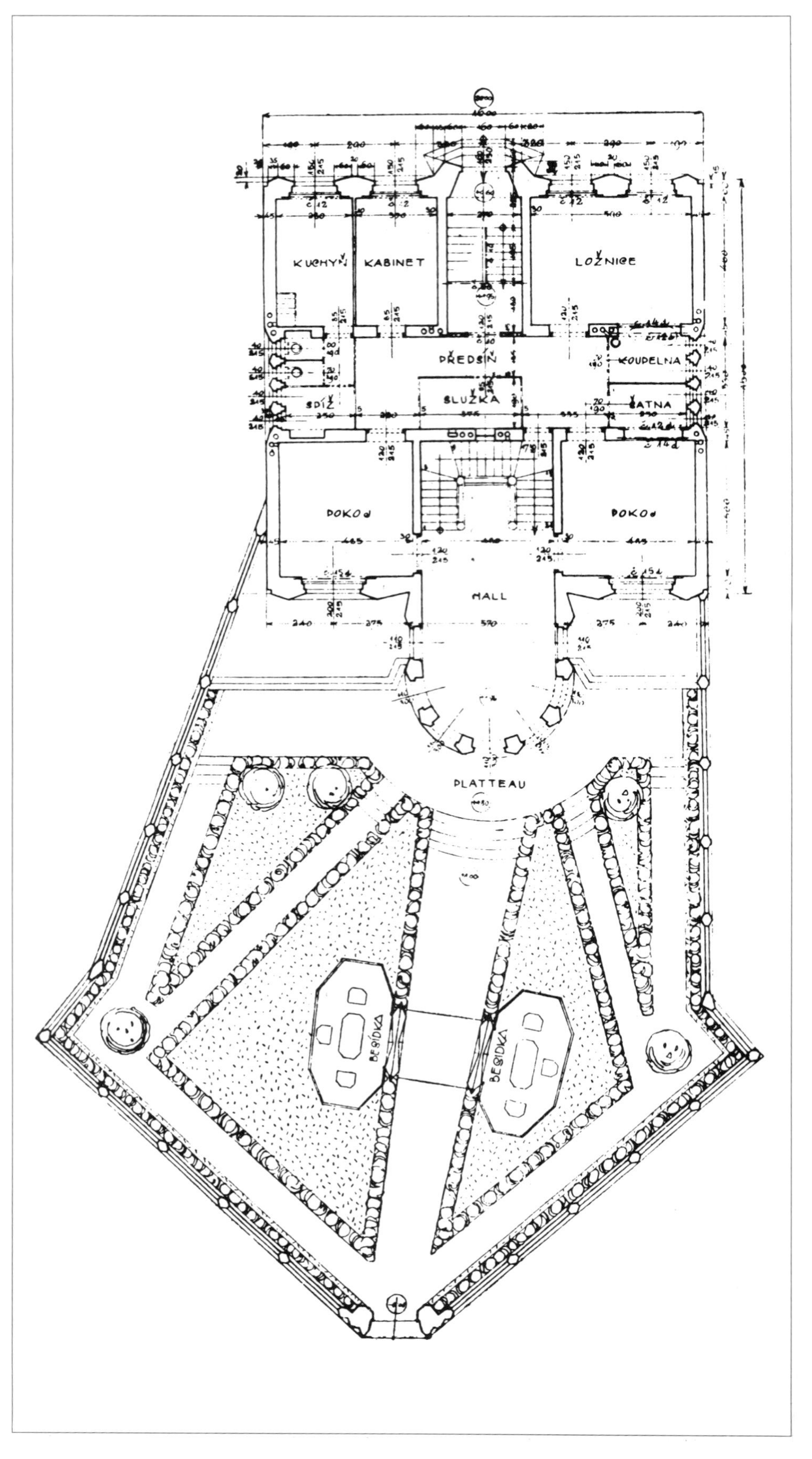

Ground-floor plan of villa, reproduction from period journal

View of garden-side facade from the Vltava River, period photograph

View of garden-side facade from the Vltava River, present condition

4.
Family triplex, 1912–1913

Rašín Embankment nos. 6/42, 8/47, and 10/71, Prague–Vyšehrad

View of street facade from the Vltava River, present condition

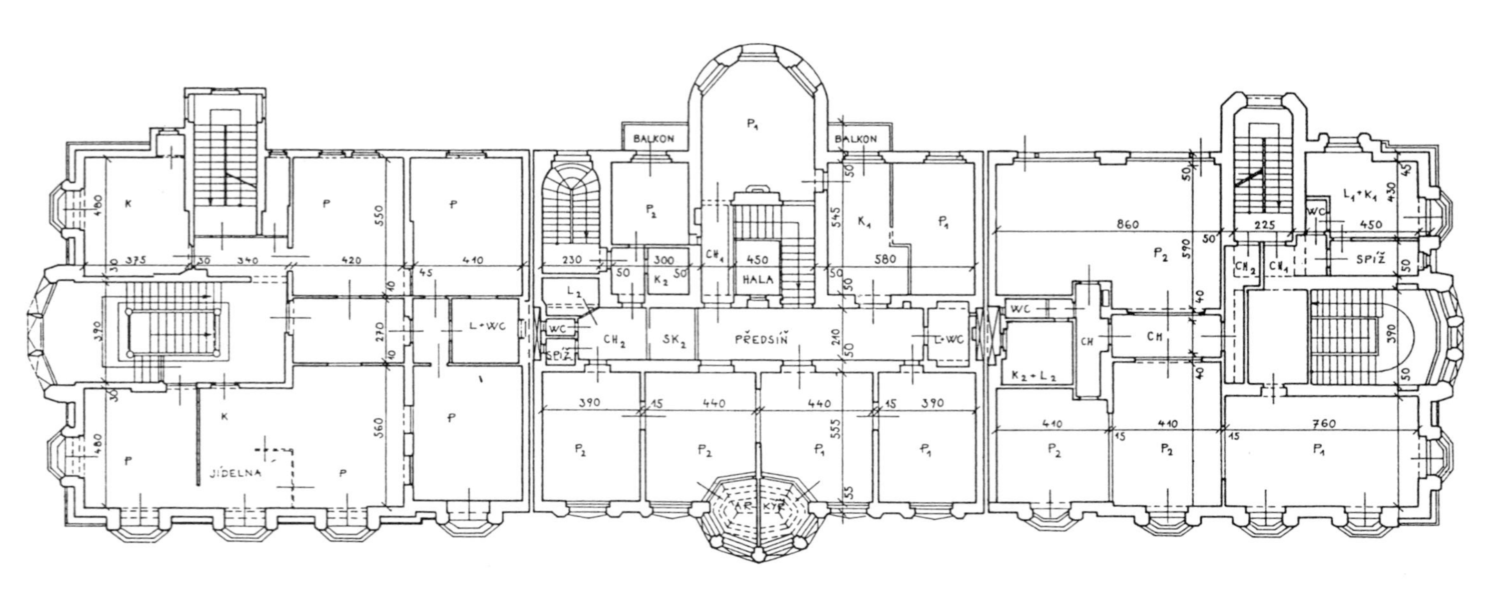

Typical floor plan

North facade, present condition

Street facade of middle house, period photograph

5.
Apartment house, 1913

Neklan Street no. 30/98, Přemysl Street no. 11, Prague–Vyšehrad

North and east elevations

Detail of corner, present condition

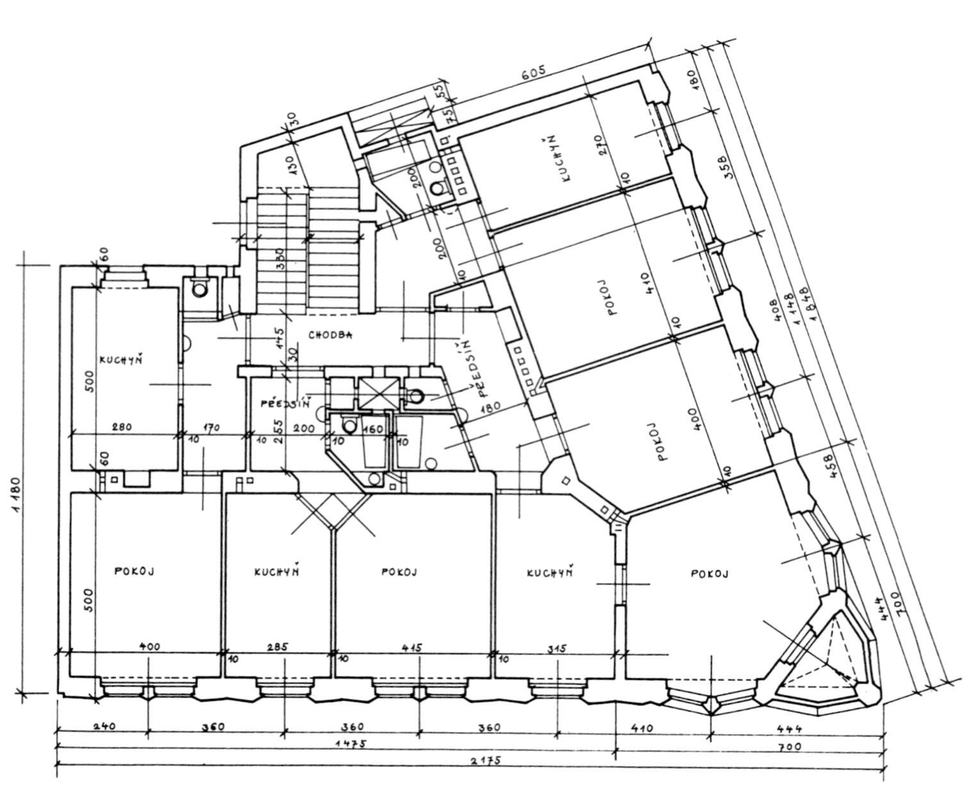

Plan of a typical floor

Corner view, period photograph

Bohuslav Fuchs and Josef Štěpánek

6.
Hydro-electric power station for the Plhák Brothers, 1921

Háj near Mohelnice

View of downstream facade of power station, period photograph

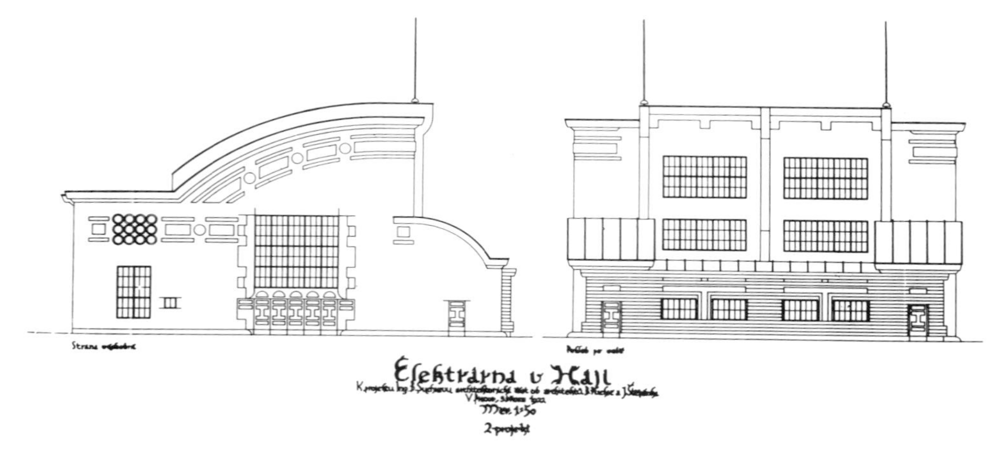

6a.
Power station at Háj, elevations of east and downstream facades, 1922

India ink
53 x 104.5 cm
Inscribed l.c.: "For the project of [Engineer] B. Sychrava architectural component by architects B. Fuchs and J. Štěpánek. In Prague, 3 March 1920"; inscribed l.l.: "East side"; inscribed l.c.: "Downstream view" and "Power station at Háj. Scale 1:50. 2nd project"
Designed for R. and K. Plhák
NTM Collection no. 126 Štěpánek
Acquired in 1964 from the architect's estate

6b.
Power station at Háj, west side and upstream view, 1922

India ink
54.5 x 103.5 cm
Inscribed l.r.: "For the project of [Engineer] B. Sychrava architectural component by architects B. Fuchs and J. Štěpánek. In Prague, 3 March 1920"; inscribed l.l.: "Upstream view"; inscribed l.c.: "West side." and "Power station at Háj. Scale 1:50. 2nd project"
Designed for R. and K. Plhák
NTM Collection no. 126 Štěpánek
Acquired in 1964 from the architect's estate

View of the villa's entrance area, original condition

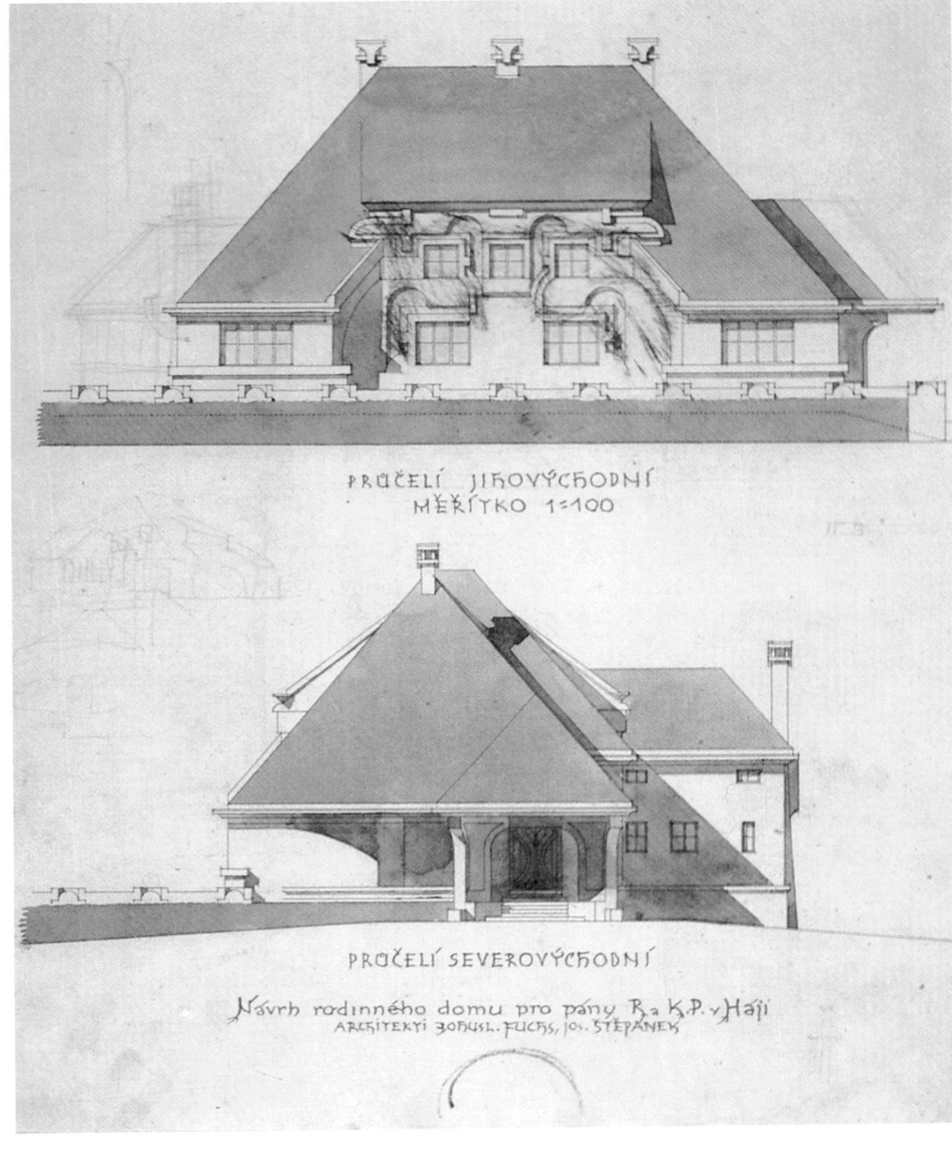

7.
Design for the Plhák brothers' villa, 1921
Háj near Mohelnice

7a.
Front and side elevations, 1921
India ink and watercolour; 51 x 41cm
Signed l.c.: "Architects Bohusl. Fuchs, Jos. Štěpánek." Inscribed c. and l.c.: "Design for residence for Messrs. R. and K. P. at Háj. Southeast facade. Northeast facade. Scale 1:100."

7b.
Southeast elevation, 1921
India ink and watercolour; 41 x 51.4 cm
Signed: "Architects B. Fuchs and J. Štěpánek. In Prague, July 1921"
Text explaining project in central column
Both 7a and 7b
Designed for R. and K. Plhák
NTM Collection no. 126 Štěpánek
Acquired in 1964 from the architect's estate

Josef Gočár

8.
U černé Matky Boží (At the Black Mother of God) department store, 1911–1912
Celetná Street no. 34, Ovocný trh Street no. 19/569, Prague–Staré Město

Exterior view, period photograph

8a.
Elevations for U černé Matky Boží department store, Celetná Street, 1912
India ink
34 x 68.9 cm
Not signed. Inscribed l.l.: "half-round"
NTM Collection no. 14 Gočár
Acquired in 1951 from the architect's estate

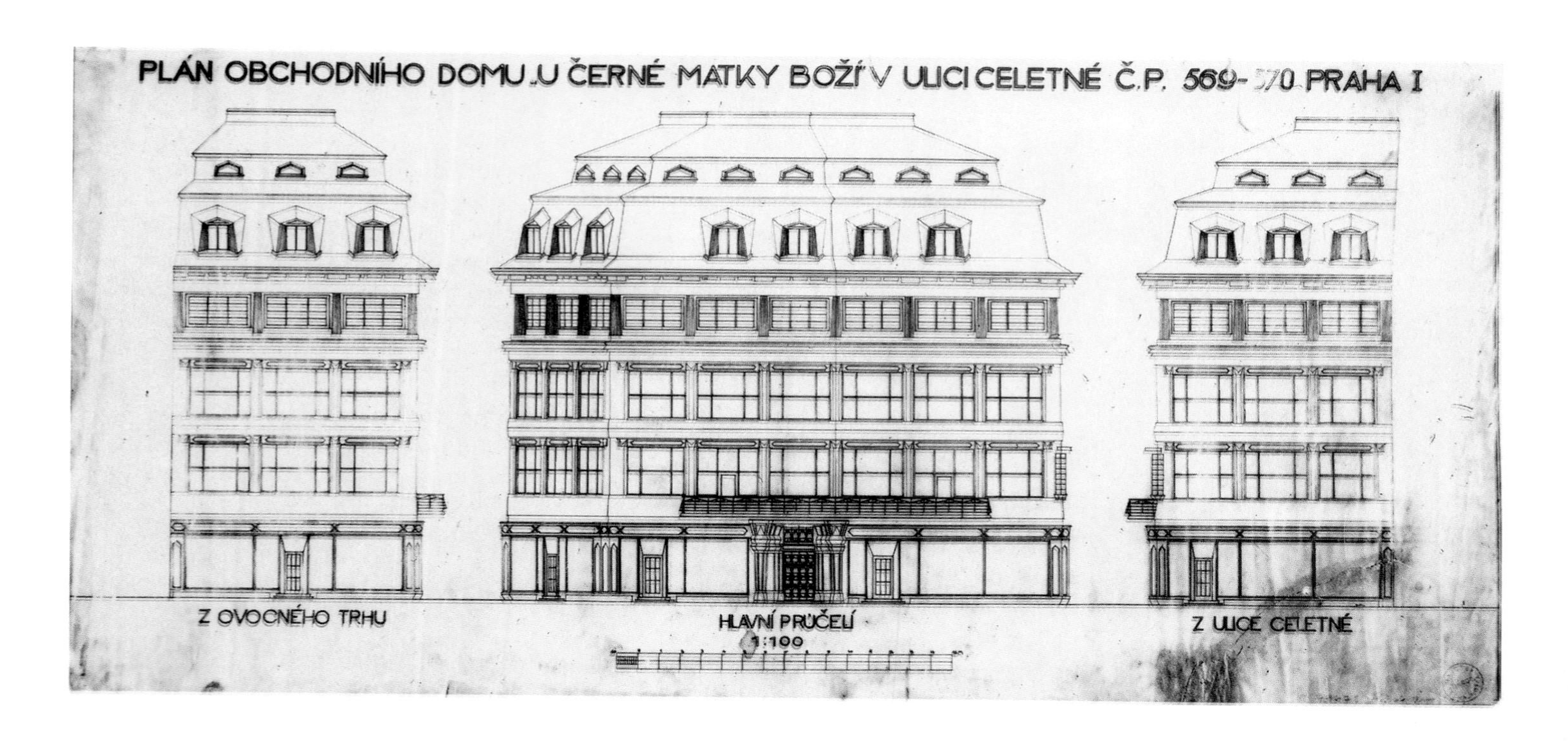

Detail of stairway railing, period photograph

Counter in café, period photograph

Interior of café, period photograph

9.
Bohdaneč spa, 1911–1912
Spa grounds, Bohdaneč, Pardubice County

Principal facade, period photograph

Interior of hall on ground floor, period photograph

10.
Family duplex, 1912–1913

Tychon Street nos. 4/268 and 6/269,
Prague–Hradčany
Project 1911–1912, realized 1912–1913

10a.
Entrance detail on Tychon Street in Prague, 1912

India ink and crayons
61 x 47.5 cm
Stamped c.r.: "Architekt Gočár, 22. srp. 12, Praha 1., Frant.nábř. č. 6"
Horizontal notation at c.: "– DETAIL OF PORTAL – VILLA OF P. HOFMANN – 1:20 –"
Designed for Messrs. Hofmann and Stach
NTM Collection no. 14 Gočár
Acquired in 1951 from the architect's estate

Entrance facade, present condition

11.
Family home for Mr. Bauer, 1912–1913

Libodřice, Kolín County

Garden-side facade, present condition

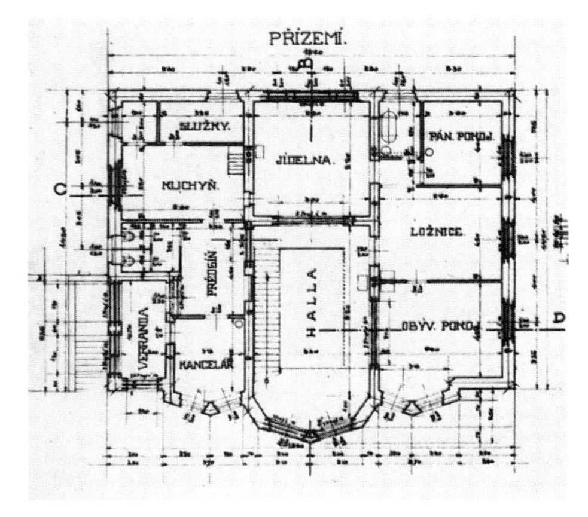

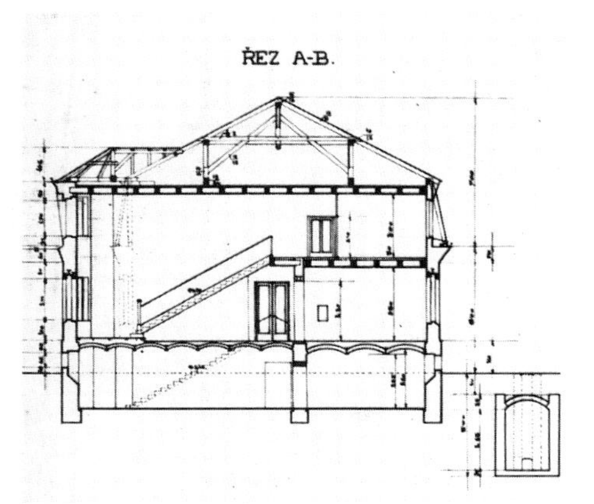

Construction drawings of villa

12.

Bank of the Czechoslovak Legion, 1922–1923

Na poříčí Street no. 24/1046, Prague–Nové Město
Design 1921, realized 1922–1923
Collaboration with sculptors Jan Štursa
and Otto Gutfreund

12a.

Competition design, main elevation, 1921

Graphite and watercolour, mounted on cardboard
44.2 x 25 cm
Inscribed l.c.: "Unity" (competition slogan)
Recommended for final competition
NTM Collection no. 14 Gočár
Acquired in 1951 from the architect's estate

12b.

Competition design, perspective, 1921

India ink and watercolour, mounted on cardboard
52 x 50 cm
Inscribed l.c.: "Unity" (competition slogan)
Recommended for final competition
NTM Collection no. 14 Gočár
Acquired in 1951 from the architect's estate
Exhib.: Prague, 1947 (cat. no. 285)

Facade study

Interior of main hall of bank, period photograph

Interior of hall, upper level, present condition

Main (north) facade, period photograph

13.
The Bank of Brno, 1922–1923
Panská Street no. 9, Jindřišská Street
no. 15/1308, Prague–Nové Město
Project 1921, realized 1922–1923
Collaboration with sculptor Karel Dvořák

Corner view, period photograph

14.
Anglo-Czechoslovak Bank, 1922–1923
Masaryk Square, Čelakovsky Street no. 642,
Hradec Králové

14a.
Design for the building of the Anglo-Czechoslovak Bank, corner perspective, 1922
Graphite and india ink
46.5 x 47.5 cm
NTM Collection no. 14 Gočár
Acquired in 1951 from the architect's estate

Corner view, period photograph

Vlastislav Hofman

15.
Cemetery Entrance with Gate and Kiosks, 1912–1913

Ďáblická Street, Prague 8 – Ďáblice

Entrance gate with kiosks, present condition

Design for entrance, architect's linocut, reproduction from period journal

Pavel Janák

16.
Family home for Mr. Jakubec, 1911–1912
Marshal Koněv Street no. 157, Jičín

16a.
Front elevation, 1911
India ink and watercolour
31.5 x 49.5 cm
Designed for Mr. Jakubec at Jičín
NTM Collection no. 85 Janák
Acquired in 1957 from the architect's estate
Exhib.: Prague, Vienna (cat. no. 37, repr.), Helsinki, 1982–1987; Tokyo, 1984 (cat. no. 110, repr.)

View of entrance facade, period photograph

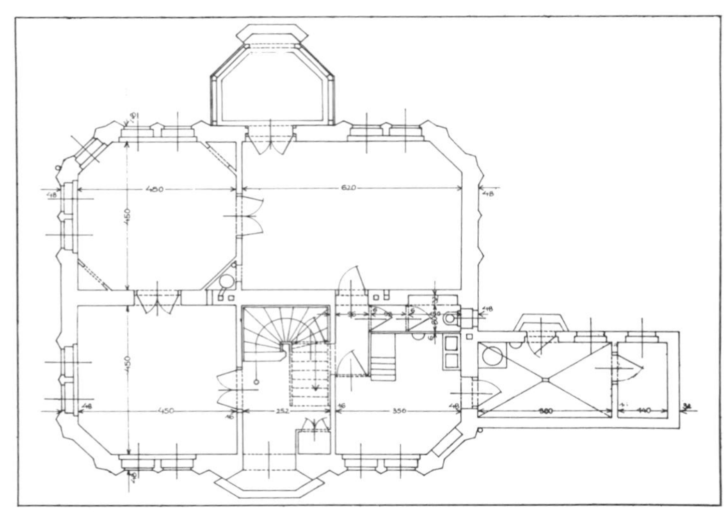

Floor plan

17.
Family residence, 1912
Strachovská Street no. 331, Pelhřimov

Garden elevation

Street facade and fence, period photograph

18.
Reconstruction of Dr. Fára's house, 1913

Masaryk Square no. 13, Pelhřimov

18a.
Elevation study, 1913

Graphite and crayon
20.8 x 34 cm
Inscribed l.r.: "17.9.1913"
Designed for V. K. Fára, M.D.
NTM Collection no. 85 Janák
Acquired in 1957 from the architect's estate
Exhib.: Prague, Vienna (cat. no. 81, repr.),
Helsinki, 1982–1987

18b.
Elevation study, 1913

Graphite, india ink, and crayons
36.4 x 46.5 cm
Inscribed verso: "sketches of facade"
Designed for V. K. Fára, M.D.
NTM Collection no. 85 Janák
Acquired in 1957 from the architect's estate
Exhib.: Prague, Vienna (cat. no. 82, repr.),
Helsinki, 1982–1987

18c.
Construction drawing of gable, 1913

Graphite
43 x 41 cm
Inscriptions c.l and u.c. regarding tiling
Designed for V. K. Fára, M.D.
NTM Collection no. 85 Janák
Acquired in 1957 from the architect's estate
Exhib.: Prague, Vienna (cat. no. 80, repr.),
Helsinki, 1982–1987; Tokyo, 1984
(cat. no. 138, repr.)

Facade facing the square, present condition

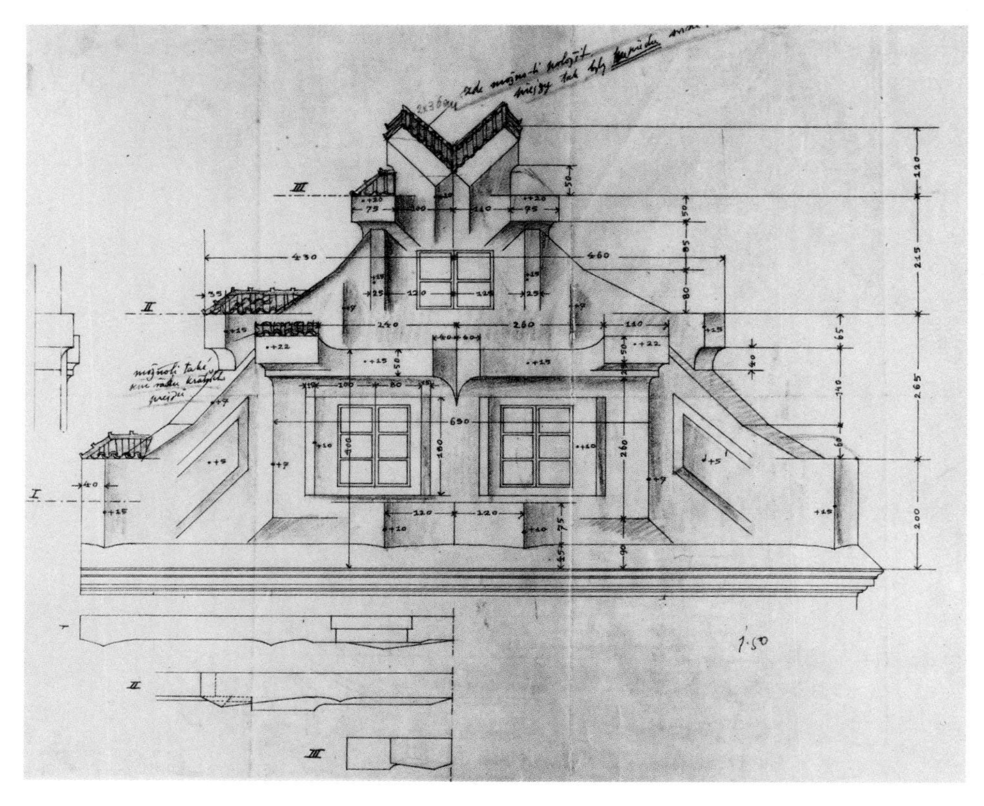

19.
Villa for Dr. Pick, 1920–1921
Jaroměřice

Exterior view, period photograph

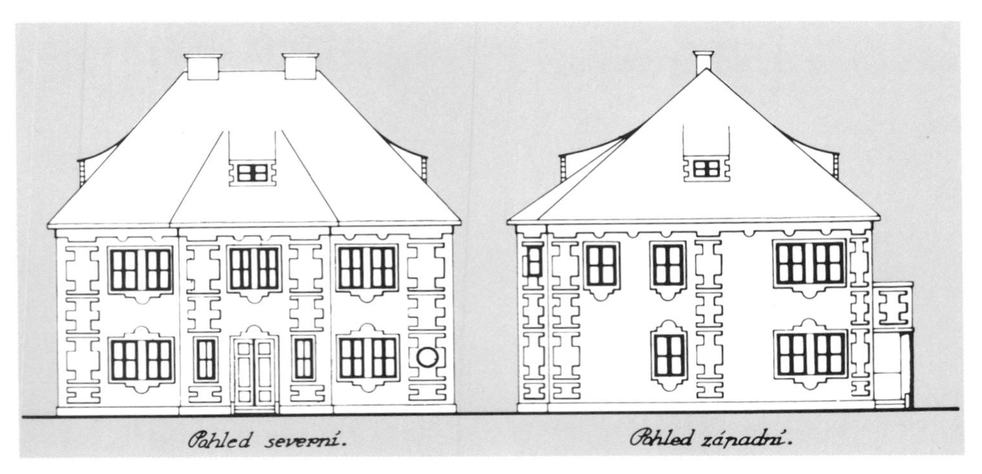

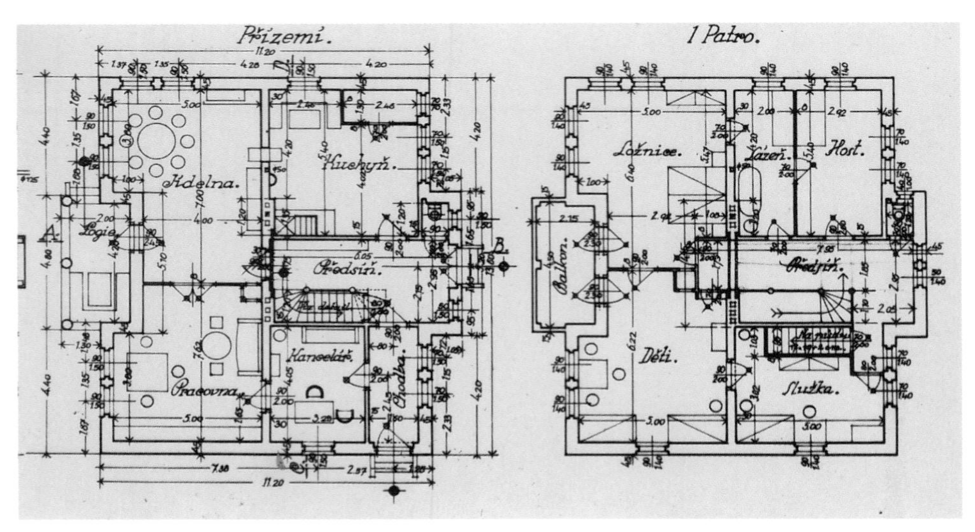

Construction drawings for villa

20.
Crematorium, 1921–1923
Pod břízkami Street no. 990, Pardubice

Entrance facade, period photograph

Floor plan of ceremonial hall

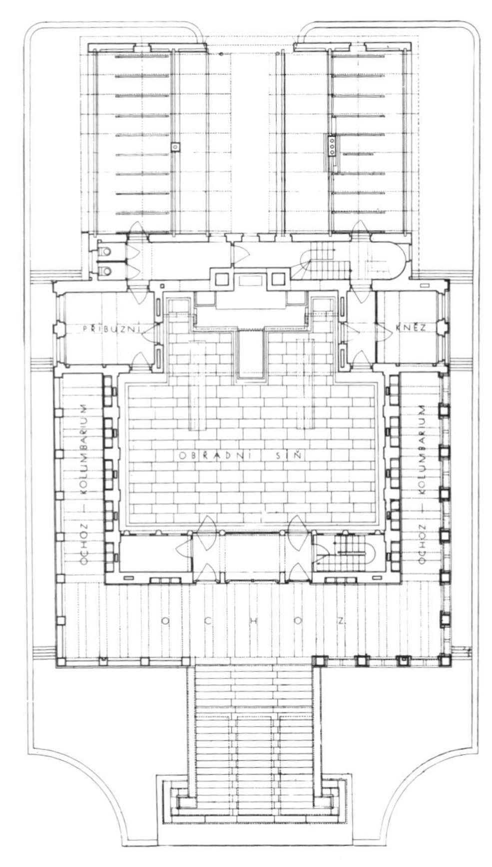

Corner view, period photograph

21.
Riunione Adriatica di Sicurtá commercial and department-store building, 1922–1924
Jungmann Street no. 31/36, Prague–Nové Město
Collaboration with Josef Zasche

Detail of facade, period photograph

Otakar Novotný

22.
Apartment buildings for the Teachers' Housing Co-operative, 1917–1919
Elišky Krásnohorské Street nos. 10, 12, 14/123, 1021, 1037, Prague–Staré Město

Corner view, period photograph

Detail of facade, present condition

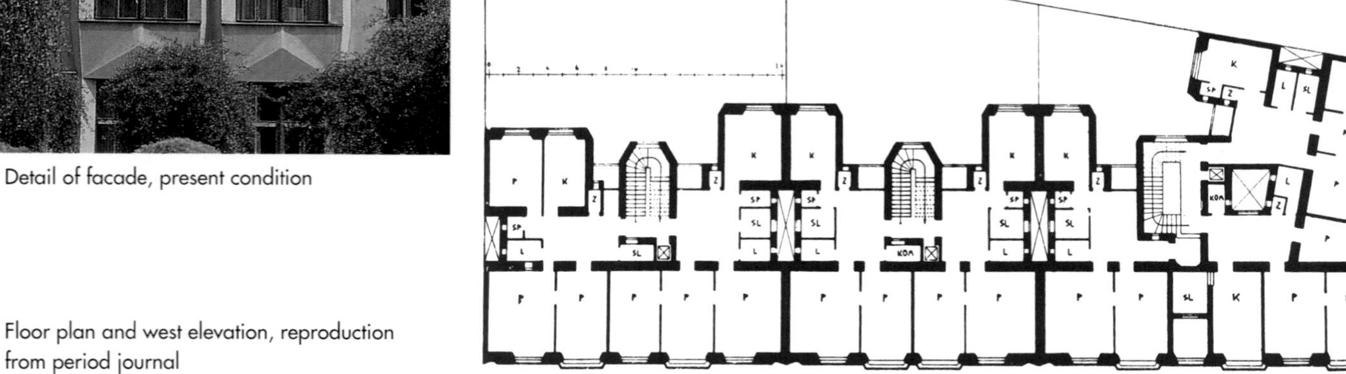

Floor plan and west elevation, reproduction from period journal

23. Managers' and workers' residences for the Domovina (Homeland) building co-operative, 1920

U Domoviny Street no. 1, General Jaroš Avenue, nos. 18, 20, 22, 24, 26, Znojmo

Street facade, present condition

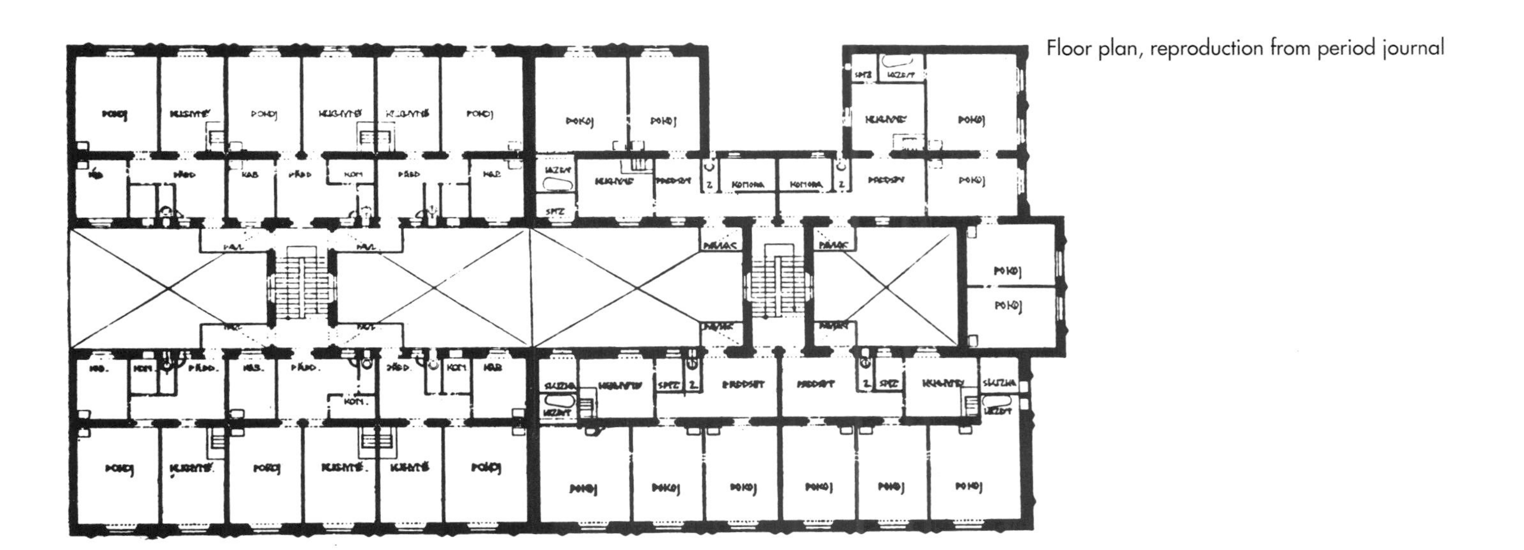

Floor plan, reproduction from period journal

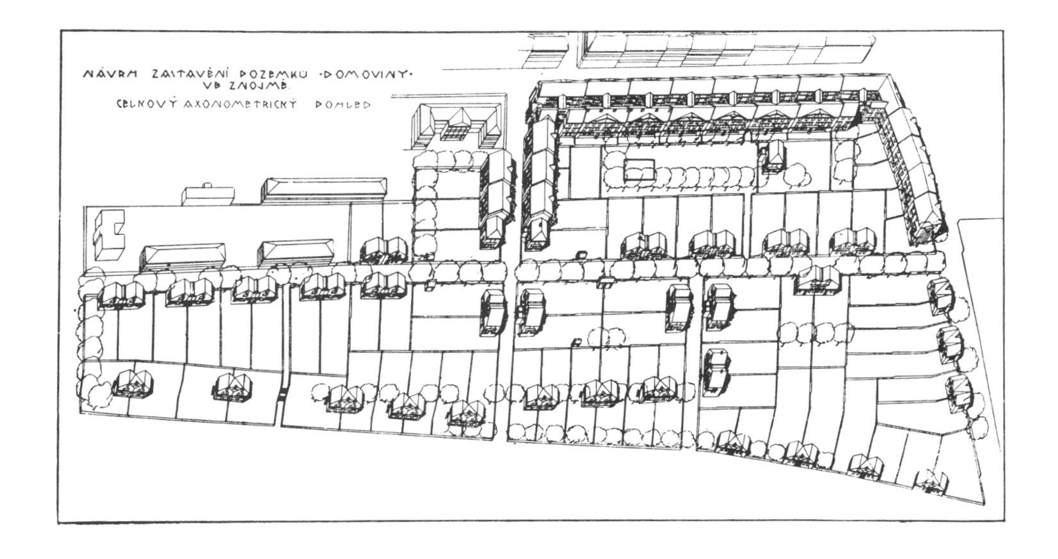

Axonometric projection, reproduction from period journal

24.
Teachers' Co-operative apartment building, 1923

Kamenická Street no. 35/811, Prague–Holešovice

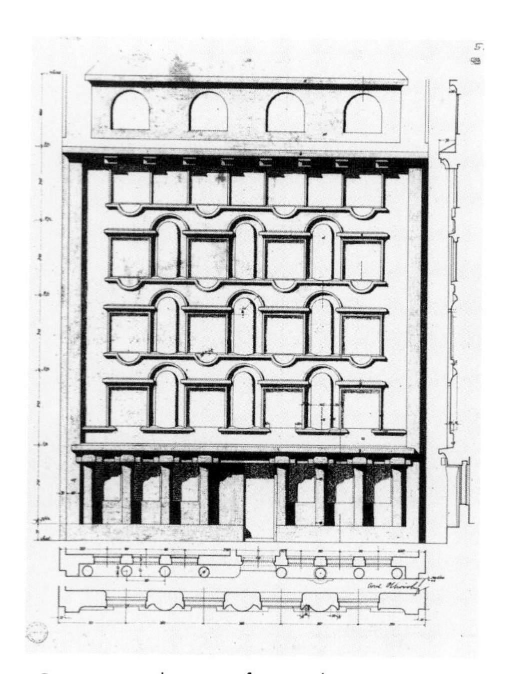

Construction drawing of street elevation

Street facade, present condition

Rudolf Stockar

25.
Reconstruction and extension of Mrs. Lipčík's house, 1918–1919
Zelená Street no. 80, Olomouc–Nová ulice

View of entrance facade, period photograph

Street facade, period photograph

26.
Office building for F. J. Materna's factory, 1920
Dělnická Street no. 20, Osadní Street no. 10/313, Prague–Holešovice

27.

Reconstruction of a commercial and apartment building, 1920–1921

October 28th Street no. 8, Jungmann Square no. 4/764, Prague–Nové Město

Facade on October 28th Street, period photograph

Facade on Jungmann Square, period photograph

Destroyed Buildings

Cat. nos. 28–34

Josef Gočár

28.
Trade-fair exhibition pavilion, 1919–1920
Lyon, France

Detail of facade, period photograph

Interior of pavilion, period photograph

Entrance facade, period photograph

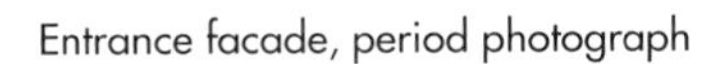

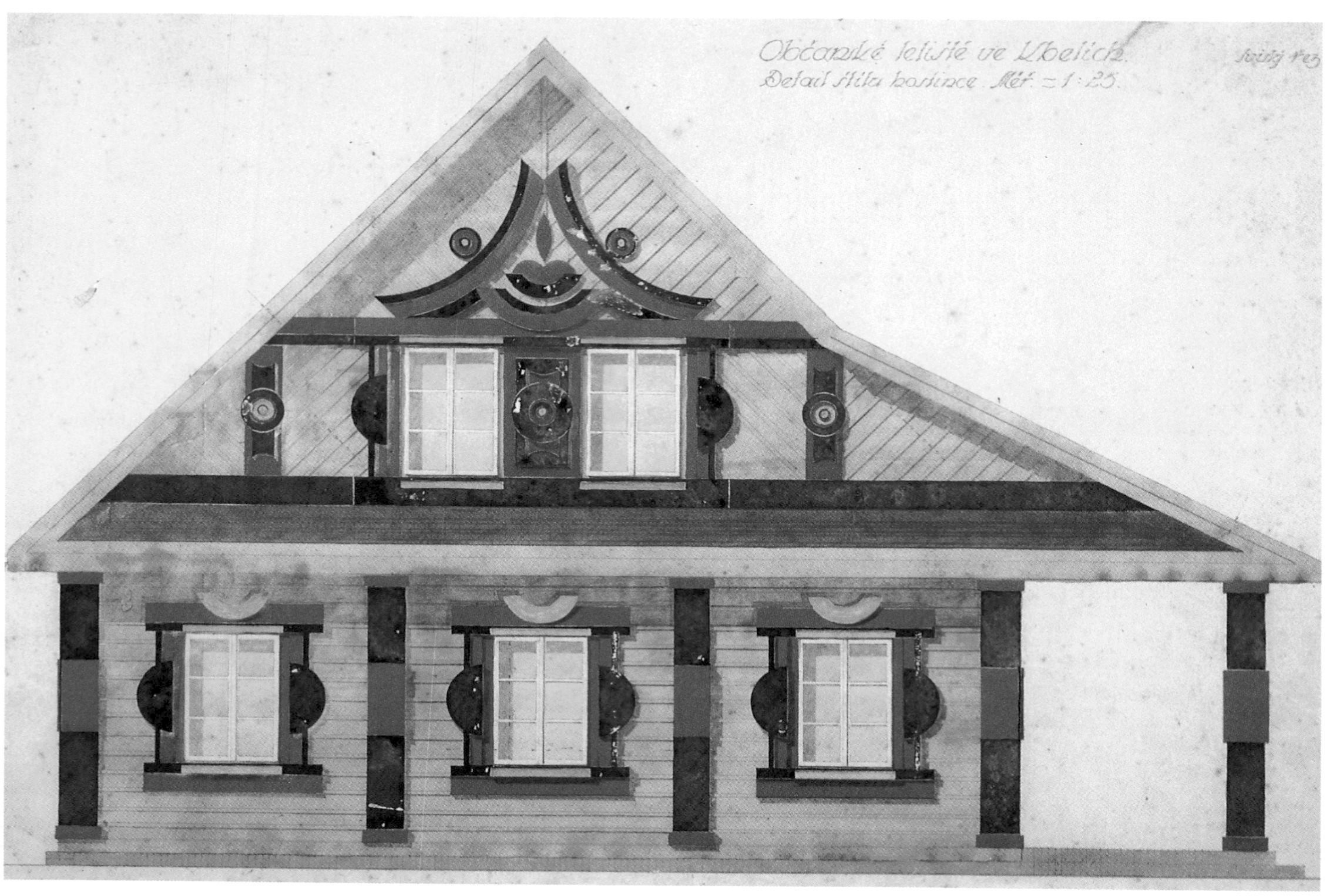

29.

Inn and manager's house at the Kbely civilian airport, 1920–1921

Prague–Kbely, moved to the grounds of the zoo in Prague–Trója in the 1970s

29a.

Design for the gable of the inn, 1920

India ink, watercolour, and tempera
42 x 62 cm
Inscribed u.r.: "Civilian airport at Kbely. Detail of gable of inn. Scale=1:25."
NTM Collection no. 14 Gočár
Acquired in 1951 from the architect's estate
Exhib: Prague, 1947 (cat. no. 260)

Entrance facade of inn, period photograph

30.
Exhibition pavilion of the Mánes Association of Plastic Artists, 1921
Vodičkova Street, Prague–Nové Město,
destroyed in the early 1930s

Entrance facade, period photograph

Vlastislav Hofman

31.
Crematorium, 1920–1922
Ostrava, destroyed in the 1970s

Entrance facade, period photograph

Pavel Janák

32.
Dam at Předměřice nad Labem, 1914–1915
Destroyed during floods in 1932

32a.
Design for the dam at Předměřice nad Labem, 1915
Graphite, india ink, tempera, and chalk
63 x 90 cm
Dated l.r.: "1915." Stamped "Architekt Pavel Janák." Inscribed u.l.: "Perspective sketch, huts have been changed since"
NTM Collection no. 85 Janák
Acquired in 1957 from the architect's estate

Upstream view, period photograph

33.
Café Juliš (rondo-cubist variant), 1925–1926
Václav Square no. 22/782, Prague–Nové Město, demolished for construction of new building in 1931

Ground-floor view, period photograph

Miloš Vaněček

34.
Building for the Kolonka emergency student colony, 1920–1922
Prague–Letná
Destroyed during construction of a streetcar loop in the 1980s
Collaboration with Otakar Záhorský

Entrance facade, period photograph

Exhibition Installations

Cat. nos. 35–37

Pavel Janák

35.
First exhibition of the Group of Plastic Artists, 1912
Municipal Hall, Prague

35a.
Design for exhibition interior, 1912
India ink and tempera
46.8 x 59.6 cm
Designed for the Group of Plastic Artists
NTM Collection no. 85 Janák
Acquired in 1957 from the architect's estate
Exhib.: Prague, Vienna (repr.), Helsinki, 1982–1987

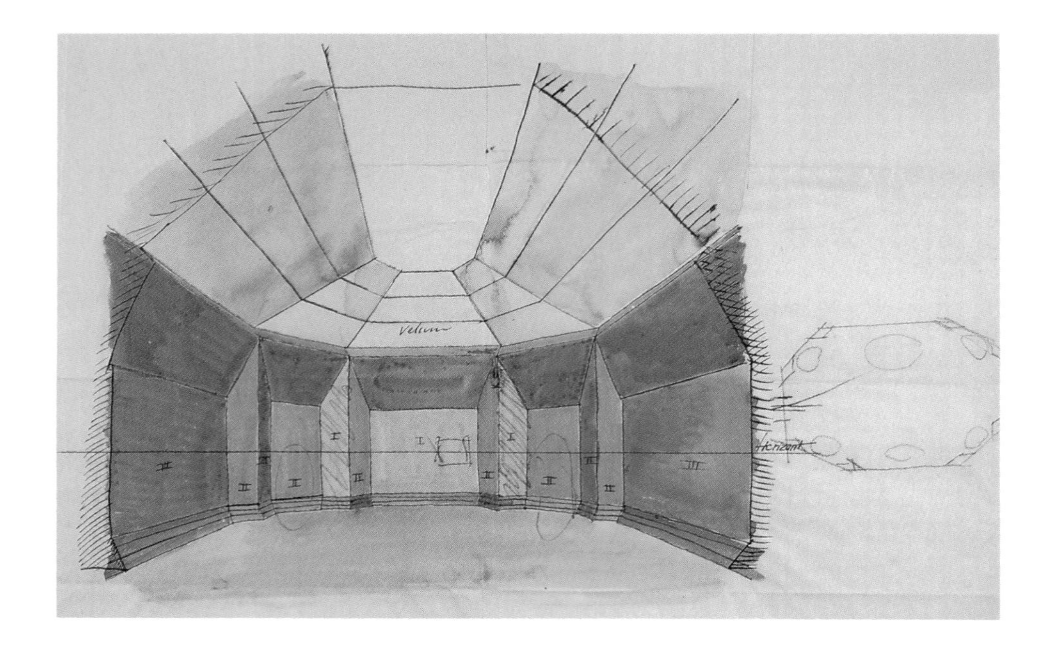

Installation of the Group's exhibition hall, photograph from period journal

Josef Gočár

36.
Second exhibition of the Group of Plastic Artists, 1912
Municipal Hall, Prague

Installation of exhibition hall, period photograph

Otakar Novotný

37.
Exhibition of the Svaz českého díla (Union of Czech Creative Work) at the Werkbund Exhibition, 1914
Austrian Pavilion, Cologne

Interior of one of the exhibition halls, period photograph

Unrealized Projects

Cat. nos. 38–87

Bedřich Feuerstein

38.
Design for a columbarium, 1912
Graphite and india ink
27 x 28.8 cm
Dated l.r.: "5 November 1912"
Designed for a competition held by the Krematorium association
NTM Collection no. 109 Feuerstein
Acquired in 1953 from the architect's estate

39.
Design for the facade of a post-office building in Pardubice, 1913
Graphite, india ink, and wash
30.2 x 47.5 cm
Stamped on verso: "Ing. arch. Bedřich Feuerstein, Praha–Bubeneč"
Designed for a public competition held by the County Committee in Pardubice
NTM Collection no. 109 Feuerstein
Acquired in 1953 from the architect's estate
Exhib.: Prague, 1956 (cat. no. 6)

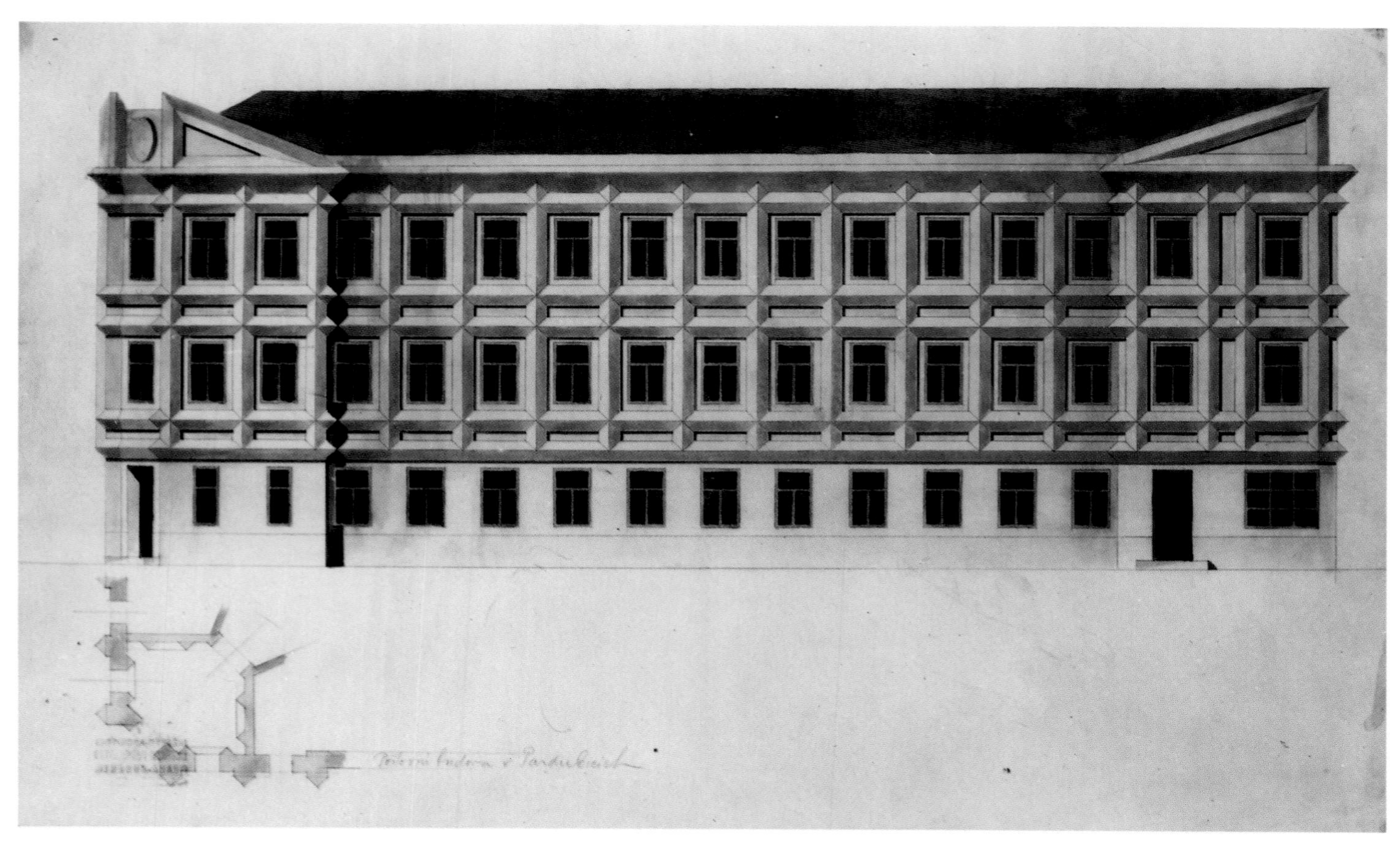

40.
Design for a memorial, 1914
India ink
20.7 x 34 cm
Inscribed l.l.: "1/II." Stamped on verso: "Ing. arch. Bedřich Feuerstein, Praha–Bubeneč"
NTM Collection no. 109 Feuerstein
Acquired in 1953 from the architect's estate
Exhib.: Prague, 1956

41.
Design for a memorial, 1914
Graphite, india ink, and wash
21.6 x 30 cm
Stamped on verso: "Ing. arch. Bedřich Feuerstein, Praha–Bubeneč"
NTM Collection no. 109 Feuerstein
Acquired in 1953 from the architect's estate
Exhib.: Prague, 1956
Lit.: A) Burkhardt & Lamarová, 1982, p. 127, repr.

42.
Competition design for a memorial to Jan Žižka at Vítkov Hill in Prague, ground plan and elevation (collaboration with O. Švec), 1914
Graphite, and india and coloured ink
45.2 x 35.4 cm
Stamped on verso: "Ing. arch. Bedřich Feuerstein, Praha–Bubeneč"
Designed for a public competition
NTM Collection no. 109 Feuerstein
Acquired in 1953 from the architect's estate
Exhib.: Prague, 1956 (cat. no. 7); Prague, 1967 (cat. no. 5)
Lit.: A) Benešová, 1984, p. 300, ill. 265

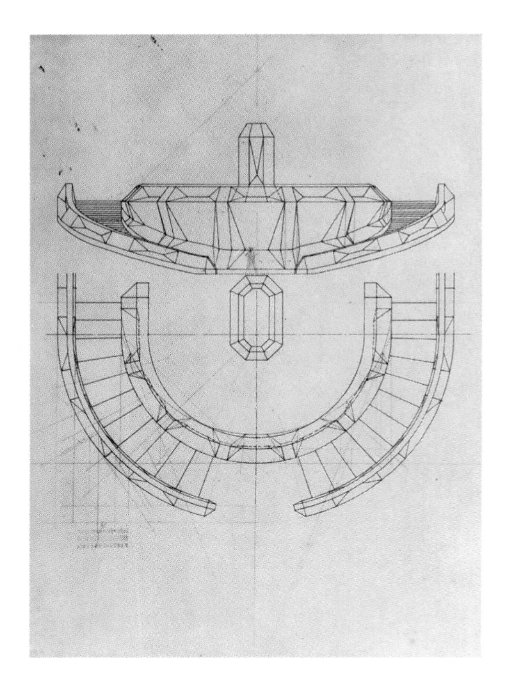

43a.

Competition design for a memorial to Dr. Rieger at Kozákov, perspective view (collaboration with Vojtěch Kerhart), 1914

Graphite and watercolour
20 x 45 cm
Stamped on verso: "Ing. arch. Bedřich Feuerstein, Praha–Bubeneč"
Designed for a public competition
NTM Collection no. 109 Feuerstein
Acquired in 1953 from the architect's estate
Exhib.: Prague, 1956
Lit.: A) Burkhardt & Lamarová, 1982, p. 129, repr.

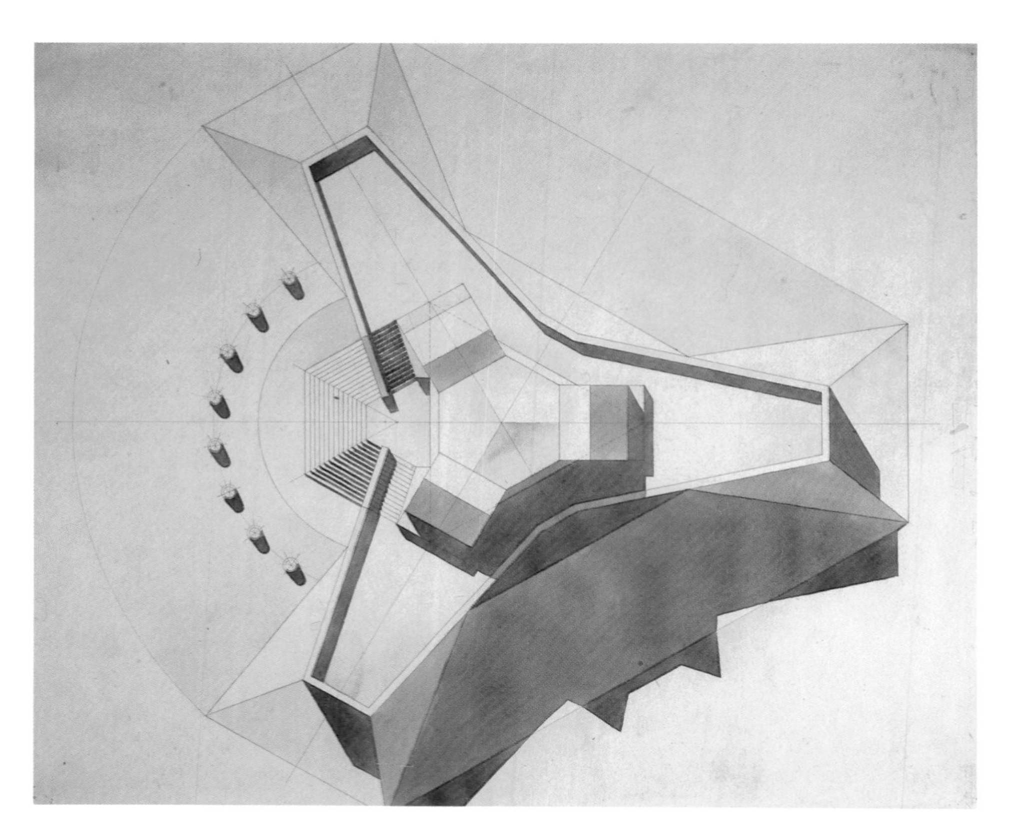

43b.

Competition design, plan (collaboration with Vojtěch Kerhart), 1914

Graphite and watercolour
63 x 52.5 cm
Stamped on verso: "Ing. arch. Bedřich Feuerstein, Praha–Bubeneč"
Designed for a public competition, sponsored by the Cooperative for the Establishment of Rieger's Barrow
NTM Collection no. 109 Feuerstein
Acquired in 1953 from the architect's estate
Exhib.: Prague, 1956; Malmö, 1982 (cat. no. 238)
Lit.: A) Burkhardt & Lamarová, 1982, p. 128, repr.

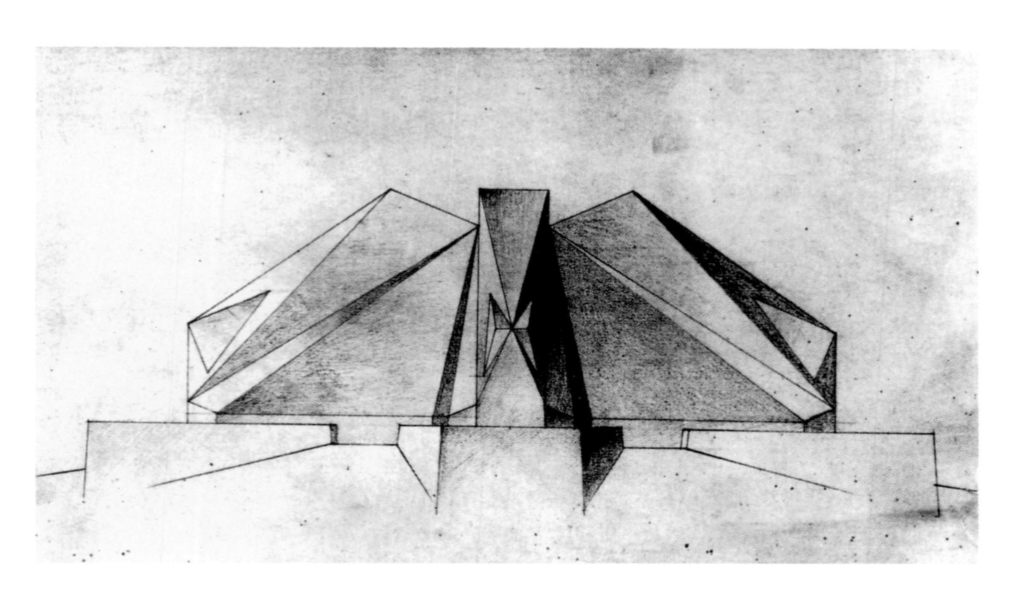

43c.

Competition design, perspective view (collaboration with Vojtěch Kerhart), 1914

Graphite
25 x 49.5 cm
Stamped on verso: "Ing. arch. Bedřich Feuerstein, Praha–Bubeneč"
Designed for a public competition
NTM Collection no. 109 Feuerstein
Acquired in 1953 from the architect's estate
Exhib.: Prague, 1956

43d.

Competition design, perspective view (collaboration with Vojtěch Kerhart), 1914

Graphite, india ink, and wash
29 x 27 cm
Stamped on verso: "Ing. arch. Bedřich Feuerstein, Praha–Bubeneč"
Designed for a public competition
NTM Collection no. 109 Feuerstein
Acquired in 1953 from the architect's estate
Exhib.: Prague, 1956 (cat. no. 12);
Tokyo, 1984 (cat. no. 160, repr.)

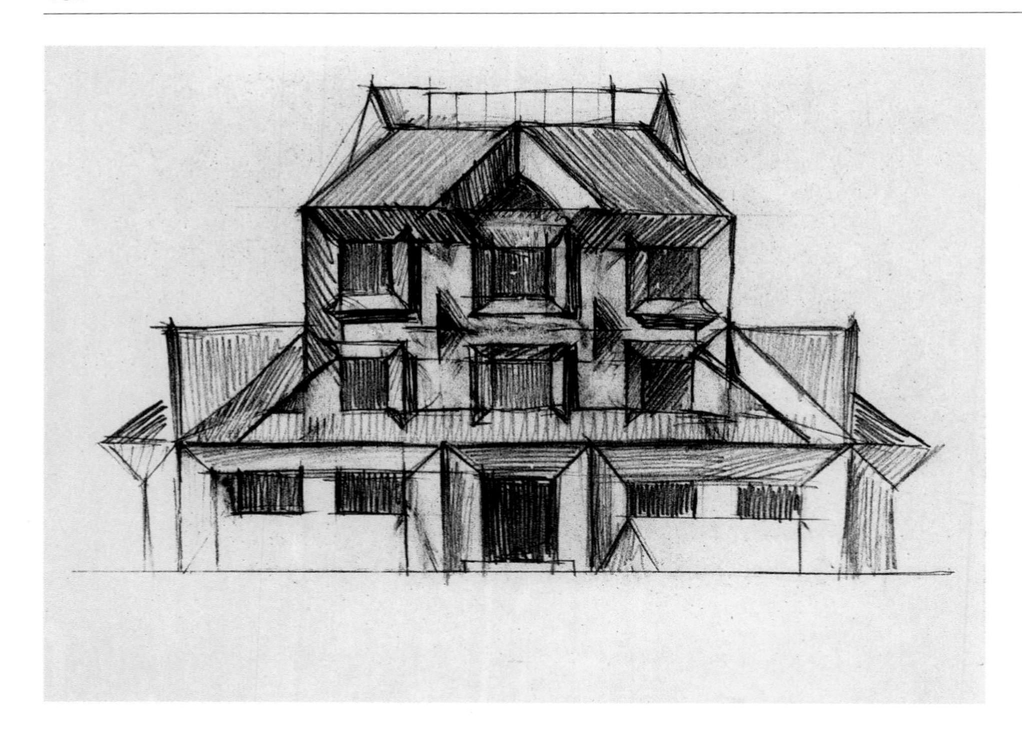

44.
Design for a facade, 1914–1918
Graphite
25.1 x 35.7 cm
Stamped on verso: "Ing. arch. Bedřich Feuerstein, Praha–Bubeneč"
NTM Collection no. 109 Feuerstein
Acquired in 1953 from the architect's estate
Exhib.: Prague, 1967b
Lit.: A) Burkhardt & Lamarová, 1982, p. 139, ill. 132

45a.
Study for church architecture, 1917
Graphite and india ink
34 x 21.2 cm
Stamped on verso: "Ing. arch. Bedřich Feuerstein, Praha–Bubeneč"
NTM Collection no. 109 Feuerstein
Acquired in 1953 from the architect's estate
Exhib.: Prague, 1956 (cat. no. 25)

45b.
Study for church architecture, 1917
Graphite, india ink, and tempera
53 x 38 cm
Stamped on verso: "Ing. arch. Bedřich Feuerstein, Praha–Bubeneč"
NTM Collection no. 109 Feuerstein
Acquired in 1953 from the architect's estate
Exhib.: Prague, 1956

46.
Design for a memorial to the fallen of the World War, perspective view, 1918
India ink and charcoal
36.5 x 51 cm
Dated l.r.: "1918." Stamped on verso: "Ing. arch. Bedřich Feuerstein, Praha–Bubeneč"
NTM Collection no. 109 Feuerstein
Acquired in 1953 from the architect's estate
Exhib.: Prague, 1956 (cat. no. 19)

47.
Design for a monument to the fallen of the World War, perspective view, 1920
India ink
34.2 x 21 cm
Dated l.r.: "1920." Stamped on verso: "Ing. arch. Bedřich Feuerstein, Praha–Bubeneč"
Designed for a Ministry of Education and National Enlightenment public competition
NTM Collection no. 109 Feuerstein
Acquired in 1953 from the architect's estate
Exhib.: Prague, 1956 (cat. no. 20)

Josef Gocár

48.
Competition design for a secondary-school building in Chotěboř, 1912
India ink, chalk, and watercolour
38 x 42.3 cm
Signed l.r.: "J. Gočár 1912"
Designed for a public competition for the elementary and secondary school in Chotěboř
NTM Collection no. 14 Gocár
Acquired in 1951 from the architect's estate
Exhib.: Prague, 1947 (cat. no. 258); Malmö, 1982 (cat. no. 250); Tokyo, 1984 (cat. no. 154, repr.)

Pavel Janák

49.
Vision of architecture, 1906
India ink, graphite, watercolour, and crayons
40 x 56 cm
Signed l.r.: "16/9 1906 Pavel Janák"
School assignment
NTM Collection no. 85 Janák
Acquired in 1957 from the architect's estate
Exhib.: Prague, Vienna (cat. no. 8, repr.), Helsinki, 1982–1987

50.
Design for a residential building, 1911
Graphite and india ink
31.7 x 37 cm
NTM Collection no. 85 Janák
Acquired in 1957 from the architect's estate
Exhib.: Prague, Vienna (cat. no. 44, repr.), Helsinki, 1982–1987

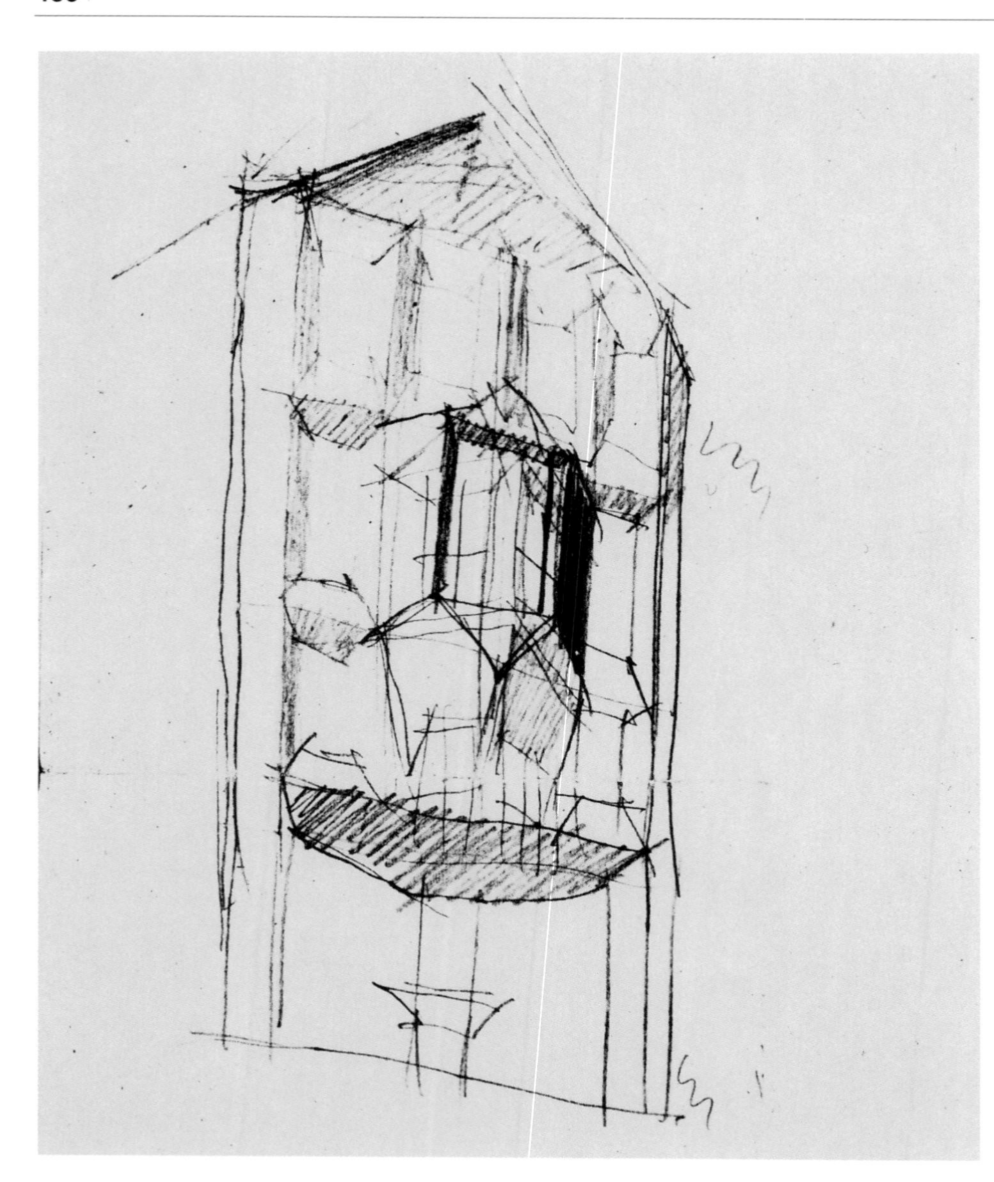

51.
Facade study, 1911
Graphite
16 x 9 cm
NTM Collection no. 85 Janák
Acquired in 1957 from the architect's estate
Exhib.: Prague, Vienna (cat. no. 35); Helsinki, 1982–1987

52.
Design for monument to Dr. Fügner and Dr. Tyrš at Letná in Prague, 1911
India ink and watercolour
17.5 x 40.5 cm
NTM Collection no. 85 Janák
Acquired in 1957 from the architect's estate
Exhib.: Prague (repr.), Vienna (cat. no. 41, repr.); Helsinki, 1982–1987

53.
Four architectural studies, 1912
India ink
15.4 x 10.2 cm each
NTM Collection no. 85 Janák
Acquired in 1957 from the architect's estate
Exhib.: Prague (repr.), Vienna (cat. no. 50, repr.), Helsinki, 1982–1987

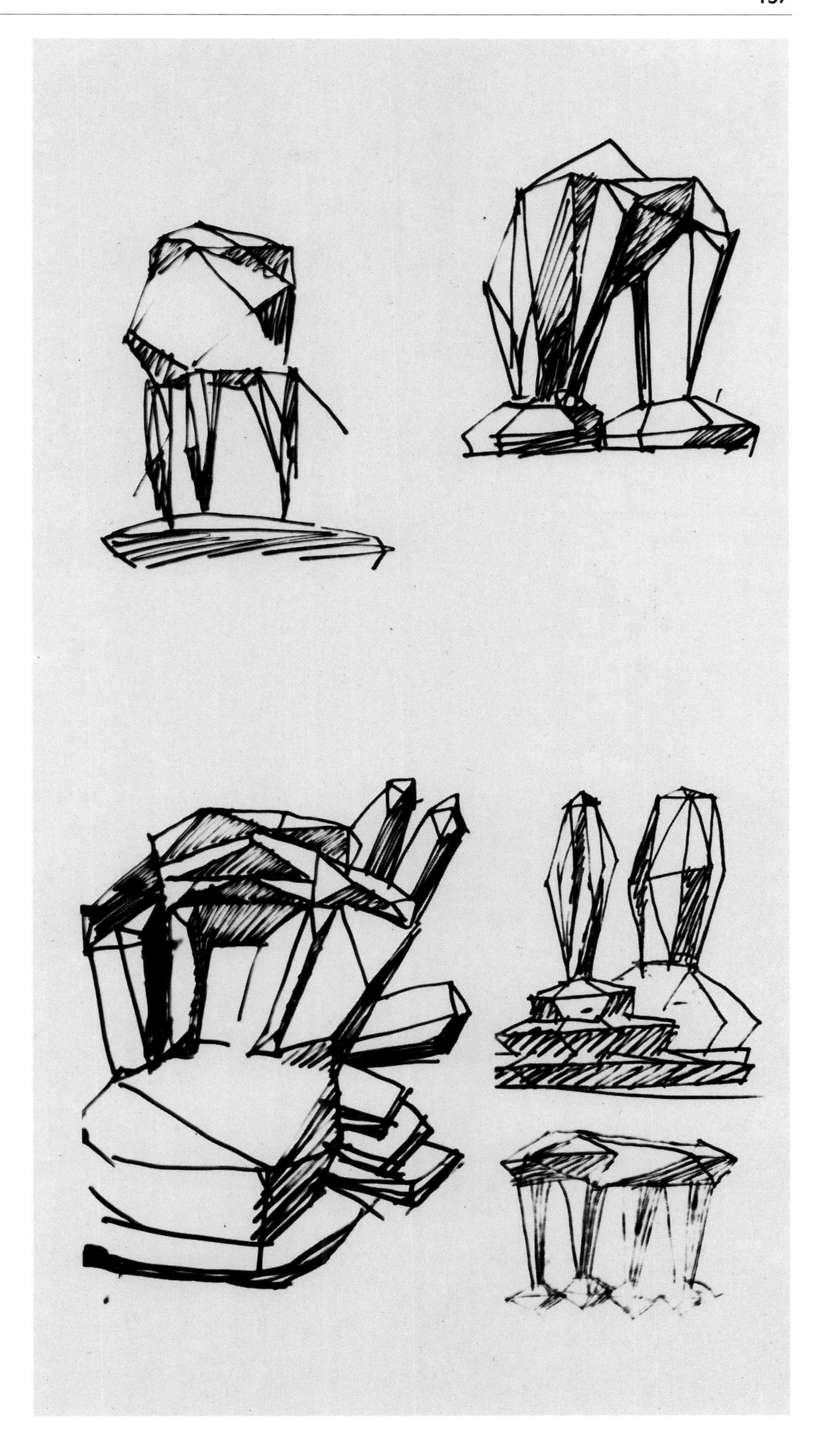

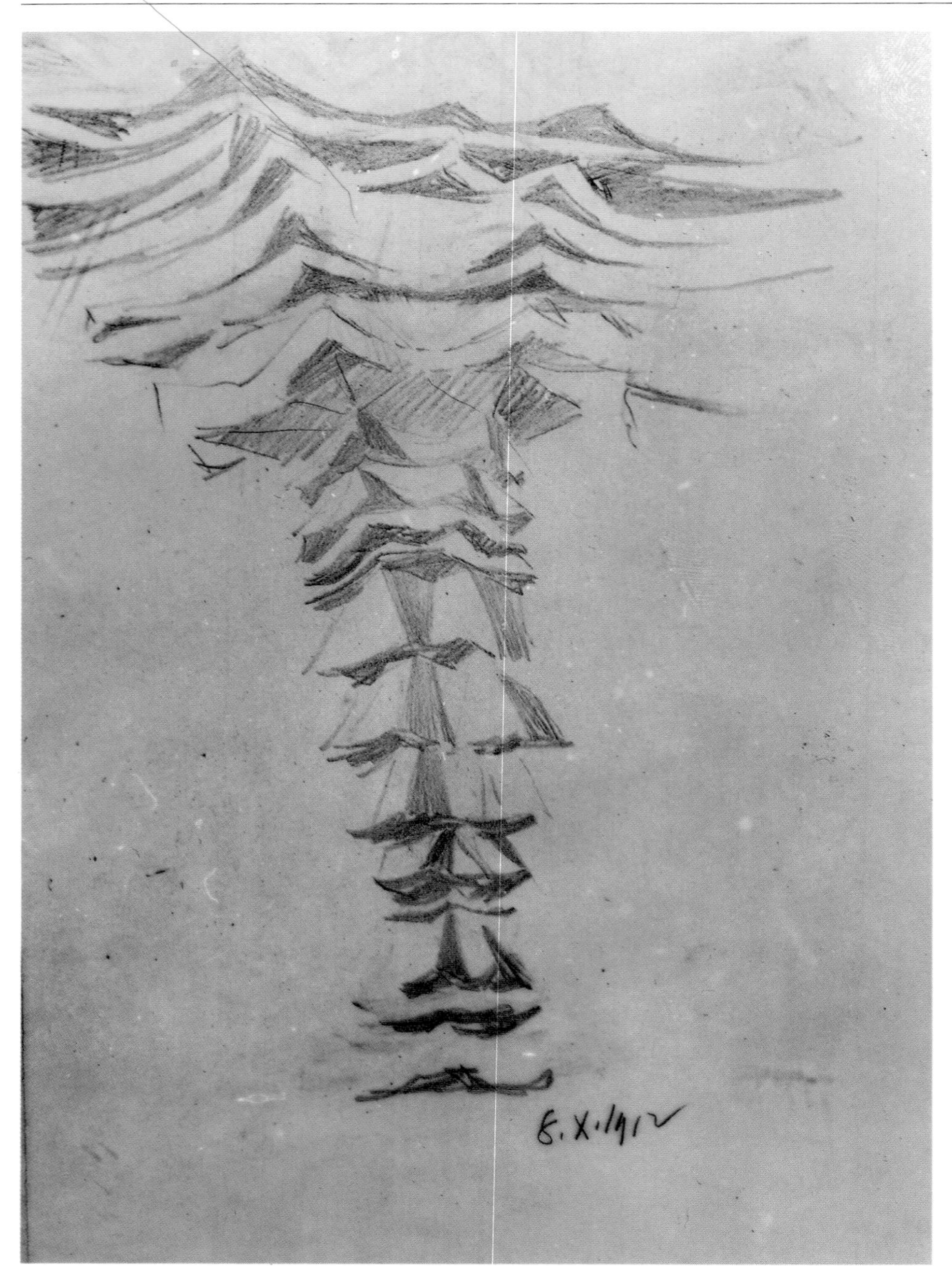

54.
Architectural study, 1912
Graphite
34 x 21 cm
Dated l.r.: "8.X.1912"
NTM Collection no. 85 Janák
Acquired in 1957 from the architect's estate
Exhib.: Prague, Vienna (cat. no. 51), Helsinki, 1982–1987

55.
Facade study for an apartment house, 1912
Graphite and india ink
30.2 x 14.7 cm
NTM Collection no. 85 Janák
Acquired in 1957 from the architect's estate
Exhib.: Prague (repr.), Vienna (cat. no. 46, repr.), Helsinki, 1982–1987

56.
Facade study, 1912
Graphite, india ink, and crayon
16.5 x 25.2 cm
Dated l.r.: "26/9 1912"
NTM Collection no. 85 Janák
Acquired in 1957 from the architect's estate
Exhib.: Prague, Vienna (cat. no. 47, repr.), Helsinki, 1982–1987

57.
Design for a facade, 1912
India ink
40 x 44.8 cm
Dated l.r.: "1912"
Stamped "Architekt Pavel Janák"
NTM Collection no. 85 Janák
Acquired in 1957 from the architect's estate
Exhib.: Prague, Vienna (cat. no. 45, repr.), Helsinki, 1982–1987

58.
Studies for a family home, 1912

Graphite; graphite and crayon
34 x 21 cm
Annotated on lower third with
calculations and other text
NTM Collection no. 85 Janák
Acquired in 1957 from the architect's estate
Exhib.: Prague, Vienna (cat. no. 69),
Helsinki, 1982–1987

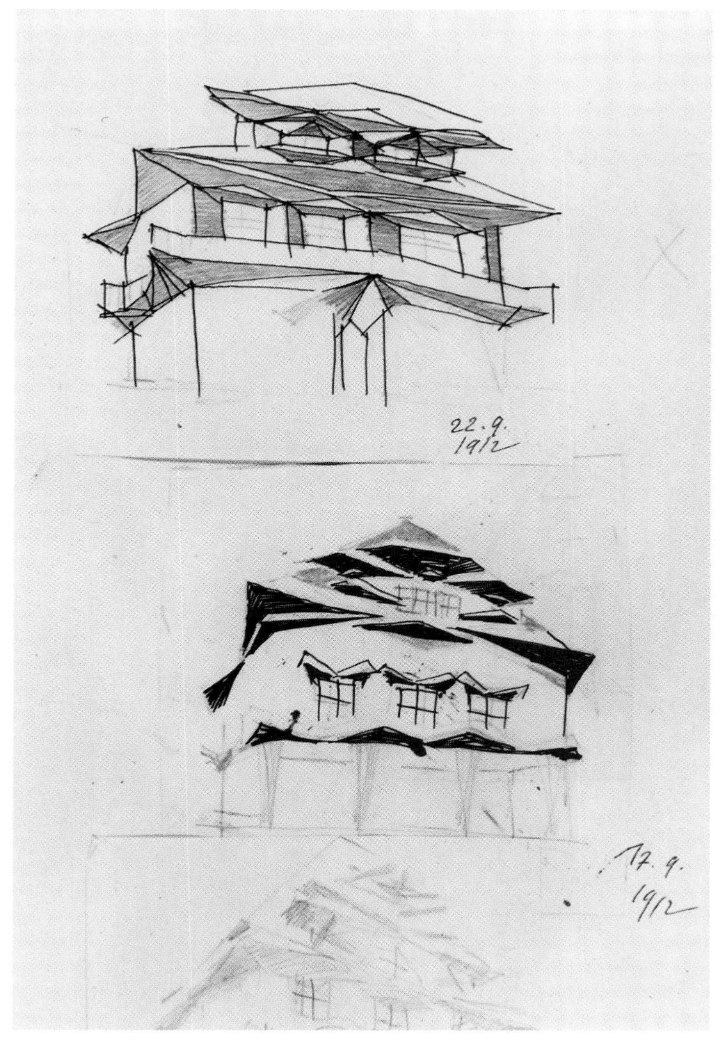

59.
Three facade studies, 1912

Graphite and india ink; graphite, india ink, and
crayon; graphite
10.5 x 13.5 cm; 12 x 12 cm; 9.5 x 12 cm
Dated l.r. of each: "22.9.1912"; "17.9.1912";
"20.9.1912"
Draft of letter on verso
NTM Collection no. 85 Janák
Acquired in 1957 from the architect's estate
Exhib.: Prague (repr.), Vienna (cat. no. 52, repr.),
Helsinki, 1982–1987

60.
Two facade studies, 1912

Graphite, india ink, and crayon
33.8 x 21 cm; 11.8 x 12 cm
Dated l.r.: "20/9 1912"; dated l.c.: "19/9 1912"
NTM Collection no. 85 Janák
Acquired in 1957 from the architect's estate
Exhib.: Tokyo, 1984 (cat. no. 133, repr.)

61.
Design for a plastic execution of a gable, 1912

India ink
35.4 x 32.5 cm
Dated l.r.: "1912"
Stamped: "Architekt Pavel Janák"
Numerical calculations on bottom edge
NTM Collection no. 85 Janák
Acquired in 1957 from the architect's estate
Exhib.: Prague, Vienna (cat. no. 45), Helsinki, 1982–1987
Lit.: A) Burkhardt & Lamarová, 1982, p. 90, ill. 78

62.
Cornice study, 1912

Graphite
33.9 x 20.8 cm
Dated l.r.: "8.X.1912"
NTM Collection no. 85 Janák
Acquired in 1957 from the architect's estate
Exhib.: Prague, Vienna (cat. no. 50), Helsinki, 1982–1987

63.
Partial facade study, 1912

Graphite and india ink
20.8 x 33.9 cm
Dated l.r.: "30.X.1912"
NTM Collection no. 85 Janák
Acquired in 1957 from the architect's estate
Exhib.: Prague, Vienna (cat. no. 65), Helsinki, 1982–1987; Tokyo, 1984 (cat. no. 120, repr.)

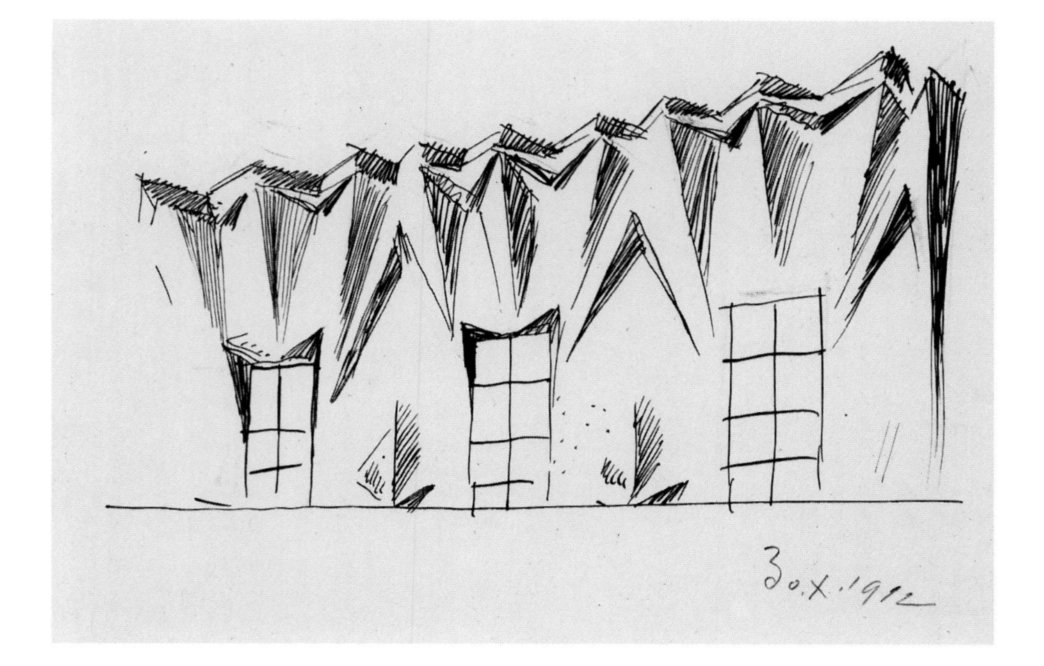

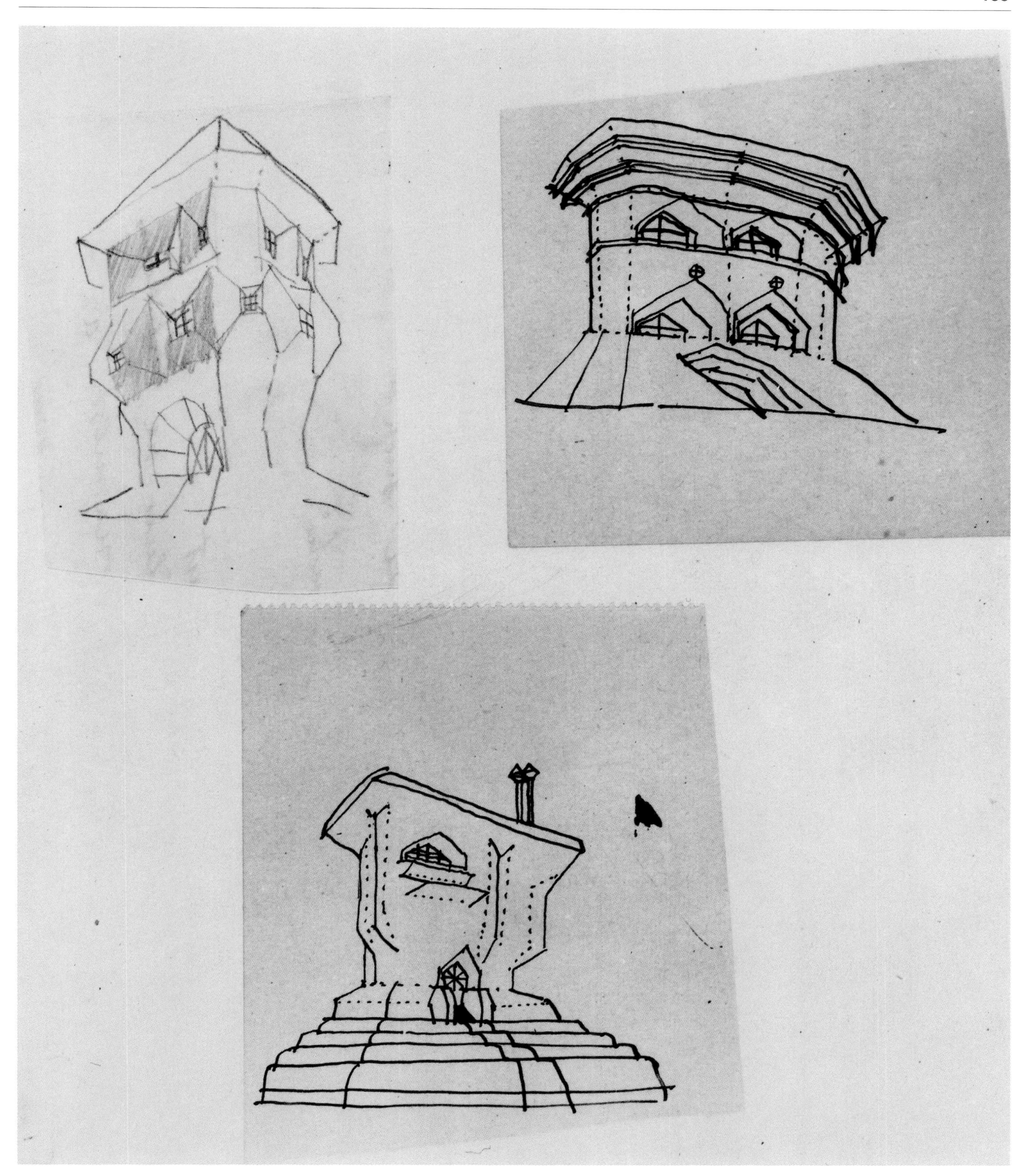

64.

Three studies for a lock, 1912

Aniline graphite; india ink; india ink
7.6 x 5.8 cm; 7.4 x 7.8 cm; 8 x 7.2 cm
NTM Collection no. 85 Janák
Acquired in 1957 from the architect's estate
Exhib.: Prague, Vienna (cat. no. 56, repr.),
Helsinki, 1982–1987

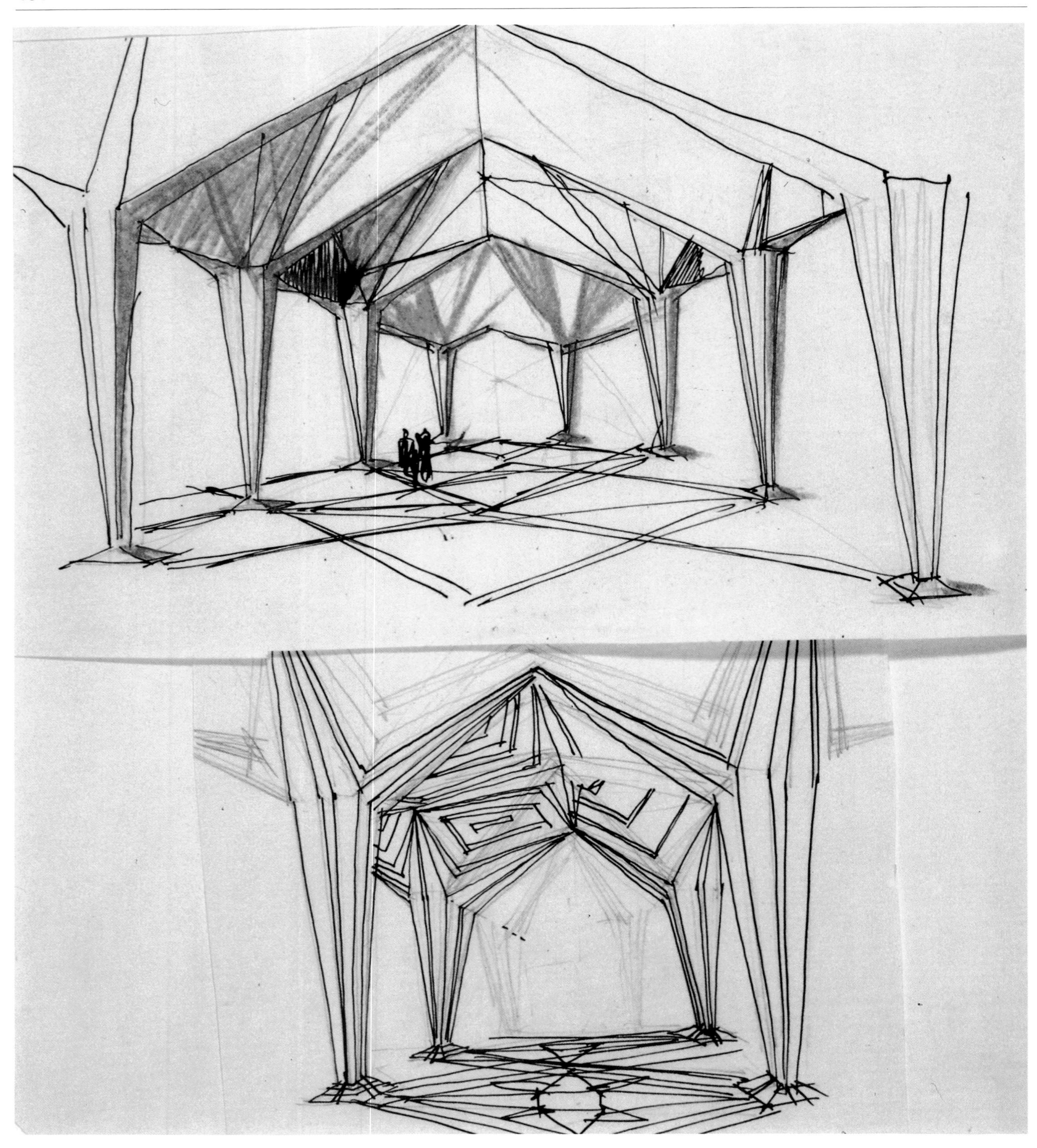

65.

Two studies for an interior, 1912

Graphite, india ink, and crayon;
graphite and india ink
12 x 19 cm; 11.8 x 13 cm
NTM Collection no. 85 Janák
Acquired in 1957 from the architect's estate
Exhib.: Prague (repr.), Vienna (cat. no. 63, repr.), Helsinki, 1982–1987; Tokyo, 1984 (cat. no. 114, repr.)
Lit.: A) Švácha 1985, p. 135, repr.

66.

Design for a monumental interior, 1912

India ink

39.5 x 42.5 cm

Dated l.r.: "7.X.1912 Janák"

Stamped: "Architekt Pavel Janák"

NTM Collection no. 85 Janák

Acquired in 1957 from the architect's estate

Exhib.: Malmö, 1982–1983 (cat. no. 302, no repr.)

Lit.: A) Burkhardt & Lamarová, 1982, p. 91;
Švácha 1985, p. 135, repr.

67a.
Design for a credit bank in Pardubice, perspective view, 1912
Graphite
46 x 45.1cm
Inscribed l.r.: "View from point A"
Designed for a public competition
NTM Collection no. 85 Janák
Acquired in 1957 from the architect's estate

67b.
Design for credit bank, facade study, 1912
Graphite
33 x 51.6 cm
Designed for a public competition
NTM Collection no. 85 Janák
Acquired in 1957 from the architect's estate

68.
Design for the town hall in Německý Brod (now Havlíčkův Brod), perspective view, 1913
India ink, watercolour, and crayon
65 x 99 cm
Designed for a public competition
NTM Collection no. 85 Janák
Acquired in 1957 from the architect's estate

69a.

Design for a monument to Jan Žižka at Vítkov Hill in Prague, perspective view from Hus Avenue, 1913

India ink and graphite
19.7 x 30 cm
Inscribed l.r.: "View from Hus Ave."
Designed for a public competition
NTM Collection no. 85 Janák
Acquired in 1957 from the architect's estate

69b.

Design for monument to Jan Žižka, perspective view and site plan, 1913

India ink, graphite
59 x 35 cm
Inscribed l.r.: "View, layout"
Designed for a public competition
NTM Collection no. 85 Janák
Acquired in 1957 from the architect's estate
Lit.: A) Burkhardt & Lamarová, 1982, p. 139, repr.

69c.

Alternate design for monument to Jan Žižka, 1913

Charcoal
58.7 x 46 cm
Inscribed u.l.: "Rampart"
Notation l.r.: "Architectural variant"
Designed for public competition
NTM Collection no. 85 Janák
Acquired in 1957 from the architect's estate
Lit.: A) Švácha 1985, p. 106, repr.

„Hradba"
Varianta architekty

70.
Studies for a war memorial, 1915
Graphite, india ink, and watercolour
33.9 x 24.5 cm
NTM Collection no. 85 Janák
Acquired in 1957 from the architect's estate
Exhib.: Prague, Vienna (cat. no. 89, repr.), Helsinki, 1982–1987; Tokyo, 1984 (cat. no. 142, repr.)

71.
Design for a church, 1915
Graphite, india ink, and watercolour
34 x 24.5 cm
Dated l.r.: "12/II 15"
NTM Collection no. 85 Janák
Acquired in 1957 from the architect's estate
Exhib.: Prague, Vienna (cat. no. 86, repr.), Helsinki, 1982–1987

72.
Facade study, 1916
Graphite, india ink, and watercolour
33.9 x 24.5 cm
Dated l.r.: "19.3.16 Marosvásárhely"
NTM Collection no. 85 Janák
Acquired in 1957 from the architect's estate
Exhib.: Prague, Vienna (cat. no. 91), Helsinki, 1982–1987; Tokyo, 1984 (cat. no. 146, repr.)

73.
Design for the facade of a hydro-electric power station in Předměřice nad Labem, 1916
Graphite, india ink, and tempera
31 x 48.2 cm
Dated l.r.: "5/XII 1916"
NTM Collection no. 85 Janák
Acquired in 1957 from the architect's estate
Exhib.: Prague, Vienna (cat. no. 93), Helsinki, 1982–1987; Tokyo, 1984 (cat. no. 147, repr.)

74.
Design for a monument to the victims of war, 1917
India ink and tempera
40 x 31.5 cm
Dated l.r.: "1917"
NTM Collection no. 85 Janák
Acquired in 1957 from the architect's estate
Exhib.: Prague, Vienna (cat. no. 95), Helsinki, 1982–1987; Tokyo, 1984 (cat. no. 149, repr.)

77.
Two facade studies, 1918
India ink and crayons
13.4 x 15 cm; 13.8 x 14 cm
Dated l.r.: "14/4 18"; "14.4.18"
Inscribed on verso: "Architecture"
NTM Collection no. 85 Janák
Acquired in 1957 from the architect's estate
Exhib.: Prague, Vienna (cat. no. 96), Helsinki, 1982–1987

75.
Facade study, 1918
Aniline graphite and india ink
16.2 x 15.2 cm
Dated l.r.: "22/9 18"
NTM Collection no. 85 Janák
Acquired in 1957 from the architect's estate
Exhib.: Prague, Vienna (cat. no. 96), Helsinki, 1982–1987

76.
Facade study, 1921
Graphite and crayons
33 x 21 cm
Dated l.r.: "7.III.1921"
NTM Collection no. 85 Janák
Acquired in 1957 from the architect's estate
Exhib.: Prague, Vienna (cat. no. 105), Helsinki, 1982–1987

14/4 18
14.4.18.

78.
Design for an opera house on Republic Square in Prague, perspective view, 1918
Graphite and india ink
21 x 33.9 cm
Dated l.r.: "17/3 18"
NTM Collection no. 85 Janák
Acquired in 1957 from the architect's estate
Exhib.: Prague, Vienna (cat. no. 99, repr.), Helsinki, 1982–1987

79.
Front and side elevations for the hydro-electric power station at Háj near Mohelnice, 1919
Watercolour
32 x 75 cm
Dated l.c.: "1919-VIII-21"
Inscribed u.c.: "Design for facade of hydro-electric power station at Háj in Moravia"
NTM Collection no. 85 Janák
Acquired in 1957 from the architect's estate

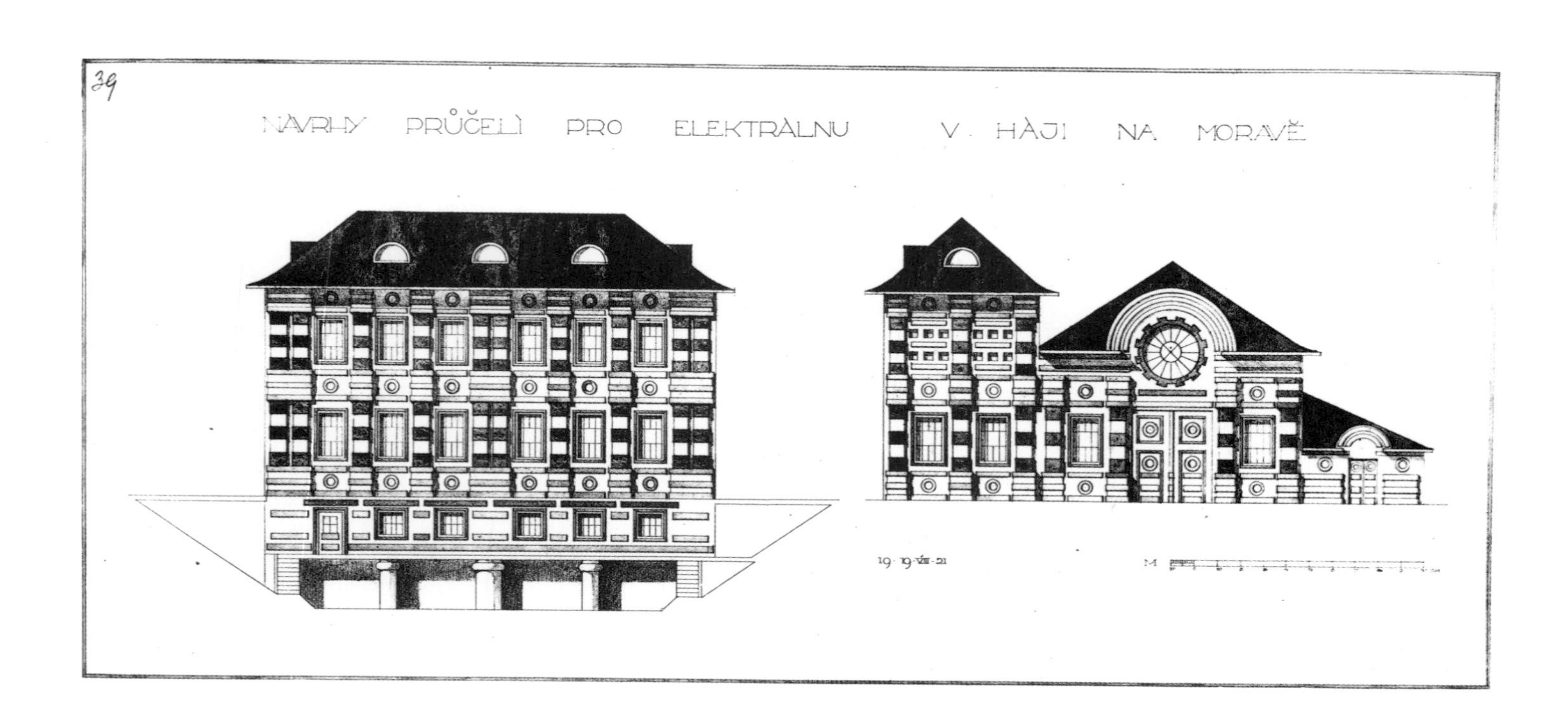

Jan Kotěra

80a.
Design for a monument to Jan Žižka at Vítkov Hill in Prague (collaboration with Jan Štursa), hilltop perspective, 1913
Graphite and india ink
30.6 x 47.6 cm
Dated l.r.: "October 1913"
Designed for a public competition
NTM Collection no. 21 Kotěra
Acquired in 1926 from the architect's estate
Exhib.: Prague, 1926 (cat. no. 349); Prague, 1943 (cat. no. 142); Prague, 1971b
Lit.: A) Novotný, 1958, p. 61

80b.
Design for monument to Jan Žižka, perspective view, 1913
Graphite and india ink
29.2 x 39.5 cm
Dated u.r.: "10.IV.1913"
Designed for a public competition
NTM Collection no. 21 Kotěra
Acquired in 1926 from the architect's estate
Exhib.: Prague, 1926 (cat. no. 347); Prague, 1943 (cat. no. 138); Prague, 1971
Lit.: A) Benešová, 1984, p. 285, ill. 249; Novotný, 1958, p. 61

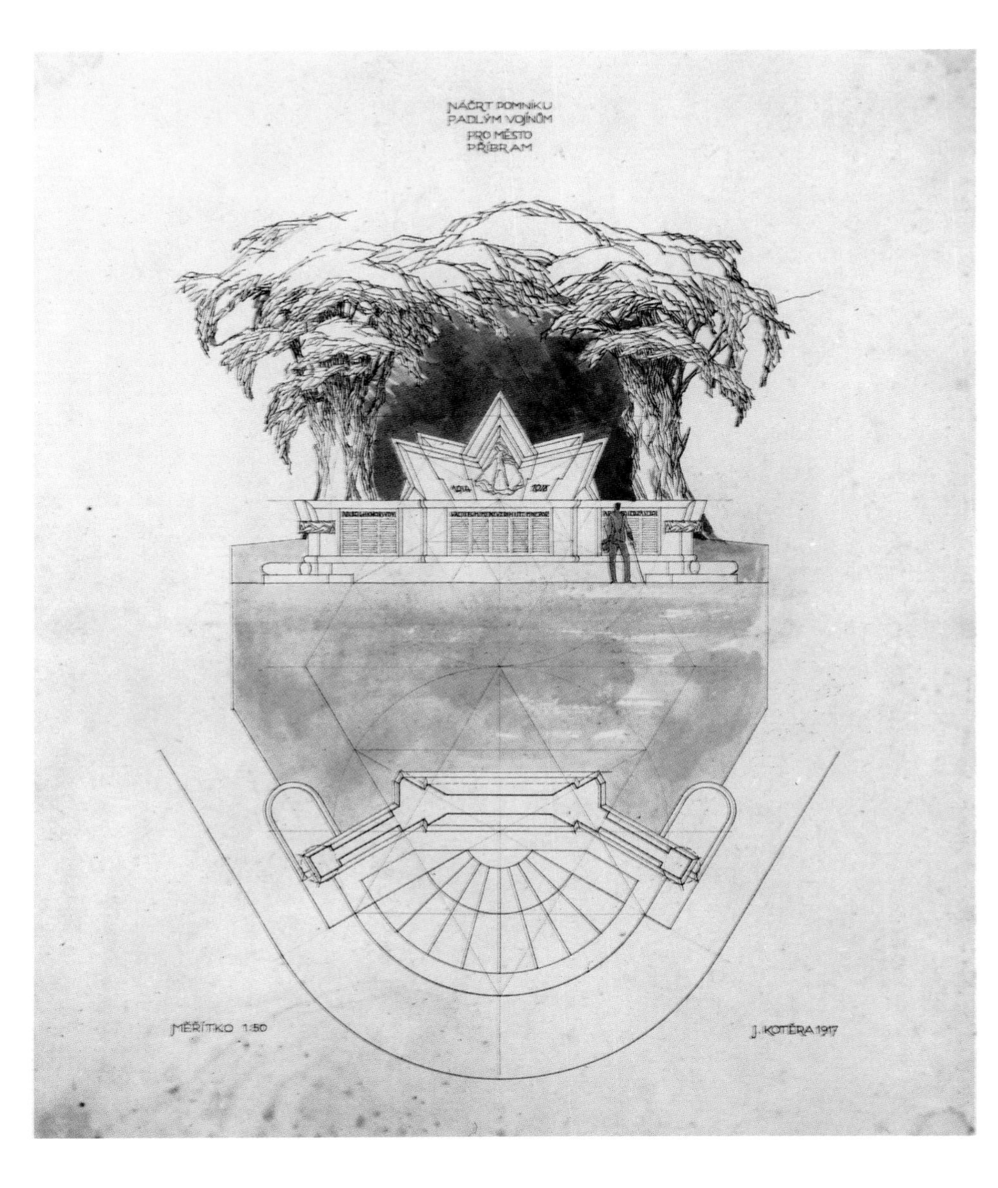

81.
Design for a monument to fallen soldiers at Příbram, 1917
Graphite, india ink, and wash
52.2 x 41.6 cm
Signed l.r.: "J. Kotěra 1917"
Inscribed u.c.: "SKETCH OF MONUMENT TO FALLEN SOLDIERS FOR THE TOWN OF PŘÍBRAM"; inscribed l.l.: "SCALE 1:50"
NTM Collection no. 21 Kotera
Acquired in 1926 from the architect's estate
Exhib.: Prague, 1926 (cat. no. 358); Prague, 1943 (cat. no. 200); Prague, 1971
Lit.: A) Novotný, 1958, p. 136, ill. 273

Jiří Kroha

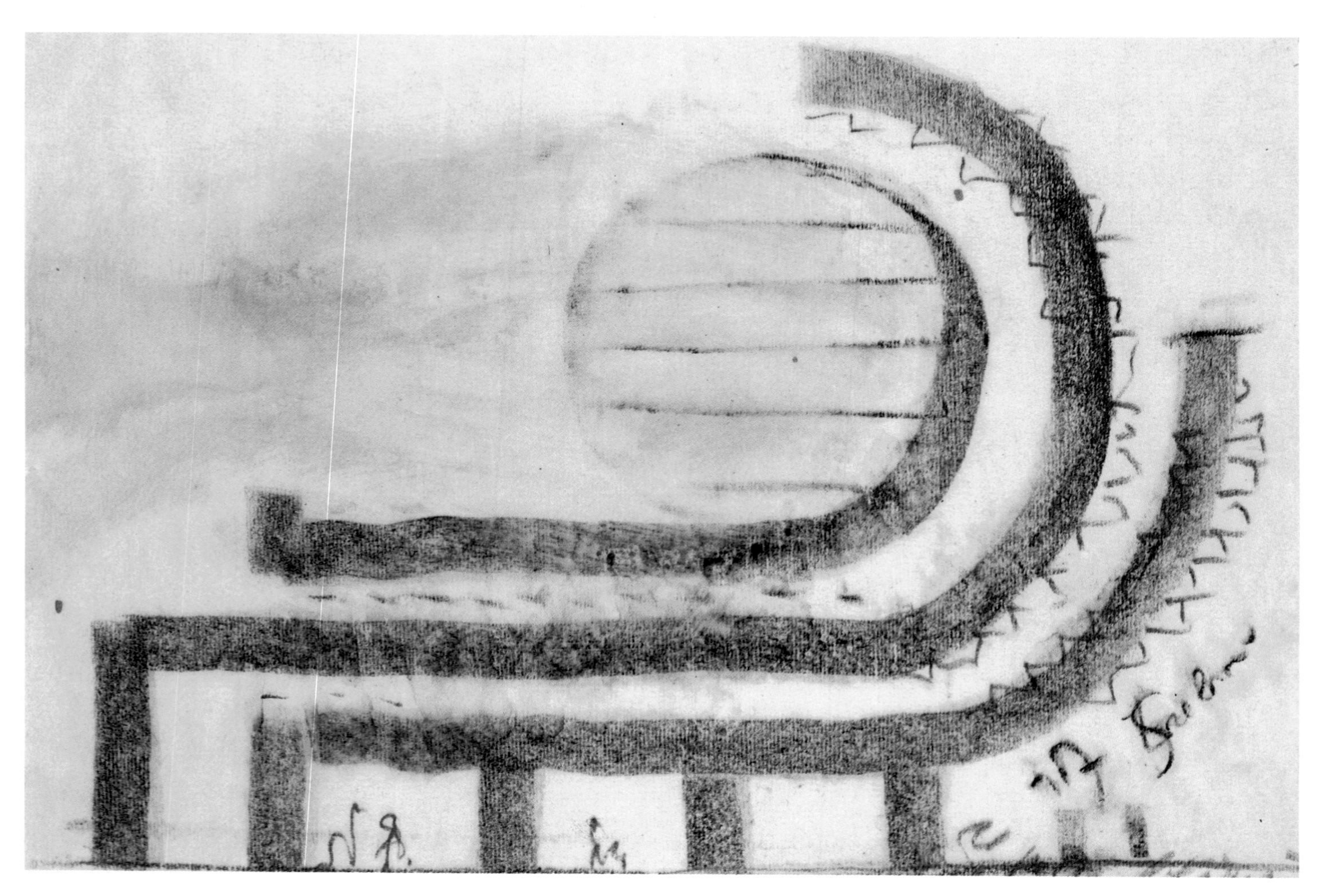

82.
Architectonic vision, 1917
Charcoal
21 x 29 cm
Inscribed l.r.: "17 Srebrno"
Project for a sea spa at Srebrno in Yugoslavia
School assignment
UPM inv. no. 92.243
Acquired in 1985
Exhib.: Prague, Brno, 1964; Darmstadt, 1988–1989 (cat. no. 317)
Lit.: A) Císařovský, 1967; Lamarová, 1987, pp. 12–14

83c.
Study for Roman Catholic church, 1918–1919
Brown pastel
26 x 21.5 cm
Study for a competition
UPM inv. no. 92.239
Exhib.: Prague, Brno, 1964

83a.

Design for a Roman Catholic church at Král. Vinohrady, 1918–1919

Coloured pastel
27.5 x 22 cm
Study for a competition
UPM inv. no. 92.238
Exhib.: Prague, Brno, 1964; Tokyo, 1984 (cat. no. 171, repr.)
Lit.: A) Císařovský, 1967

83b.

Design for Roman Catholic church, 1918–1919

Graphite and coloured pastel
34 x 42 cm
Study for a competition
UPM inv. no. 92.237
Exhib.: Prague, Brno, 1964; Tokyo, 1984 (cat. no. 172, repr.)

Eugen Linhart

84.
Facade study, 1922
Graphite, india ink, and watercolour
52.8 x 36.2 cm
Signed l.r.: "Eugen Linhart"
NTM Collection no. 153 Linhart
Acquired in 1976 from the architect's estate

Josef Štěpánek

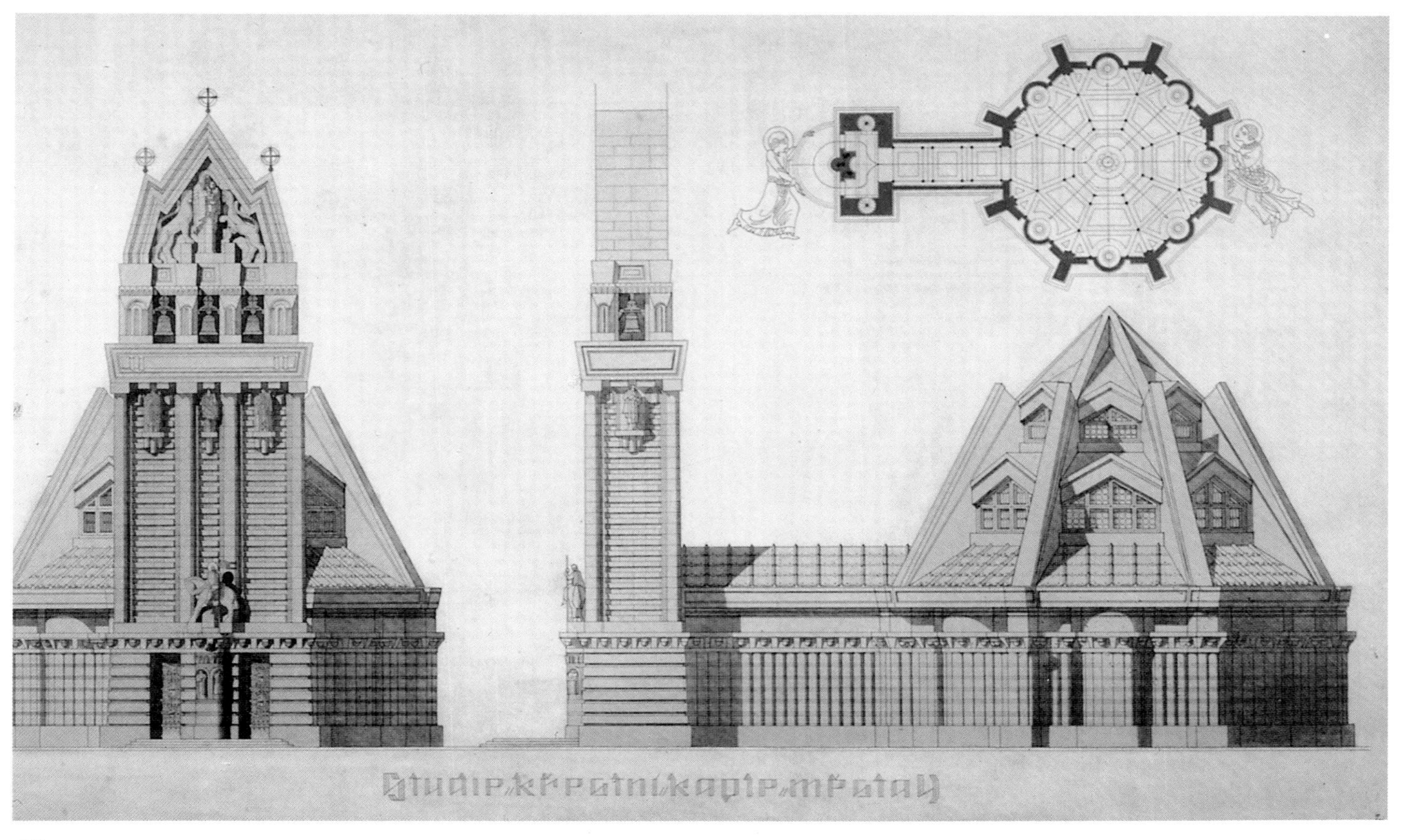

85.
Design for a baptismal chapel for the City "Y," elevations and partial plan, 1912
India ink, watercolour, and crayons
53.5 x 92.4 cm
Signed l.r.: "Josef Štěpánek 1912"
Inscribed l.c.: "Study of a baptismal chapel for the City 'Y'"
School assignment
NTM Collection no. 126 Štěpánek
Acquired in 1964 from the architect's estate
Lit.: B) *Styl*, vol. 4, p. 190, repr.

86.
Facade study, 1919
India ink and pastel

34 x 25 cm
NTM Collection no. 126 Štěpánek
Acquired in 1964 from the architect's estate

87a.
Design for the Arts Centre for the City of Brno, perspective view from Lužánky Street, 1921
India ink. 43.6 x 41.1 cm
Inscribed: "From Lužánky Street. Morava Slogan. 9."
Designed for public competition
NTM Collection no. 126 Štěpánek
Acquired in 1964 from the architect's estate

87b.
Design for Arts Centre, two facades, 1921
Graphite. 32.8 x 37.3 cm
Notations (technical notes and elevations) over the entire drawing
Designed for a public competition
NTM Collection no. 126 Štěpánek
Acquired in 1964 from the architect's estate

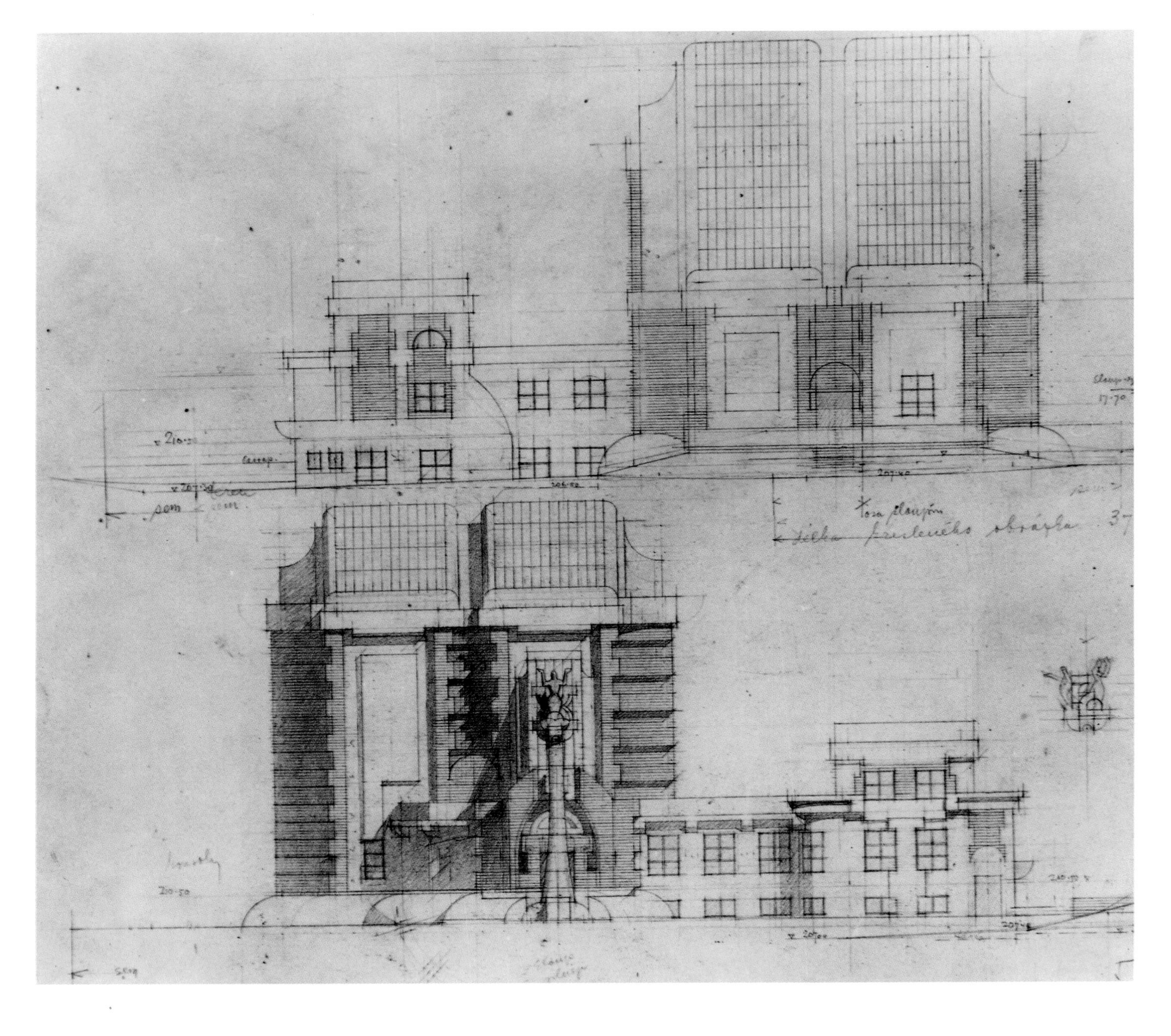

Furniture

Josef Chochol

Seating group, 1911
Cat. nos. 88–90
Designed for the English Circle at the Municipal Hall in Prague
Manufactured by PUD
UPM inv. no. 76.201, 203–4
Acquired in 1972 from the estate of the sculptor Fr. Barták

88.
Armchair, 1911
Black-stained oak, upholstered, with cover
Restored in 1973
110 x 65 x 59.5 cm
UPM inv. no. 76.201
Exhib.: Prague, 1976 (cat. nos. 88–89, repr.); Tokyo, 1984 (cat. no. 007, repr.)
Lit.: A) Burkhardt & Lamarová, 1982, repr. no. 158; A) Lamač, 1988, repr. no. 231

Period photograph, SÚPPOP Archive, Štenc Collection

89.
Settee, 1911
Black-stained oak, upholstered, with cover
Restored in 1973
110 x 131 x 60 cm
UPM inv. no. 76.203
Exhib.: Prague, 1976 (cat. no. 90, repr.)
Lit.: A) Burkhardt & Lamarová, 1982, repr. no. 157

90.
Small table, 1911
Black-stained oak, veneered
76 x 53 x 53 cm
UPM inv. no. 76.204
Exhib.: Prague, 1976 (cat. no. 91, repr.)
Lit.: B) Hofman, 1911–1912, p. 215

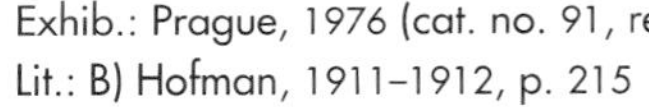

Period photograph, SÚPPOP Archive, Štenc Collection

Josef Gočár

Dining room and part of bedroom, 1912–1913
Cat. nos. 91–100
Designed for artist's own apartment
Manufactured by PUD
Museum Hradec Králové inv. no.
E-N 253–255, 266, 268–273
Acquired in 1946

91.
Sideboard, 1912–1913
Brown-red-stained oak, interior
mahogany, veneered
200 x 140 x 58 cm
Museum Hradec Králové inv. no. E-N 273
Exhib.: Cologne, 1914; Prague, 1947 (unnumb., no repr.); Paris, 1966; Prague, 1967a; Prague, 1971a; Prague, 1976 (cat. no. 30, repr.); Jaroměř, 1983 (cat. no. 9, repr.)
Lit.: B) Janák 1912–1913a, p. 8; *Umělecký měsíčník* 3, 1914, p. 72; A) Wirth, 1930, repr. p. 29; A) Benešová, 1958, repr. no. 18; B) Benešová, 1967, repr. no. 19; B) Vokoun, 1966a; B) Vokoun, 1966b, repr. no. 7; A) Burkhardt & Lamarová, 1982, repr. no. 164, A) Lamač, 1988, repr. no. 312, detail 314, 315.

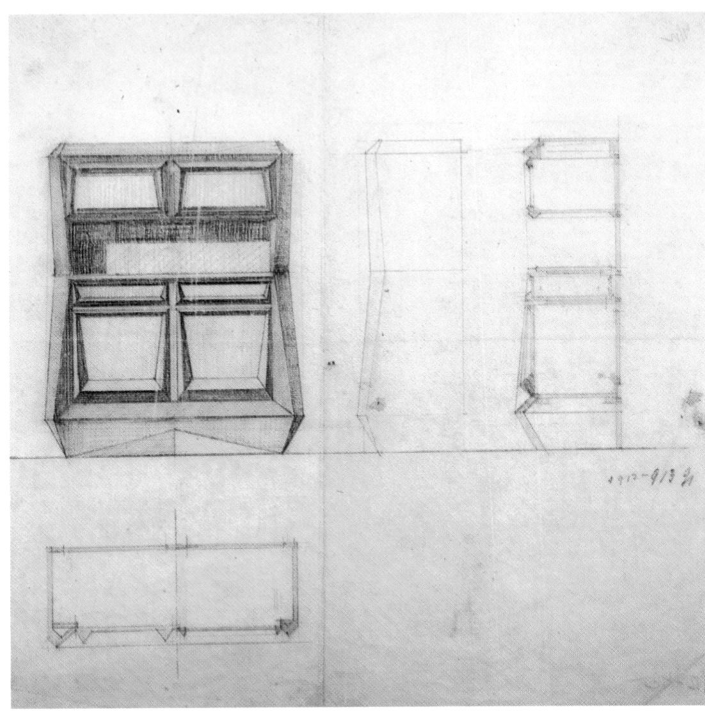

91a.
Design for a sideboard, 1912
Graphite and crayon
47 x 52.5 cm
Dated l.r. in graphite: "1912 G"
NTM Collection no. 14
Acquired in 1951
Lit.: A) Burkhardt & Lamarová, 1982, rep. no. 163

91b.
Design for a sideboard (variation), 1912
Graphite and crayon
54 x 56.5 cm
Dated c.r. in graphite: "1912–1913 G"
NTM Collection no. 14
Acquired in 1951

92.
Cabinet, 1912–1913

Red-brown-stained oak, interior mahogany, veneered, and glass
193 x 110 x 60 cm
Museum Hradec Králové inv. no. E-N 269
Exhib.: Cologne, 1914; Liberec, 1967; London, 1970; Prague, 1976 (cat. no. 31, repr.); Jaroměř, 1983 (cat. no. 1, repr.)
Lit.: B) Janák, 1912/13a, p. 9; *Umělečky měsíčník* 3, 1914, p. 72; A) Wirth, 1930, repr. p. 29; A) Burkhardt & Lamarová, 1982, repr. no. 165; B) Behal, 1987, repr. no. 9; B) Behal, 1988, p. 170; A) Lamač, 1988, repr. no. 311

PUD exhibit at the Werkbund Exhibition at Cologne, 1914, period photograph

Period photograph, SÚPPOP Archive, Prague, Štenc Collection

93.
Small conference table
Brown-stained oak, veneered,
and black opaque glass
80 x 60 x 60 cm
Restored in 1975
Museum Hradec Králové inv. no. E-N 254
Exhib.: Prague, 1976 (cat. no. 42, repr.);
Jaroměř, 1983 (cat. no. 4, repr.)

93a.
Design for small conference table, 1913
Graphite and crayon
27 x 23.5 cm
Inscribed l.r. in graphite: "Own furn. 1913 G"
NTM Collection no. 14
Acquired in 1951

94.
Commode, 1912–1913
Brown-red-stained oak, interior
mahogany, veneered
120 x 175 x 80 cm
Museum Hradec Králové inv. no. E-N 270
Exhib.: Prague, 1976 (cat. no. 49, repr.)

95.
Bookcase, 1912–1913
Red-brown-stained oak, partly veneered
141 x 70 x 25 cm
Museum Hradec Králové inv. no. E-N 266
Exhib.: Prague, 1976 (cat. no. 44, repr.);
Jaroměř, 1983 (cat. no. 6, repr.); Tokyo,
1984 (cat. no. 016, repr.)
Lit.: A) Burkhardt & Lamarová, 1982, repr.
no. 168; A) Lamač, 1988, repr. no. 323

V. Glücklich's apartment, period photograph,
SÚPPOP Archive, Štenc Collection

96.
Small conference table, 1912–1913
American pearwood, veneered,
and opaque glass
80.5 x 70 x 70 cm
Museum Hradec Králové inv. no. E-N 253
Exhib.: Prague, 1976 (cat. no. 43, repr.);
Jaroměř, 1983 (cat. no. 5, repr.); Tokyo,
1984 (cat. no. 009, repr.)
Lit.: A) Burkhardt & Lamarová, 1982, repr.
no. 167; A) Lamač, 1988, repr. no. 319

97.
Armoire, 1912–1913
Brown-stained oak, veneered
198 x 180 x 66 cm
Museum Hradec Králové inv. no. E-N 268
Exhib.: Prague, 1969 (unnumb., no repr.);
Prague, 1976 (cat. no. 50, repr.)
Lit.: *Umělecký měsíčník* 2, 1913, p. 7

98.
Night table, 1912–1913
Brown-stained oak, interior mahogany,
veneered, and opaque glass
79 x 40 x 38 cm
Museum Hradec Králové inv. no. E-N 255
Exhib.: Prague, 1976 (cat. nos. 47–48, repr.);
Jaroměř, 1983 (cat. no. 8, no repr.); Tokyo,
1984 (cat. no. 008, repr.)

99.

Dressing table, 1912–1913

Brown-stained oak, veneered,
and mirrored glass (replaced)
140 x 129 x 45 cm
Museum Hradec Králové inv. no. E-N 271
Exhib.: Prague, 1976 (cat. no. 46, repr.)
Lit.: A) Wirth, 1930, repr. p. 28

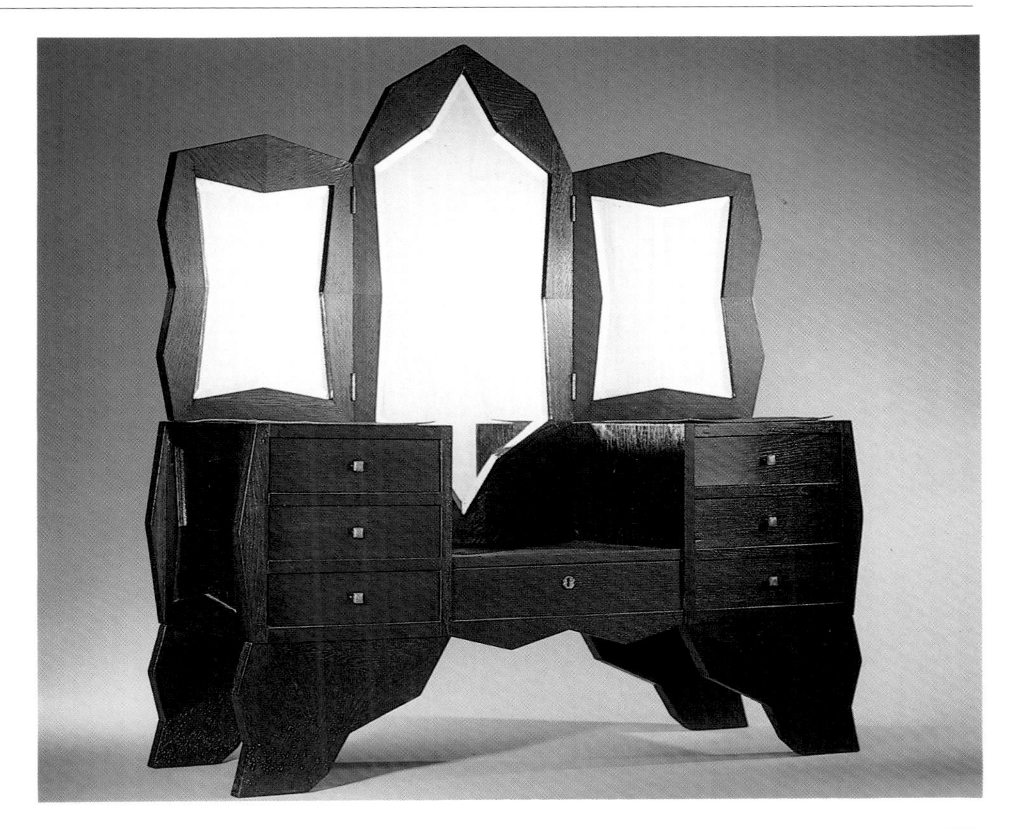

Josef Gočár's apartment, period photograph, taken in 1919, SÚPPOP Archive, Štenc Collection

100.
Portable commode, 1913
Brown-red-stained oak, veneered
80 x 56.5 x 40 cm
Museum Hradec Králové inv. no. E-N 272
Exhib.: Prague, 1976 (cat. no. 45, repr.);
Jaroměř, 1983 (cat. no. 7, repr.)
Lit.: A) Burkhardt & Lamarová, 1982,
repr. no. 166

101.
Pedestal, 1912
Walnut, veneered, painted brown
110 x 72 x 50 cm
Designed for exhibition of
the Group of Plastic Artists
Manufactured by PUD
UPM inv. no. 62.621
Acquired in 1964
Exhib.: Prague, 1976 (cat. no. 58, repr.);
Jaroměř, 1983 (cat. no. 10, repr.)
Lit.: A) Burkhardt & Lamarová, 1982,
repr. no. 178

102.
Side chair, 1912–1915
Brown oak, upholstered
90 x 48 x 48 cm
Designed for the painter E. Filla
Manufactured by PUD
MG Brno inv. no. 16.687
Acquired in 1962

Period photograph, SÚPPOP Archive, Štenc Collection

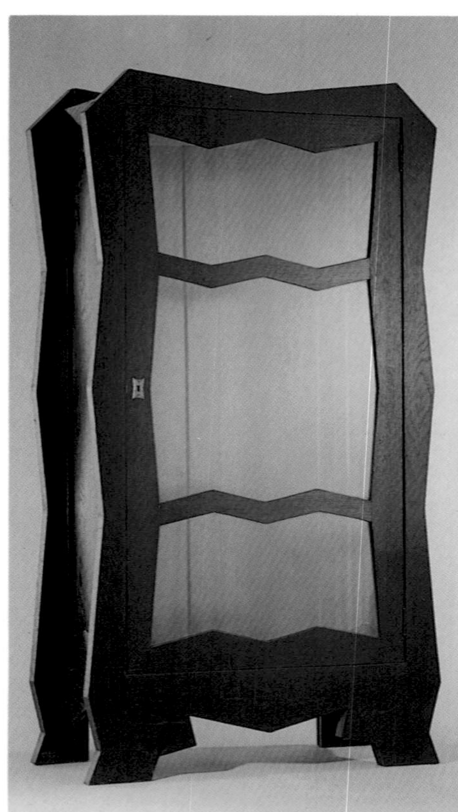
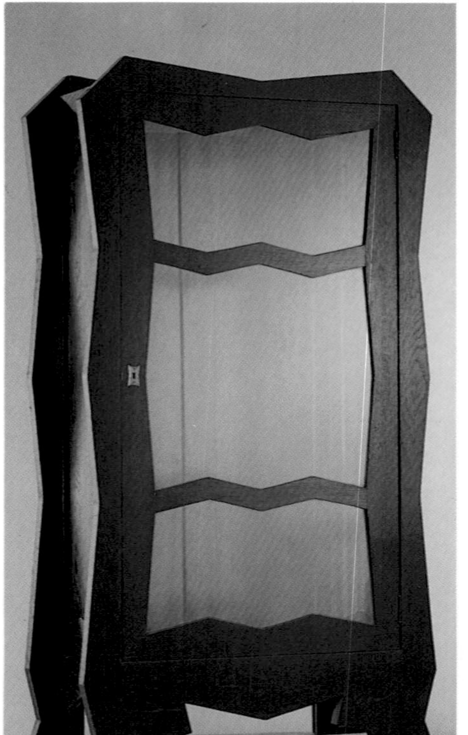

Bedroom and study (partial), 1913

Cat. nos. 103–112
Designed for the actor Otto Boleška
Manufactured by PUD
UPM dep. 1388/1–13ab
Acquired in 1955 by transfer from
the National Museum in Prague

103.
Bookcase, 1913
Black-stained oak, interior mahogany, veneered
165.5 x 88 x 40 cm
UPM dep. 1388/4
Exhib.: Prague, 1976 (cat. no. 69, repr.); Jaroměř, 1983 (cat. no. 13, repr.); Tokyo, 1984 (cat. no. 015, repr.)
Lit.: A) Burkhardt & Lamarová, 1982, repr. no. 177

104.
Bed, 1913
Black-stained oak, veneered
99.5 x 100 x 190 cm
UPM dep. 1388/5ab
Exhib.: Prague, 1976 (cat. no. 59, repr.); Jaroměř, 1983 (cat. no. 16, repr.); Tokyo, 1984 (cat. no. 014, repr.)
Lit.:A) Burkhardt & Lamarová, 1982, repr. no. 171

105.
Night table, 1913
Black-stained oak, interior mahogany, veneered, and marble
98.5 x 45 x 34.5 cm
UPM dep. 1388/6
Exhib.: Prague, 1976 (cat. no. 60, repr.)
Lit.:A) Burkhardt & Lamarová, 1982, repr. no. 172

106.
Washstand, 1913
Black-stained oak, interior mahogany, veneered, and marble
173 x 90 x 60 cm
UPM dep. 1388/7
Exhib.: Prague, 1976 (cat. no. 61, repr.); Jaroměř, 1983 (cat. no. 12, repr.)

107.
Writing desk, 1913
Black-stained oak, veneered, and grey fabric
Height 110 cm, desktop 97.5 x 65 cm
UPM dep. 1388/8
Exhib.: Prague, 1976 (cat. no. 63, repr.); Jaroměř, 1983 (cat. no. 11, repr.); Tokyo, 1984 (cat. no. 011, repr.)
Lit.: A) Lamač, 1988, repr. no. 317

108.
Armchair, 1913
Black-stained oak, upholstered
(Fabric design by F. Kysela)
100 x 57 x 52 cm
UPM dep. 1388/9
Exhib.: Prague, 1976 (cat. no. 64, repr.); Jaroměř, 1983 (cat. no. 17, repr.); Tokyo, 1984 (cat. no. 012, repr.)
Lit.: A) Burkhardt & Lamarová, 1982, repr. no. 173

109.
Sofa, 1913
Black-stained oak, veneered, upholstered
(Fabric design by F. Kysela)
118.5 x 230 x 75 cm
UPM dep. 1388/12
Exhib.: Prague, 1976 (cat. no. 65, repr.); Jaroměř, 1983 (cat. no. 14, repr.)
Lit.: A) Burkhardt & Lamarová, 1982, repr. no. 180; A) Adlerová, 1983, repr. no. 4

110.
Furniture design for the actor Otto Boleška, 1913
Graphite, pen, and india ink
46 x 63 cm

Inscribed l.r. in graphite: "Boleška 1913 G"
NTM Collection no. 14
Acquired in 1951
Exhib.: Jaroměř, 1983 (cat. no. 29, repr.); Tokyo, 1984 (cat. no. 155, repr.)

111.
Side chair, 1913
Black-stained oak
92 x 46 x 48 cm
UPM dep. 1388/10
Exhib.: Prague, 1976
(cat. nos. 67–68, repr.)

112.
Smoking table, 1913
Black-stained oak, veneered
82 x 44 x 50.5 cm
UPM dep. 1388/13
Exhib.: Prague, 1976 (cat. no. 66, repr.); Jaroměř, 1983 (cat. no. 18, repr.); Tokyo, 1984 (cat. no. 013, repr.)
Lit.: A) Burkhardt & Lamarová, 1982, repr. no. 173

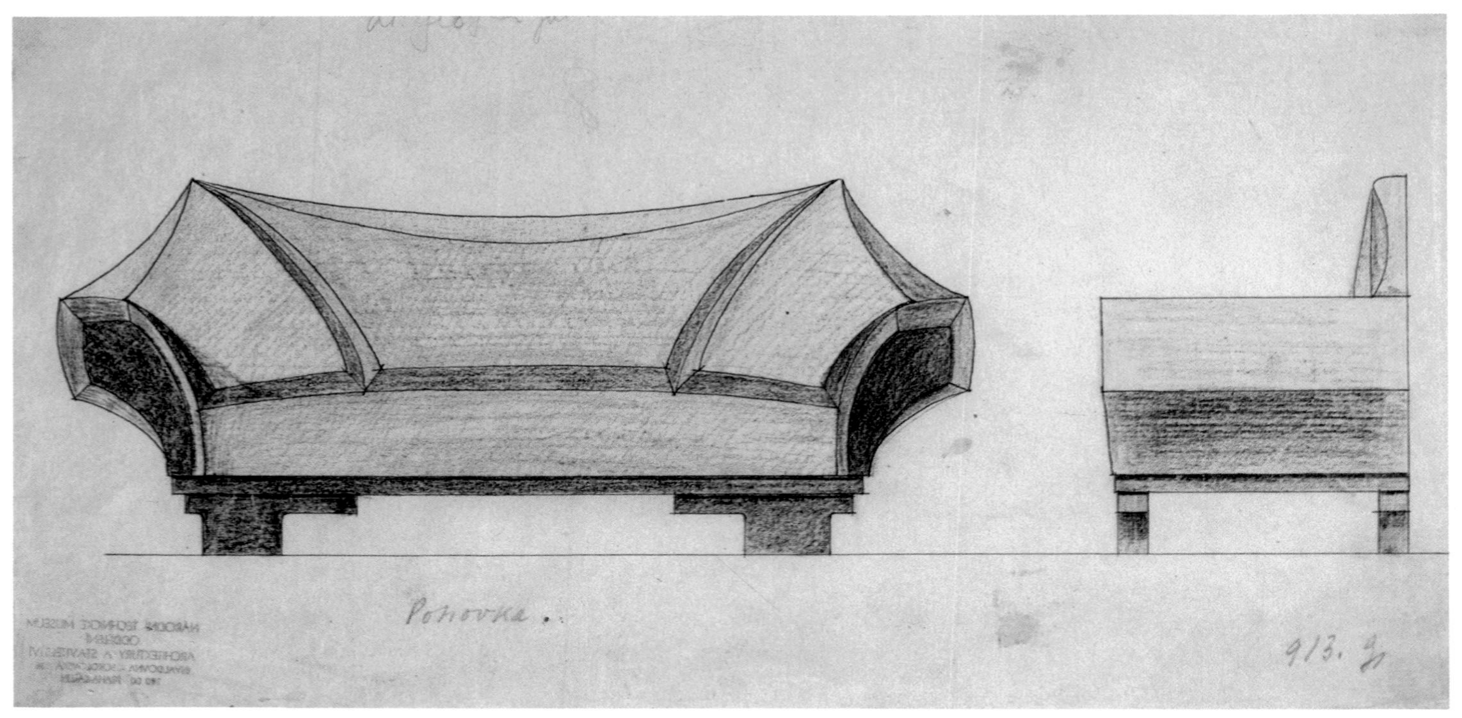

113.
Design for a sofa and armchair, 1913
Graphite and crayon
21 x 42.5 cm
Designed for Dr. J. Grégr

Inscribed l.r. in graphite: "913 G"; inscribed u. and l. in graphite: "Dr. Grégr's Jul Sofa"
NTM Collection no. 14
Acquired in 1951
Exhib.: Tokyo, 1984 (cat. no. 158, repr.)

Dr. Grégr's apartment, period photograph, SÚPPOP Archive, Štenc Collection

Dining room and study (partial), 1914
Cat. nos. 114–118
Designed for the art historian V. V. Štech
Manufactured by PUD
UPM 62.101, 76.046–51
Acquired in 1964 and 1972

114.
Sofa, 1914
Softwood, upholstered
(Fabric design by F. Kysela)
124 x 246 x 90 cm
UPM inv. no. 62.101
Exhib.: Cologne, 1914; Paris, 1966; Prague, 1971; Prague, 1976 (cat. no. 55, repr.); Tokyo, 1984 (cat. no. 010, repr.)
Lit.: B) Janák, 1912-1913a (repr. of the original upholstery-fabric design); *Umělecký měsíčník* 3, 1914; B) Brožová, 1967, repr. no. 367;
A) Burkhardt & Lamarová, 1982, repr. no. 179;
A) Lamač, 1988, repr. no. 318

115.

Chaise longue, 1914

Beech, softwood, upholstered
(Fabric design by F. Kysela)
83 x 68 x 190 cm
UPM inv. no. 76.047
Exhib.: Prague, 1976 (cat. no. 56, repr.)
Lit.: B) Janák, 1912–1913a, p. 145 (repr. of the original upholstery-fabric design); A) Burkhardt & Lamarová, 1982, repr. no. 186

116.
Cupboard, 1914
Black-stained oak, veneered
190 x 120 x 50 cm
UPM inv. no. 76.049
Exhib.: Prague, 1976 (cat. no. 57, repr.)

117.
Sideboard, 1914
Black-stained oak, veneered, and glass
185 x 180 x 68 cm
UPM inv. no. 76.048
Exhib.: Prague, 1976 (cat. no. 51, repr.)

118.

Writing desk, 1914

Black-stained oak, veneered

124 x 145 x 80 cm

UPM inv. no. 76.051

Exhib.: Prague, 1976 (cat. no. 54, repr.)

119.
Dressing table, 1915
Imported pine, veneered
152 x 119 x 39 cm
Designed for Helena Johnová
Manufactured by PUD
UPM inv. no. 63.959
Acquired in 1965 from the estate of H. Johnová
Exhib.: Prague, 1976 (cat. no. 83, repr.)
Lit.: A) Burkhardt & Lamarová, 1982, repr. no. 185

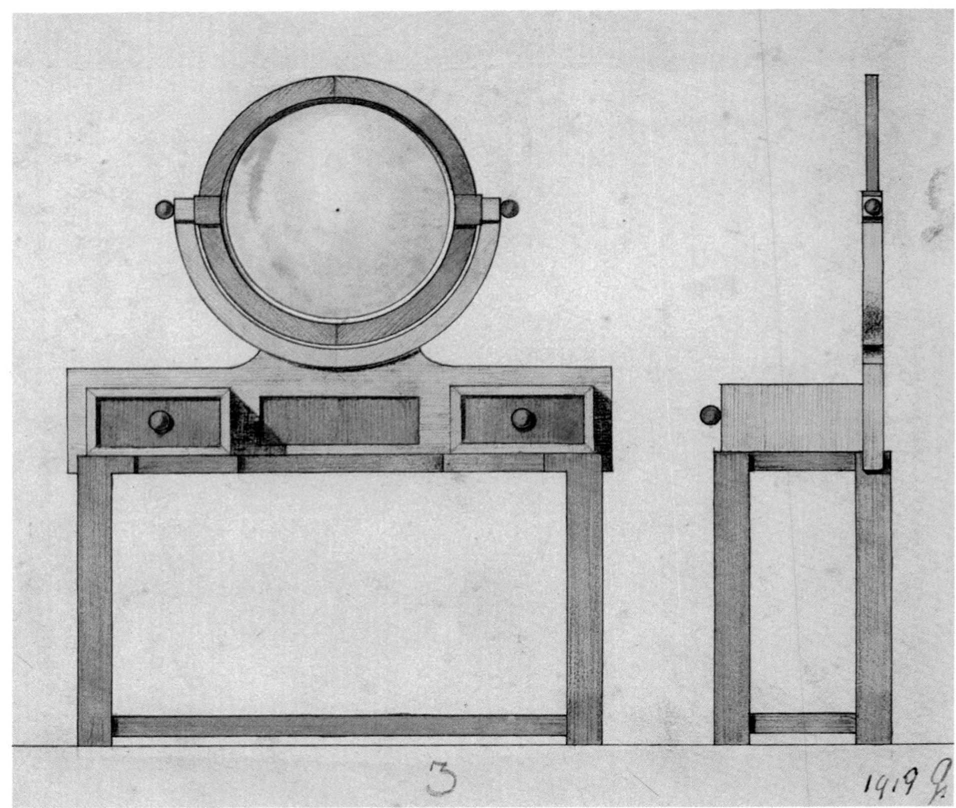

120.
Design for a dressing table, 1919
India ink and watercolour
31.5 x 24 cm
Dated l.r. in ink: "1919 G"
NTM Collection no. 14
Acquired in 1951

121.
Design for a bed and bedside table, 1919
India ink and watercolour
31.5 x 24 cm
Dated l.r. in ink: "1919 G"
NTM Collection no. 14
Acquired in 1951

122.
Design for a small table and sofa, 1919
India ink and watercolour
31.5 x 24 cm
Inscribed l.r. in ink: "[1]919 G"
NTM Collection no. 14
Acquired in 1951

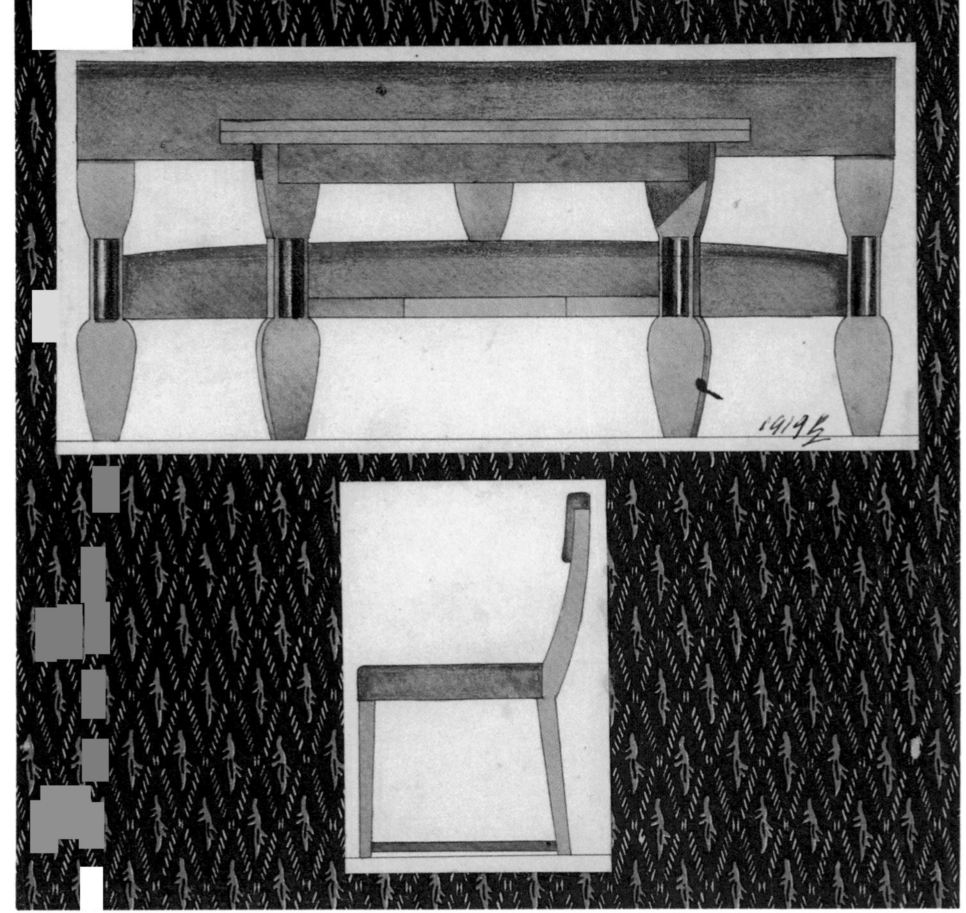

123.
Design for a bench, table, and chair, 1919
India ink and watercolour
31.5 x 24 cm
Dated l.r. in ink: "1919 G"
NTM Collection no. 14
Acquired in 1951

124.
Bookcase, 1922
Black-stained oak, light ash, and frosted glass
150 x 250 x 45 cm
UPM inv. no. 95.685
Acquired in 1985

125.
Small conference table, 1922
Black-stained oak, light ash, and glass
80 x 80 x 80 cm
UPM inv. no. 95.675
Acquired in 1985
Lit.: A) Adlerová, 1983, repr. no. 25

126.
Armchair, 1922
Black-stained oak, light ash, and leather
88 x 87 x 84 cm
MG Brno inv. no. 26.300
Acquired in 1976
Lit.: A) Adlerová, 1983, repr. no. 25

127.
Sofa, 1922
Dark-stained oak, light ash, and leather
89 x 148 x 75 cm
MG Brno, inv. no. 26.299
Acquired in 1976
Lit.: A) Adlerová, 1983, repr. no. 25

Furniture group, ca. 1922
Cat. nos. 128–130
Manufactured by PUD
UPM inv. no. 96.558–60
Acquired in 1989

128.
Vitrine, ca. 1922
Brown-stained oak, light ash, and glass
154 x 41 x 30 cm
UPM inv. no. 96.558
Acquired in 1989

129.
Writing desk, ca. 1922
Brown-stained oak and light ash
80 x 194 x 90 cm
UPM inv. no. 96.559
Acquired in 1989

130.
Armchair, ca. 1922
Brown-stained oak, light ash, and leather
84 x 83 x 87 cm
UPM inv. no. 96.560
Acquired in 1989

Vlastislav Hofman

Dining-room group (partial), 1911–1912
Cat. nos. 131–132
Designed for the sculptor Josef Mařatka
Manufactured by PUD
UPM inv. no. 40.488–9, 40.492
Acquired in 1956 from Zdeňka Mařatková

131.
Side chair, 1911–1912
Black-stained oak, veneered, and leather
90 x 43 x 46 cm
UPM inv. no. 40.488–9
Exhib.: Prague, 1972 (cat. no. 76, repr.); Prague, 1976 (cat. nos. 94–97)
Lit.: A) Burkhardt & Lamarová, 1982, repr. no. 183; A) Lamač, 1988, repr. no. 237; B) Behal, 1988, p. 171

Vlastislav Hofman, sketches for a sofa, armchair, and small table, 1912

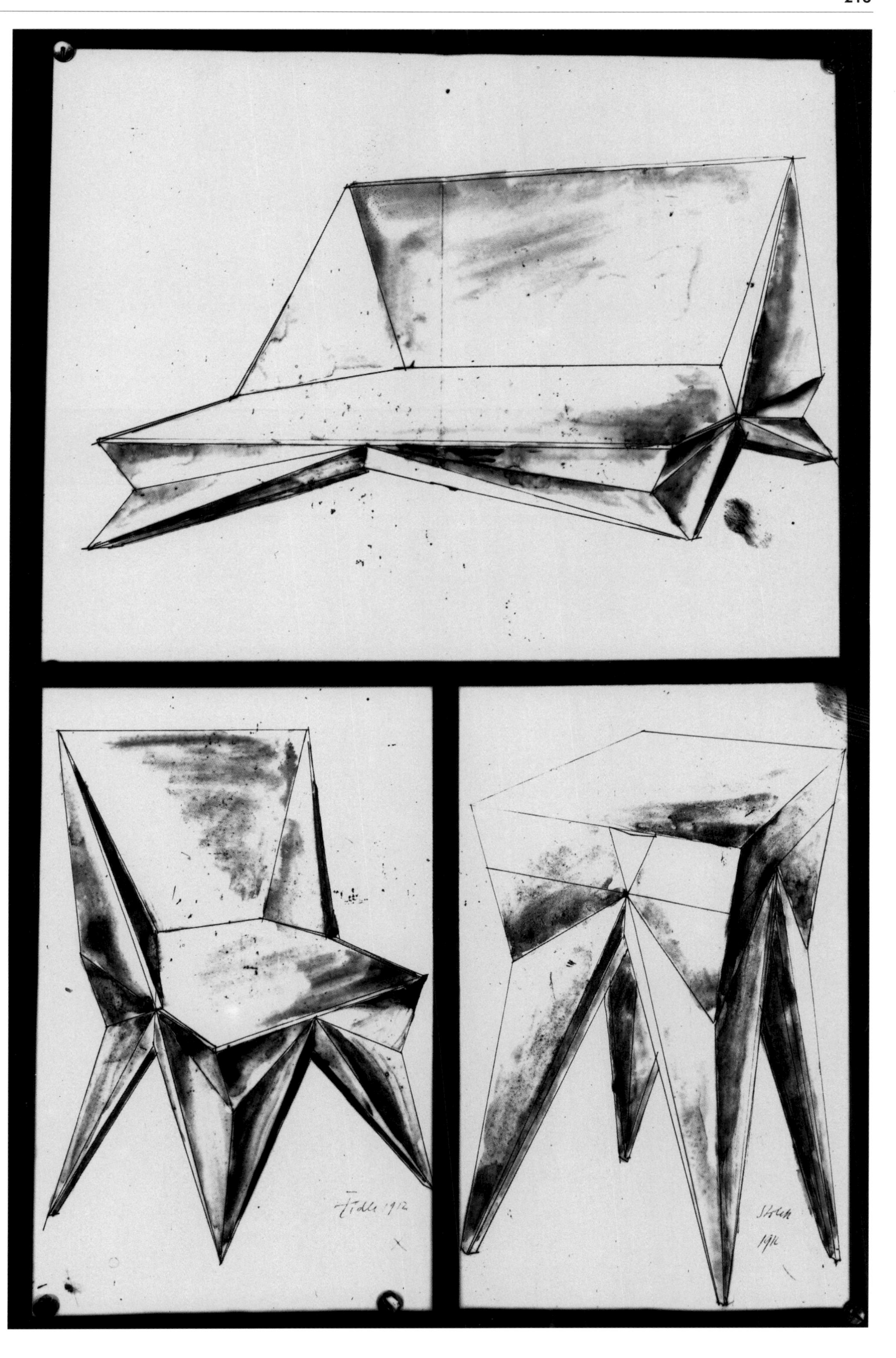

Period photograph, SÚPPOP Archive, Štenc Collection

132.
Armchair, 1911–1912
Black-stained oak, veneered, and leather
90 x 57 x 53 cm
UPM inv. no. 40.492
Exhib.: Prague, 1976 (cat. nos. 98–99, repr.)
Lit.: A) Burkhardt & Lamarová, 1982, repr. no. 184; A) Lamač, 1988, repr. no. 238

133.
Dining table, 1912
Black-stained oak, veneered
81.5 x 130 x 150 cm
UPM inv. no. 74.848
Exhib.: Prague, 1976 (cat. no. 101, repr.)

Seating group, 1912
Cat. nos. 133–135
Designed for National Theatre
director Vojta Novák
Manufactured by the workshops
of the National Theatre
UPM inv. no. 74.848–50
Acquired in 1971

134.
Side chair, 1912
Black-stained oak, veneered, upholstered
101 x 48 x 50 cm
UPM inv. no. 74.850
Exhib.: Prague, 1976 (cat. nos. 102–105, no repr.)

135.
Sofa, 1912
Black-stained oak, veneered, upholstered
Restored in 1991
129 x 46 x 83 cm
UPM inv. no. 74.849
Exhib.: Prague, 1976 (cat. no. 100, repr.)

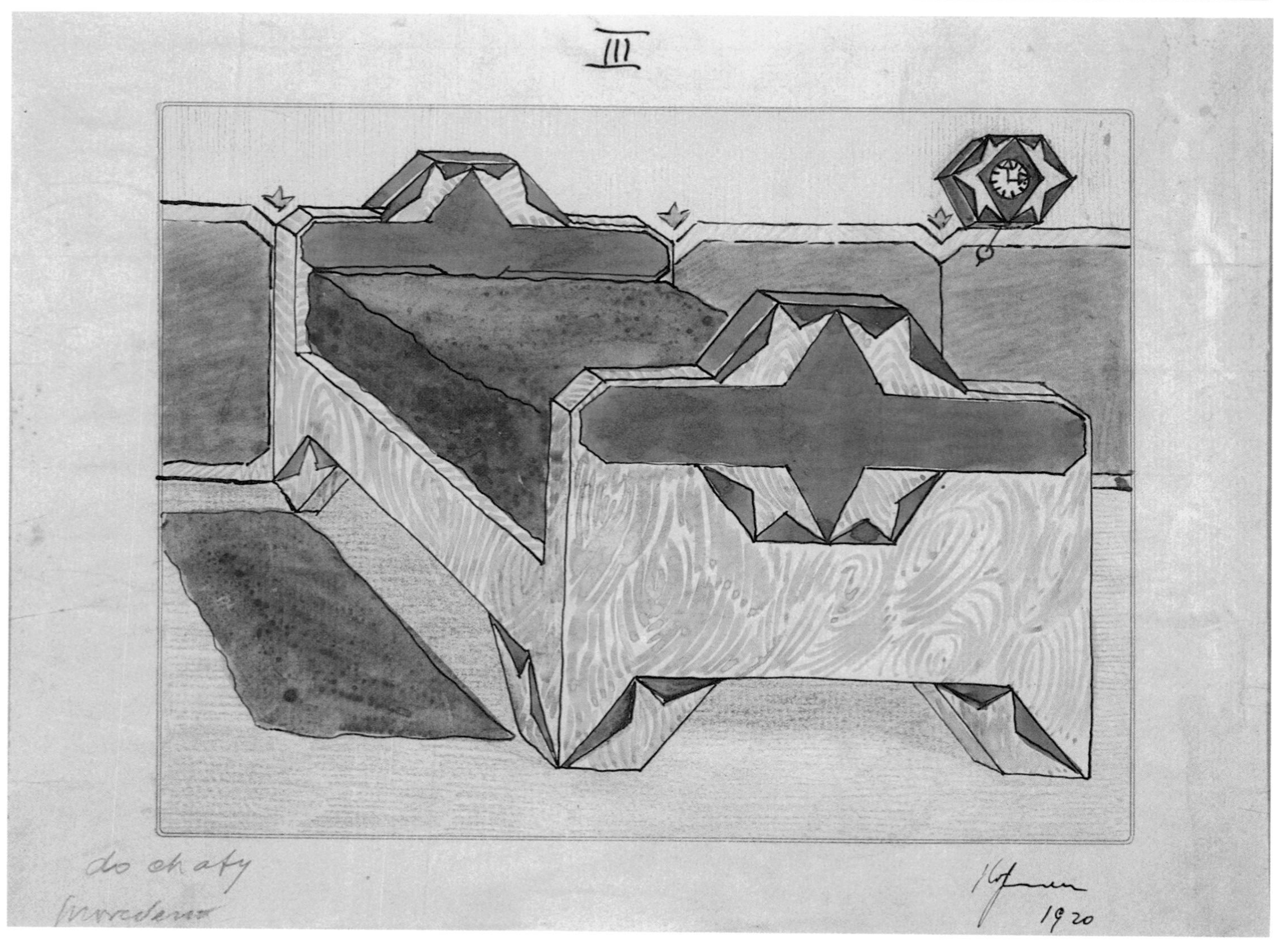

136.
Design for a cottage bed, 1920
India ink, crayon, and watercolour
26 x 36 cm
Signed l.r.: "Hofman 1920"
Inscribed l.l.: "for cottage produced"
Private archive

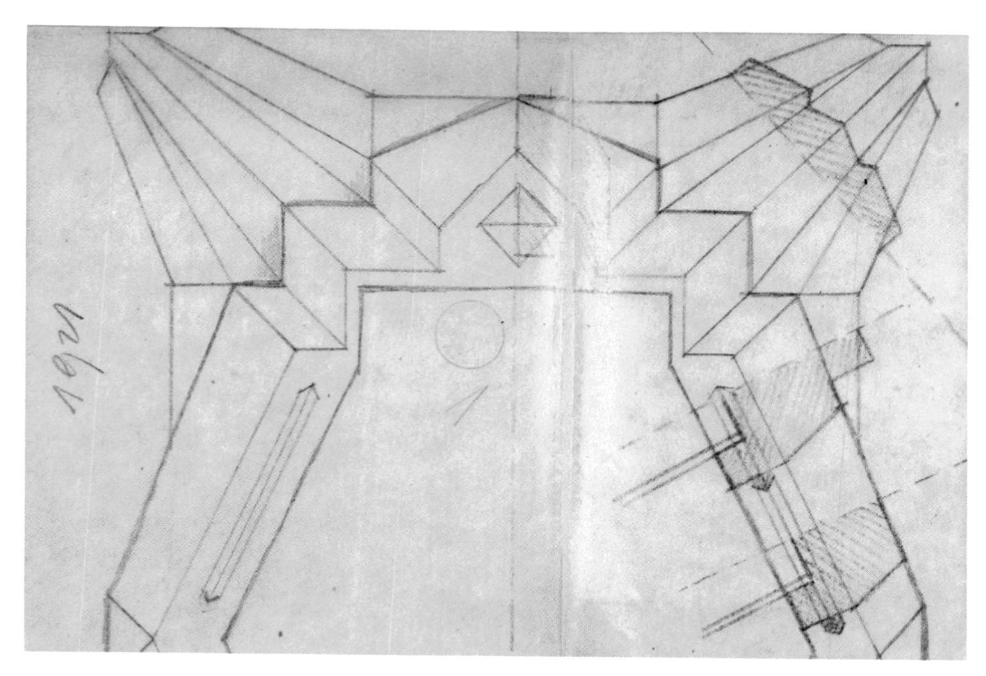

137.
Design for a mirror, 1921
Graphite and crayon
23 x 35 cm
Dated c.l.: "1921"
Private archive

138.
Design for a carpet, 1922
Watercolour
27 x 39 cm
Dated u.l. in graphite: "1922"
Private archive
Exhib.: Berlin, 1982 (unnumb., repr.)

Pavel Janák

Gentleman's room, 1911–1912
Cat. nos. 139–142
Designed for Dr. Josef Borovička
Manufactured by PUD
UPM inv. no. 41.703–6
Acquired in 1957 from Dr. J. Borovička

Period photograph, SÚPPOP Archive, Štenc Collection

139.
Writing desk, 1911–1912
Dark-stained polished oak with white-painted panels, interior mahogany, veneered
78 x 160 x 78 cm
UPM inv. no. 41.703
Exhib.: Prague, 1969 (unnumb., repr.); Prague, 1976 (cat. no. 2, repr.)
Lit.: B) Janák, 1912–1913, p. 97; A) Burkhardt & Lamarová, 1982, repr. no. 151; A) Lamač, 1988, repr. no. 230

140.
Bookcase, 1911–1912
Softwood, white-painted exterior, black-lacquered interior, and glass
155.5 x 224 x 45 cm
UPM inv. no. 41.706
Exhib.: Prague, 1969 (unnumb., repr.); Prague, 1976 (cat. no. 1, repr.)
Lit.: B) Janák, 1912–1913, p. 97

141.
Side chair, 1911–1912
Brown-stained oak
95 x 45 x 43 cm
UPM inv. no. 41.704
Exhib.: Paris, 1966; Prague, 1967a; Prague, 1969 (cat. no. 110, no repr.); London, 1970; Prague, 1972 (cat. no. 74, repr.); Prague, 1976 (cat. no. 4, repr.); Tokyo, 1984 (cat. no. 001, repr.); Prague, Vienna, Helsinki, 1982–1987 (cat. no. 1, repr.)
Lit.: B) Janák, 1912–1913, p. 97; B) Vokoun, 1966b, repr. no. 5; A) Burkhardt & Lamarová, 1982, repr. no. 153; B) Behal, 1987, repr. no. 5; A) Lamač, 1988, repr. no. 232

142.
Armchair, 1911–1912
Softwood, white lacquer, upholstered
94 x 65 x 55 cm
UPM inv. no. 41.705
Exhib.: Prague, 1969 (unnumb., repr.); Prague, 1976 (cat. no. 3, repr.)
Lit.: B) Janák, 1912–1913a, p. 97

143.
Commode, 1912

Dark-stained oak, interior mahogany, veneered
97 x 141 x 60 cm
UPM inv. no. 72.036
Exhib.: Prague, 1971; Prague, 1976 (cat. no. 6, repr.); Tokyo, 1984 (cat. no. 003, repr.)
Lit.: A) Burkhardt & Lamarová, 1982, repr. no. 18; A) Lamač, 1988, repr. no. 233

144.
Table mirror, 1912

Dark-stained oak, interior mahogany, veneered, and gilding
73 x 88 x 29 cm
UPM inv. no. 72.037
Exhib.: Prague, 1971; Prague, 1976 (cat. no. 7, repr.); Prague, Vienna, Helsinki, 1982–1987 (cat. no. 3, repr.)
Lit.: A) Burkhardt & Lamarová, 1982, repr. no. 157

Furniture group, 1912

Cat. nos. 143–146
Designed for Růžena Jakubcová in Jičín
Manufactured by PUD
UPM inv. nos. 72.036–37, 39–40
Acquired in 1967

145.
Dining table, 1912
Dark-brown-stained oak
77.5 x 110 x 110 cm
UPM inv. no. 72.039
Exhib.: Prague, 1976 (cat. no. 8, repr.)

145a.
Design for a table and chair, 1912
India ink and watercolour
17 x 22 cm
NTM Collection no. 85
Acquired in 1957

146.
Side chair, 1912
Light-brown-stained oak, upholstered (restored)
99 x 44 x 47 cm
UPM inv. no. 72.040
Exhib.: Prague, 1971; Prague, 1976 (cat. nos. 9–12, repr.); Tokyo, 1984 (cat. no. 002, repr.); Prague, Vienna, Helsinki, 1982–1987 (cat. no. 4, repr.)
Lit.: A) Burkhardt & Lamarová, 1982, repr. no. 152

147.
Small table, 1912
Polished oak, veneered
60 x 35 x 35 cm
UPM inv. no. 91.762
Acquired in 1984

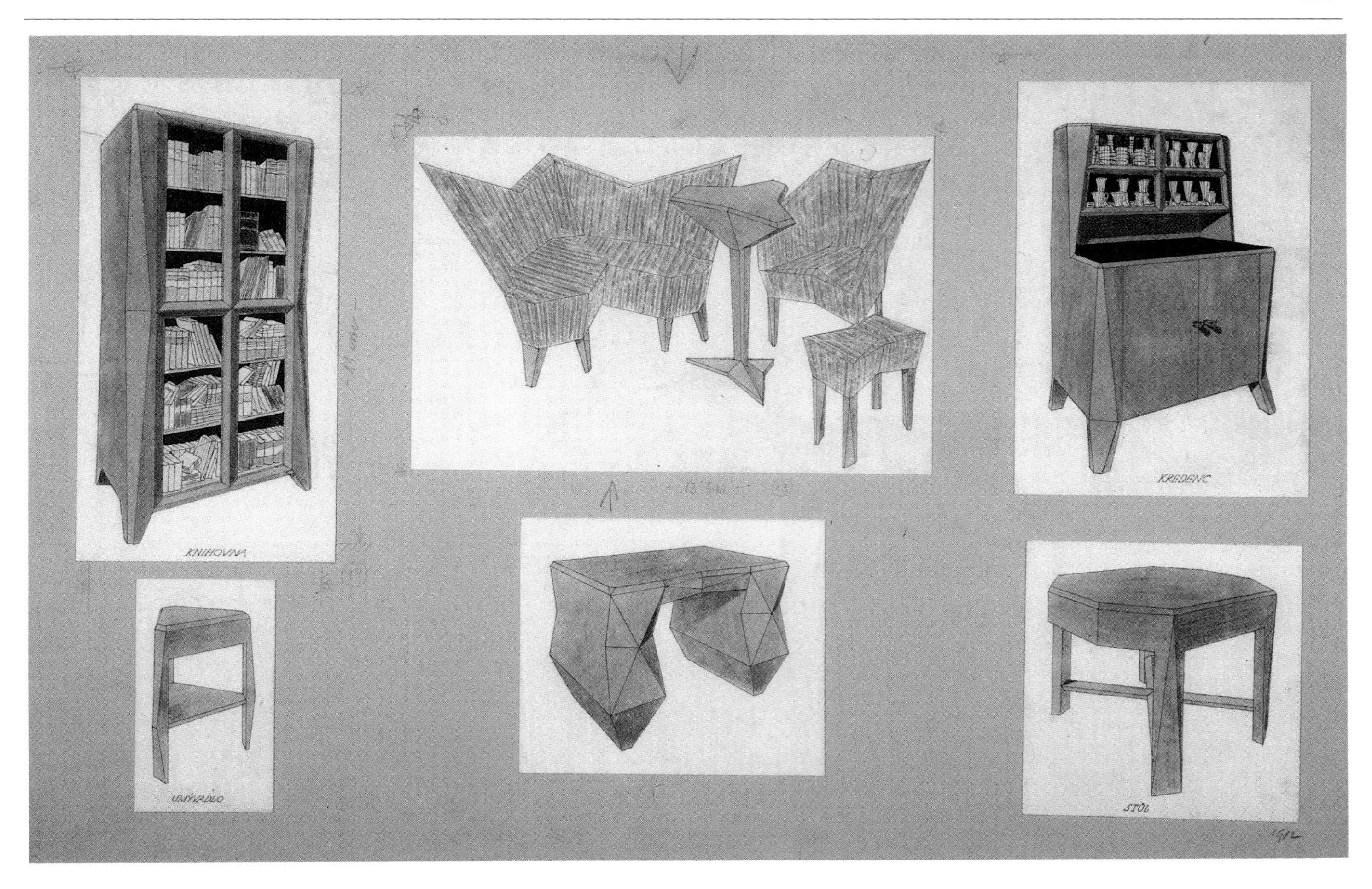

148.

Designs for furniture, 1912

Bookcase, washstand, sideboard,
seating set, tables
India ink, watercolour, and crayon
50 x 75 cm
Dated l.r. in graphite: "1912"
Stamped: "Architekt Pavel Janák"
Technical notations and short descriptions, l. and c.
NTM Collection no. 85
Acquired in 1957

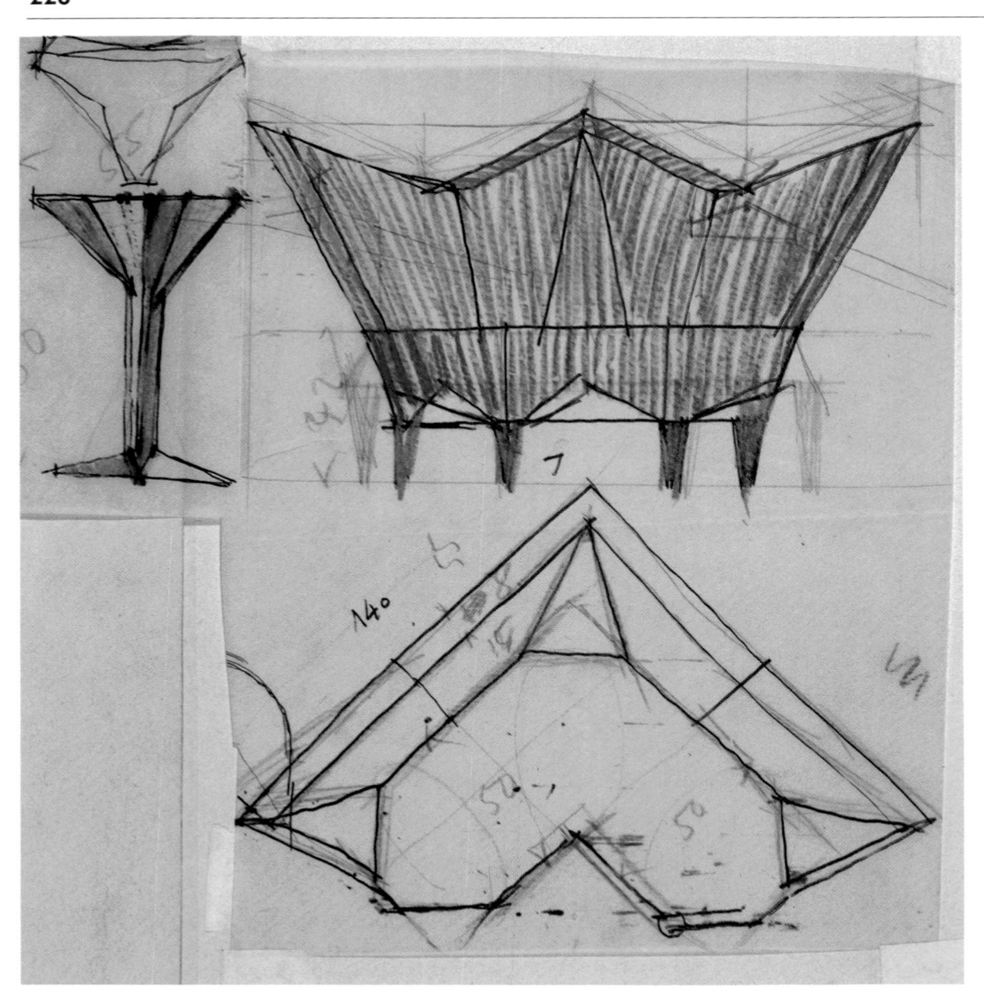

149.
Design for a sofa and table, 1912
India ink, graphite, and crayon
27 x 27.5 cm
Technical numerical notations
NTM Collection no. 85
Acquired in 1957
Exhib.: Prague, Vienna, Helsinki, 1982–1987
(unnumb., repr.)

Dining room in Dr. F. Závišek's apartment, period photograph, SÚPPOP Archive, Štenc Collection

150.
Design for an upholstered side chair, 1912
Graphite, india ink, and watercolour
21.5 x 7.5 cm
NTM Collection no. 85
Acquired in 1957
Exhib.: Tokyo, 1984 (cat. no. 116, repr.)

151.
Furniture studies, 1912
Aniline graphite
34 x 21 cm
NTM Collection no. 85
Acquired in 1957

Furniture for a gentleman's room, 1912–1913
Cat. nos. 152–155
Manufactured by PUD
UPM inv. no. 43.405, 45.681–2,4
Acquired in 1957

152.
Bookcase, 1912–1913
Light polished ash, veneered, interior stained black, and glass
159 x 86 x 40 cm
UPM inv. no. 43.405
Exhib.: Prague, 1976 (cat. no. 14, repr.); Prague, Vienna, Helsinki, 1982–1987 (unnumb., repr.)
Lit.: A) Burkhardt & Lamarová, 1982, repr. no. 155

153.
Writing desk, 1912
Light-stained oak, interior mahogany, veneered
Restored in 1991
80 x 110 x 65 cm
UPM inv. no. 45.681
Exhib.: Prague, 1976 (cat. no. 15, repr.)

154.
Side chair, 1912
Light-stained ash, upholstered
90 x 47 x 46 cm
UPM inv. no. 45.684
Exhib.: Prague, 1976 (cat. no. 17, repr.)

155.
Conference table, 1912
Natural polished oak, veneered
80 x 110 x 69 cm
UPM inv. no. 45.682
Exhib.: Prague, 1967a; London, 1970; Prague, 1976 (cat. no. 16, repr.)

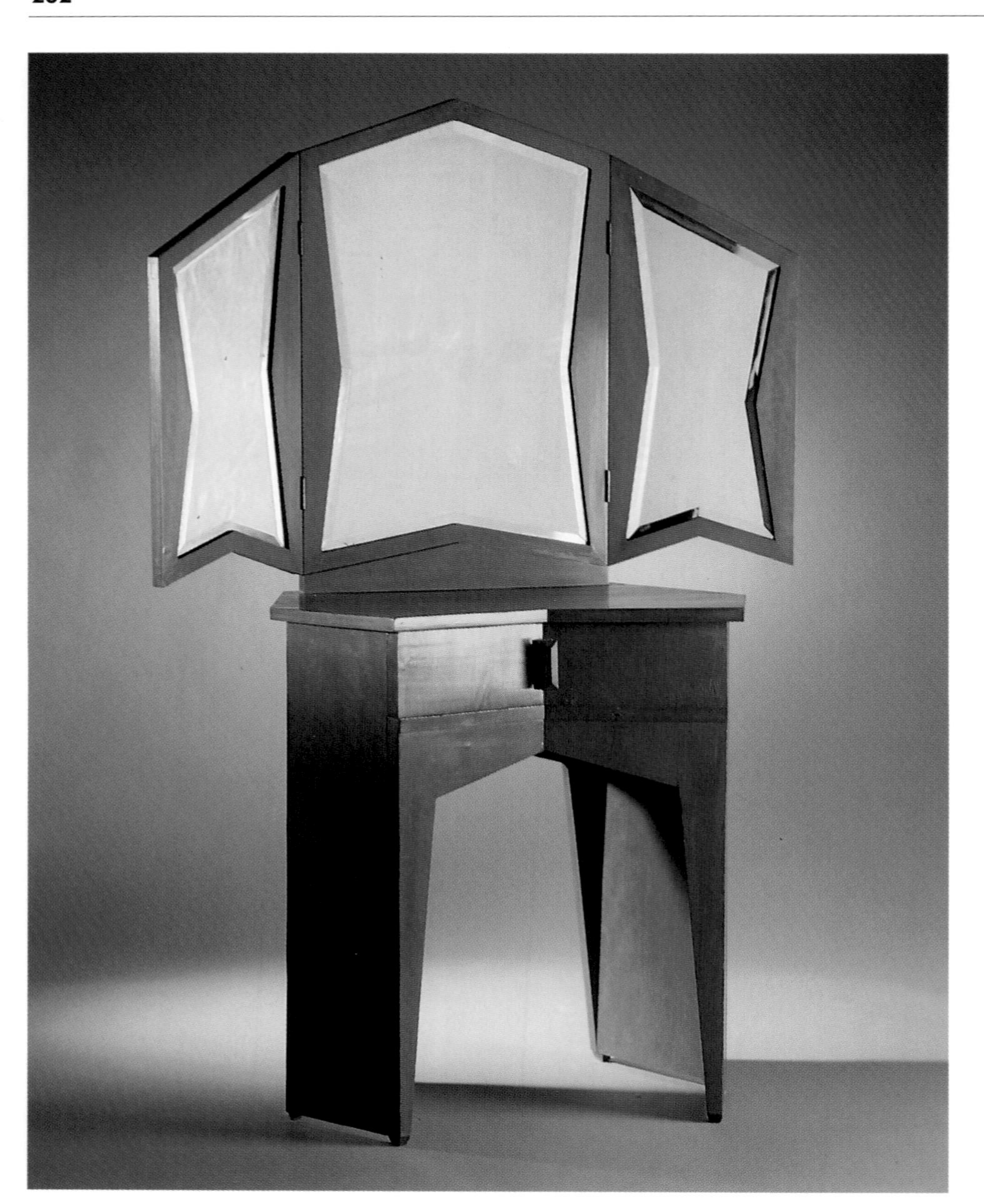

Furniture for a lady's room (partial), 1912–1914

Cat. nos. 156–157
Designed for National Theatre director Vojta Novák
Manufactured by PUD
UPM inv. no. 74.855–6
Acquired in 1971

156.
Dressing table, 1912–1914
Pearwood, veneered, and mirrored glass
158 x 76 x 55 cm
UPM inv. no. 74.855
Exhib.: Prague, 1976 (cat. no. 27, repr.); Tokyo, 1984 (cat. no. 004, repr.)
Lit.: A) Burkhardt & Lamarová, 1982, repr. no. 156; A) Lamač, 1988, repr. no. 321

157.
Armchair, 1912–1914
Walnut
85 x 65 x 59 cm
UPM inv. no. 74.856
Exhib.: Prague, 1976 (cat. nos. 28–29, repr.)

Furniture group (partial), 1913
Cat. nos. 158–159
Designed for Dr. K. Hoch
Manufactured by PUD
UPM inv. no. 88.302–3
Acquired in 1980

158.
Side chair, 1913
Black-stained oak and black leather
95 x 45 x 47 cm
UPM inv. no. 88.302
Exhib.: Tokyo, 1984 (cat. no. 005, repr.); Prague, Vienna, Helsinki, 1982–1987 (cat. no. 10, repr.)

Period photograph, SÚPPOP Archive, Štenc Collection

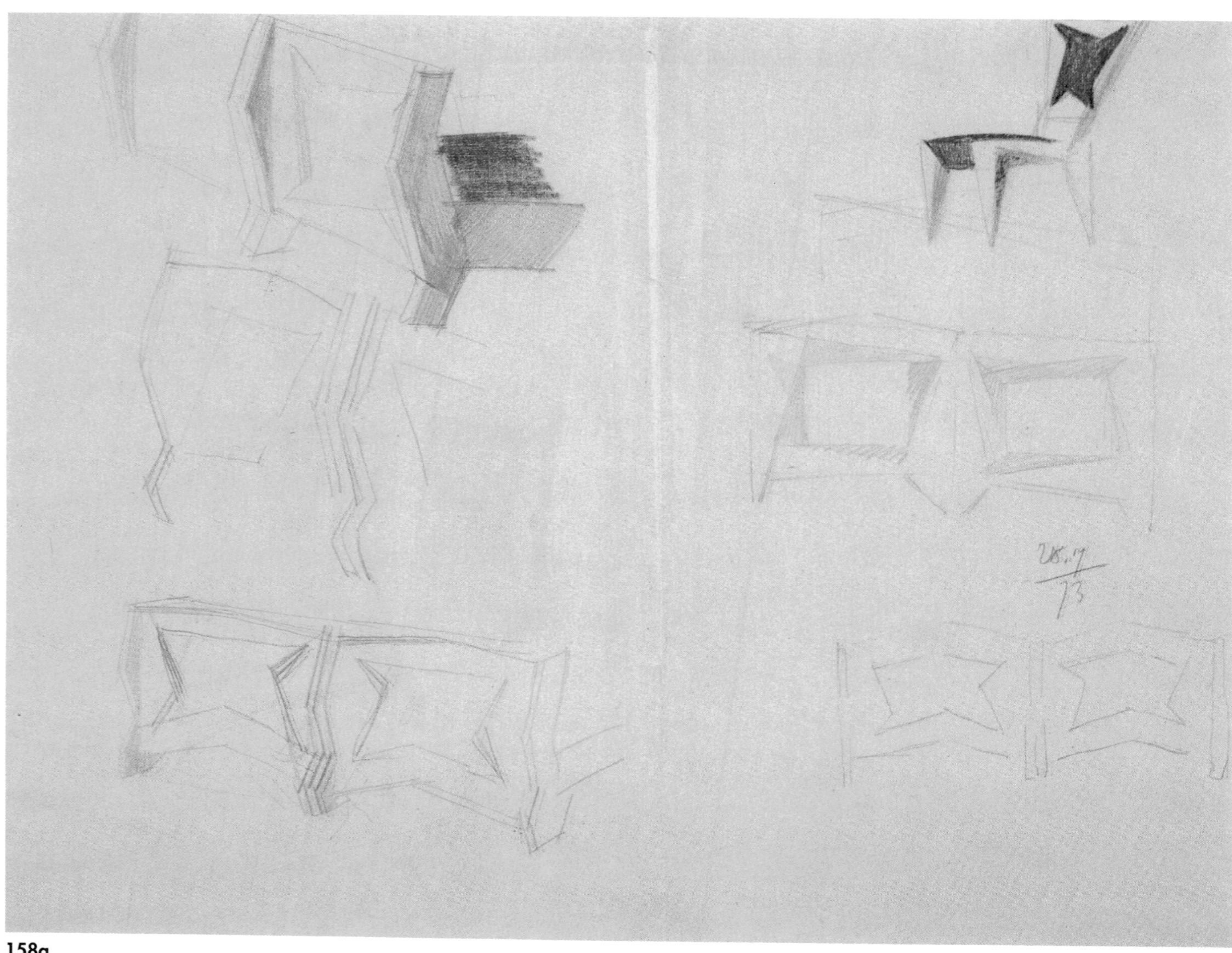

158a.
Studies for bedroom furniture, 1913
Aniline graphite and red crayon
34 x 42 cm
NTM Collection no. 85
Acquired in 1957
Exhib.: Prague, Vienna, Helsinki,
1982–1987 (cat. no. 78, no repr.)

159.
Mirror, 1913
Black-stained oak and mirrored glass
100 x 60 x 3 cm
UPM inv. no. 88.303
Exhib.: Tokyo, 1984 (cat. no. 006, repr.)

160.
Dining-room table, 1913–1914
Natural oak, veneered
73.5 x 119 x 118 cm
Designed for the painter Pravoslav Kotík
Manufactured by PUD
UPM inv. no. 55.860
Acquired in 1962 from Vendula Kotíková
Exhib.: Prague, 1976 (cat. no. 22, repr.)

161.

Design for wallpaper, 1911

Watercolour

74 x 55 cm

Inscribed at u.c. in india ink: "White in white. Thicker drawn lines could also be in black, but then they would have to be of course thinner, about the same as the others. The whole drawing could also be black, of course in very thin lines."

NTM Collection no. 85

Acquired in 1957

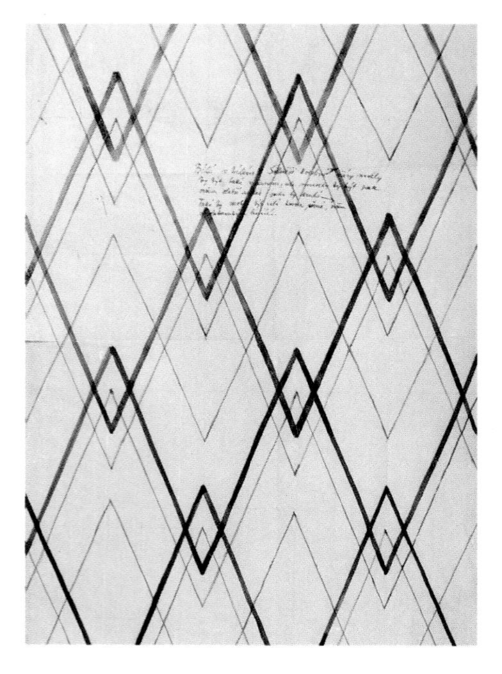

162.

Design for a washstand and two chairs, 1910–1912

India ink, graphite, and crayon

22.5 x 21 cm

NTM Collection no. 85

Acquired in 1957

Exhib.: Prague, Vienna, Helsinki, 1982–1987 (cat. no. 43)

163.
Study for a commode, 1912
Aniline graphite, india ink, and crayon
22 x 28.5 cm
Dated u.r. in graphite: "1912"
NTM Collection no. 85
Acquired in 1957
Exhib.: Prague, Vienna, Helsinki, 1982–1987 (cat. no. 76, no repr.)

164.
Designs for furniture, 1912
Armoires, bed, bedside tables, dresser, washstand, dressing table
India ink, watercolour, and crayon
50 x 75 cm
Dated l.r. in graphite: "1912"
Stamped: "Architekt Pavel Janák"
NTM Collection no. 85
Acquired in 1957
Exhib.: Prague, Vienna, Helsinki, 1982–1987 (cat. no. 62, repr. [dresser, washstand]); Tokyo, 1984 (cat. no. 118, repr.)

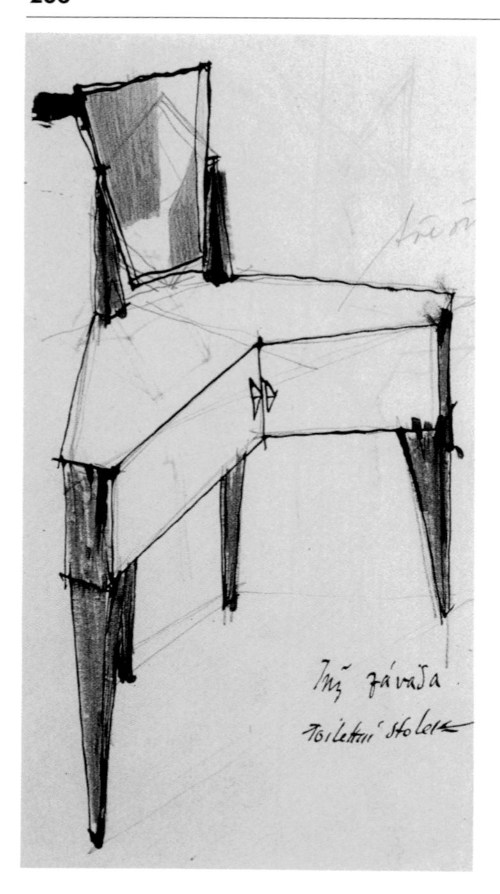

165.
Studies for a dressing table, 1912
India ink and crayon
21 x 13 cm
Designed for Mr. Závada
Inscribed u.r. in graphite: "cherries"; inscribed l.r. in india ink: "Inž. Závada dressing table"
NTM Collection no. 85
Acquired in 1957
Exhib.: Tokyo, 1984 (cat. no. 117, repr.)

166.
Design for a carpet, 1912
India ink, coloured
20.5 x 27 cm
Stamped l.r.
NTM Collection no. 70
Acquired in 1957
Exhib.: Tokyo, 1984 (cat. no. 136, repr.)

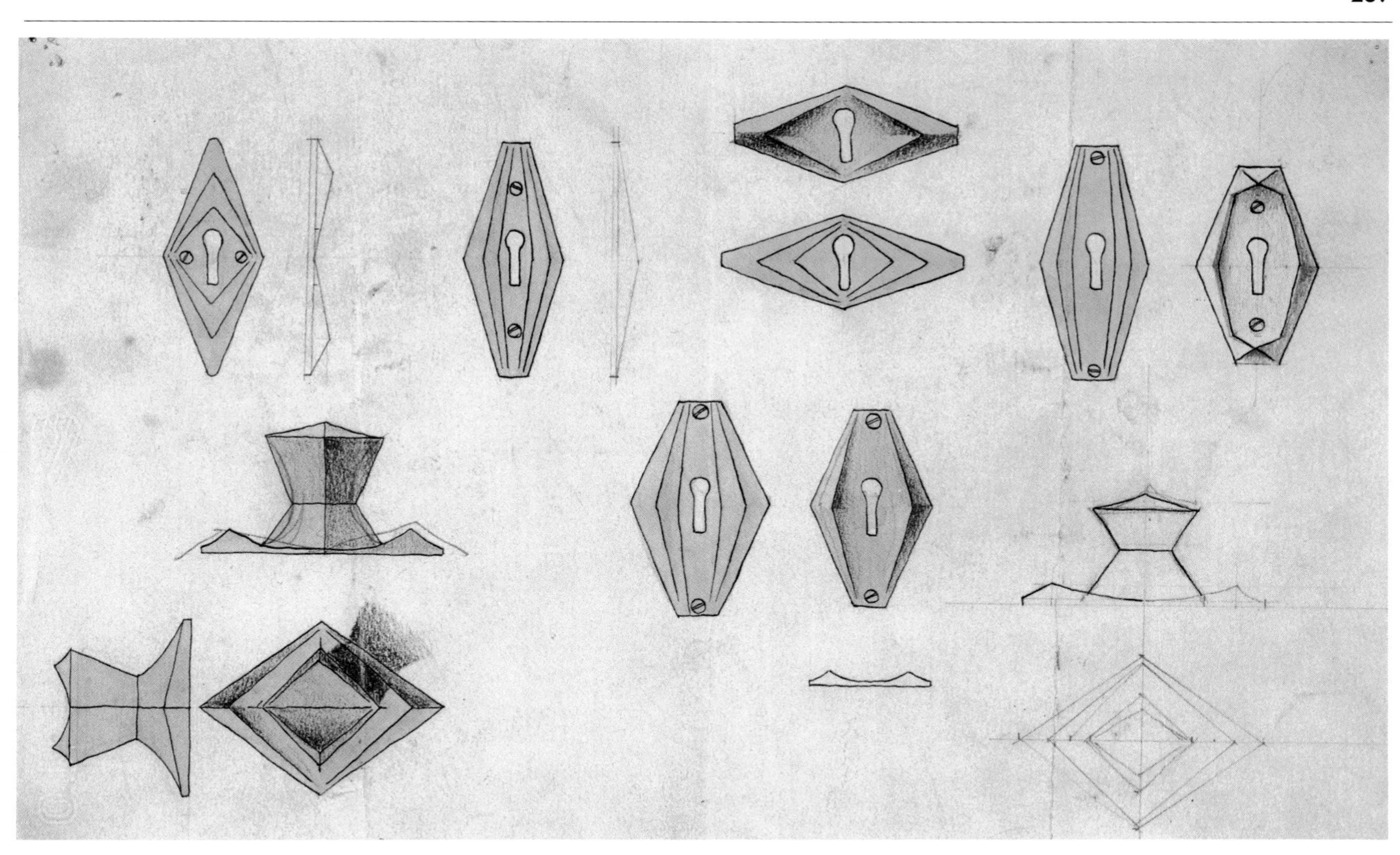

167.
Hardware studies, 1912
Graphite and watercolour
22 x 34.6 cm
NTM Collection no. 85
Acquired in 1957
Exhib.: Prague, Vienna, Helsinki, 1982–1987 (unnumb., repr.)

168.
Design for dress material, 1918

Graphite, watercolour, and india ink
50.5 x 21 cm
Inscribed l.r. in india ink: "Printed. Dress material quite good, I think"
NTM Collection no. 85
Acquired in 1957

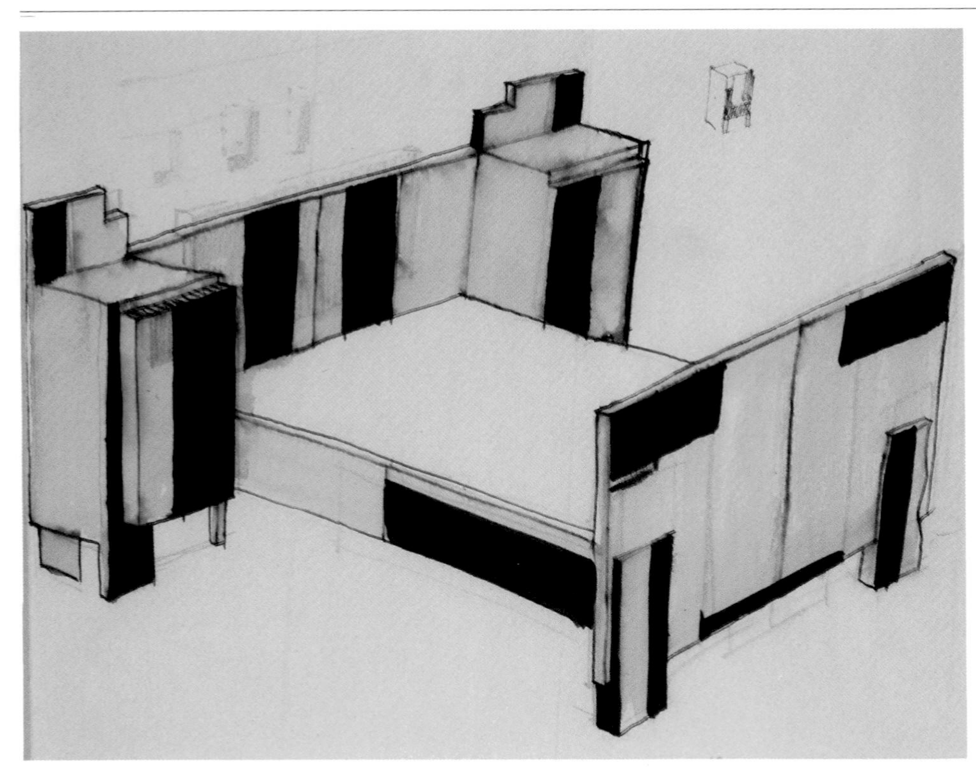

169.
Design for a bed, 1915
India ink, coloured
34 x 24.5 cm
Dated l.r. in graphite: "12. 11. 15."
NTM Collection no. 85
Acquired in 1957
Exhib.: Prague, Vienna, Helsinki, 1982–1987 (cat. no. 86, repr.)

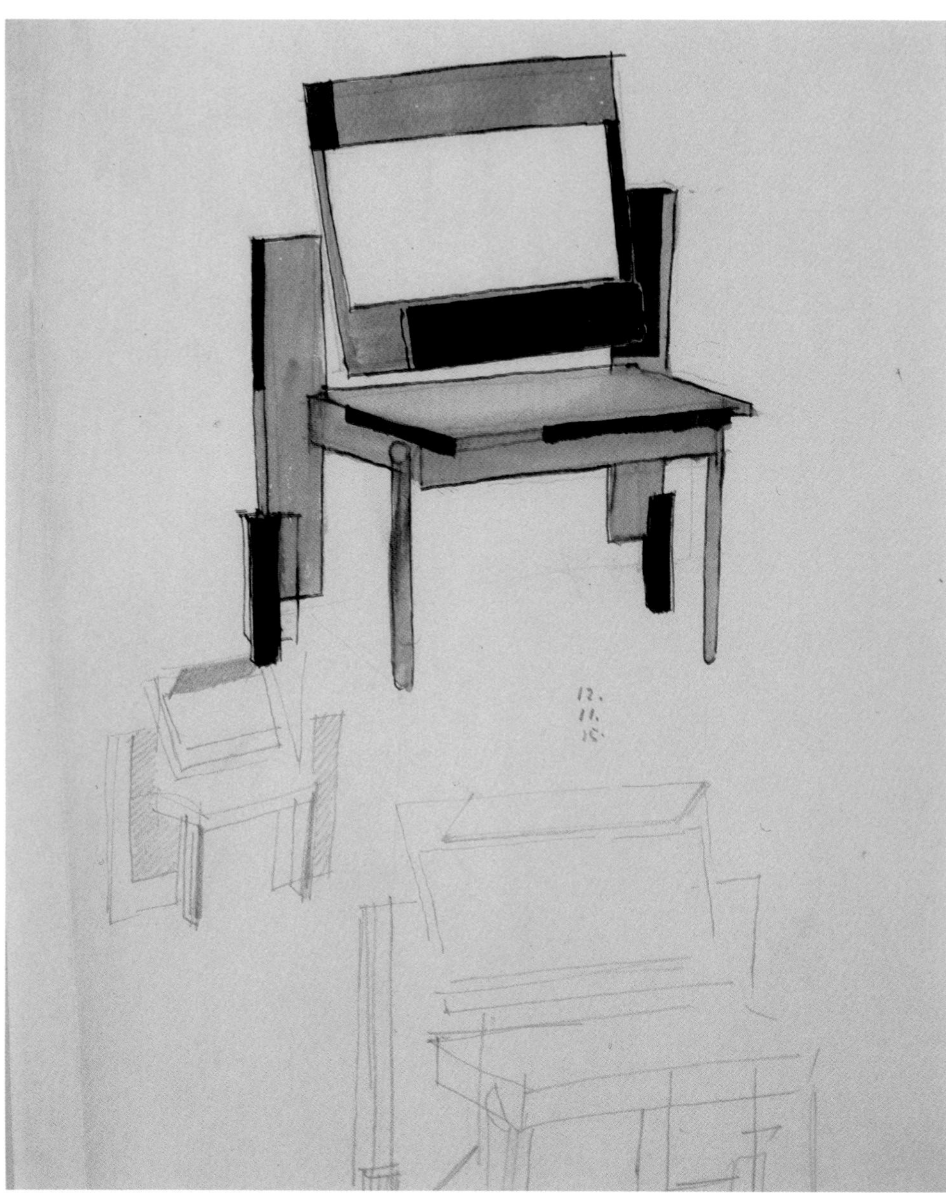

170.
Design for a dressing table, 1915
India ink and watercolour
34 x 25 cm
Dated c. in graphite: "12. 11. 15."
NTM Collection no. 85
Acquired in 1957
Exhib.: Prague, Vienna, Helsinki, 1982–1987 (cat. no. 87, no repr.)

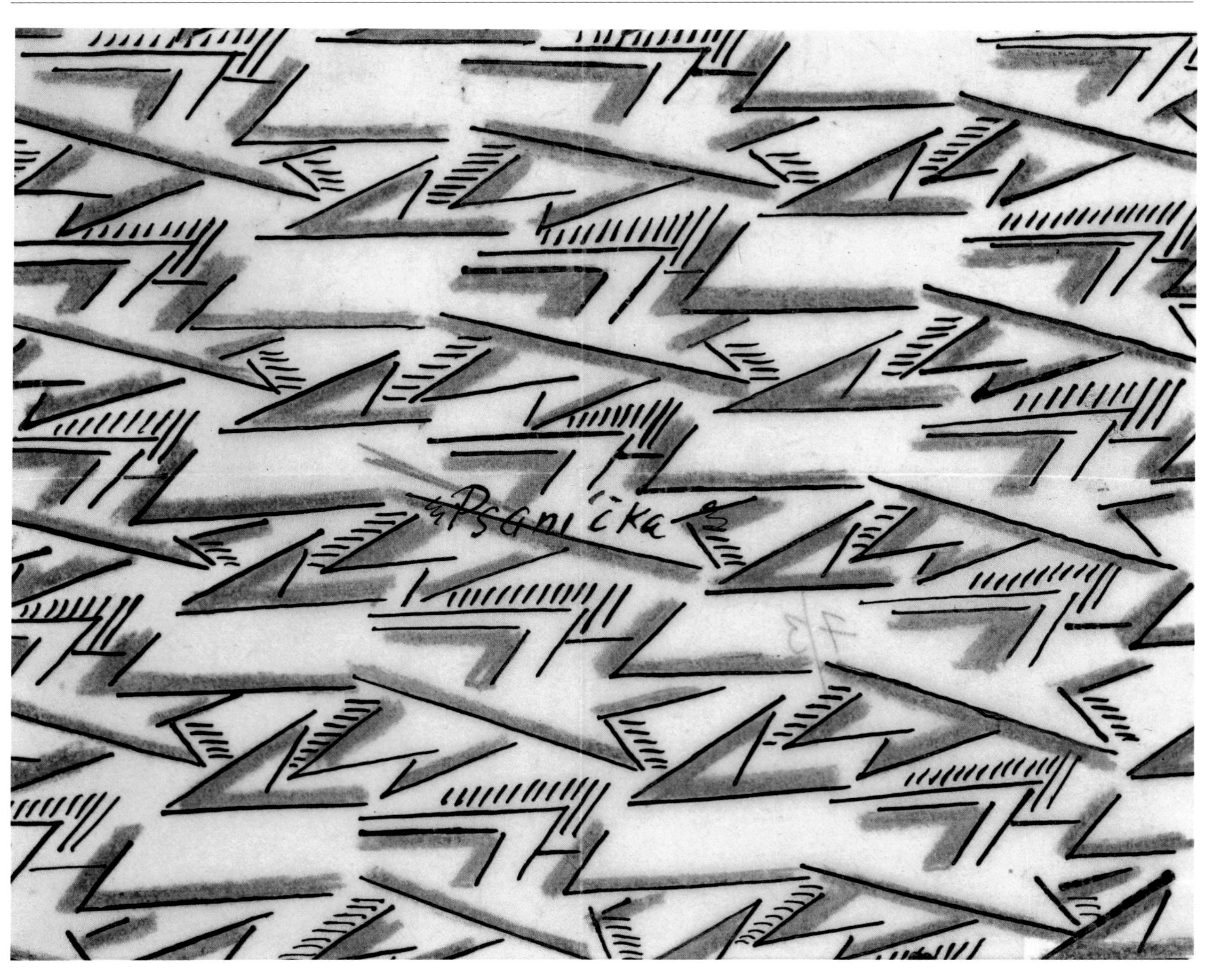

171.
Design for fabric "Psaníčka" (little letters), 1918
Graphite, pen, and watercolour
50.5 x 21cm
Inscribed c.: "Psaníčka"
NTM Collection no. 85
Acquired in 1957
Exhib.: Prague, Vienna, Helsinki, 1982–1987 (cat. no. 27, repr.)

Jiří Kroha

172.
Design for a drawing cabinet, 1917–1918
Red chalk
22 x 27 cm
Signed l.r.: "K."
Inscribed l.r. in red chalk: "Drawing cabinet"
UPM inv. no. 92.244
Acquired in 1985
Exhib.: Darmstadt, 1988–1989
(cat. no. 319, repr.)
Lit.: B) Lamarová, 1985, repr. p. 24

173.
Primary plan, 1917–1919
Pastels
26 x 44 cm
Inscribed l.r.: "JK 17"
UPM inv. no. 92.236
Acquired in 1985
Exhib.: Tokyo, 1984 (cat. no. 168, repr.),
Darmstadt, 1988–1989 (cat. no. 318, repr.)
Lit.: A) Císařovský, 1967; B) Lamarová, 1985,
repr. p. 24

174.
Furniture studies, 1917–1919
Graphite and pen, coloured
27 x 44.5 cm
Page 30 dated l.r. in india ink: "12 August 1917"
From a 30-page sketch book on cardboard,
pp. 30, 6, 5, 21
UPM inv. no. 92.254
Acquired 1985
Exhib.: Darmstadt, 1988–1989
(cat. no. 321, repr.)
Lit.: B) Lamarová, 1985, repr. p. 24

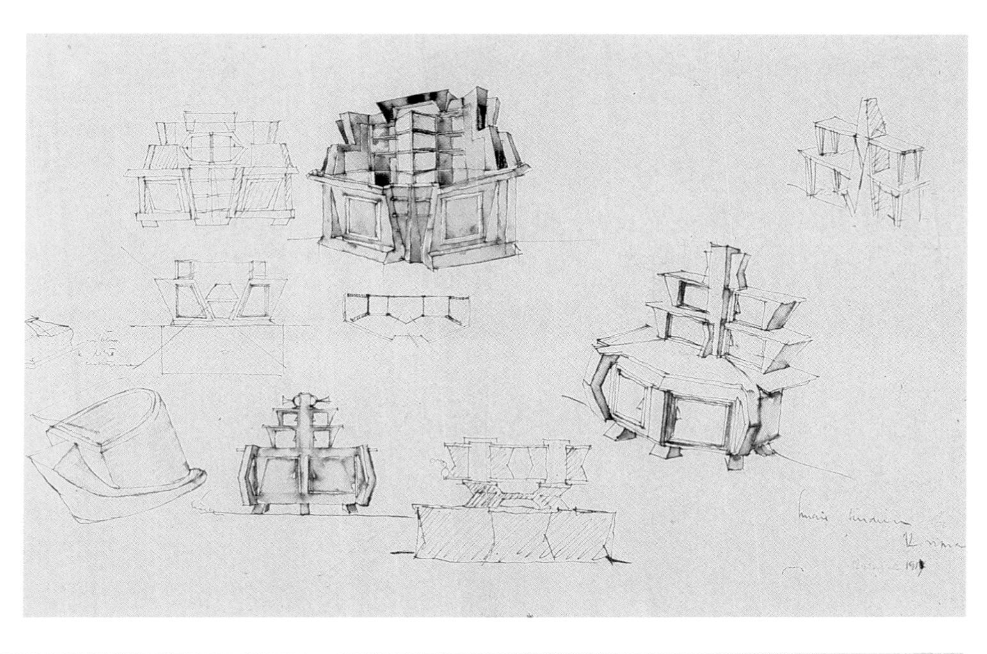

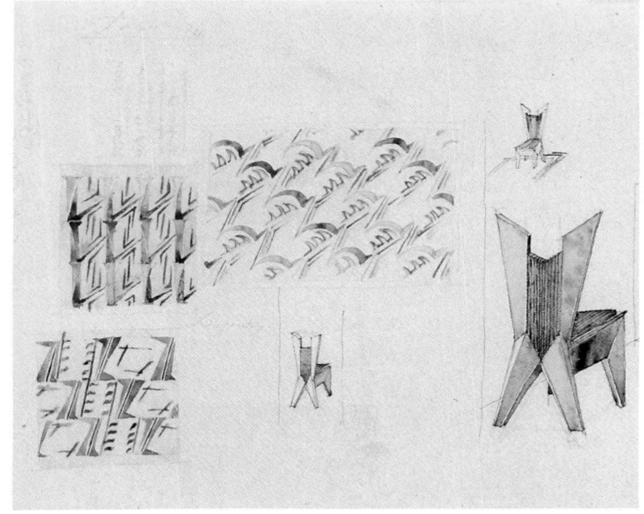

177.
Spatial study of dynamic property, 1918
Pastels
39 x 24.5 cm
Signed l.r. in pastel: "Kroha 18"
UPM inv. no. 92.247
Acquired in 1985
Exhib.: Tokyo, 1984 (cat. no. 170, repr.)

Interior of the Cabaret Montmartre, period photograph, private archive

175.
Study for a ceiling and walls, 1918
Pastels and tempera
28.5 x 43 cm
Study for the Cabaret Montmartre
UPM inv. no. 92.250
Acquired in 1985
Exhib.: Tokyo, 1984 (cat. no. 173, repr.)

176.
Detail study for a wall console, 1918
Pastels
28.5 x 43 cm
Designed for Cabaret Montmartre
UPM inv. no. 92.249
Acquired in 1985
Exhib.: Tokyo, 1984 (cat. no. 176, repr.);
Darmstadt, 1988–1989 (cat. no. 320, repr.)
Lit.: A) Císařovský, 1967; B) Lamarová, 1987

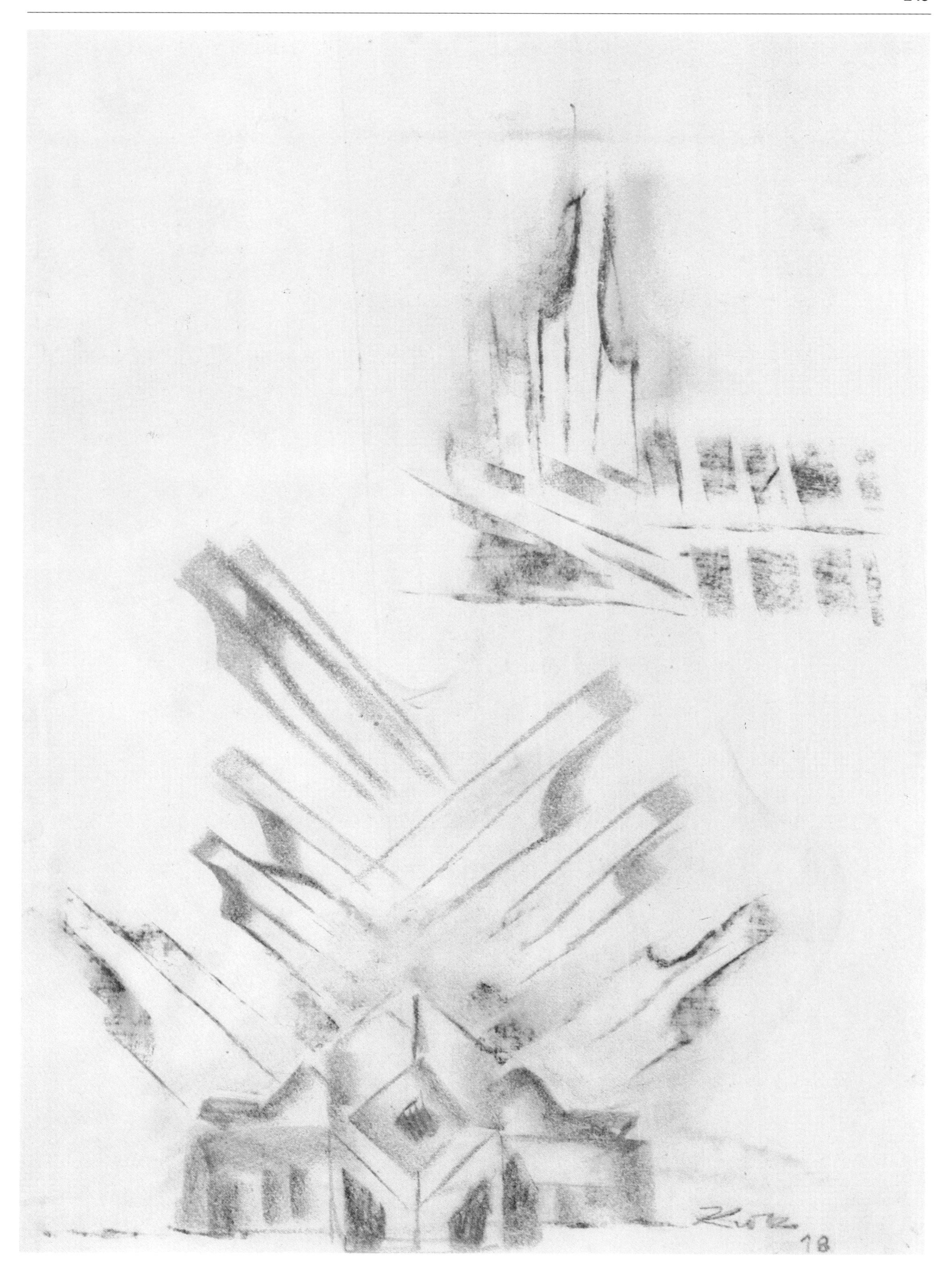

Otakar Novotný

Study and dining room, 1922
Cat. nos. 178–183
Designed for Dr. Ledeč
Manufactured by PUD
UPM inv. no. 66.541–6
Acquired in 1965 from the estate of Dr. Ledeč

178.
Sideboard, 1922
Black-stained oak, veneered, and glass
177 x 151 x 60 cm
UPM inv. no. 66.541
Exhib.: Prague, 1976 (cat. no. 110, repr.)

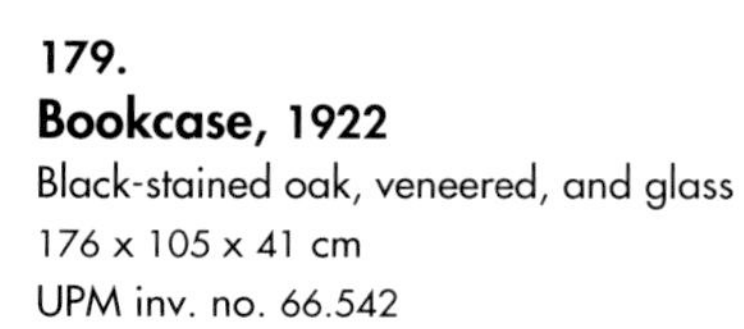

179.
Bookcase, 1922
Black-stained oak, veneered, and glass
176 x 105 x 41 cm
UPM inv. no. 66.542
Exhib.: Prague, 1976 (cat. no. 106, repr.)

180.
Armchair for writing desk, 1922
Black-stained oak, veneered, upholstered (Fabric design by F. Kysela, made by M. Teinitzerová)
112 x 59 x 65 cm
UPM inv. no. 66.544
Exhib.: Prague, 1971a; Prague, 1976 (cat. no. 108, repr.); Tokyo, 1984 (cat. no. 021, repr.); Darmstadt, 1988–1989 (cat. no. 430, repr.)
Lit.: A) Adlerová, 1983, repr. no. 26

181.

Dining-room side chairs, 1922

Black-stained oak, veneered, upholstered
(Fabric design by F. Kysela,
made by M. Teinitzerová)
110 x 43 x 43 cm
UPM inv. no. 66.546

Exhib.: Prague, 1967a; London, 1970; Prague, 1972 (cat. no. 75, repr.); Prague, 1976 (cat. nos. 112–115, repr.); Tokyo, 1984 (cat. no. 022, repr.); Darmstadt, 1988–1989 (cat. no. 431, repr.)
Lit.: A) Burkhardt & Lamarová, 1982; A) Adlerová, 1983, repr. no. 26

182.
Dining-room table, 1922
Black-stained oak, veneered
Height 77.5 cm, diameter 120 cm
UPM inv. no. 66.545
Exhib.: Prague, 1976 (cat. no. 111, repr.)

183.
Games table, 1922
Black-stained oak, veneered
78 x 60 x 60 cm
UPM inv. no. 66.650
Exhib.: Prague, 1976 (cat. no. 109, repr.)

Antonín Procházka

Studies for armchairs, 1911–1914
Cat. nos. 184a–d
MG Brno inv. nos. B 3456, 3467, 3454, 3458
Acquired in 1951 from Linka Procházková

184a.
Study for an armchair, 1911–1914
India ink
29 x 23 cm
MG Brno, inv. no. B 3456

184b.
Study for an armchair, 1911–1914
Graphite and india ink
29 x 23 cm
MG Brno, inv. no. B 3467

184c.
Study for an armchair, 1911–1914
Graphite and india ink
28.9 x 23 cm
MG Brno, inv. no. B 3454
Lit.: A) Burkhardt & Lamarová, 1982, repr. no. 159; A) Lamač, 1988, rep. no. 427

184d.
Studies for armchairs, 1911–1914
Graphite
29.1 x 23 cm
MG Brno, inv. no. B 3458

184.
Armchair, 1919
Black-stained oak
90 x 67 x 70 cm
Designed for the actress Nina Balcarová
MG Brno inv. no. 27.995
Acquired in 1983 from the estate of N. Balcarová

185.
Stool, 1919
Black-stained oak
47 x 47 x 47 cm
Designed for the actress Nina Balcarová
MG Brno inv. no. 28.421
Acquired in 1985

186.
Design for an armoire, ca. 1916
India ink and watercolour
29 x 22.9 cm
MG Brno inv. no. B 3449
Acquired in 1951 from Linka Procházková
Lit.: A) Burkhardt & Lamarová, 1982, repr. no. 20; A) Lamač, 1988, repr. no. 428

187.
Design for a table and chandelier, 1916
India ink and watercolour
29 x 22.9 cm
MG Brno inv. no. B 3452
Acquired in 1951 from Linka Procházková
Lit.: A) Burkhardt & Lamarová, 1982, repr. no. 21

188.
Design for an armchair and sofa, ca. 1916
(originally dated 1910, dating questionable)
India ink, watercolour, and crayon
23 x 29.1 cm
MG Brno inv. no. B 3463
Acquired in 1951 from Linka Procházková

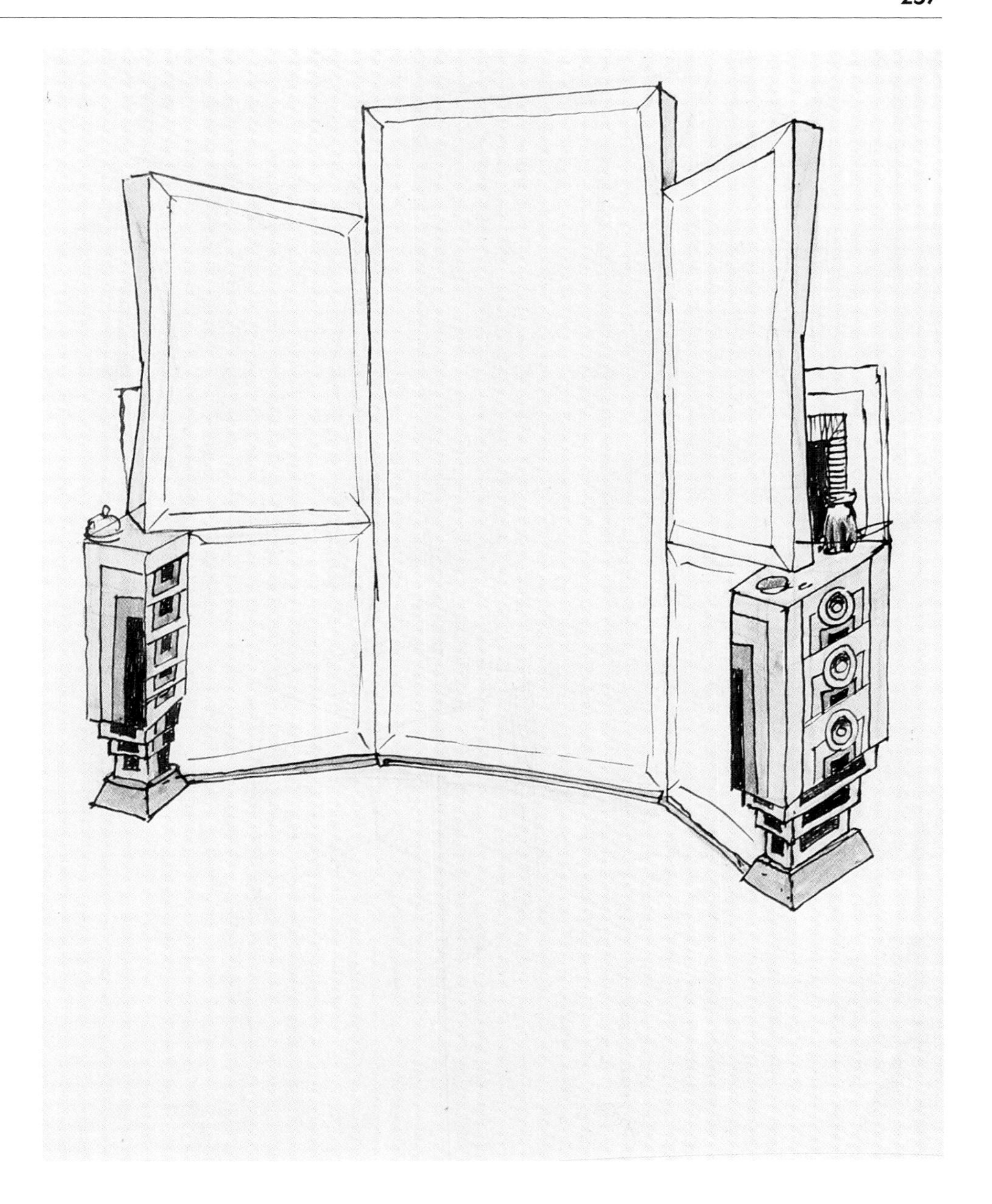

189.
Design for a mirror, ca. 1916
(originally dated 1910, dating questionable)
India ink and watercolour
29 x 23 cm
MG Brno inv. no. B 3443
Acquired in 1951 from Linka Procházková

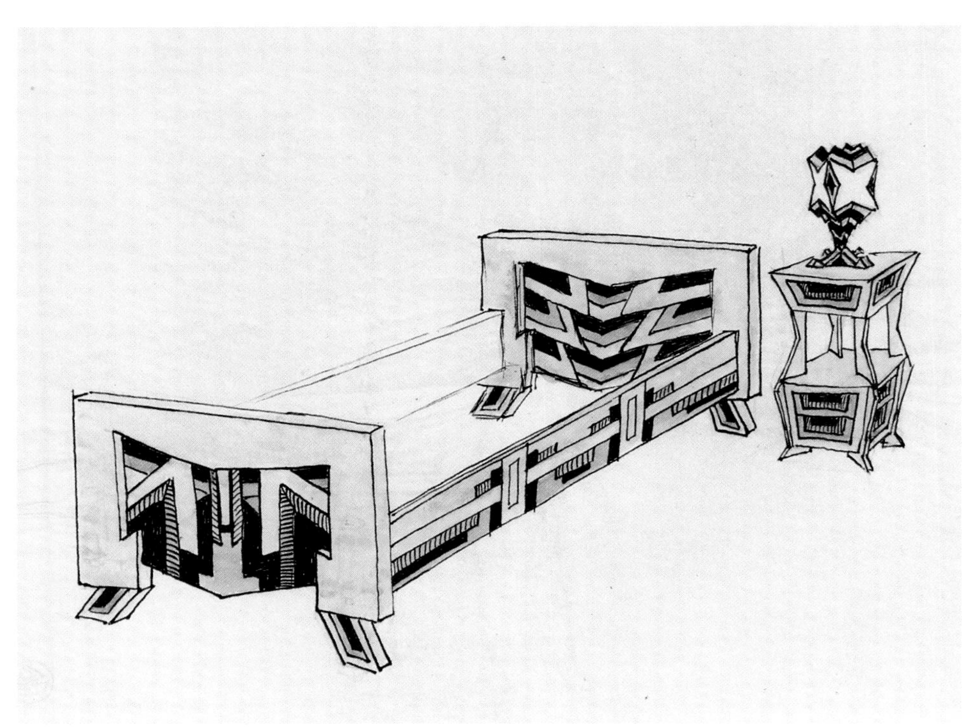

190.
Design for a bed and bedside table, ca. 1916
(originally dated 1910, dating questionable)
Graphite, india ink, and watercolour
22.8 x 29 cm
MG Brno inv. no. B 9937
Acquired in 1973

193.
Design for an armchair, 1917
India ink and watercolour
29 x 23 cm
Inscribed at l.c. in graphite:
"Armchair: light, golden-brown veneer
dark brown and black varnish"
MG Brno inv. no. 28.208
Acquired in 1951

191.
Design for a bookcase, ca. 1916
(originally dated 1910, dating questionable)
India ink and watercolour
22.8 x 29 cm
MG Brno inv. no. B 9937
Acquired in 1973

192.
Design for a writing desk, 1917–1919
India ink and watercolour
23 x 29 cm
MG Brno inv. no. B 3444
Acquired in 1951 from Linka Procházková

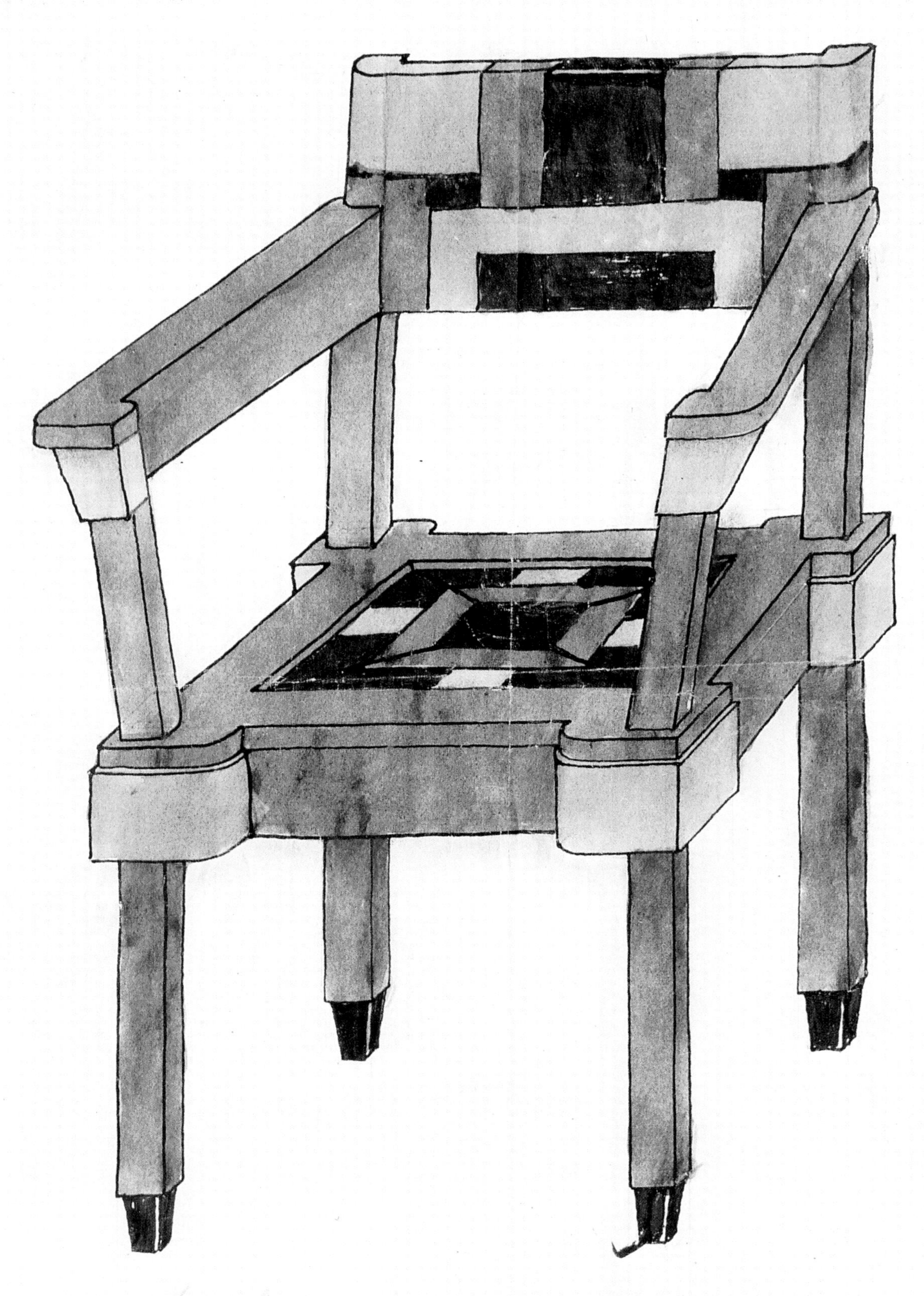
Křeslo : světlý,
černá politura

Rudolf Stockar

194.
Small table, 1910–1914
Brown-stained oak, brass, and opaque glass
79 x 90 x 60 cm
Manufactured by PUD
UPM inv. no. 89.718
Acquired in 1982
Exhib.: Malmö, 1982–1983 (cat. no. 326, repr.); Tokyo, 1984 (cat. no. 023, repr.); Darmstadt, 1988–1989 (cat. no. 578, repr.)

195.
Armchair, 1923
Polished rosewood, upholstered
73 x 58 x 54 cm
Designed for Jan Masaryk
UPM inv. no. 70.515
Acquired in 1965
Exhib.: Prague, 1972 (cat. no. 77, repr.); Tokyo, 1984 (cat. no. 024, repr.); Darmstadt, 1988–1989 (cat. no. 576, repr.)

Ceramics

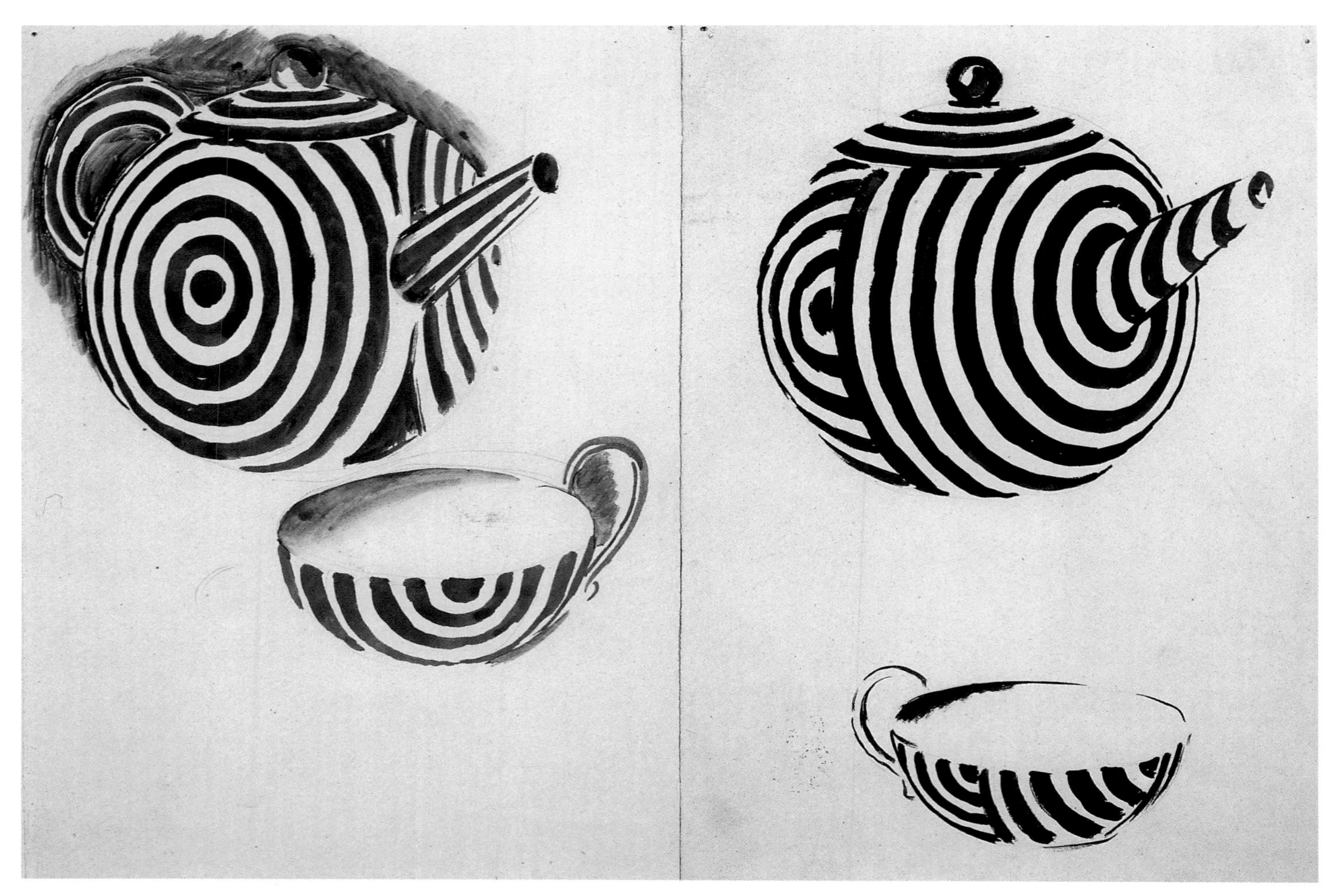

Bedřich Feuerstein

196.
Design for a tea set, 1919
Watercolour
32 x 42 cm
NTM Collection no. 109
Acquired in 1953 from J. Feuersteinová
Exhib.: Prague, 1967b

Ceramics produced by the Artěl Co-operative, manufactured by the firm Rydl and Thon in Svijany-Podolí, base marked with the Artěl logo

Josef Havlíček

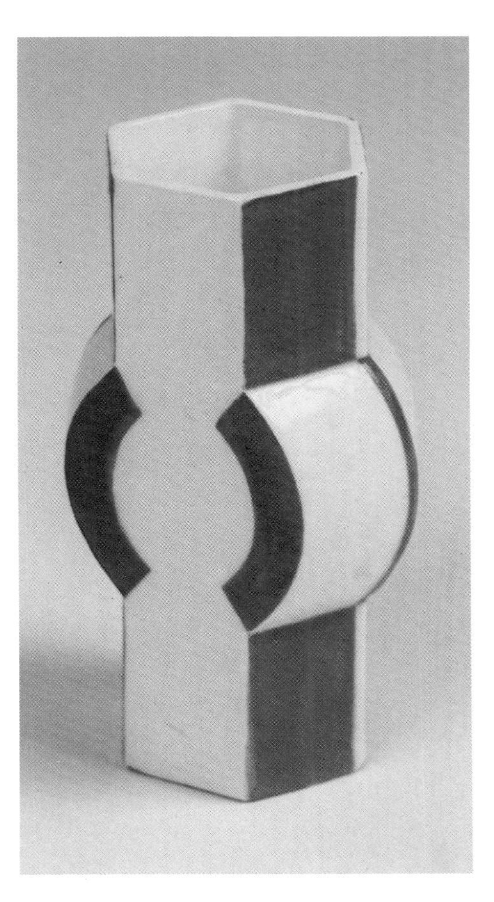

197.
Vase, ca. 1920
Earthenware, with painted
underglazing decoration
Height 20.5 cm
UPM inv. no. 30.833
Marked
Acquired in 1950
Exhib.: Prague, 1969 (cat. no. 45, no repr.),
London, 1970; Prague, 1976 (cat. no. 142, repr.)
Lit.: *Drobné umění*, no. 3, 1922, p. 7; B)
Vondráčková, 1968, p. 85

198.
Vase, ca. 1920
Earthenware, with green-grey glaze
Height 14 cm
Marked
UPM inv. no. 30.834
Acquired in 1950; since 1967, on long-term
loan for the MG Brno exhibition

Vlastislav Hofman

199.
Vase, 1911
Earthenware, with light-yellow glaze
Height 29.5 cm
Marked
UPM inv. no. 30.829
Exhib.: Paris, 1966 (cat. no. 137, repr.); Prague, 1976 (cat. no. 116, repr.); Tokyo, 1984 (cat. no. 056, repr.)
Lit.: *Styl* 5, 1912, p. 22; B) Vondráčková, 1968, p. 83; A) Neuwirth, 1974, p. 309; A) Burkhardt & Lamarová, 1982, p. 54; B) Behal, 1987b, repr. no. 3; B) Behal, 1988, p. 167

All objects designed by V. Hofman were acquired in 1950

200.
Creamer from a tea set, 1911
Earthenware, with white and red glaze
Height 14 cm
Marked
UPM inv. no. 30.852/1
Exhib.: Prague, 1976 (cat. no. 118, repr.); Tokyo, 1984 (cat. no. 057, repr.)
Lit.: *Umělecký měsíčník* 1, 1911–1912, p. 140; B) Vondráčková, 1968, p. 82; A) Lamač, 1988, repr. no. 228

201.
Coffee and tea set, 1911
Earthenware, with white glaze
and red decoration
Height of coffee pot 16.5 cm, height of teapot 12 cm, height of cup 4 cm, diameter of plate 18 cm
Marked
UPM inv. nos. 30.853/1, 2ab, 3, 4
Exhib.: Paris, 1966 (cat. no. 130, repr.); Prague, 1969 (cat. no. 47, repr.); Prague, 1976 (cat. no. 119, repr.); Tokyo, 1984 (cat. no. 059, repr.)
Lit.: *Umělecký měsíčník* 1, 1911–1912, p. 138; B) Brožová, 1967, p. 204

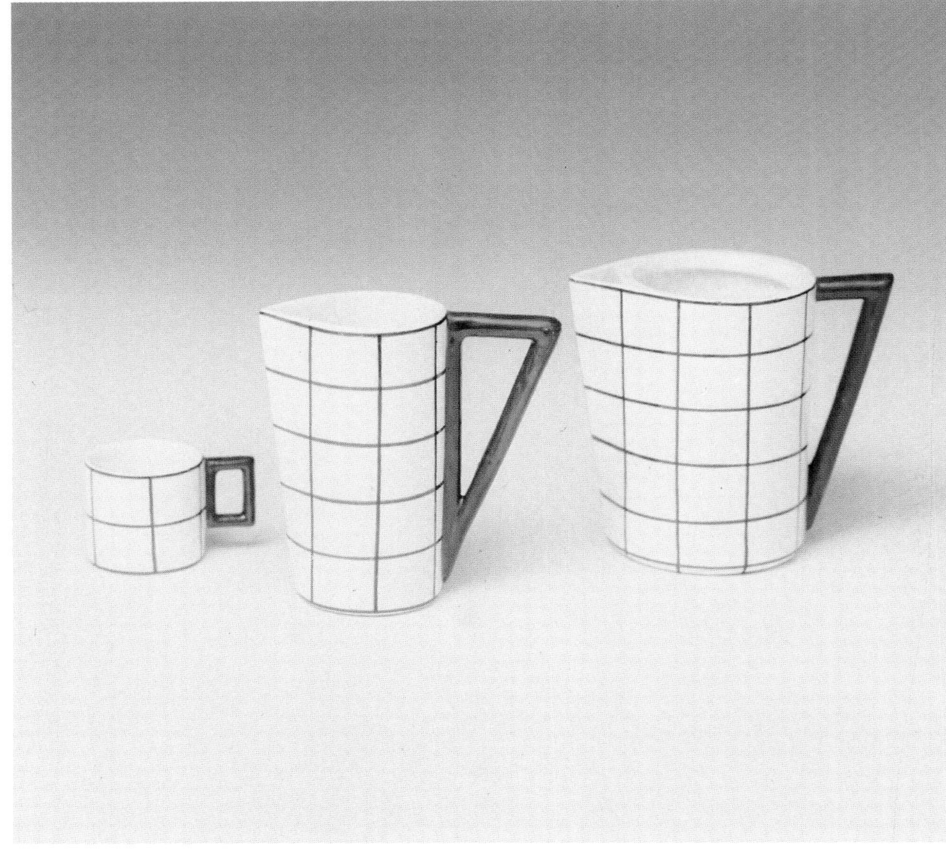

202.
Tea and coffee set, 1911
Earthenware, with white glaze
and red decoration
Height of creamer 14.5 cm, height of cup 5.5 cm, height of teapot 14.5 cm
Marked
UPM inv. nos. 30.854/1, 2, 51.583
Exhib.: Paris, 1966 (cat. no. 13, repr.); Prague, 1969 (cat. no. 46, repr.); Prague, 1976 (cat. no. 120, repr.); Tokyo, 1984 (cat. no. 058, repr.)
Lit.: *Umělecký měsíčník* 1, 1911–1912, p. 138

203.
Ashtray, ca. 1912
Earthenware, with black and white glaze
Height 4 cm
Marked
UPM inv. no. 30.842
Exhib.: Prague, 1976 (cat. no. 122, repr.);
Tokyo, 1984 (cat. no. 062, repr.)
Lit.: A) Burkhardt & Lamarová, 1982; A) Lamač,
1988, repr. no. 223

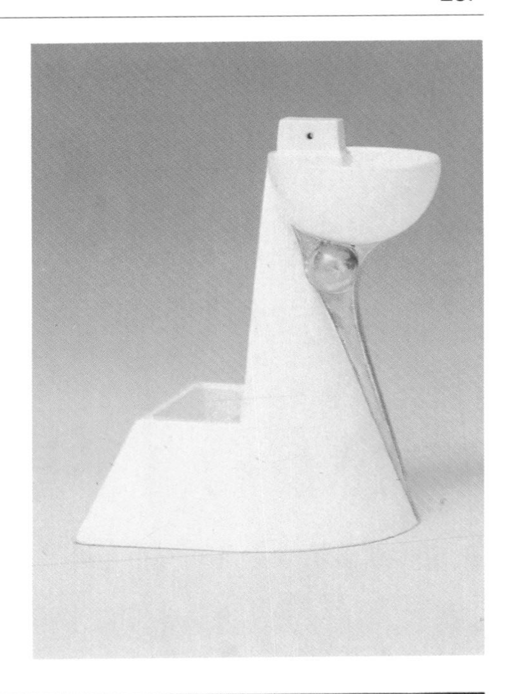

204.
Ashtray, ca. 1912
Earthenware, with white glaze
and gold decoration
Height 21 cm
UPM inv. no. 30.843
Exhib.: Prague, 1976 (cat. no. 123, repr.);
Tokyo, 1984 (cat. no. 061, repr.)
Lit.: B) Vondráčková, 1968, p. 85

205.
Coffee set, 1913
Earthenware, with ivory-coloured glaze
Height of coffee pot 17.5 cm, height of
creamer 11 cm, height of sugar bowl 11 cm,
height of mug 5 cm
UPM inv. no. 30.851/1ab, 2, 3–4ab, 7–8ab; on
long-term loan for the MG Brno exhibition

206.
Coffee set, 1913–1914
Earthenware, with white glaze
and black decoration
Height of coffee pot 17.5 cm, height of creamer 11 cm, height of sugar bowl 11 cm, height of mug 5 cm
Marked
UPM no. 30.850/1ab, 2, 3–5ab
Exhib.: Prague, 1967a; Prague, 1969 (unnumb., repr.); London, 1970; Prague, 1976 (cat. no. 124, repr.); Tokyo, 1984 (cat. no. 063, repr.)
Lit.: B) Vondráčková, 1968, p. 85 (mistakenly attributed to P. Janák); A) Burkhardt & Lamarová, 1982, repr. no. 203

207.
Small vase, ca. 1914
Earthenware, with white glaze
and red-brown decoration
Height 15 cm
Marked
UPM no. 30.836
Exhib.: Paris, 1966 (cat. no. 136, repr.); Prague, 1969; Prague, 1976 (cat. no. 126, repr.); Tokyo, 1984 (cat. no. 064, repr.)
Lit.: B) Vondráčková, 1968, p. 84 (mistakenly attributed to P. Janák); A) Burkhardt & Lamarová, 1982, repr. no. 196; A) Lamač, 1988, repr. no. 224

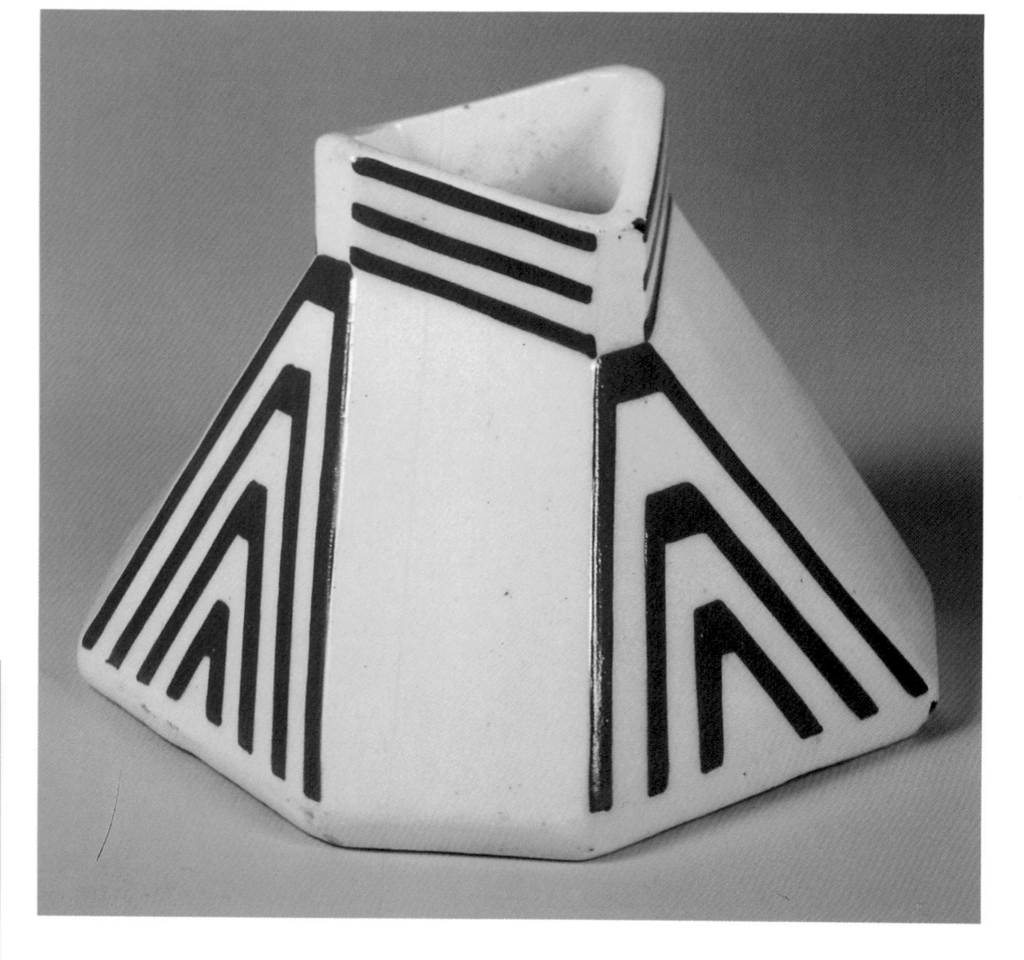

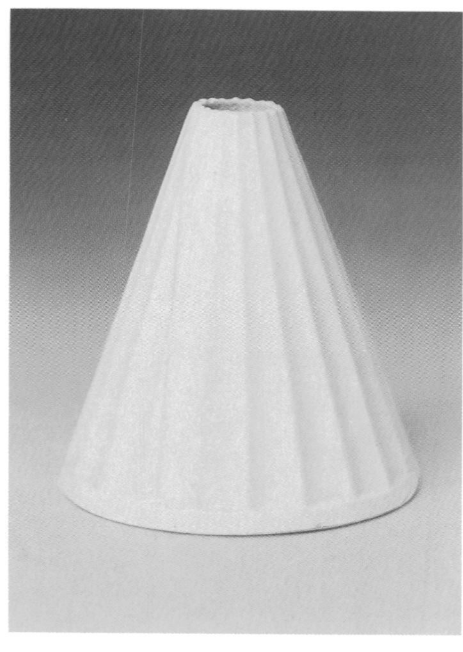

208.
Vase, 1916
Earthenware, with ivory-coloured glaze
Height 23 cm
UPM no. 30.837
Exhib.: Paris, 1966 (cat. no. 136, repr.); Prague, 1969 (cat. no. 53, repr.); Prague, 1976 (cat. no. 117, repr.); Tokyo, 1984 (cat. no. 065, repr.)

209.
Two inkwells, 1916
Earthenware, with white and cobalt glaze and green and gold decoration
Height 7 cm
Marked
UPM inv. nos. 30.841/1, 2
Exhib.: Prague, 1976 (cat. no. 121 repr.); Tokyo, 1984 (cat. no. 066, repr.)

210.
Wooden model of a vase, ca. 1918
Wood, with white lacquer and black decoration
Height 25 cm
UPM inv. no. 30.835
Exhib.: Prague, 1976 (cat. no. 149, repr.)

211.
Two vases, ca. 1919
Stoneware, with white glaze
and black decoration
Height 25 cm
Marked
Private collection

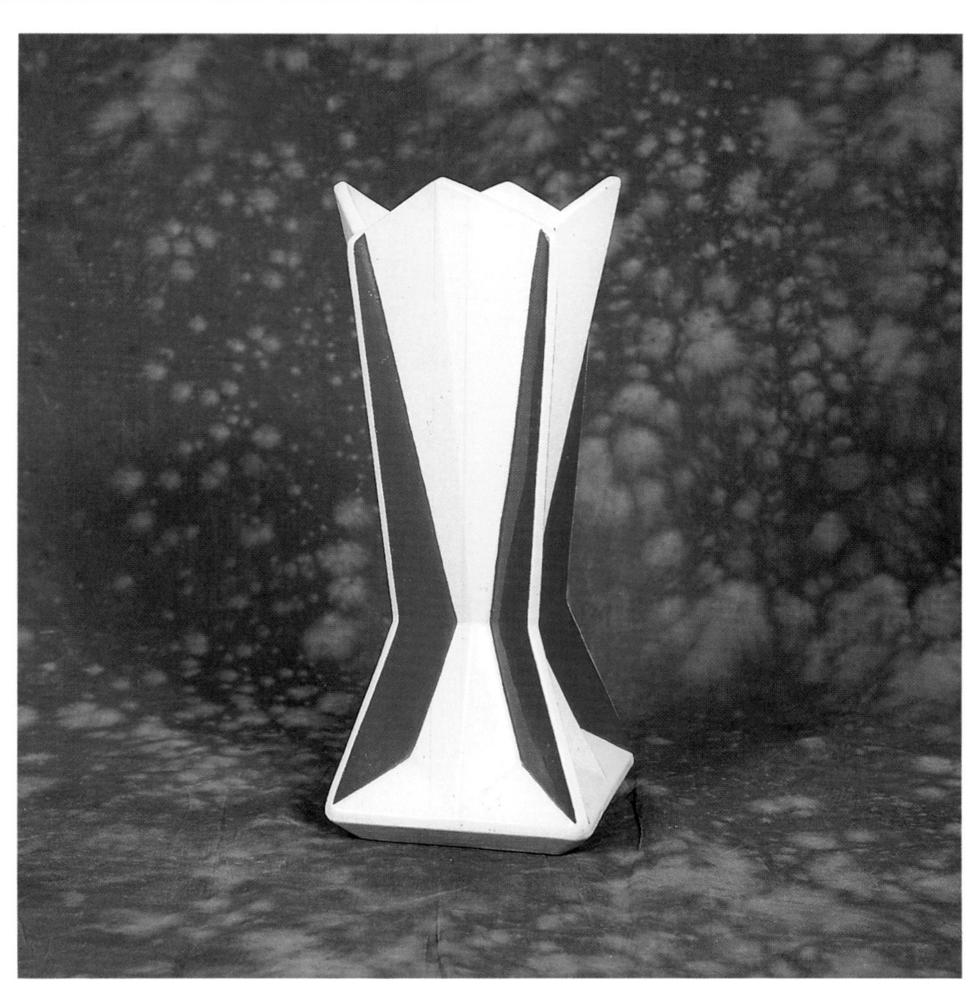

212.
Vase, 1919
Stoneware, with white glaze and red decoration
Height 38 cm
Marked
Notation on base in india ink
Sales exhibition of Artěl at the Museum of
the Industrial Arts in Prague in 1919
Private collection

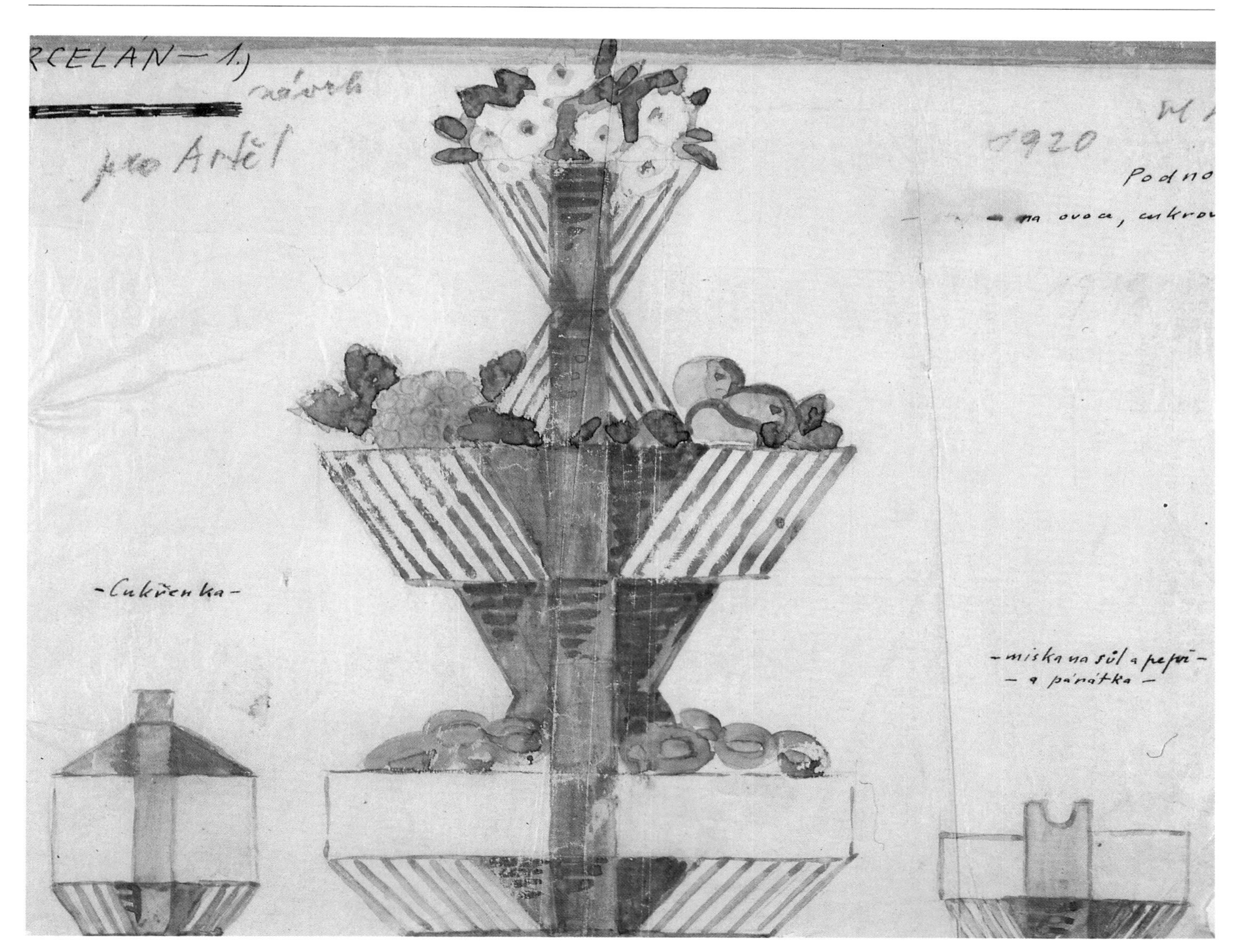

213.
Design for a porcelain table service, 1920
Watercolour
19 x 24 cm
Signed u.r. in graphite: "1920 Vl H"
Inscribed u.l. in pen and graphite:
"Porcelain 1) design for Artěl"
Descriptions in india ink
Designed for Artěl
Private archive

Jaroslav Horejc

214.
Vase, 1911
Earthenware, with black and white glaze
Height 21 cm
Marked
UPM inv. no. 30.827
Acquired in 1950
Exhib.: Paris, 1966; Prague, 1969 (cat. no. 49 [mistakenly attributed to V. Hofman]); Prague, 1976 (cat. no. 141, repr.); Tokyo, 1984 (cat. no. 068, repr.)
Lit.: B) Vondráčková, 1968 (under no. 248 mistakenly attributed to V. Hofman); A) Neuwirth, 1974, p. 311; A) Burkhardt & Lamarová, 1982, repr. no. 197; B) Behal, 1988, p. 173

215.
Vase, 1911
Earthenware, with blue and white glaze
Height 26 cm
UPM inv. no. 30.825/1
Acquired in 1950; from 1967, on long-term loan for the MG Brno exhibition
Lit.: A) Neuwirth, 1974, p. 311

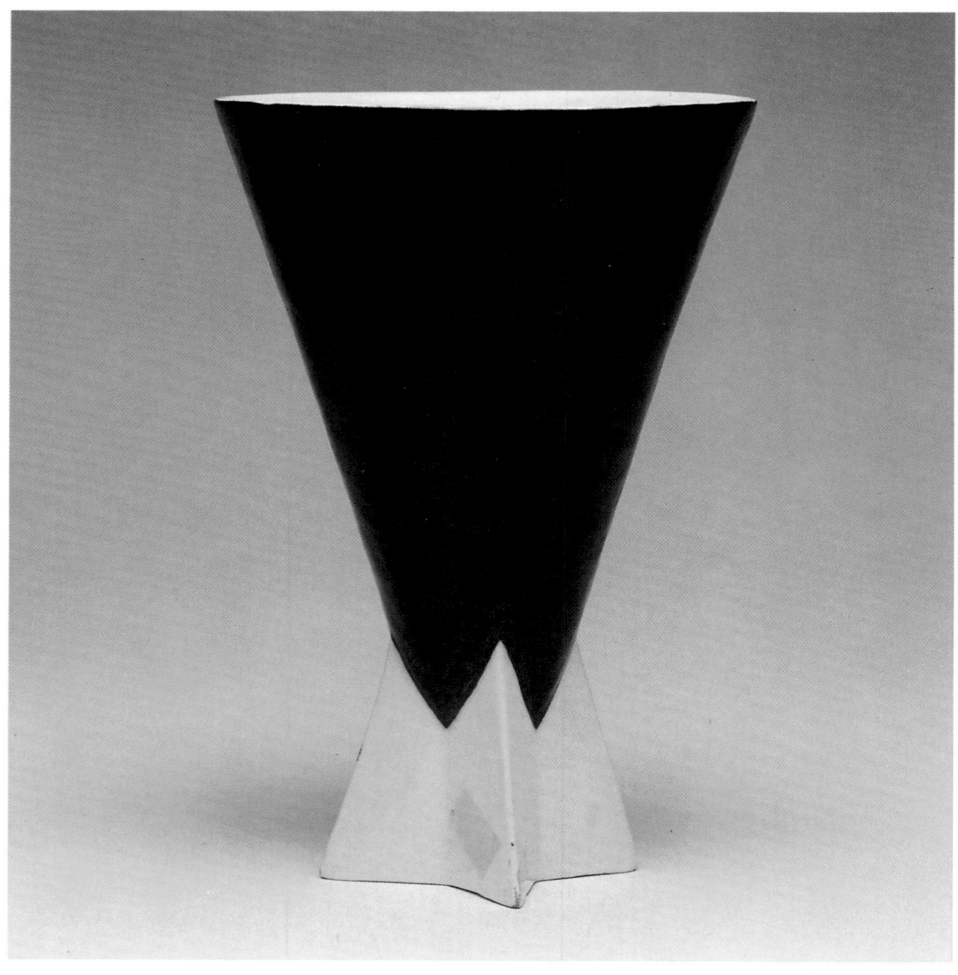

Pavel Janák

216.
Two designs for covered boxes, 1910
Graphite, india ink, and watercolour
19 x 13 cm; 12.5 x 11 cm

NTM Collection no. 85
Acquired in 1957
Exhib.: Prague, Vienna, Helsinki, 1982–1987 (cat. no. 32, no repr.)

217.
Covered box, 1911

Earthenware, with ivory-coloured glaze and black decoration
Height 9 cm
UPM inv. no. 75.894
Acquired in 1972
Exhib.: Prague, 1976 (cat. no. 127, repr.); Prague, Vienna, Helsinki, 1982–1987 (cat. no. 6, repr.); Tokyo, 1984 (cat. no. 036, repr.)
Lit.: A) Burkhardt & Lamarová, 1982, repr. no. 191; A) Adlerová, 1983, repr. no. 5; A) Lamač, 1988, repr. no. 212

218.
Covered box, 1911
Earthenware, white glaze, black decoration
Height 13 cm
Marked: "MG Brno, inv. no. 20.892"
Acquired in 1969

219.
Covered box, 1911
Earthenware, white glaze, black decoration
Height 12 cm
Marked
UPM inv. no. 30.844/1
Acquired in 1950
Exhib.: Paris, 1966 (cat. nos. 141, 142, repr.); London, 1970; Prague, 1976 (cat. no. 128, repr.); Prague, Vienna, Helsinki, 1982–1987 (cat. no. 7, repr.)
Lit.: *Umělecký měsíčník* 1, 1911–1912, p. 136; B) Vondráčková, 1968, p. 85; B) Behal, 1988, p. 166

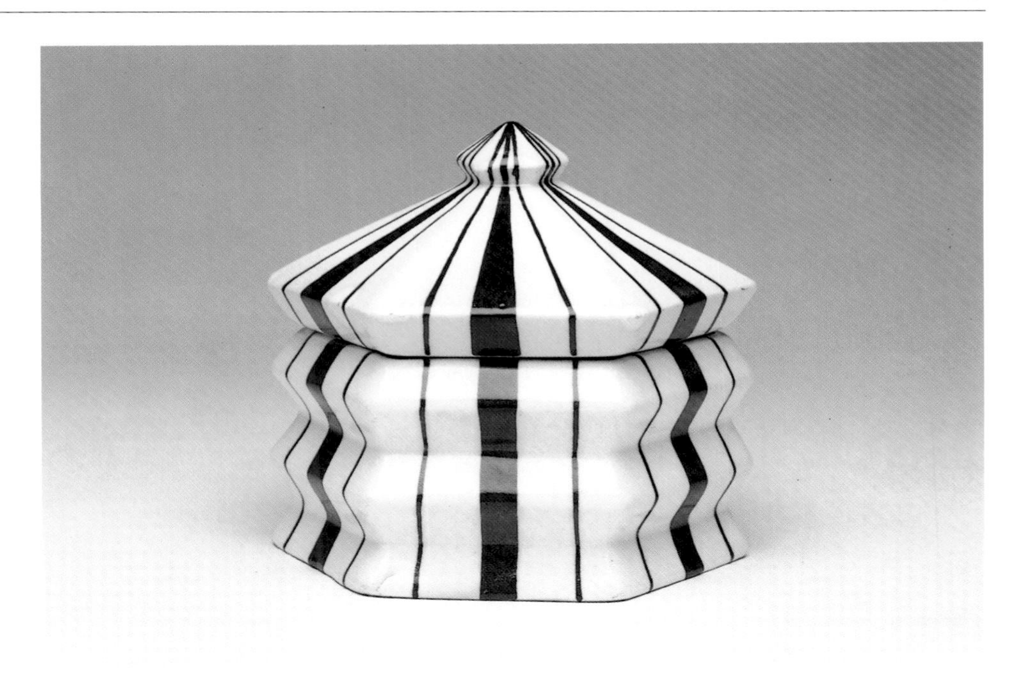

220.
Six covered boxes, 1911
Earthenware, with white glaze and black, blue, brown, and gold decoration
30.844/2–5ab height 12 cm, 30.844/6ab height 8.5 cm, 30.844/7ab height 8 cm
Marked
UPM inv. nos. 30.844/2–7ab
Acquired in 1950
Exhib.: Paris, 1966 (cat. nos. 141, 142, repr.); London, 1970 (cat. no. 128, repr.); Prague, 1976 (cat. no. 128, repr.); Prague, Vienna, Helsinki, 1982–1987 (cat. no. 7, repr.)
Lit.: B) Vondráčková, 1968, p. 85

221.
Covered box, 1911
Earthenware, with white glaze
and green decoration
Height 12 cm
Marked
UPM inv. no. 16.179
Acquired in 1927
Exhib.: Tokyo, 1984 (cat. no. 041, repr.)
Lit.: Lamač, 1988, repr. no. 217

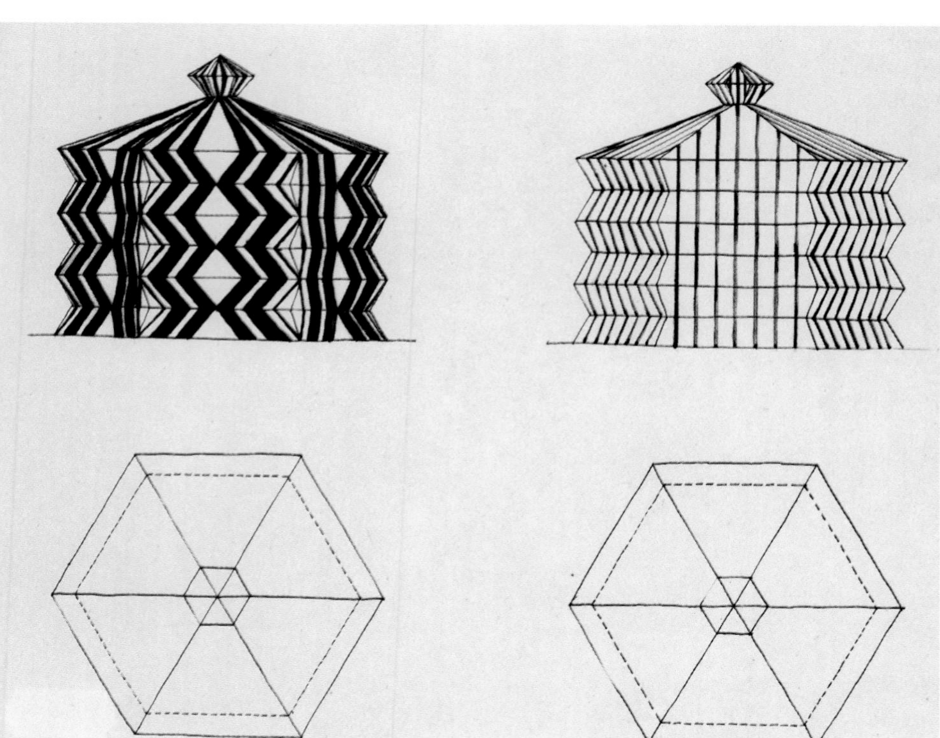

222.
Design for a covered box, ca. 1910
India ink
42 x 46 cm
NTM Collection no. 85
Acquired in 1957
Exhib.: Tokyo, 1984 (cat. no. 108, repr.)

223.
Coffee set (partial), 1911
Earthenware, with white and black glaze
Coffee cup with saucer height 7 cm, sugar bowl height 8.5 cm, smaller pot with lid height 15.5 cm, large pot height 21.5 cm
Marked
UPM inv. nos. 95.217/5ab, 95.216ab, 66.503ab, 66.501ab
Acquired in 1950
Exhib.: Prague, 1976 (cat. no. 133, repr.); Tokyo, 1984 (cat. no. 047, repr.)

224.
Coffee set (partial), 1911
Earthenware, with white glaze
and gold decoration
Pot height 21 cm, cup height 7 cm
Marked
UPM inv. no. 30.845/1ab–3
Acquired in 1950
Exhib.: Tokyo, 1984 (cat. no. 049, repr.)

225.
Coffee set (partial), 1911
Earthenware, with white glaze
and black decoration
Coffee pot with lid height 22 cm, creamer with lid height 14 cm, sugar bowl height 11.5 cm, cup with saucer height 6.8 cm
Marked
UPM inv. no. 30.846/1ab, 73.520ab,
73.521ab, 52.190ab
Acquired in 1950
Exhib.: Prague, 1976 (cat. no. 132, repr.); Tokyo, 1984 (cat. no. 048, repr.); Prague, Vienna, Helsinki, 1982–1987 (cat. no. 5, repr.)
Lit.: *Umělecký měsíčník* 1, 1911–1912, p. 9; *Drobné umění* 2, 1921, p. 31; A) Burkhardt & Lamarová, 1982, repr. no. 195; A) Lamač, 1988, repr. no. 222

226.

Vase, 1911

Earthenware, with ivory-colored glaze
Height 23.5 cm
Marked
UPM inv. no. 30.826
Acquired in 1950
Exhib.: Paris, 1966 (cat. no. 148, repr.); Prague, 1967; Prague, 1969 (cat. no. 64, repr.); Prague, 1976 (cat. no. 140, repr.); Tokyo, 1984 (cat. no. 033, repr.)
Lit.: *Umelecky mesícník* 1, 1911–1912, p. 6

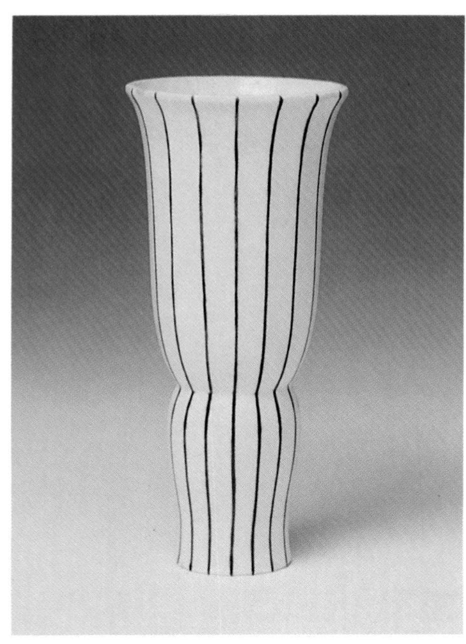

227.

Vase, 1911

Earthenware, with white glaze and black decoration
Height 29 cm
Marked
UPM inv. no. 54.976
Acquired in 1962
Exhib.: Paris, 1966; Prague, 1969 (cat. no. 63, repr.); Prague, 1976 (cat. no. 139, repr.); Tokyo, 1984 (cat. no. 034, repr.)
Lit.: *Umelecky mesícník* 1, 1911–1912, p. 6; A) Neuwirth, 1974, p. 214; A) Lamac, 1988, repr. no. 218

228.

Compotier, 1911

Earthenware, with ivory-coloured glaze and black decoration
Height 13 cm
UPM inv. no. 30.855
Acquired in 1950
Exhib.: Paris, 1966 (cat. no. 141, repr.); Prague, 1969 (cat. no. 64, repr.); Prague, Vienna, Helsinki, 1982–1987 (cat. no. 2, repr.); Tokyo, 1984 (cat. no. 050, repr.)
Lit.: *Umělecký měsíčník* 1, 1911–1912, p. 6; *Drobné umění* 2, 1921, p. 32; A) Lamač, 1988, repr. no. 218

229.
Compotier, 1911
Earthenware, with ivory-coloured glaze and black decoration
Height 12.3 cm
Marked
UPM inv. no. 73.270
Acquired in 1969
Exhib.: Prague, Vienna, Helsinki, 1982–1987 (cat. no. 2, repr.)
Lit.: A) Lamač, 1988, repr. no. 218

Period photograph, SÚPPOP Archive, Štenc Collection

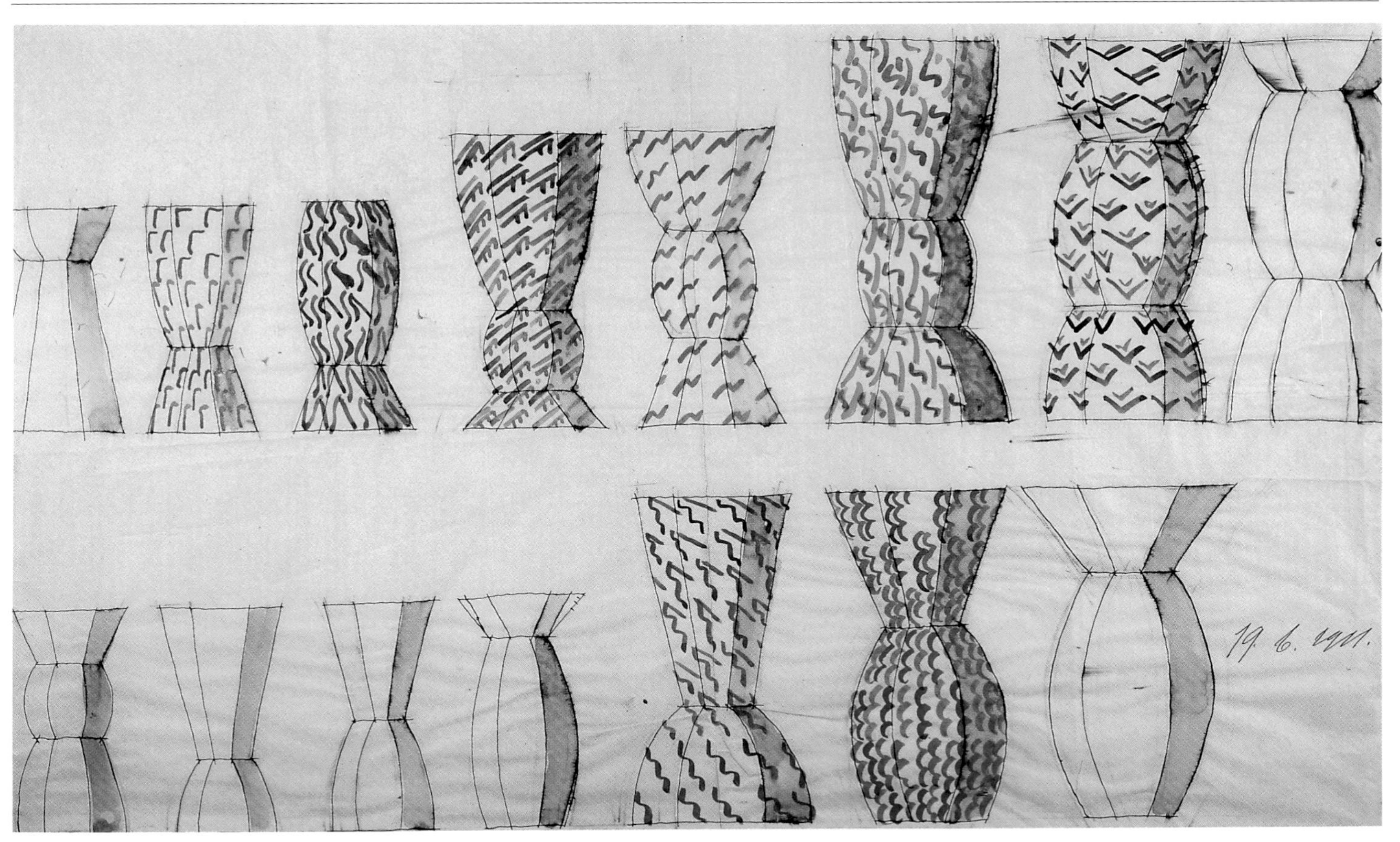

230.
Designs for ceramic vases, 1911
India ink and watercolour
79.5 x 53.5 cm
Dated l.r. in india ink: "19.6.1911"
NTM Collection no. 85
Acquired in 1957
Exhib.: Prague, Vienna, Helsinki,
1982–1987 (cat. no. 36, repr.)
A) Burkhardt & Lamarová, 1982, repr. no. 194

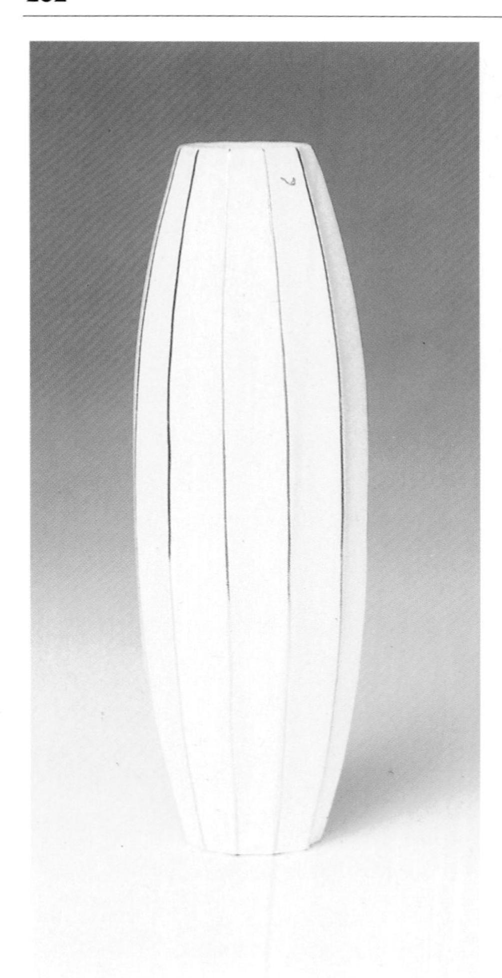

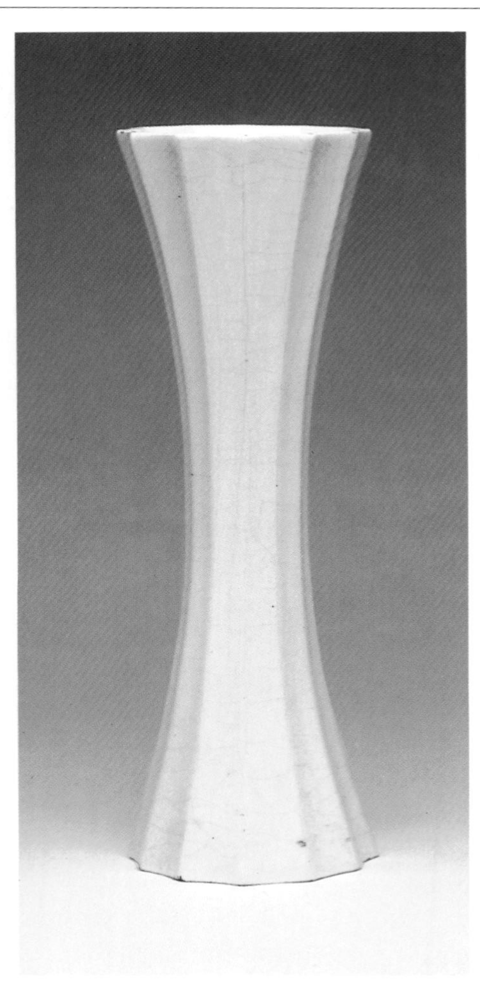

232.
Vase, 1911
Stoneware, with white glaze
Height 33 cm
MG Brno inv. no. 15.099
Acquired in 1958

231.
Vase, 1911
Earthenware, with white glaze
and gold decoration
Height 31.8 cm
Embossed: "159 1"
UPM inv. no. 45.170
Acquired in 1957
Exhib.: Prague, 1976 (cat. no. 13, repr.);
Tokyo, 1984 (cat. no. 051, repr.)

233.
Two vases, 1911
Stoneware, with white glaze and gold decoration
Height 24 cm
Marked
UPM inv. no. 30.598/1, 2
Acquired in 1949
Exhib.: Paris, 1966 (cat. no. 145, repr.); Prague,
1969 (cat. no. 61, no repr.); London, 1970;
Prague, 1976 (cat. no. 137, repr.)
Lit.: *Umělecký měsíčník* 1, 1911–1912, p. 7;
B) Vondráčková, 1968, p. 83; A) Lamač, 1988,
repr. no. 221

235.
Four vases, 1911
Porcelain, with black glaze and white decoration
Height 32.5 cm, 26 cm, 13.5 cm
Manufactured by J. Schnabel, Desná
UPM inv. no. 96.588, 45.168–9, 86.540
Acquired in 1988

236.
Two vases, 1911
Earthenware, with black and white glaze
Height 12.6 cm
Marked
UPM inv. no. 96.587–8
Acquired in 1990

234.
Two vases, 1911
Earthenware, with black and white glaze
Height 30 cm, 13.5 cm
One vase marked: "inv. no. 45.167"
UPM inv. no. 90.379, 45.167
Acquired in 1983, 1957
Exhib.: Prague, 1969 (cat. no. 60, repr. [smaller vase]); Prague, Vienna, Helsinki, 1982–1987 (cat. no. 2, repr.)

Period photograph, SÚPPOP Archive, Štenc Collection

237.

Two vases, 1911

Earthenware, with black and white glaze
Height 32 cm
Marked
UPM inv. no. 96.584–5
Acquired in 1988

238.
Covered box, 1912

Earthenware, with ivory-coloured glaze and black and gold decoration
Height 11.5 cm
Marked
UPM inv. no. 65.994
Acquired in 1965
Exhib.: London, 1970; Prague, 1976 (cat. no. 131, repr.); Prague, Vienna, Helsinki, 1982–1987 (cat. no. 12, repr.); Tokyo, 1984 (cat. no. 045, repr.)
Lit.: A) Burkhardt & Lamarová, 1982, repr. no. 202

239.
Coffee set (partial), 1912

Earthenware, with white glaze and blue decoration
Larger pot with lid height 19 cm, smaller pot with lid height 15 cm, sugar bowl height 13 cm, diameter of plate 15 cm
Marked
UPM inv. no. 30.849/1–4
Acquired in 1950
Exhib.: Prague, 1976 (cat. no. 135, repr.); Tokyo, 1984 (cat. no. 053, repr.)

240.
Covered box, 1914
Stoneware, with white glaze and red, green, black, and gold decoration
(Ornamental design by F. Kysela)
Height 11.5 cm
UPM inv. no. 89.850ab
Acquired in 1982
Exhib.: Tokyo, 1984 (cat. no. 042, repr.)

241.
Covered box, 1915
Earthenware, with white glaze and brown and gold decoration
Height 21 cm
Marked
UPM inv. no. 92.941ab
Acquired in 1965
Exhib.: Tokyo, 1984 (cat. no. 046, repr.); Darmstadt, 1988–1989 (cat. no. 244, repr.)

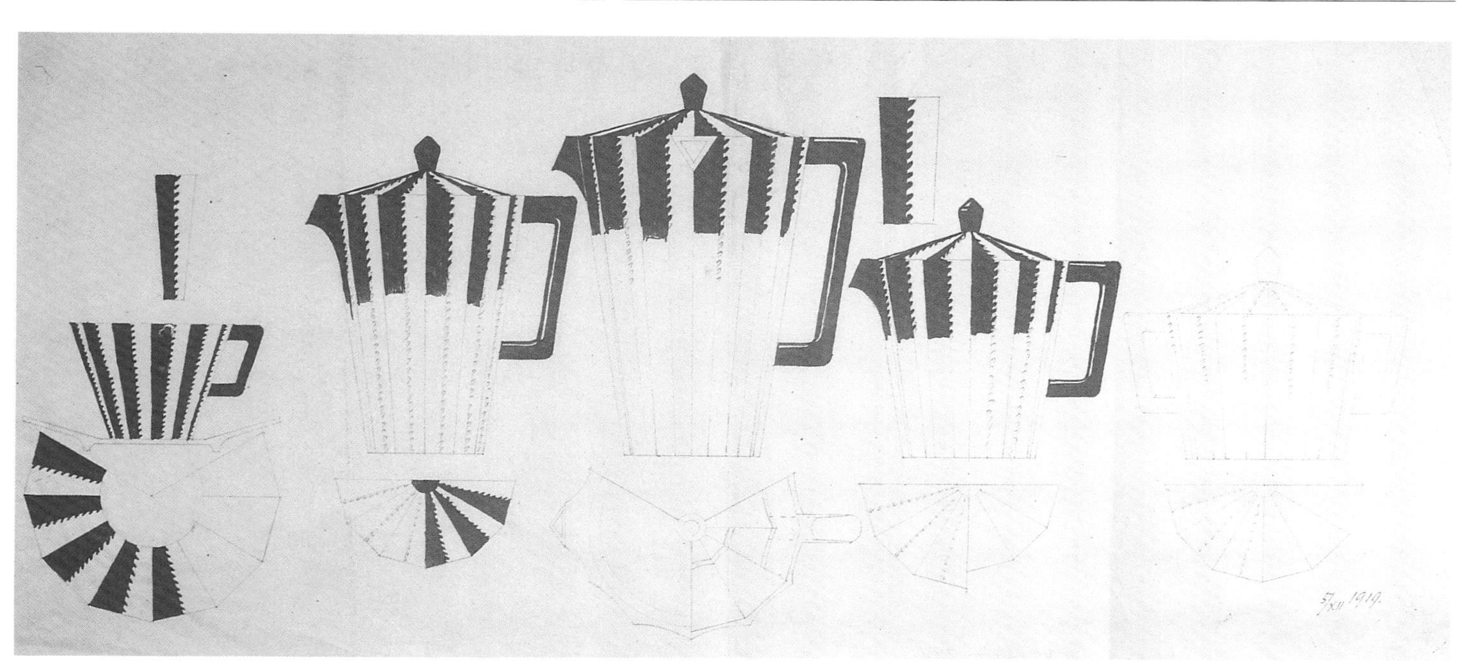

242.
Coffee set (partial), 1919
Three coffee pots with lids
Earthenware, with white glaze
and red decoration
Height 22 cm, 19 cm, 15 cm
Marked

UPM inv. no. 30.848/1–3
Acquired in 1950
Exhib.: Prague, 1976 (cat. no. 134, repr.);
Tokyo, 1984 (cat. no. 052, repr.); Darmstadt,
1988–1989 (cat. no. 242, repr.)
Lit.: A) Burkhardt & Lamarová, 1982,
repr. no. 199

242a.
Design for a coffee set, 1919
Graphite and watercolour
38.5 x 84.5 cm
Dated u.l.: "5.XII.1919"
NTM Collection no. 85
Acquired in 1957
Exhib.: Tokyo, 1984 (cat. no. 152, repr.)

243.
Two covered boxes, ca. 1915
Earthenware, with white glaze and red, green, blue, and gold decoration
Height 21.5 cm, 17 cm
UPM inv. no. 30.862/1, 2ab
Acquired in 1950
Exhib.: Malmö, 1982–1983 (cat. no. 306, repr.); Tokyo, 1984 (cat. nos. 043, 044 repr.); Darmstadt, 1988–1989 (cat. no. 243, repr.)
Lit.: B) Brožová, 1967, pp. 202–208; A) Burkhardt & Lamarová, 1982, repr. no. 204; A) Adlerová, 1983, pp. 222–223

Jiří Kroha

245.
Ceramics studies, 1917–1919
Graphite and india ink, coloured
27 x 46.5 cm
Signed u.l.: "K"
From a 30-page sketch book
on cardboard, p. 11
UPM inv. no. 92.254
Acquired in 1985

244.
Coffee set, ca. 1920
Porcelain, with black and white
glaze and blue decoration
Height of coffee pot 14.8 cm, height of
sugar bowl 11.5 cm, height of cup 5 cm
Manufactured by J. Schnabel, Desná
Marked with manufacturer's stamp
UPM inv. no. 63.032ab-3,4,6,8ab
Acquired in 1964
Exhib.: Tokyo, 1984 (cat. no. 054, repr.);
Darmstadt, 1988–1989 (cat. no. 244, repr.)

246.
Three coloured studies, 1917–1919
Graphite, charcoal, and pastel
a. 15 x 22 cm, b. 19 x 27.5 cm, c. 20 x 16 cm
Signed l.r.: "JK"
UPM inv. no. 92.245/a, b, c
Acquired in 1985
Exhib.: Tokyo, 1984 (cat. no. 174, repr. [drawings a and b only])

247.

Designs for vessels and lamps, 1918

Graphite and pastel
19.5 x 25 cm
Illegible notation in graphite l.l.
UPM inv. no. 92.257/a,b
Acquired in 1985
Exhib.: Darmstadt, 1988–1989
(cat. no. 324, repr.)

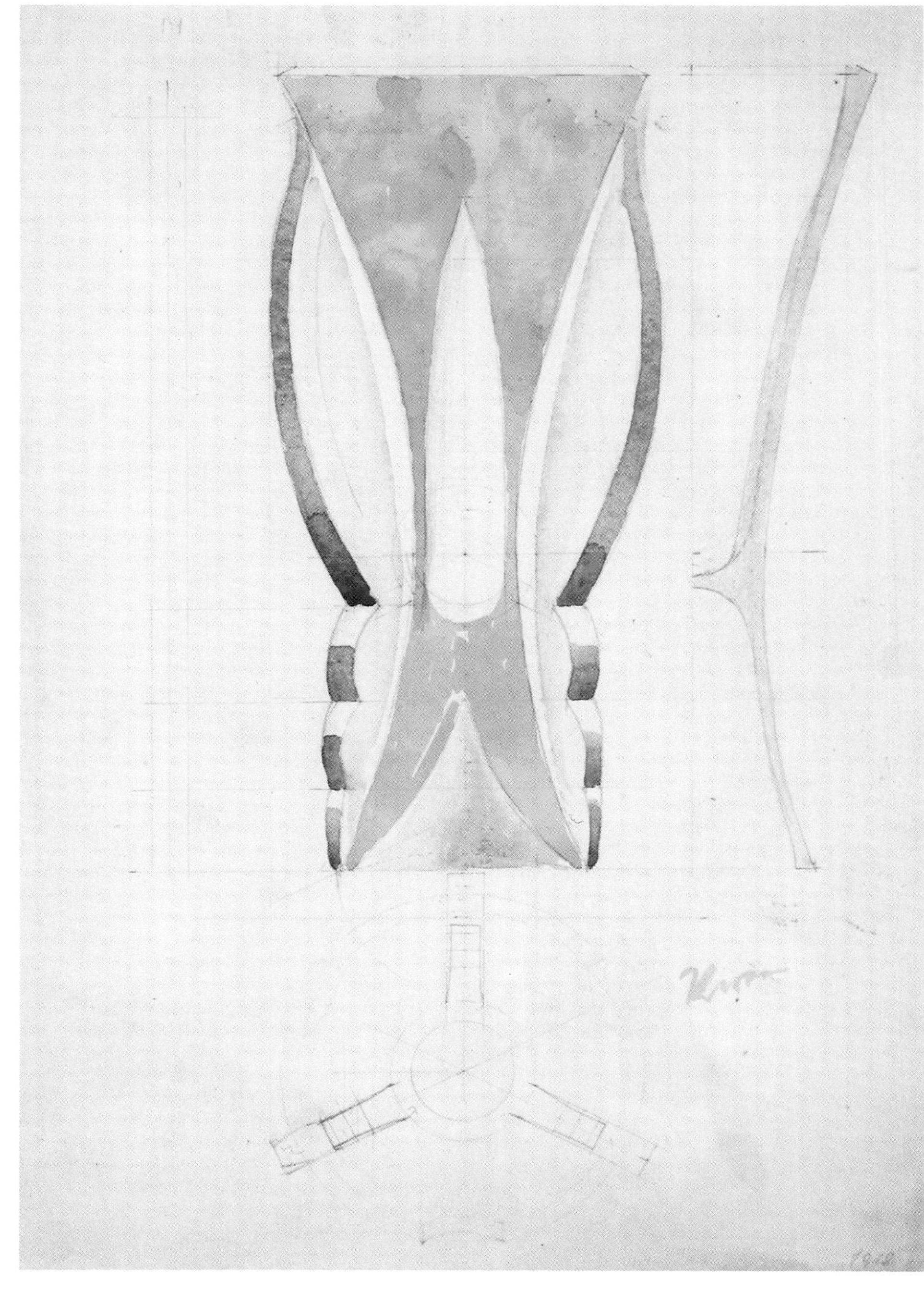

248.

Design for a vase, 1918

Graphite and watercolour
44 x 29.5 cm
Signed l.r. in graphite: "Kroha 1918"
UPM inv. no. 92.252
Acquired in 1985

249.
Two designs for an inkwell, 1918
Graphite and watercolour
22 x 29.5 cm
Inscribed in graphite, drawing b,
u.r.: "inkwell, glass, metal"
UPM inv. no. 92.241/a,b
Acquired in 1985

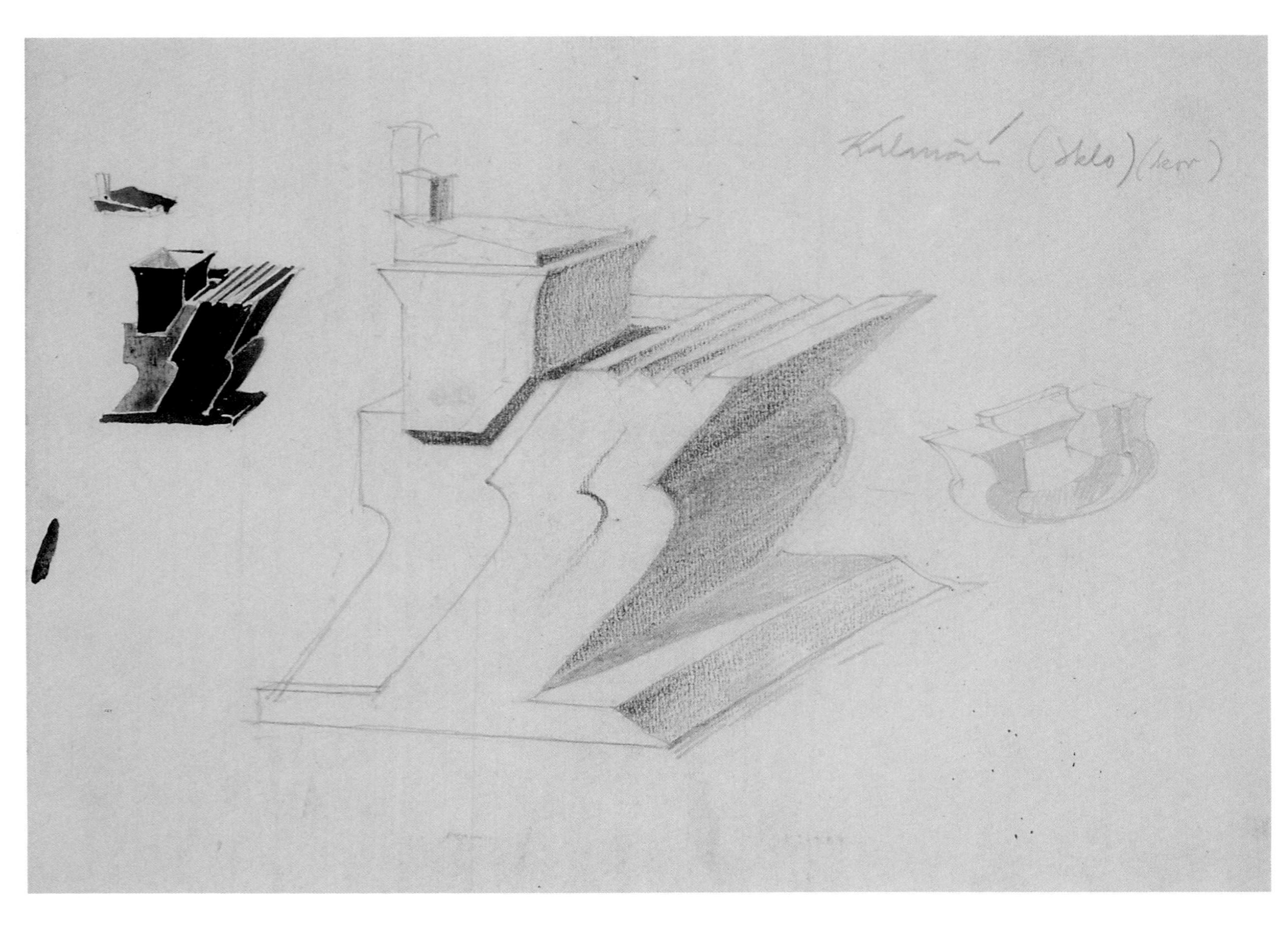

250.
Studies for vessels, 1918–1919
Pastel
31.5 x 47.5 cm
Signed l.r. in graphite: "1918–1919 Jiří Kroha"
UPM inv. no. 92.255
Acquired in 1985
Exhib.: Darmstadt, 1988–1989
(cat. no. 323, repr.)
Lit.: B) Lamarová, 1985, p. 25

Antonín Procházka

251.
Design for a vase, 1916
India ink
29 x 23 cm
MG Brno inv. no. B 3450
Acquired in 1951 from Linka Procházková
Lit.: A) Burkhardt & Lamarová, 1982,
repr. no. 210

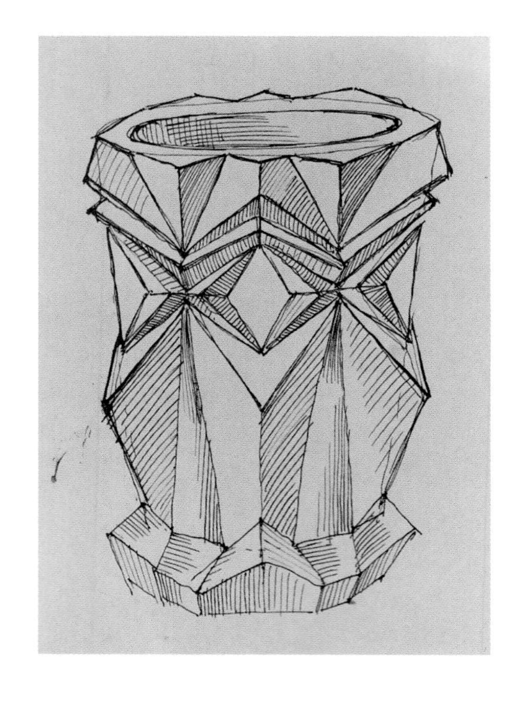

252a.
Design for a vase, 1925
India ink and watercolour
29 x 23 cm
MG Brno inv. no. B 3448
Acquired in 1951 from Linka Procházková

252.
Vase, 1925–1930
Stoneware, with coloured glaze
Height 23 cm
MG Brno inv. no. 20.893
Acquired in 1969

Rudolf Stockar

253.
Coffee and tea set (partial), ca. 1920
Earthenware, with white glaze
and gold decoration
Pots with lids height 14 cm and 15 cm,
cup height 6 cm
Marked
UPM inv. no. 30.857/1-2ab, 3
Acquired in 1950
Exhib.: Tokyo, 1984 (cat. no. 078, repr.)

Metal

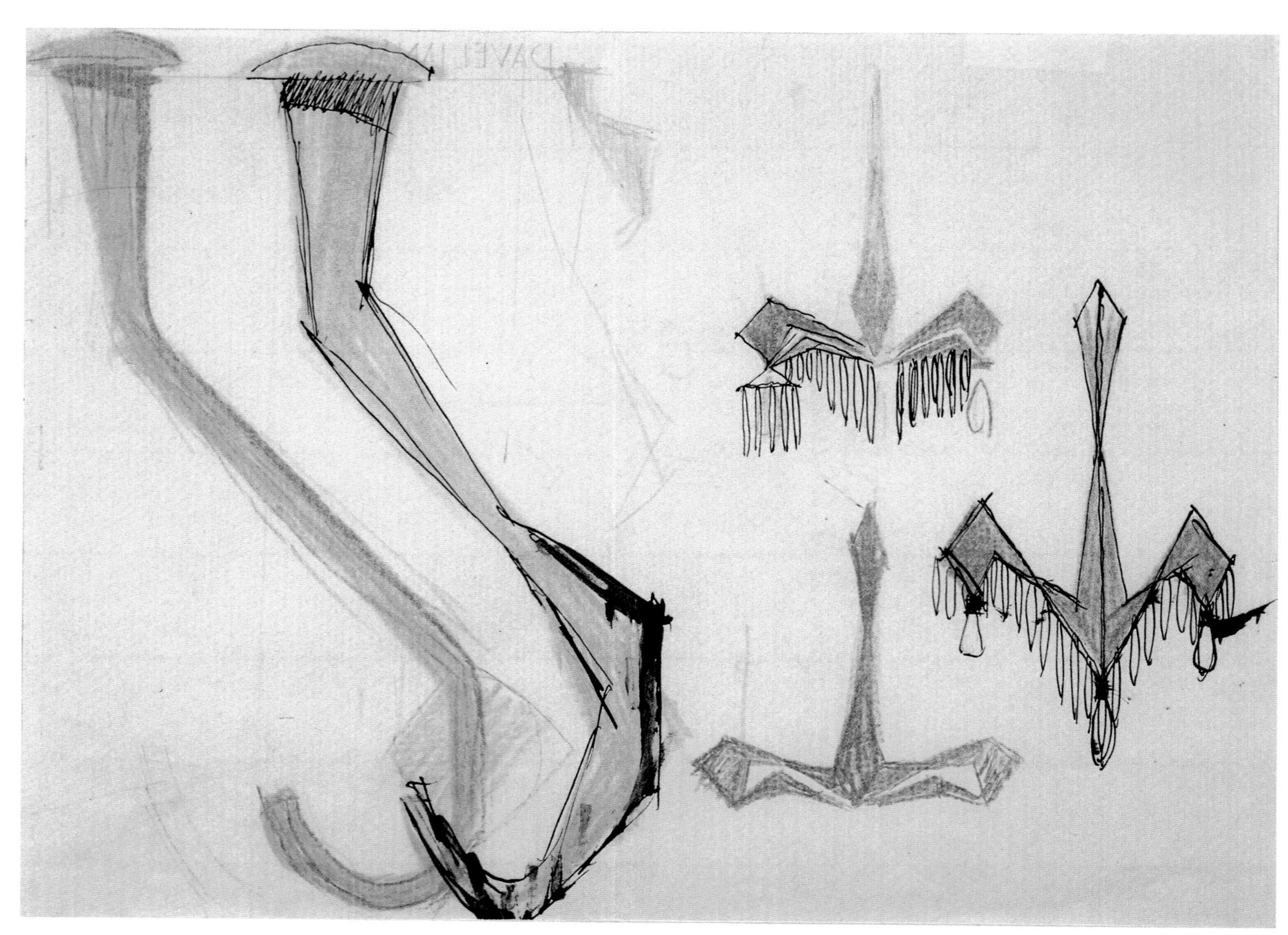

Josef Gocár

254.
Studies for metal objects, 1912
India ink and crayon
24 x 30 cm
NTM Collection no. 14
Acquired in 1951

Chandelier in a villa in Bruska, period photograph, SÚPPOP Archive, Štenc Collection

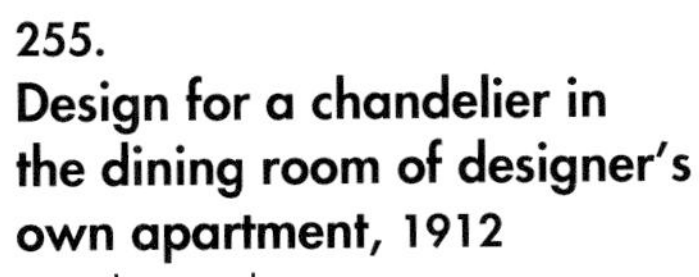

255.
Design for a chandelier in the dining room of designer's own apartment, 1912
Graphite and crayon
49.5 x 26.5 cm
Stamped l.r.: "Architekt J. Gočár"
Inscribed in graphite u.r. (illegible);
inscribed l.: "Chandelier for dining room centre for lowering 4 fixtures immovable"
NTM Collection no. 14
Acquired in 1951

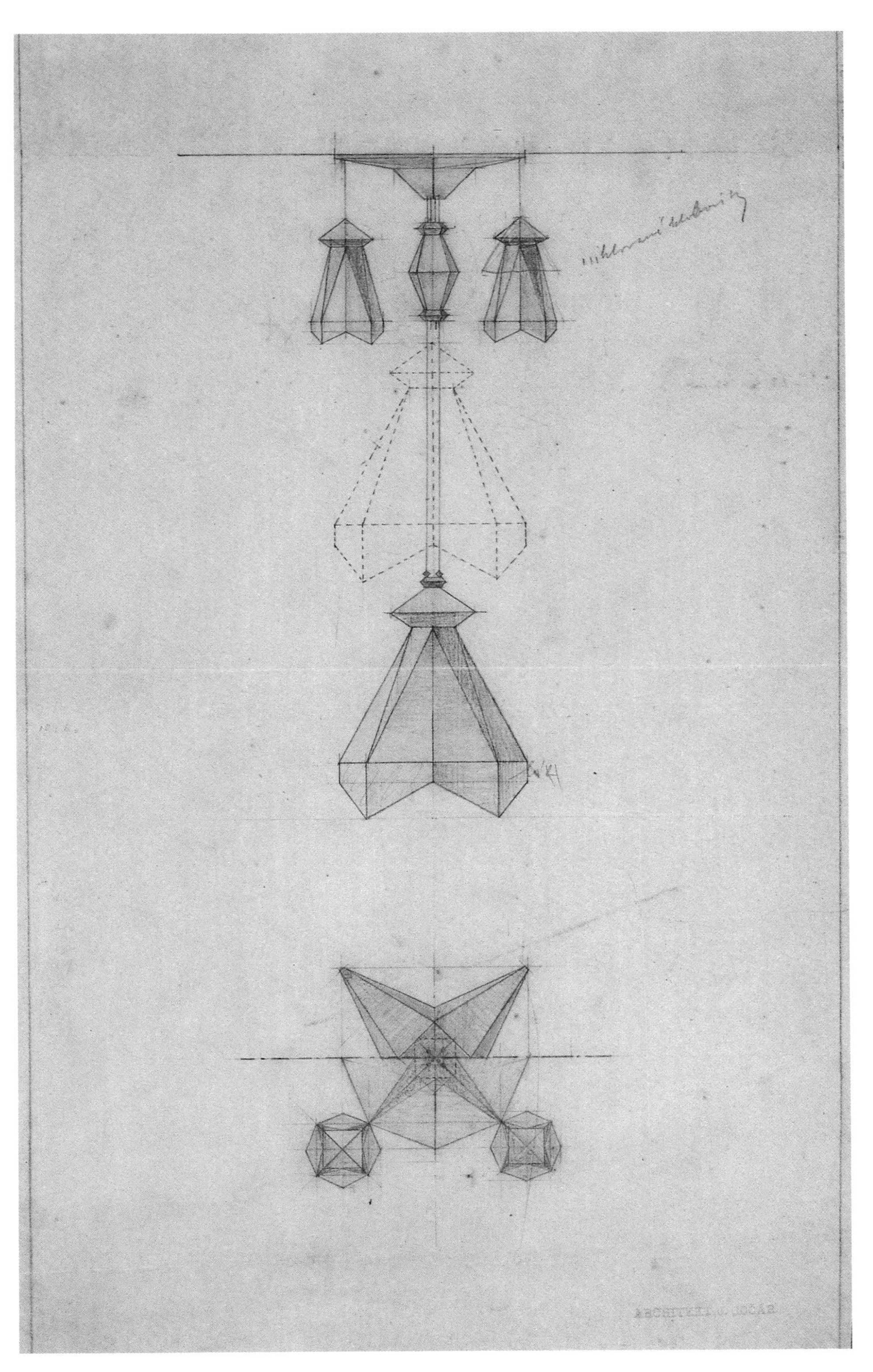

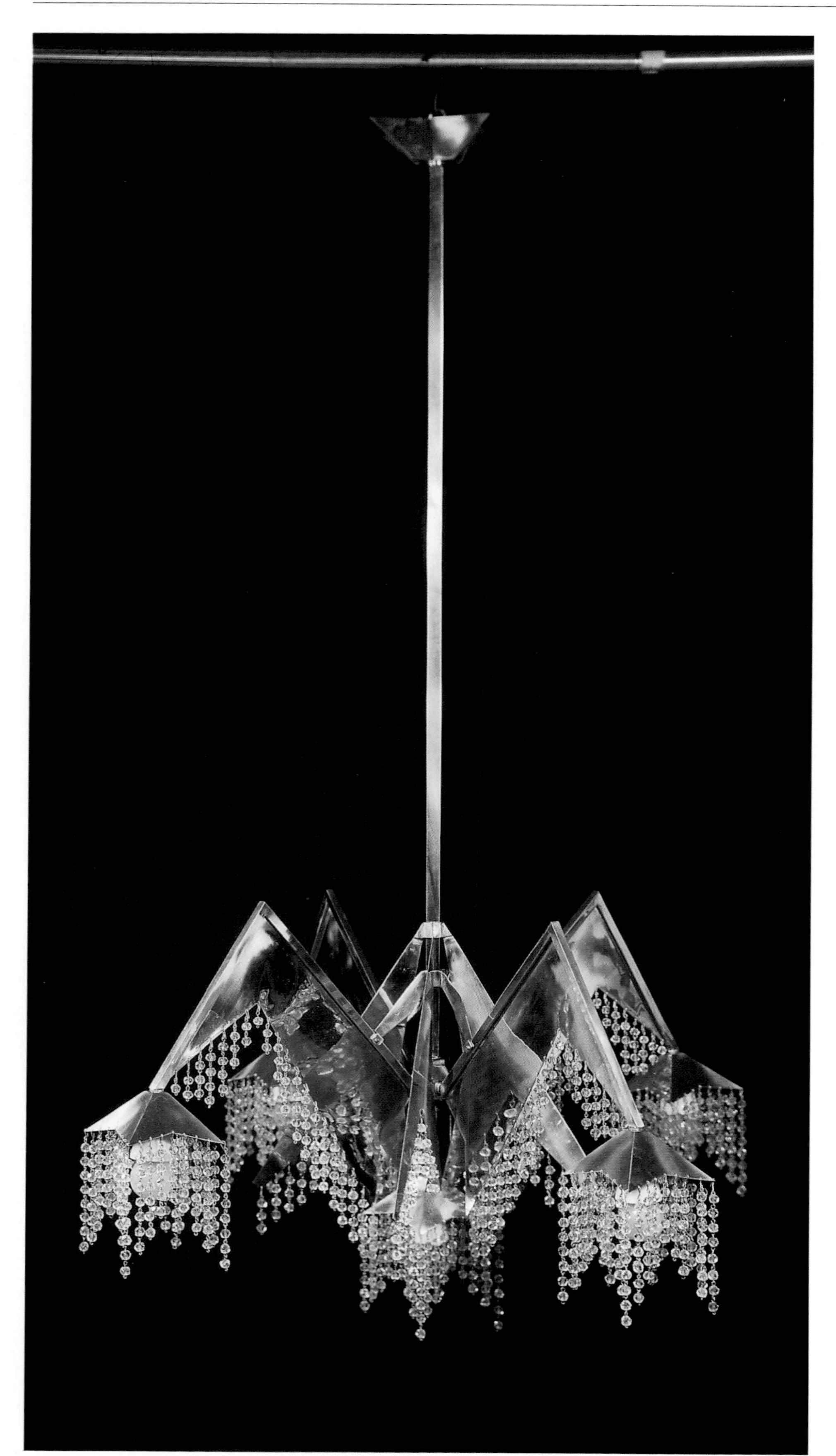

256.

Chandelier, 1913

Polished brass and glass
Height 105 cm, width 77 cm
Designed for the actor Otto Boleška
Manufactured by PUD
UPM inv. no. 50.895
Acquired in 1955
Exhib.: Cologne, 1914; London, 1970; Prague, 1976 (cat. nos. 70–71); Jaroměř, 1983 (cat. no. 20, repr.); Tokyo, 1984 (cat. no. 017, repr.)

257.
Clock, 1913
Brass
24 x 29 x 13.5 cm
Designed for the actor Otto Boleška
Manufactured by PUD
UPM dep. 1388/3
Acquired in 1955

Exhib.: Paris, 1966 (cat. no. 129, repr.); Prague, 1967; London, 1970; Prague, 1976 (cat. no. 73, repr.); Jaroměř, 1983 (cat. no. 21, repr.); Tokyo, 1984 (cat. no. 020, repr.)
Lit.: B) Janák, 1912–1913a, p. 280; A) Wirth, 1930, repr. p. 24; B) Vokoun, 1966a, repr. no. 6; B) Czagan, 1969; A) Burkhardt & Lamarová, 1982, repr. no. 206; A) Lamač, 1988, repr. no. 313

Vlastislav Hofman

258.
Covered tobacco box, 1918
Red tombac, with black decoration
Height 15.7 cm. Marked: "V.H."
Designed for Artěl
Manufactured by A. Štolba, Prague
UPM inv. no. 30.869
Acquired in 1950
Exhib.: Paris, 1966 (cat. no. 138, repr.); Prague, 1969 (cat. no. 55, repr.); Prague, 1976 (cat. no. 148, repr.); Tokyo, 1984 (cat. no. 179, repr.)

259.
Two covered boxes, 1918–1920
Brass, with engraved decoration
Height 12 cm, 7 cm
Marked: "Artěl Praha V.H. 1918"
Designed for Artěl
Manufactured by A. Štolba, Prague
UPM inv. nos. 30.864/1–2
Acquired in 1950
Exhib.: Prague, 1969 (cat. no. 56, repr.); Prague, 1976 (cat. no. 146, repr.); Malmö, 1982–1983; Darmstadt, 1988–1989 (cat. no. 186, repr.)
Lit.: B) Brožová, 1967, pp. 203–208; Burkhardt & Lamarová, 1982, repr. no. 188

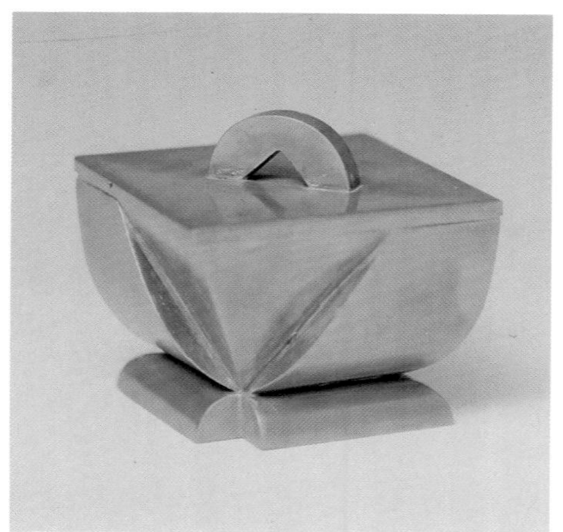

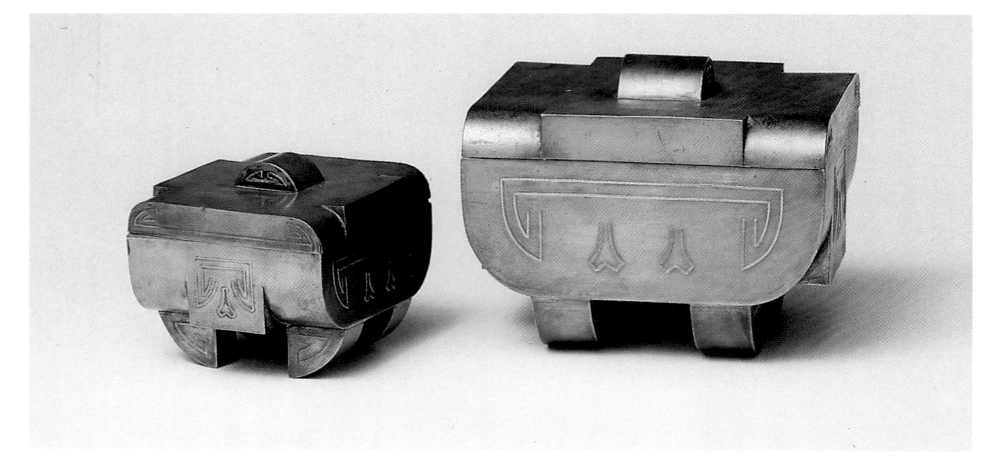

260.
Covered box, 1919
Brass
Height 6 cm
Marked: "Artěl Praha V.H. 1919"
Designed for Artěl
Manufactured by A. Štolba, Prague
UPM inv. no. 30.870
Acquired in 1950
Exhib.: Paris, 1966; Prague, 1976 (cat. no. 148, repr.); Malmö, 1982–1983 (cat. no. 283, repr.); Darmstadt, 1988–1989 (cat. no. 187, repr.)
Lit.: B) Brožová, 1967, pp. 203–208; A) Adlerová, 1983, repr. no. 77

261.
Covered box, 1919
Brass, with rose-quartz finial
Height 6 cm
Designed for Artěl
Manufactured by A. Štolba, Prague
UPM inv. no. 66.510
Acquired in 1965
Exhib.: Prague, 1976 (cat. no. 148, repr.); Darmstadt, 1988–1989 (cat. no. 188, repr.)

262.
Ashtray, ca. 1920
Copper, with engraved decoration
Height 6.5 cm
Marked: "Artěl Praha 711 H"
Designed for Artěl
Manufactured by A. Štolba, Prague
UPM inv. no. 30.865
Acquired in 1950
Exhib.: Paris, 1966 (cat. no. 139, repr.);
Prague, 1976 (cat. no. 140, repr.)
Lit.: Burkhardt & Lamarová, 1982, repr. no. 211

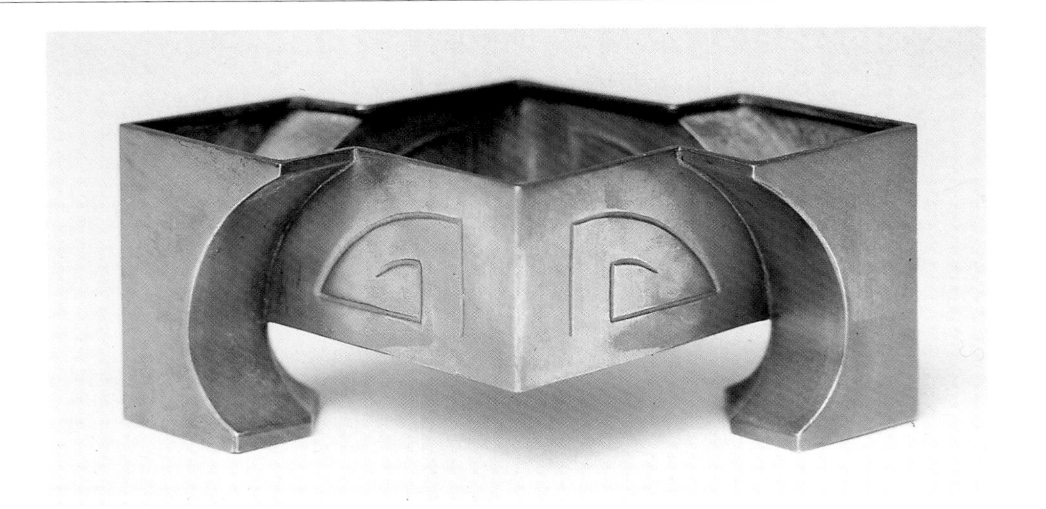

263.
Ashtray, ca. 1920
Brass, with engraved decoration
Height 8 cm
Marked: "Artěl Praha"
Designed for Artěl
Manufactured by A. Štolba, Prague
UPM inv. no. 30.867
Acquired in 1950
Exhib.: Paris, 1966 (cat. no. 140, repr.);
Prague, 1976 (cat. no. 147, repr.);
Tokyo, 1984 (cat. no. 080, repr.);
Darmstadt, 1988–1989 (cat. no. 190, repr.)
Lit.: B) Lamarová 1978, pp. 44–53

264.
Covered box, ca. 1920
Copper
Height 8 cm
Designed for Artěl
Manufactured by A. Štolba, Prague
UPM inv. no. 77.680
Acquired in 1945
Exhib.: Prague, 1976 (cat. no. 144, repr.);
Tokyo, 1984 (cat. no. 081, repr.);
Darmstadt, 1988–1989 (cat. no. 189, repr.)
Lit.: B) Behal, 1987a, repr. no. 12

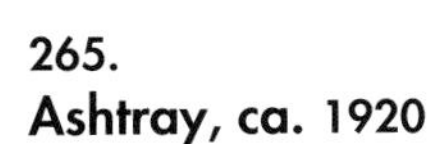

265.
Ashtray, ca. 1920
Brass
Height 15 cm
Designed for Artěl
Manufactured by A. Štolba, Prague
UPM inv. no. 30.866
Acquired in 1950
Exhib.: Prague, 1969 (cat. no. 54, repr.);
Prague, 1976 (cat. no. 147, repr.);
Darmstadt, 1988–1989 (cat. no. 191, repr.)

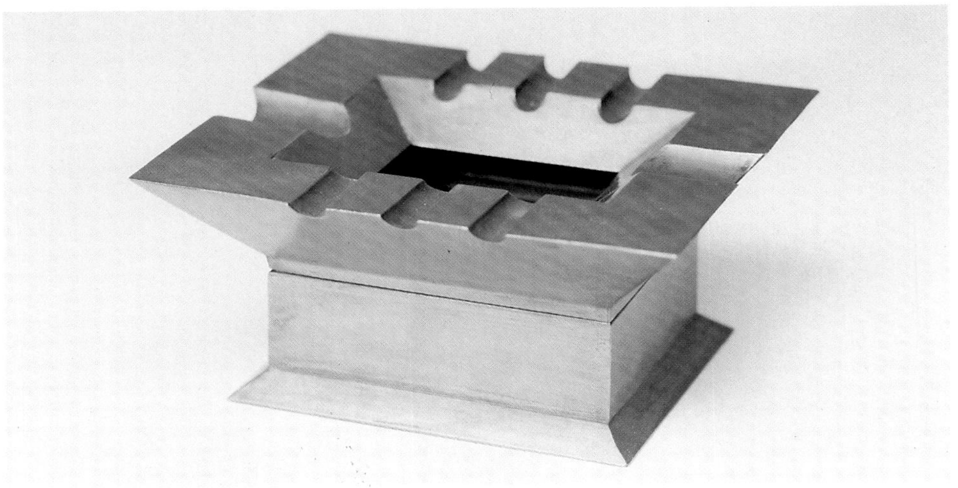

Jiří Kroha

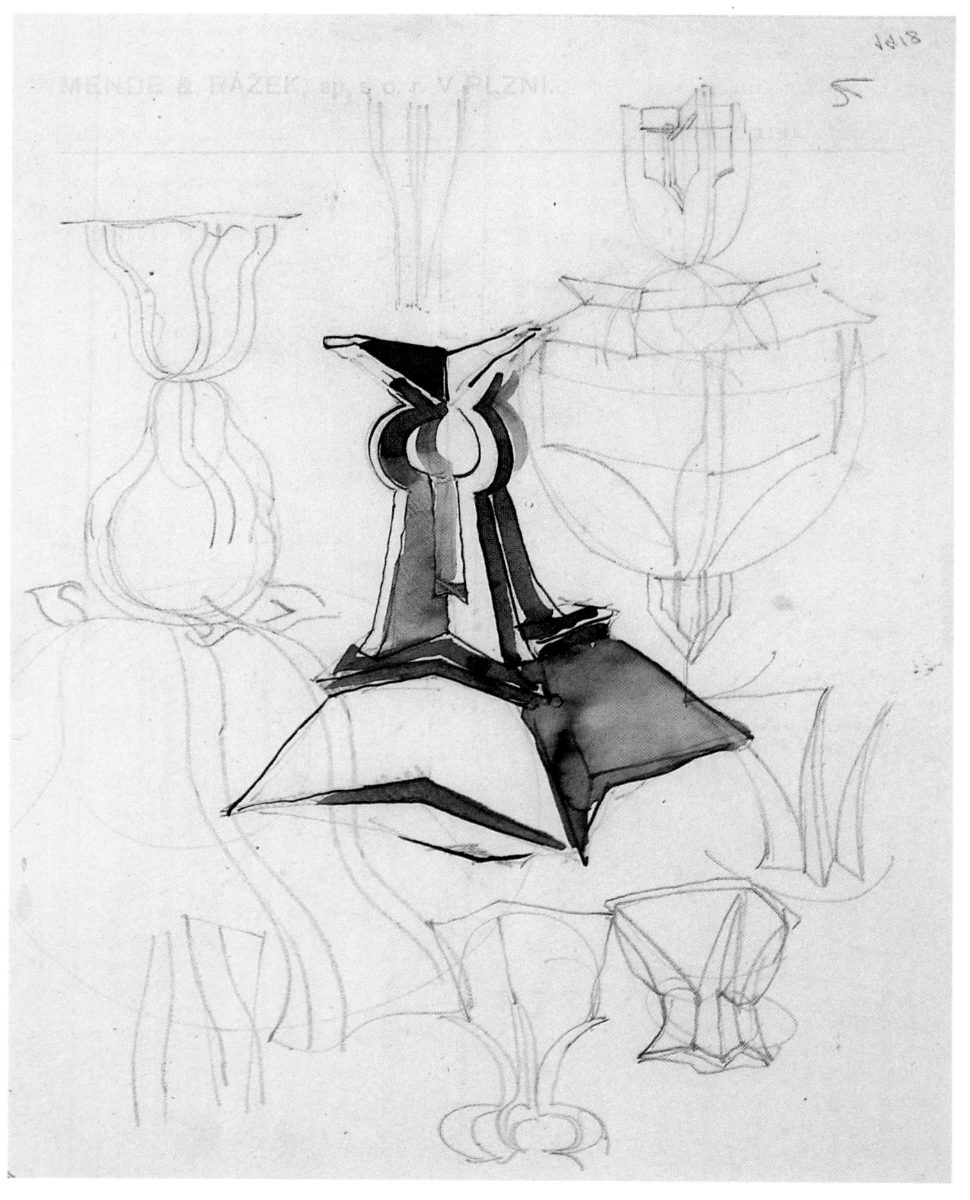

266.
Studies for lighting fixtures, 1918
Graphite and india ink, coloured
25 x 19.5 cm
Signed l.r.: "JK"
UPM inv. no. 92.257a, b
Acquired in 1985

267.
Candleholder, ca. 1925
Brass
Height 15 cm
Designed for Artěl
UPM inv. no. 92.253
Acquired in 1985
Exhib.: Darmstadt, 1988–1989
(cat. no. 330, repr.)
Lit.: B) Lamarová, 1985, repr. no. 23

Rudolf Stockar

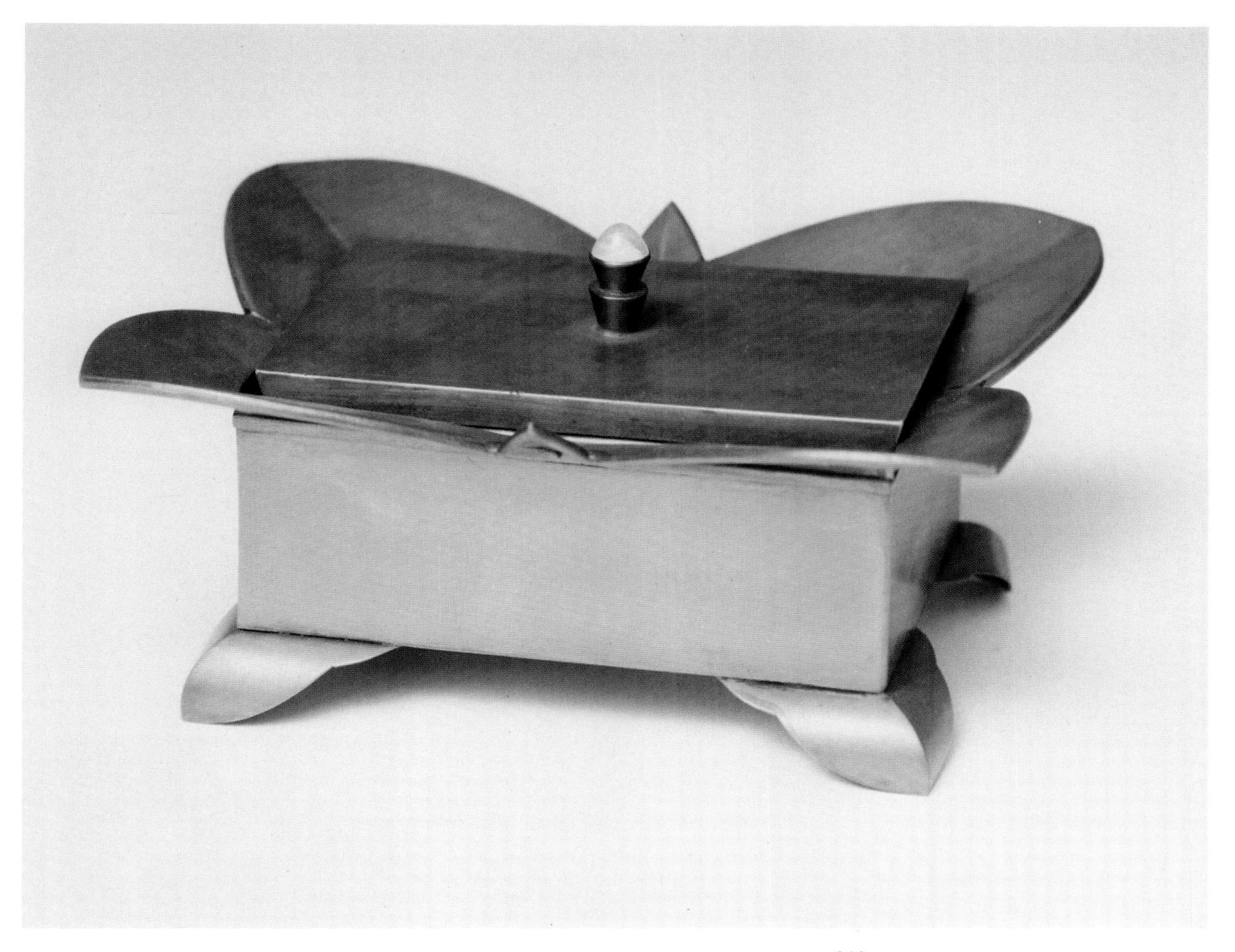

268.
Covered box, ca. 1920
Brass, with pink-quartz finial
Height 7.5 cm
Marked: "Artěl Praha"
Designed for Artěl
Manufactured by A. Štolba, Prague
UPM inv. no. 30.868
Acquired in 1950
Exhib.: Prague, 1976 (cat. no. 145);
Tokyo, 1984 (cat. no. 082, repr.)

Posters

Jaroslav Benda

269.
The Old Graphics Masters, 44th Exhibition of the Mánes Association of Plastic Artists, 1913
Poster, colour lithograph
41 x 120 cm
UPM inv. no. GP 15.740
Exhib.: Prague, 1971 (cat. no. 10, repr.)

270.
47th Exhibition of the Mánes Association of Plastic Artists, 1916
Poster, colour lithograph
93 x 63 cm
Marked l.c.: "B"
UPM inv. no. GP 23.659

271.
The Parks at Letna, Skating Rink of the Lawn-Tennis Circle, ca. 1914
Poster, lithograph
95 x 63 cm
Marked l.c.: "B"
UPM inv. no. GP 21.825
Exhib.: Prague, 1988

Vincenc Beneš

272.
Exhibition of the Mod[ern] Art School
Beneš–Nejedlý, 1914
Poster, linocut
66.5 x 41 cm
UPM inv. no. GP 15.794

Antonín Brunner

273.
The Municipal Mud Baths Bohdaneč, 1913
Poster, colour lithograph
89 x 59 cm
Marked l.r.: "Ant. Brunner"
UPM inv. no. GP 17.530

Vratislav Hugo Brunner

274.
Forty-third Members' Exhibition of Mánes Association of Plastic Artists, 1913
Poster, colour lithograph
150 x 105 cm
Marked l.r.: "VHB"
UPM inv. no. GP 15.919
Exhib.: Prague, 1971c (cat. no. 15, repr.); Tokyo, 1984 (cat. no. 098, repr.)
Lit.: A) Lamač, 1988, repr. no. 302

275.
Montmartre, American Bar, 1914
Poster, colour lithograph
63 x 95 cm
UPM inv. no. GP 19.198

Josef Čapek

276.
Radicals, Read "June," 1918
Poster, colour lithograph
95 x 63 cm
Marked l.r.: "Č"
UPM inv. no. GP 12.314
Exhib.: Prague, 1984; Darmstadt, 1988–1989 (cat. no. 34, repr.)
Lit.: B) Kroutvor, 1987, repr. no. 49

277.
Arnošt Dvořák, The Dead [Girl], 1920
Poster, colour lithograph
95 x 63 cm
Marked l.r.: "J. Čapek"
UPM inv. no. GP 13.316
Exhib.: Prague, 1984; Tokyo, 1984 (cat. no. 099, repr.); Prague, 1988 (cat. no. 13, repr.); Pardubice, 1990 (cat. no. 27, repr.)
Lit.: B) Kroutvor, 1985, repr. no. 58

Jiří Dréman

278.
The Red Seven Theatre, Hotel Central, 1919
Poster, colour lithograph
125 x 95 cm
Marked l.r.: "Dréman"
UPM inv. no. GP 16.585
Exhib.: Prague, 1984; Darmstadt, 1988–1989 (cat. no. 57, repr.)

Jindřich Hlavín

279.
74. Jahres-Ausstellung des Kunstvereines Prag, 1914
Poster, colour lithograph
126 x 94 cm
Marked l.c.: "H"
UPM inv. no. GP 19.581
Exhib.: Prague, 1971c (cat. no. 28, repr.); Tokyo, 1984 (cat. no. 100, repr.)

Oldřich Koníček

280.
Assn. of Plast. Art. Mánes, 1914
Poster, colour lithograph
125 x 95 cm
Marked l.l.: "Koníček"
UPM inv. no. GP 6041
Exhib.: Prague, 1971c (cat. no. 46, repr.); Tokyo, 1984 (cat. no. 101, repr.)

Jiří Kroha

282.
Montmartre, Waltner, 1919
Poster, colour lithograph
126 x 95 cm
Marked l.l.: "Kroha 1919"
UPM inv. no. GP 17.844
Exhib.: Prague, 1984; Tokyo, 1984 (cat. no. 102, repr.); Prague, 1988 (cat. no. 5, repr.); Pardubice, 1990 (cat. no. 19, repr.)

281.
Design for a poster for cabaret of the Red Seven, 1918
Pastels
46 x 28.5 cm
UPM inv. no. 92.248
Exhib.: Tokyo, 1984 (cat. no. 178, repr.)

MONTMARTRE

10 hodin

10 hodin

PRAHA

ŘETEZOVÁ

ŘETEZOVÁ

Kroha
1919

V. NEUBERT
SMÍCHOV

WALTNER

283.
Krasoumná jednota (The Beaux-Arts Fellowship), Exhibition of the Veraikon, Modern Art, 1920
Poster, colour lithograph
63 x 47 cm
Marked l.r.: "Kroha"
UPM inv. no. GP 16.575
Exhib.: Prague, 1984; Tokyo, 1984
(cat. no. 103, repr.)
Lit.: A) Kroutvor, 1985, repr. no. 57

284.
Arnošt Dvořák, The New Oresteia, 1923
Colour lithograph
160 x 114 cm
Marked l.r.: "Kroha"
UPM inv. no. GP 17.132
Exhib.: Prague, 1984; Darmstadt, 1988–1989 (cat. no. 325, repr.)
Lit.: A) Kroutvor, 1985, repr. no. 64

ARNOŠT DVOŘÁK:
Duben 13. 14. 15.
NOVÁ
REŽIE JIŘÍ KROHA:
ORESTEIA
KROHA

František Kysela

285.
Group of Plast. Artists, Exhibition. Drawings of Z. Kratochvíl, 1912
Poster, colour linocut
62 x 95 cm
UPM inv. no. GP 21.877

286.
The Competition of Display Windows in Prague, 1912
Poster, colour lithograph
122 x 95 cm
Marked l.c.: "K"
UPM inv. no. GP 21.832

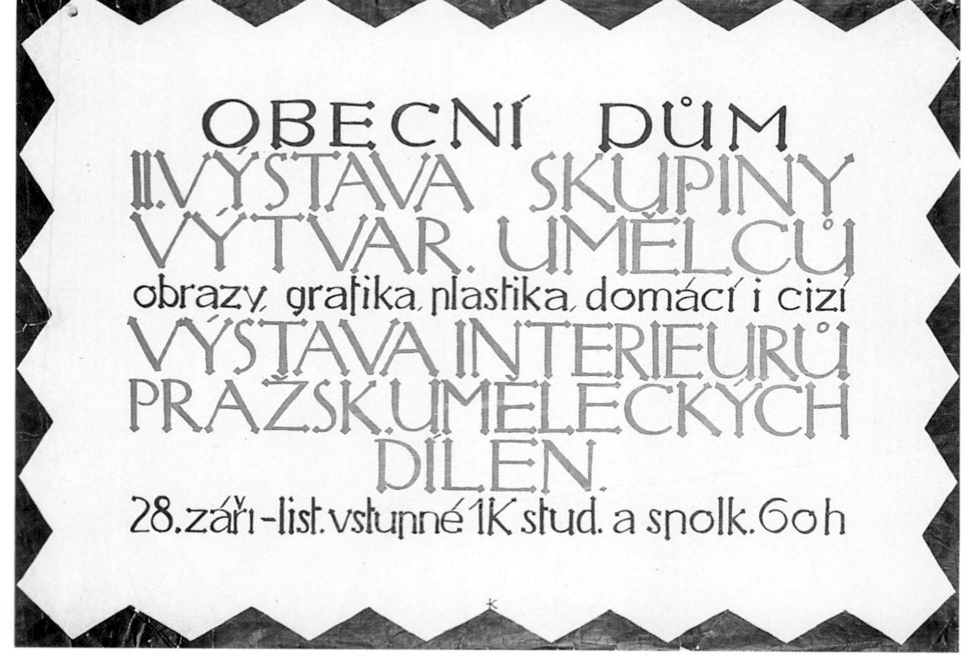

287.
Second Exhibition of the Group of Plast. Artists, Exhibition of Interiors by Prague Art Workshops, 1912
Poster, colour lithograph
78 x 108 cm
Marked l.c.: "K"
UPM inv. no. GP 15.776
Exhib.: Tokyo, 1984 (cat. no. 097, repr. [mistakenly identified as poster by Benda])

288.
Third Exhibition of the Group P.A., 1913
Poster, colour lithograph
142 x 108 cm
Marked l.c.: "K"
UPM inv. no. GP 15.992
Exhib.: Prague, 1971 (cat. no. 63, repr.)
Lit.: A) Lamač, 1988, repr. no. 296

III. VÝSTAVA SKUPINY V.U.
PICASSO, BRAQUE
DERAIN
MODERNÍ GRAFIKA STARÁ GRAFIKA a
PLASTIKA LIDOVÉ a EXOTICKÉ UMĚNÍ
Květen-Červen
1K-Stud. a spolk. 60 h
9-6 hod
OBECNÍ DŮM u PRAŠNÉ VĚŽE

Emil Artur Longen

289.
Ivan Olbracht: Fifth Act, 1921
Colour lithograph
95 x 64 cm
UPM inv. no. GP 16.485
Exhib.: Tokyo, 1984 (cat. no. 104, repr.)

Augusta Nekolová-Jarešová

290.
Concert Gustav Dörfl, **1914**
Poster, lithograph
128 x 92 cm
Marked l.r.: "JN"
UPM inv. no. GP 21.884
Exhib.: Prague, 1988 (cat. no. 99, repr.)
Lit.: A) Kroutvor 1985, repr. no. 50

Václav Špála

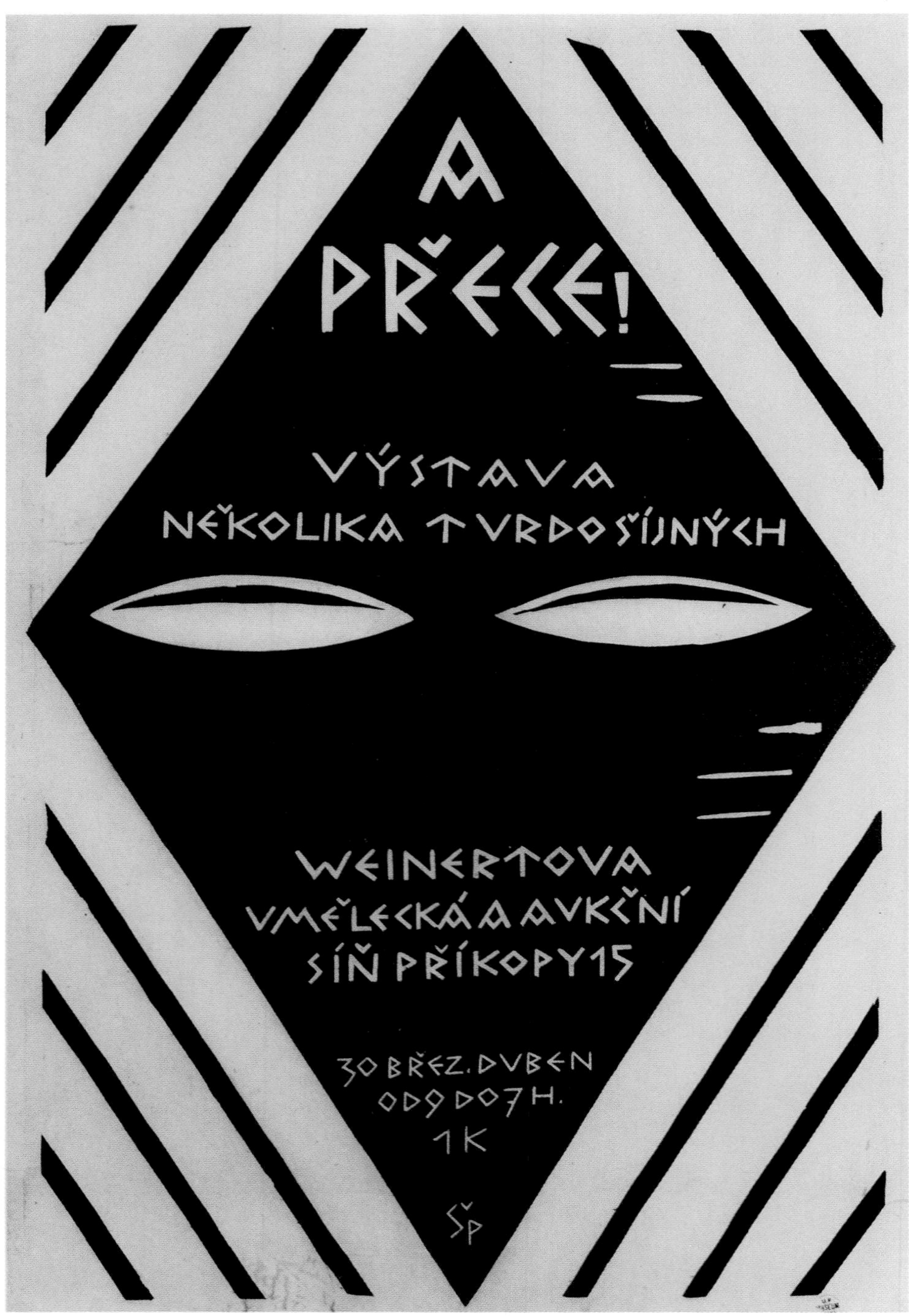

291.
And Yet! An Exhibition of a Few Stiffnecked, 1918
Poster, linocut
95 x 63 cm
Marked: "S"
UPM inv. no. GP 10.083
Exhib.: Prague, 1988 (cat. no. 1, repr.); Pardubice, 1990 (cat. no. 29, repr.)
Lit.: A) Kroutvor, 1985, repr. no. 53

292.
150th Exhibition of the Mánes Association of Plastic Artists, 1929
Poster, colour lithograph
126 x 93 cm
Marked l.r.: "S 29"
UPM inv. no. GP 20.678
Exhib.: Prague, 1984 (unnumb., no repr.); Tokyo, 1984 (cat. no. 105, repr.); Darmstadt, 1988–1989 (cat. no. 563, repr.)

150
S.V.U. MÁNES
VÝSTAVA
ČLENSKÁ
OBECNÍ DŮM
Š29
VSTUPNÉ 5 Kč. OD 5. ŘÍJNA – 17. LISTOPADU OD 9–18 HOD.

Jan Zrzavý

293.
Posthumous Exhibition of Bohumil Kubišta, 1920
Poster, colour lithograph
94 x 60.5 cm
UPM inv. no. GP 15.784
Exhib.: Tokyo, 1984 (cat. no. 106, repr.)

Addenda

Biographies

Jaroslav Benda
27 April 1882 (Prague)–12 January 1970 (Prague)

Studied with A. Hofbauer at the School of Decorative Arts in Prague from 1901 to 1904, and at the Academy of Fine Arts until 1906. Professor at the School of Decorative Arts from 1920 to 1941. In 1908, was one of the founders of the Artěl Co-operative. Worked principally as a typographer and book designer. Like V. H. Brunner and F. Kysela, Benda explored cubism in applied graphics and typography. Designed series of books for such publishing houses as J. Laichter and J. Štenc. Was also concerned with the theory and practice of typography; published a study, "Písmo a nápis" (Writing and Sign), in 1931. Designed postage stamps, bank notes, posters, and, with O. Španiel, the Czech national emblem. Designed textiles for upholstery and tapestries. Also worked in mosaics and glass, including windows (e.g., the burial chapel of J. A. Komensky in Naarden in 1935).

Vincenc Beneš
22 January 1883 (Lišice near Chlumce nad Cidlinou)–27 March 1979 (Prague)

Studied at the School of Decorative Arts from 1902 to 1904, and with V. Bukovac and R. Ottenfeld at the Academy of Fine Arts in Prague from 1904 to 1907. In 1907, visited Dresden, Berlin, Munich, and Paris, where he stayed until 1908. In June, 1908, participated in the second exhibition of the Group of Eight at the Topic Salon in Prague. At this time, was mainly associated with B. Kubišta. In 1909, joined the Mánes Association of Plastic Artists. In 1911, resigned and became a member of the Group of Plastic Artists. Published theoretical studies in *Umělecký měsíčník*. In 1912, participated in the Sonderbund exhibition in Cologne. In October 1912, took part in the prestigious exhibition of contemporary avant-garde art at the Goltz Salon of New Art in Munich; in April 1913, participated in the third exhibition of the Group of Eight in the same venue. In 1913, founded, with O. Nejedlý, a private school for painters. In 1917, returned to Mánes. Beneš was a firm proponent of cubism in his theoretical and practical work, but in 1915 there was a radical break in his own production. He became more inclined to work from sensory perceptions and experiences from nature; he went through a neo-classicist phase, and in the 1930s his model was Bonnard's colourism.

Matěj Blecha
16 July 1861 (Štítary)–18 December 1919 (Prague)

Builder and architect, owner of a construction firm in Prague. Studied at the Prague and Vienna technical universities and at the Vienna Academy of Fine Arts. Was active in public life, as a member of the city council, and in the Czech Academy of Science, Literature, and Arts. Collaborated with the sculptor Celda Klouček, and employed in his office the architects Emil Králicek and Oldřich Tyl. Designed and realized a significant number of important buildings in Prague in the historicist, secessionist, and cubist styles, including the Credit Bank in Prague (1900–1902), the Kalous pharmacy (1911–1913), the Golden Goose Hotel (1911–1913), the Diamant department store and apartment building on Spálena Street, and Šupich's Department Store on Václav Square (1913–1916); outside of Prague, he built the sanatorium at Pleš, the Academy of Fine Arts in Belgrade, and bank buildings in Lvov and in Brody in Galicia.

Antonín Brunner
13 June 1881 (Prague)–date of death unknown

Painter, graphic artist, and restorer. Studied at the School of Decorative Arts in Prague from 1901 to 1903, and in Paris. In 1905 and 1906, exhibited at the Paris Salon, in 1907 at the Topic Salon in Prague. In 1908, returned to Prague. Studied folk art in Slovakia. Created the portrait of T. G. Masaryk for the assembly hall in Náchod. Worked for the industrialist Barton. Brunner also designed diplomas, posters, and ex libris. From 1929, lived permanently in Náchod.

Vratislav Hugo Brunner
15 October 1886 (Prague)–13 July 1928 (Lomnice u Jílového)

Studied with V. Bukovac and M. Pirner at the Prague Academy of Fine Arts from 1903 to 1906. In 1906, spent a year studying in Munich. Became a member of the Mánes Association of Plastic Artists in 1908. Was a co-founder of the Artěl Co-operative in 1908, and was a principal designer for it (toys, painted gingerbreads, souvenirs, painted glass, etc.). In 1911, resigned from Mánes and joined the executive of the newly established Group of Plastic Artists. In 1912, went on a study trip to Leipzig. At the end of 1912, resigned from the Group and returned to Mánes. From 1919, was a professor at the School of Decorative Arts in Prague, where he headed the department of decorative and ornamental drawing; in 1928, was named rector of the School for Decorative Arts. Dedicated a significant part of his career to book design, collaborating with a number of important publishers, including Kamila Neumannova's imprint Books by Good Authors, K. H. Hilar, and especially Aventinum. Also produced drawings and illustrations for a large number of magazines (*Šibeničky, Prager Presse, Rozpravy Aventina*). At the International Exhibition of Decorative Art in Paris in 1925, was awarded the Grand Prix and gold medal for his book designs. Designed Czechoslovak postage stamps in 1918, and worked on designs for decorative wall paintings. Brunner created a number of important posters and catalogue designs, through which he contributed significantly to the establishment of cubist principles in applied graphics.

Josef Čapek
23 March 1887 (Hronov nad Metují)–April 1945 (Bergen-Belsen concentration camp)

Studied with E. Díte, A. Hofbauer, and K. V. Mašek at the School of Decorative Arts in Prague from 1904 to 1910. Published very early, co-writing some articles with his brother, Karel. The two published a somewhat negative review of the second exhibition of the Group of Eight, "Synteza a výstava osmi" (Synthesis and the Exhibition of the Eight), in *Snaha* in 1908. In 1910–1911, he and Karel lived in Paris. In 1911, visited Marseilles and Spain; in 1912, briefly attended the Académie Colarossi in Paris with V. Hofman. In 1911, joined the Group of Plastic Artists and began to edit *Umělecký měsíčník*. In 1912, resigned from the Group and joined the Mánes Association of Plastic Artists. In 1913, joined the executive and, with A. Matějček, edited the twenty-seventh volume of *Volné směry*. Helped to establish the literary Almanach in 1914 and S. K. Neumann's magazine *Červen* in 1918. Was a member of the Stiffnecked (the Tvrdošíjní group), which held its first exhibition in April, 1918. From 1929, exhibited with Umělecka beseda and helped to edit the magazine *Zivot*. Was an editor for the newspaper *Lidove noviny*. Čapek's activity was exceptionally wide-ranging: in addition to his important *œuvre* as painter and author, he worked in scenography and the graphic arts. Collaborated with a number of publishing houses, among them Aventinum, Melantrich, Družstevní práce, and Odeon, and contributed to the journal *Bytová kultura*. His reflections in this area are contained in a collection of writings, *Nejskromnější umění* (The Humblest Art).

Josef Chochol

Josef Chochol
13 December 1880 (Písek)–6 July 1956 (Prague)

Studied with J. Schulz at the Czech Technical University in Prague, and with O. Wagner at the Academy of Fine Arts in Vienna. In 1911, left the Mánes Association of Plastic Artists and joined the Group of Plastic Artists. In 1912, was one of the initiators of the Prague Artistic Workshops. At the end of 1912, left the Group and returned to Mánes. Member of the Devětsil Artists' Association and, from 1923, of its architecture section, Ardev. Was a founding member of the Left Front, in 1929, and of the Association of Socialist Architects, in 1933. As a leading proponent of cubism in architecture and applied arts (designed furniture for the English Circle at the Municipal Hall), Chochol anticipated in some measure Czech postwar purism, as he expressed in 1913 in his principal treatise "K funkci architektonického článku" (On the Function of the Architectural Link) (*Styl*, vol. 5). In the 1920s, he was strongly influenced by Soviet constructivism, as is demonstrated in his remarkable design of the building of the Liberated Theatre (1927).

Jiří Dréman (pen name of Josef Nerad)
1892–1946

Where Dréman studied is not known. He was connected with the cabaret The Red Seven, for which he created a poster and set designs. He was inspired by expressionism and cubism.

Bedřich Feuerstein
15 January 1892 (Dobrovice)–10 May 1936 (Prague)

Studied at the Prague Technical University from 1911 to 1917; in 1921, was awarded a French government scholarship to study at École du Louvre. In 1922, joined the Devětsil Artists' Association; in 1923, became member of its architecture section, Ardev. Worked at the Paris studio of August Perret on projects for the theatre at the International Exhibition of Decorative Art in 1925. From 1926 to 1930, worked at Antonin Raymond's studio in Tokyo, where he designed the Soviet Embassy building and St. Luke Hospital. Made study trips to the U.S., and visited China (1930) and the U.S.S.R. (1931). From 1932, was a member of the Mánes Association of Plastic Artists. The point of departure of Feuerstein's work was cubism, as evidenced in his studies and designs. His first effort was the design for Žižka's monument at Vítkov Hill in 1913; he also participated in the competition for Dr. Rieger's Barrow at Kozákov in 1914. An important architect of the Czech purist movement, he also designed the building of the Military Geographical Institution in Prague–Dejvice (1921) and the crematorium building in Nymburk (1921–1923). Scenography was another major component of his production; Feuerstein worked for both the National Theatre and the Liberated Theatre.

Bedřich Feuerstein

Josef Gočár

Josef Gočár
13 March 1880 (Semín near Pardubice)–
10 September 1945 (Jičín)

Studied at the Higher National Technical School and, from 1902 to 1905, with J. Kotěra at the School of Decorative Arts; from 1906 to 1908, worked in Kotěra's studio. In 1908, became a member of the Union of Architects of the Mánes Association of Plastic Artists and helped to edit the magazine *Styl*. In 1910, participated in the competition for the design of the town hall in Prague–Staré Město. In 1911, left Mánes and became the first chairman of the Group of Plastic Artists; collaborated on the editing of *Umělecký měsíčník*. In 1912, was one of the founders of the Prague Artistic Workshops. In 1913, participated in the competition for Žižka's monument at Vítkov Hill. Returned to Mánes in 1917. Until 1924, was chairman of the Union of Czech Accomplishment; from 1922 to 1939 was a professor at the Academy of Fine Arts in Prague. In 1925, received the Grand Prix for the design of the Czechoslovak Pavilion at the International Exhibition of Decorative Art in Paris. Gočár was a proponent of Czech modernism and of cubism, rondo-cubism, and functionalism in architecture and applied arts, and an important urbanist.

Josef Havlíček
5 May 1899 (Prague)–30 December 1961 (Prague)

Studied at the Czech Technical University from 1916 to 1924, and with J. Gočár at the Academy of Fine Arts from 1924 to 1926. Member of the architecture section of the Devětsil Artists' Association; in 1929 joined the Left Front, in 1933 the Association of Socialist Architects; from 1929, was a member of the Congrès internationaux d'architecture moderne (CIAM); from 1945 to 1947, was a member of the world council of CIAM. In 1948, became the first director of the Prague Projects Institute. An important representative of the Czech avant-garde, particularly the functionalists, in the interwar period, Havlíček collaborated with Karel Honzík from 1928 to 1936; their most famous realization is the General Pensions Institution in Prague–Žižkov (1929–1934). In addition to his activity as architect, urbanist, and theoretician, he worked in the applied arts (from 1918, he worked for the Artěl Co-operative).

Bohuslav Fuchs

Bohuslav Fuchs
24 March 1895 (Všechovice near Holešov)–
18 September 1972 (Brno)

Studied with J. Kotěra at the Academy of Fine Arts in Prague from 1916 to 1923, and worked in Kotěra's studio until 1923. In 1925, became a member of the Mánes Association of Plastic Artists; in 1929, joined the group Index; in 1930, became a member of the Left Front; in 1933, joined the Association of Socialist Architects. Was also a member of the Czech branch of CIAM; in 1937, became an honourary member and correspondent of the Royal Institute of British Architects. From 1926, worked at the Building Office in Brno. From 1938, was a professor at the School of Decorative Arts in Zlín; in 1945, was appointed professor at the Technical University at Brno. Fuchs's first influences were cubism and Dutch brick architecture. He was an important figure in the architectural avant-garde of Brno and a leading proponent of Czech functionalism (e.g., the hotel Avion in Brno). His work was unusually wide-ranging; he realized about 200 buildings, and made significant contributions in urbanism and furniture design.

Jindřich Hlavín
29 September 1877 (Prague)–8 February 1958 (Prague)

Painter, graphic artist, and art restorer. Studied with J. Schikaneder and K. V. Mašek at the School of Decorative Arts in Prague. In 1912, studied in Italy; then travelled in Germany, France, and Belgium. In 1916–1917, created a monumental cycle from the lives of Czech patron saints for a church in Bohnice, and designed the windows. Exhibited at the Munich Secession and at the Topic Salon in Prague. Carried out restoration work in Czech chateaux. His poster designs won several first prizes at public competitions. Although his style originated in the ideas of the Secession, he incorporated modern elements.

Vlastislav Hofman

Pavel Janák

Jan Kotěra

Vlastislav Hofman
6 February 1884 (Jičín)–28 August 1964 (Prague)

Studied with J. Fanta, J. E. Koula, and J. Schulz at the Czech Technical University from 1902 to 1907. Worked at the building department of the Prague magistrate. Was a member of the Artěl Co-operative and the Mánes Association of Plastic Artists. Left Mánes in 1911, and joined the Group of Plastic Artists. Wrote a substantial number of theoretical essays for the magazines *Volné směry*, *Styl*, and *Umělecký měsíčník*. At the end of 1912, left the Group and returned to Mánes. In 1913, participated in the competition for Žižka's monument at Vítkov Hill. Took part in the first exhibition of the Stiffnecked in 1918. Won a gold medal at the International Exhibition of Decorative Art in Paris in 1925, the Grand Prix at the Exhibition of Arts and Technology in Paris in 1937, and the Grand Prize at the Triennial Exhibition in Milan in 1940. Was one of the founders of the Czech modern movement. Hofman's wide-ranging activity included architecture, applied arts, painting, and, from 1919, scenography, primarily in collaboration with Karel Hilar. His contribution to the development of Czech cubism was significant and included theoretical treatises, architecture, and design.

Jaroslav Horejc
15 June 1886 (Prague)–3 January 1983 (Prague)

A master engraver, he studied first at a technical school, then with E. Novák, S. Sucharda, and J. Drahoňovsky at the School of Decorative Arts in Prague from 1906 to 1910; at the same time he worked as a plasterer. Was a member of the Artěl Co-operative from 1909, of the Mánes Association of Plastic Artists from 1911, and of the Association of Czech Accomplishment from 1914. Was a guest participant in the exhibition of the group Sursum at the Prague Municipal Hall in 1912. From 1918 to 1948, was a professor at the School of Decorative Arts in Prague, and chairman of its department of artistic metal working. Won the Grand Prix for his collection of glass at the International Exhibition of Decorative Art in Paris in 1925. Horejc is the creator of important sculptural works, metal objects (including numerous figurative grilles), ceramics, and cut and engraved glass for the firm of J. and L. Lobmeyr.

Pavel Janák
12 March 1882 (Prague)–1 August 1956 (Prague)

Studied with J. Schulz at the Czech Technical University; also audited at the German Technical University in Prague with J. Zitek from 1899 to 1905, then with O. Wagner at the Academy of Fine Arts in Vienna from 1906 to 1908; worked in Kotěra's studio in Prague in 1908 and 1909. In 1908, became a member of the Union of Architects of the Mánes Association of Plastic Artists; in the same year, participated in the founding of the Artěl Co-operative. In 1911, resigned from Mánes and joined the executive of the Group of Plastic Artists, working also in the editorial circle of *Umělecký měsíčník*, was the architect of the first exhibition of the Group in 1912. Also in that year, was a co-founder of the Prague Artistic Workshops. Participated in the competition for Žižka's monument at Vítkov Hill in 1913. Was founding member of the Association of Czech Accomplishment in 1914; from 1924, was chairman of SČSD. In 1917, returned to Mánes. Editor of the magazine *Výtvarná práce* from 1921 to 1925. Professor of architecture at the School of Decorative Arts in Prague from 1921 to 1942. In 1936, took over from Josip Plečnik as chief architect for the Prague Castle. Designed a number of reconstructions of historical objects, and was an important urbanist.

Oldřich Koníček
12 October 1886 (Kutná Hora)–17 July 1932 (Žebroň near Podebrad)

Studied at the Prague Academy from 1907 to 1912. Lived in Paris for a year. In 1910, joined the Mánes Association of Plastic Artists. First influence was French impressionism, but later development was influenced by Matisse and Derain. In 1920, there was a retrospective exhibition of his work in Prague. There were also exhibitions abroad, in Paris, Zurich, Bern, Bolzano, Venice, Rome, Vienna, and London. In 1932, Mánes mounted a posthumous exhibition of Koníček's work. He occasionally designed posters.

Jan Kotěra
18 December 1871 (Brno)–17 April 1923 (Prague)

The founder of modern Czech architecture. Studied at the German Technical Secondary School in Plzeň, then with O. Wagner at the Academy of Fine Arts in Vienna from 1894 to 1897. In 1897, received the Prix de Rome. Member of the Mánes Association of Plastic Artists, founding member of the Union of Architects of Mánes and of the magazine *Styl*. In 1902, designed the pavilion for Rodin's exhibition in Prague. In 1903, travelled to the U.S. for the St. Louis World Fair. The evolution of his work was also affected by journeys to Holland and England (between 1906 and 1914 he used red-brick architecture). In 1913, participated in the competition for Žižka's monument at Vítkov Hill. Was the general commissioner of the art exhibitions in Venice (1910), Rome (1911), and Munich. Kotěra taught two generations of Czech architects, first at the School of Decorative Arts in Prague, then from 1910 to 1923 at the Academy of Fine Arts.

Emil Králíček

Emil Králíček
1877 (Německý Brod)–ca. 1930 (Prague)

Studied privately with Antonín Balšánek in Prague, and with Joseph Maria Olbrich in Darmstadt. Worked for various building companies in Prague (e.g., at the offices of Matěj Blecha). Was among the first to use cubist forms in architecture. Recently, Králíček's work has become the subject of renewed research interest.

Jiří Kroha
5 June 1893 (Prague)–7 June 1974 (Prague)

Studied with J. Koula, J. Fanta, and A. Balšánek at the Czech Technical University from 1911 to 1916. Member of the Mánes Association of Plastic Artists. In 1920, co-founded the magazine *Socialistická scéna* and in 1927, *Horizont*, a journal of contemporary culture. In 1925, was named professor at the Technical University in Brno. Member of the Left Front; in 1933, became a founding member and chairman of the Association of Socialist Architects. Kroha was an important representative of the Czech avant-garde and a versatile artist: he was an architect, theoretician, scenographer, and significant contributor in the area of applied arts. From cubism and expressionism, he turned, via neo-plasticism, to functionalism. Kroha's substantial output was accompanied from the outset by influential theoretical work: in 1920, he published a key article, "O prostoru architektonickém a jeho mezích" (On Architectural Space and Its Limits), in *Veraikon*; in 1933 he published *Sociologický fragment bydlení* (Sociological Fragment on Habitation); in 1934, *Ekonomický fragment bydlení* (Economic Fragment on Habitation), and a concluding work, *Socialistické bydlení* (Socialist Habitation).

František Kysela
4 September 1881 (Kouřim)–20 February 1941 (Prague)

Studied with K. Mašek at the School of Decorative Arts from 1900 to 1904 and from 1905 to 1908. In 1904–1905, studied at the Academy of Fine Arts with H. Schwaigr. In 1913, became an instructor and in 1917 a professor at the School of Decorative Arts; from 1921, led a special class of applied graphics. In 1908, joined the Mánes Association of Plastic Artists; was elected to the executive in 1909. Was a member of the Artěl Co-operative. Left Mánes in 1911 and became a member of the Group of Plastic Artists; worked in the editorial offices of *Umělecký měsíčník*. In 1917, rejoined Mánes. Won the Grand Prix and gold medal at the International Exhibition of Decorative Art in Paris in 1925. Kysela's designs were realized in various media, especially in the applied arts. He designed posters for many of the most famous exhibitions of his time; he also designed and illustrated books, and designed postage stamps, bank notes, and diplomas. In addition, Kysela created frescoes, paintings on glass windows, textile designs for clothing and upholstery fabric, jewellery, and tapestries. He was an important scenographer and costume designer (for example, he designed the costumes for all of Smetana's operas at the National Theatre).

Jiří Kroha

Eugen Linhart

Eugen Linhart
20 March 1898 (Kouřim)–29 December 1949 (Prague)

Studied at the Czech Technical University from 1918 to 1924. Was a member of Ardev, the architectural section of the Devětsil Artists' Association; from 1927, belonged to the Architects' Club and to the Mánes Association of Plastic Artists. Was one of the "Purist Foursome" (along with V. Obrtel, K. Honzík, and J. Fragner). Is credited with promoting purism and functionalism in Czech architecture. Among Linhart's important realizations are the Na Babě family villas in Prague and the former commercial high school in Dejvice.

Longen (pen name of Emil Artur Pitterman)
29 July 1885 (Pardubice)–24 April 1936 (Benešov)

Studied with F. Thiele at the Academy of Fine Arts in Prague from 1902 to 1906. Participated anonymously in the first exhibition of the Group of Eight; his works appeared there behind a curtain, since, as a student at the Academy, he was not allowed to exhibit. In 1909 and 1910, lived in Paris and Provence. In 1910, appeared as a cabaret performer in Berlin, under the name Artur Longen. In 1920, founded the Revolutionary Scene in Prague. In 1922, co-founded the Wilde Bühne in Berlin. Belonged to the anarchist circle of the Prague bohemians. Worked as an actor in Munich, Dresden, and Vienna; played Colonel Redl in a Czech sound feature film. As a visual artist, Longen's first influence was expressionism. To date, his work has not yet been sufficiently studied.

Augusta Nekolová-Jarešová
7 July 1890 (Jablonná near Neveklov)–15 September 1919 (Kutná Hora)

Studied at the School of Decorative Arts in Prague from 1904 to 1909. Created a number of paintings and illustrations for Jírasek's novel *Temno*. A posthumous exhibition of her work took place in 1922 at the Prague Municipal Hall. She designed posters only occasionally. Expressionism and cubism are the most noticeable influences in her work.

Otakar Novotný

Otakar Novotný
11 January 1880 (Benešov)–4 April 1959 (Prague)

Studied with J. Kotěra at the School of Decorative Arts in Prague; graduated in 1903, then worked in Kotěra's studio. Became a member of the Mánes Association of Plastic Artists in 1902 (was its chairman 1913–1915 and 1920–1932). From 1929 to 1954, was a professor at the School of Decorative Arts in Prague. Won the Grand Prix at the International Exhibition of Decorative Art in Paris. Was the state commissioner of exhibitions in Paris, Rome, and Vienna. Also did important theoretical work: in addition to articles in *Volné Směry*, *Styl*, *Výtvarná práce*, and *Architektura ČSR*, he wrote a monograph on Jan Kotěra. Notable in his early work was the Štenc house in Prague, influenced by the brick architecture of Berlage. Novotný was an important proponent of cubism in architecture and design; for instance, he designed the exhibition halls for the Association of Czech Accomplishment at the exhibition of the German Werkbund in Cologne. Another important commission was the design of the Mánes Association building (1927–1930), a notable example of Czech functionalism.

Antonín Procházka
5 June 1882 (Važany near Vyškov)–9 June 1945 (Brno)

Studied at the School of Decorative Arts in Prague from 1902 to 1904, and with V. Bukovac and H. Schwaigr at the Academy of Fine Arts until 1906. In 1906, he and Emil Filla took a study trip through Europe; he then took numerous other trips with his wife, Linka Scheithauerova. Participated in the first and second exhibitions of the Group of Eight, in 1907 and 1908, respectively. In 1909, his and Kubišta's paintings were not accepted for the 29th Exhibition of the Mánes Association of Plastic Artists, in which members of the Group of Eight were supposed to participate for the first time. In 1910, he and Kubišta were accepted into Mánes. In that year, he became a substitute teacher of drawing in Ostrava; he and his wife left Prague. (In 1924, he settled permanently in Brno.) In 1911, left Mánes and joined the Group of Plastic Artists. In 1912, participated in the exhibition of the Sonderbund in Cologne. Did not return to Mánes until 1922. After a fauvist-expressionist period, he was one of the first to react to cubism, through cubo-expressionist paintings and works bordering on analytical cubism; around 1915, his work approached orphism. In the 1920s, he turned to neo-primitivism and neo-classicism (best known are his paintings with encaustic elements). His cubist architecture and furniture designs comprise a remarkable chapter in his work.

Václav Špála
24 August 1885 (Žlunice near Nový Bydžov)–12 May 1946 (Prague)

Studied privately with F. Engelmüller, and with V. Bukovac and F. Thiele at the Prague Academy. In 1906, visited Dubrovnik several times to receive medical treatment, but also to paint. In 1909, joined the Mánes Association of Plastic Artists. In 1911, left Mánes and joined the Group of Plastic Artists. In that year, travelled to Paris. At the end of 1912, left the Group and returned to Mánes; became the association's chairman in 1936. In 1913, Špála was awarded the Turek Fellowship and travelled to Italy. In 1918, participated in the first exhibition of the Stiffnecked (the Tvrdošíjní group). In 1935, 1945, and 1947 (posthumously), important one-man exhibitions of his work were mounted. His work as a painter developed into a unique synthesis of the most important artistic movements of his time—fauvism, expressionism, futurism, and orphism. Occasionally, Špála got involved in certain areas of applied art: he designed posters, and in the 1920s he collaborated with the Artěl Co-operative (producing toys, painted glass, flyleafs with cubist ornamentation, suffused with the idea of a national style).

Rudolf Stockar

Josef Štěpánek
8 September 1889 (Horice)–4 April 1964 (Prague)

Architect and sculptor active in Prague. Studied at Plečnik's technical school, at a school specializing in stone-masonry in Hořice, and with J. Kotěra at the Academy of Fine Arts in Prague. Despite successes in important Prague competitions in the late 1920s and early 1930s (the Tyrš house in 1922, development of the Letná field in Prague in 1928—first prize; the sports stadium in Bráník in 1919—first prize; small apartments at Prague–Pankrác in 1930—first prize; special mention in the competition for the hospital in Motol), relatively few of his projects were realized. Those built included the Ke Klimentce family villa in Prague, the power station and a villa in Háj near Mohelnice, the lock in Predměřice, and the villa of the sculptor Pelikán in Olomouc. Štěpánek was a member of the Mánes Association of Plastic Artists, and belonged to the circle of contributors to the magazine *Stavitel.*

Rudolf Stockar
28 May 1886 (Doloplazy in Moravia)–19 December 1957 (Prague)

Studied architecture at the Czech Technical University from 1904 to 1909. In addition to his work as a freelance architect, he designed interiors, furniture, and various utilitarian objects. From 1915 to 1930, he was director of the Artěl Co-operative and was commissioner of the exhibition of applied art in Milan-Monza in 1923. At the outset, Stockar's work was somewhat influenced by cubism, but his decorative talent soon brought him to Art Deco. His life and work have so far not been adequately evaluated.

Jan Zrzavý
5 November 1890 (Vadin near Havlíčkuv Brod)–12 October 1977 (Prague)

Arrived in Prague in 1906 and studied at private schools; in 1907, registered at the School of Decorative Arts, and that same year travelled to Paris. In 1909, Zrzavý was expelled from the School of Decorative Arts and unsuccessfully tried for admission to the Academy. In 1911, he was the founding member of the Sursum association; and in 1912, he participated in the exhibition of this group at the Municipal Hall. In 1917, he resigned from the Mánes Association of Plastic Artists. In 1918, he participated in the first exhibition of the Stiffnecked (the Tvrdošíjní group). Zrzavý's first one-man show was mounted in 1918 at the Topic Salon. He organized the posthumous exhibition of Kubišta's work at the Topic Salon. In 1923, he became a member of the Umělecka beseda. He travelled frequently to France, especially to Brittany, and also to Italy. Zrzavý's first influence was symbolism, but he was soon quite attracted to other contemporary styles, such as fauvism, expressionism, cubism, and neo-classicism. He always maintained the originality and integrity of his own forms and symbols.

Chronology

1887
The Mánes Association of Plastic Artists is founded.

1896
Publication of the arts magazine *Volné směry* commences.

1898
First exhibition by Mánes; a programmatic essay on the nature and mission of modern art is published in *Volné směry*.

1902
The Auguste Rodin exhibition in Prague is organized by Mánes in an exhibition pavilion designed by J. Kotěra; it manifests the orientation of Czech modern art toward France and is a landmark in the history of Czech modern art.

1904
F. X. Šalda publishes an essay, "Problém národnosti v umění" (The Problem of Nationality in Art), in *Volné směry*.

1905
The Edvard Munch Exhibition in Prague is organized by Mánes; it is very controversial.

1907
April 18, opening of the first exhibition of the Group of Eight; showing are F. Feigl, E. Filla, M. Horb, O. Kubín, B. Kubišta, W. Nowak, A. Procházka, and, anonymously, A. Pitterman. Critical and public response is essentially negative; the only positive review is written by Max Brod ("Jaro v Praze" [Spring in Prague], *Die Gegenwart*, 1907).

October–November, the exhibition of French impressionists in Prague is organized by Mánes (works by Daumier, Boudin, Monticelli, Manet, Renoir, Monet, Pissarro, Sisley, Cézanne, Degas, Cassat, Vuillard, Bonnard, Gauguin, van Gogh, Bernard, Signac, and others).

Pablo Picasso paints *Les Demoiselles d'Avignon.*

1908
June–July, second exhibition of the Group of Eight at the Topic Salon, without the participation of M. Horb (d. 1907) and O. Kubín; new participants are L. Scheithauerová-Procházková and V. Beneš (Pitterman is not mentioned in the catalogue); again, a negative critical response.

Establishment of the Union of Architects of Mánes (members include J. Gočár, P. Janák, O. Novotný); the appearance of *Styl*, a monthly for architecture, the artistic crafts, and urban aesthetics, edited by Z. Wirth.

Founding of the Artěl Co-operative; following the example of the Wiener Werkstätte, its objective is the revival of applied arts. The proclamation of Artěl is signed by J. Benda, V. H. Brunner, J. Dyk, P. Janák, H. Johnová, J. Konůpek, and M. Teinitzerová. Janák designs the sales booth; a shop is established in 1909.

1909
February–March, Mánes organizes an exhibition of Bourdelle's work in Prague; the artist gives a lecture, garnering considerable response (especially to the call for architecturally built form).

Through the intervention of J. Kotěra, M. Jiránek, and J. Preisler, the members of the Group of Eight are invited to participate in the 29th Exhibition of Mánes.

Exhibition of Émile Bernard's work, organized by Mánes, elicits a negative response from the members of the Group of Eight; a negative review is written by B. Kubišta in *Volné směry.*

The third competition for the completion of the Old City Hall in Prague takes place; participants include P. Janák and J. Gočár, among others (design by the latter is received with particular indignation).

1910
February–March, the exhibition of Les Indépendants is organized by Mánes (showing, among others, Bonnard, Braque, Derain, van Dongen, Friesz, Maillol, Manguin, Marquet, Matisse, Redon, Vlaminck, Vallotton). Through a subscription in Prague's cafés, 800 crowns are raised for the purchase of Derain's painting *Bathing* from the exhibition; the work inspires the young artists and has a rather negative effect on the older ones. The young artists are mainly attracted to Braque. (Picasso is not represented at the exhibition.)

E. Filla and A. Matějček are editors of *Volné směry.*

P. Janák publishes his programmatic essay "Od moderní architektury k architektuře" (From Modern Architecture to Architecture) in *Styl*, vol. 2; it contains a critique of Otto Wagner's teaching.

1911
Works by the young artists raise controversy at the January exhibition of Mánes. E. Filla publishes an article, "O ctnosti novoprimitivismu" (On the Virtue of Neo-primitivism), in *Volné směry*, illustrated by Picasso; the situation at Mánes comes to a head and an open generational conflict ensues. Among those resigning from the association are V. Beneš, V. H. Brunner, E. Filla, J. Gočár, V. Hofman, P. Janák, O. Kubín, B. Kubišta, A. Procházka, and V. Špála. Many of them form the core of the Group of Plastic Artists, which commences activities on 20 November. Writers and theoreticians such as K. Čapek, F. Langer, and V. V. Štech also join the Group. J. Gočár is elected the Group's first chairman. B. Kubišta does not join the Group due to a difference of opinions. O. Kubín returns to Mánes almost immediately.

Umělecký měsíčník, the magazine of the Group, appears; it is edited by J. Čapek and an editorial board. In 1911–1912, it publishes Janák's fundamental theoretical essay "Hranol a pyramida" (The Prism and the Pyramid).

P. Janák designs his emblematic covered box with crystal-shaped finial.

March, Adolf Loos delivers his programmatic speech "Ornament a zločin" (Ornament and Crime) at the German Technical University in Prague.

Vincenc Kramář acquires a number of Cubist paintings, which form the basis of his famous collection (Picasso, Braque, Derain).

1912
January–February, first exhibition of the Group of Plastic Artists at the Prague Municipal Hall under the auspices of the Art Exhibition; organized by JUV, Mánes, and the Group of Plastic Artists. P. Janák is the architect of the exhibition.

P. Janák and F. Langer assume the editorial duties at *Umělecký měsíčník.*

The Prague Artistic Workshops (PUD) are established; the programme involves the revival of artistic industries. The principal initiators are J. Chochol, J. Gočár, and P. Janák.

Exhibition of the Sonderbund in Cologne (participants include V. Beneš, E. Filla, B. Kubišta, W. Nowak, and A. Procházka).

September–November, second exhibition of the Group of Plastic Artists. The exhibition is far more representative and varied. J. Gočár designs the exhibition. J. Chochol introduces his model of a villa below Vyšehrad, J. Gočár the spa building in Bohdaneč and the building called U černé Matky Boží (At the Black Mother of God). There is also an exhibition of paintings by Die Brücke.

At the end of the year, V. H. Brunner, the Čapek brothers, J. Chochol, V. Hofman, L. Šíma, and V. Špála resign from the Group after a disagreement.

Raymond Duchamp-Villon creates the "Cubist house" project, the only known analogue of Czech Cubist architecture.

1913
B. Kubišta goes on active service for economic reasons and, as an officer, leaves for Pula.

April, the third exhibition of the Group of Plastic Artists takes place at the Goltz Salon "New Art" in Munich (participants are V. Beneš, E. Filla, J. Gočár, O. Gutfreund, P. Janák, A. Procházka).

May, the fourth exhibition of the Group of Plastic Artists takes place at the Prague Municipal Hall. Paintings by Braque, Derain, Gris, and Picasso are shown, along with examples of folk art, exotic art, and ancient art, highlighting the relationship of the Group to these sources.

V. Beneš, E. Filla, O. Gutfreund, O. Kubín, and A. Procházka take part in the First German Autumn Salon in Berlin, organized by Walden's gallery Der Sturm. The magazine *Der Sturm* publishes avant-garde Czech graphic work and articles. (It continues to do so in later years.)

The fifth exhibition of the Group of Plastic Artists is mounted at Der Sturm gallery in Berlin.

The competition for Žižka's monument at Vítkov Hill in Prague. P. Janák and J. Gočár participate, both in collaboration with O. Gutfreund; L. Machoň participates in collaboration with J. Horejc; J. Kotěra participates with J. Štursa; V. Hofman, B. Feuerstein, and others also participate.

An exhibition of Italian futurists is mounted at the Mozarteum in Prague.

J. Chochol publishes the article "K funkci architektonického článku" (On the Function of the Architectural Link) in *Styl*, vol. 5.

1914

February, the Modern Art exhibition is organized by Mánes; the selection is made by the French poet A. Mercereau.

The sixth exhibition of the Group of Plastic Artists takes place at the Prague Municipal Hall. Gutfreund is mentioned as the director of the Group. The confrontation of the two exhibitions leads to another controversy on the nature of avant-garde art.

At J. Kotěra's instigation, the Association of Czech Accomplishment is founded.

May, the exhibition of the Werkbund takes place in Cologne. The architectural arrangement of the areas taken up by the Association of Czech Accomplishment, located in the Austrian Pavilion, is designed by O. Novotný. One of the rooms is dedicated to the work of PUD. The Czech exhibit receives a remarkable response.

The competition for Rieger's barrow at Kozákov, with participation by B. Feuerstein and V. Hofman.

Umělecký měsíčník ceases publication.

The Group of Plastic Artists dissolves.

1915

PUD publishes Štech's work *Čechische Bestrebungen um ein modernes Interieur* with the works of J. Gočár, P. Janák, and F. Kysela.

1916

The Exhibition of Czech Artistic Industry takes place at the Prague Municipal Hall, with the participation of PUD and Artěl.

1917

Members of the Group join Mánes.

1918

S. K. Neumann begins publication of the magazine *Červen.*

April, the first exhibition of the Tvrdošíjní (The Stiffnecked) at Weinert's Art Exhibition Hall (participants are J. Čapek, V. Hofman, R. Kremlička, O. Marvánek, V. Špála, J. Zrzavý).

November 27, B. Kubišta dies.

J. Kroha designs the interior of the Montmartre nightclub, the meeting place of the Prague avant-garde.

1920

May, the Association of Czech Accomplishment is revived as the Association of Czechoslovak Accomplishment; J. Gočár becomes chairman, P. Janák secretary. The Factual Programme of the Association of Czech Accomplishment is published, comprising seventeen points.

J. Kroha publishes a fundamental essay of principle, "O prostoru architektonickém a jeho mezích" (On Architectural Space and its Limits), in *Veraikon.*

October 5, the Devětsil Artistic Association is founded.

1921

The United Industrial Art Manufacturers is established, with the purpose of building standardized furniture and furnishing accessories.

J. Gočár creates a competition design for the Bank of the Czechoslovak Legions; the building is erected in 1922–1923 with sculptural decoration by O. Gutfreund and J. Štursa.

Artěl becomes a public company.

First exhibition of the Czechoslovak Artistic Industry at the Museum of Decorative Arts, organized by the Association of Czechoslovak Accomplishment; the architect of the installation is O. Novotný.

1922

First Spring Exhibition of Devětsil.

1923

The exhibition "Bazaar of Modern Art" at the Rudolfinum in Prague, organized by Devětsil.

The architecture section of Devětsil, Ardev, is established through the initiative of K. Teige and others; under the chairmanship of K. Honzík, it leans toward purism and rationalism and includes among its members B. Feuerstein, J. Fragner, J. Havlíček, J. Chochol, and E. Linhart.

The International Exhibition of Decorative and Industrial Art, Milan–Monza; R. Stockar is the curator of the exhibition.

Second Exhibition of Czechoslovak Industrial Art at the Museum of Decorative Arts, organized by the Association of Czechoslovak Accomplishment; installation by P. Janák and V. Ložek.

1924

The Association of Czechoslovak Accomplishment establishes a sample room with a permanent exhibition of works by its members at the Museum of Decorative Arts.

1925

In January, Le Corbusier lectures in Prague.

The International Exhibition of Decorative and Industrial Art in Paris; installation by O. Novotný and V. Ložek. J. Gočár receives the Grand Prix for the design of the Czechoslovak national pavilion. The Czechoslovak exhibition is successful, but it is also the final manifestation of Czech decorativism.

Bibliography

A – Books and Publications

Adlerová, 1983
Adlerová, A. *České uzité umění 1918–1938*. Prague, 1983.

Apollinaire, 1965
Apollinaire, G. *Méditations esthétiques. Les peintres cubistes*. Paris, 1965.

Apollinaire, 1974
Apollinaire, G. *O novém umění*. Prague, 1974.

Barr, 1936
Barr, A. *Cubism and Abstract Art*. New York, 1936.

Benešová, 1958
Benešová, M. *Josef Gočár*. Prague, 1958

Benešová, 1959
Benešová, M. *Pavel Janák*. Prague, 1959.

Benešová, 1984
Benešová, M. *Česká architektura v proměnách dvou století*. Prague, 1984.

Burckhardt, 1980
Burckhardt, L. *The Werkbund. Studies in the History and Ideology of the Deustcher Werkbund 1907–1933*. London, 1980.

Burkhardt & Lamarová, 1982
Burkhardt, F., and M. Lamarová. *Cubismo cecoslovacco—architetture e interni*. Milan, 1982.

Čapek, 1958
Čapek, J. *Moderní výtvarný výraz*. Prague, 1958.

Černousek, 1981
Černousek, T., V. Šlapeta, and P. Zatloukal. *Olomoucká architektura 1900–1950*. Olomouc, 1981.

Císařovský, 1962
Císařovský, J. *Otto Gutfreund*. Prague, 1962.

Císařovský, 1967
Císařovský, J. *Jiří Kroha a meziválečná avantgarda*. Prague, 1967.

Collective. *Bedřich Feuerstein*. Prague, 1936.

Cooper, 1970
Cooper, D. *The Cubist Epoch*. London, 1970.

de Micheli, 1964
de Micheli, M. *Umělecké avantgardy dvacátého století*. Prague, 1964.

Descargues, 1956
Descargues, P. *Le cubisme*. Paris, 1956.

Deutsche Form im Kriegsjahr. Die Ausstellung Köln 1914. Munich, 1915.

Filla, 1948
Filla, E. *O umění výtvarném*. Prague, 1948.

Fry, 1966
Fry, E. *Der Kubismus*. Cologne, 1966.

Gleizes, 1912
Gleizes, A., and J. Metzinger. *Du cubisme*. Paris, 1912.

Golding, 1959
Golding, J. *Cubism*. London, 1959.

Gordon, 1974
Gordon, D. E. *Modern Art. Exhibitions 1900–1916*. Monaco, 1974.

Gray, 1953
Gray, C. *Cubist Aesthetic Theories*. Baltimore, 1953.

Haas, 1968
Haas, F. *Moderná svetová architektúra*. Bratislava, 1968.

Habasque, 1959
Habasque, G. *Le cubisme*. Geneva, 1959.

Henry, 1920
Henry, D. *Der Weg zum Kubismus*. Munich, 1920.

Hyan, 1928
Hyan, J., and J. S. Weger. *V. Nekvasil 1868–1928*. Prague, 1928.

Janák, 1985
Janák, P., et al. *Acta UPM XIX Pavel Janák*. Prague, 1985.

Koula, 1940
Koula, J. E. *Nová česká architektura a její vývoj ve XX. století*. Prague, 1940.

Kramář, 1921
Kramář, V. *Kubismus*. Brno, 1921.

Krejcar, 1928
Krejcar, J. *L'architecture contemporaine en Tchécoslovaquie*. Prague, 1928.

Kroutvor, 1985
Kroutvor, J. *Prazský chodec*. Prague, 1985.

Kubišta, 1947
Kubišta, B. *Předpoklady slohu*. Prague, 1947.

Kudělka, 1966
Kudělka, Z. *Bohuslav Fuchs*. Prague, 1966.

Kupka, 1969
Kupka, F. *Úvahy*. Prague, 1969.

Kutal, 1959
Kutal, A. *Antonín Procházka*. Prague, 1959.

Lamač, 1988
Lamač, M. *Osma a Skupina výtvarnych umělcu 1907–1917*. Prague, 1988.

Lamač, 1989
Lamač, M. *Myšlenky moderních malířů*. Prague, 1989.

L'année 1913. Paris: Éditions Klinkgsieck, 1971.

Lukeš, 1985
Lukeš, Z., and J. Svoboda. *Praha 7–100 let moderní architektury 1885–1985*. Prague, 1985.

Mádl, 1922
Mádl, K. B. *Jan Kotěra*. Prague, 1922.

Maenz, 1974
Maenz, P. *Art Deco. Formen zwischen zwei Kriegen*. Cologne, 1974.

Margolius, 1979
Margolius, I. *Cubism in Architecture and the Applied Arts, Bohemia and France 1910–1914*. London-Vermont, 1979.

Nash, 1974
Nash, J. M. *Cubism, Futurism and Constructivism*. London, 1974.

Nebesky, 1923
Nebesky, N. M. *L'art moderne tchécoslovaque*. Paris, 1923.

Neuwirth, 1974
Neuwirth, W. *Österreichische Keramik des Jugendstils. Sammlung des Österreichischen Museums für angewandte Kunst Wien*. Munich, 1974.

Novotný, 1923
Novotný, O. *L'architecture et l'art décoratif moderne en Tchécoslovaquie*. Paris, 1923.

Novotný, 1947
Novotný, O. *Věci a lidé*. Prague, 1947.

Novotný, 1958
Novotný, O. *Jan Kotěra a jeho doba*. Prague, 1958.

Padrta, 1968
Padrta, J. *Ohniska české avantgardy II*. Prague, 1968 (unpublished manuscript).

Pečírka, 1931
Pečírka, J. *Otakar Novotný*. Geneva, 1931.

Pehnt, 1973
Pehnt, W. *Die Architektur des Expressionismus*. Stuttgart, 1973.

Rosenblum, 1960
Rosenblum, R. *Cubism and Twentieth Century Art*. London, 1960.

Šetlík, 1963
Šetlík, J. *Skupina umělců výtvarných/kandidátská práce/*. Prague, 1963.

Šetlík, 1989
Šetlík, J. *Otto Gutfreund, zázemí tvorby*. Prague, 1989.

Sharp, 1966
Sharp, D. *Modern Architecture and Expressionism*. New York, 1966.

Šlapeta, 1978
Šlapeta, V. *Praha 1900–1978. Průvodce po moderní architektuře.* Prague, 1978.

Sombart, 1912
Sombart, W. *Umělecký průmysl a kultura.* Prague, 1912.

Štech, 1915
Štech, V. V. *Čechische Bestrebungen um ein modernes Interieur—Werkbund Ausstellung in Köln 1914.* Prague, 1915.

Štech, 1921
Štech, V. V. *Včera. Výbor z článků 1910–1920.* Prague, 1921.

Štech, 1970
Štech, V. V. *Za plotem domova.* Prague, 1970.

Švácha, 1985
Švácha, R. *Od moderny k funkcionalismu. Proměny prazské architektury první poloviny 20. století.* Prague, 1985.

Svrček, 1960
Svrček, J. B. *Národní umělec Jiří Kroha.* Prague, 1960.

Syrový, 1967
Syrový, B., et al. *Architektura svědectví dob.* Prague, 1967.

Tafuri, 1967
Tafuri, M. F., and F. Dal Co. *Architettura contemporanea.* Milan, 1967.

Teige, 1966
Teige, K. *Vývojové proměny v umění.* Prague, 1966.

Teige, 1969
Teige, K. J. *Kroha, Avantgardní architektura.* Prague, 1969.

Trier, 1971
Trier, E. *Bildhaurer Theorien im 20. Jahrhundert.* Berlin, 1971.

Troy, 1983
Troy, N. J. *The De Stijl Environment.* London, 1983.

van de Velde, 1923
van de Velde, H. *Formule d'une esthétique moderne.* Paris, 1923.

Wagner, 1914
Wagner, O. *Moderne Architektur.* Vienna, 1914.

Wirth, 1928
Wirth, Z. *Josef Gočár—Hradec Králové.* Vienna, Berlin, 1928.

Wirth, 1930
Wirth, Z. *Josef Gočár.* Prague, Geneva, 1930.

Worringer, 1908
Worringer, W. *Abstraktion und Einfühlung.* Munich, 1908.

Zevi, 1951
Zevi, B. *Verso una architettura organica.* Turin, 1951.

B – Articles in Magazines and Anthologies

Behal, 1987a
Behal, V. "Artěl—das Atelier für Kunstgewerbe in Prag." *Zeitschrift für Kunst* 1 (1987): 116–130.

Behal, 1987b
Behal, V. "Das tschechische kubistische Kunstgewerbe 'Artěl-Atelier für die darstellende Arbeit in Prag' und die 'Prager Kunstwerkstätten.'" *Mitteilungen Wien*, no. 3 (1987).

Behal, 1988
Behal, V. "Czech Cubism in Arts and Crafts 'Artěl-Studio for the Plastic Arts in Prague' and 'the Prague Art Workshop.'" *Kosmas. Journal of Czechoslovak and Central European Studies* (Vienna) 17, nos. 1, 2 (1988).

Behne, 1914–1915
Behne, A. "Biologie und Kubismus." *Der Sturm* (Berlin) 5, nos. 11–12 (1914–1915): 68–71.

Benešová, 1966
Benešová, M. "O kubismu v české architektuře." *Architektura ČSR*, no. 3 (1966): 171–184.

Benešová, 1967
Benešová, M. "Architettura cubista in Boemia." *Casabella*, no. 314 (1967).

Benešová, 1969
Benešová, M. "Rondokubismus." *Architektura ČSR*, no. 5 (1969): 303–317.

Bentley, 1989
Bentley, G. B. "Cubist Architecture in Prague 1911–1921." *Arquitectonica* (Bilbao), no. 4, (1989).

Brožová, 1967
Brožová, J. "Artěl, mezník ve vývoji českého užitého umění." *Umění a řemesla*, no. 6 (1967): 202–208.

Burkhardt, 1978
Burkhardt, F. "Appunti sul cubismo nell architettura cecoslovacca." *Lotus International*, no. 20 (1978).

Čapek, 1908
Čapek, J. "Syntéza a výstava Osmi." *Snaha*, 21 July 1908.

Čapek, 1913
Čapek, K., and V. Hofman. "Indická architektura." *Styl* 5 (1913): 5–92.

Čapek, 1914–1915
Čapek, J. "Moderne Architektur." *Der Sturm* (1914–1915).

Chochol, 1913
Chochol, J. "K funkci architektonického článku." *Styl* 1, no. 5 (1913): 93–99.

Coppens, 1985
Coppens, B. "Jozef Peeters et ses contemporains. Dessins et œuvre graphique." In *Une collection de dessins, œuvres graphiques et documents de Jozef Peeters, Jan Cockx, Jos Leonard, Karel Maes et Edmond Van Dooren.* Koninklijke Musea voor schone Kunsten van Belgie, Museum voor Moderne Kunst, 1986.

Czagan, 1969
Czagan, F. "Kubistische Architektur in Böhmen." *Werk* 56, no. 2 (1969): 75–79.

Filla, 1911
Filla, E. "O ctnosti novoprimitivismu." *Volné směry* 15 (1911): 69–70.

Fuchs, 1910–1911
Fuchs, R. "Die neue Kunstanschauung." *Der Sturm* (Berlin) 1, no. 63 (1910–1911): 502.

Henderson, 1971
Henderson, L. D. "A New Facet of Cubism: The Fourth Dimension and Non-Euclidean Geometry Reinterpreted." *Art Quarterly* 34 (1971): 410–433.

Herbenová, 1973
Herbenová, O. "Česky nábýtek z let 1911–1915 ve sbírkách UPM v Praze." *Sborník statí na počest 70. výročí narození E. Pocheho. Acta UPM VIII-C, Commentationes* 1 (1973): 112–125.

Herbenová, 1977
Herbenová, O. "Česky kubisticky nábýtek." *Umění a řemesla*, no. 1 (1977): 13–18.

Hildebrand, 1909
Hildebrand, A. "Tesání do kamene." *Volné směry* 13 (1909): 367.

Hlušička, 1984
Hlušička, J. "Kubistická lekce." *Výtvarná kultura* 8, no. 6 (1984): 23–30.

Hofman, 1911–1912
Hofman, V. "Poznámky k nábytku." *Umělecký měsíčník* 1, no. 2 (1911–1912): 58.

Hofman, 1913
Hofman, V. "K podstatě architektury." *Volné směry* 17 (1913): 53–56.

Hofman, 1913
Hofman, V. "Nový princip v architektuře." *Styl* 1, no. 5 (1913): 13–24.

Hofman, 1914
Hofman, V. "Individualizující forma v architektuře." *Volné směry* 18 (1914): 241–253.

Hofman, 1918
Hofman, V. "O dalším vývoji naší moderní architektury." *Volné směry* 19 (1918): 193–206.

Holešovský, 1982
Holešovský, K. "Antonín Procházka a umělecká řemesla." *Umění a řemesla* (1982): 11–12.

Janák, 1908–1909
Janák, P. "Otto Wagner." *Styl* 1 (1908–1909): 41–48.

Janák, 1910
Janák, P. "Jak může být zachován Braunův dům?" *Za starou Prahu* 1, no. 8 (1910): 60–61.

Janák, 1910
Janák, P. "Od moderní architektury k architektuře." *Styl* 2 (1910): 105–109.

Janák, 1911–1912
Janák, P. "Proti náladě v architektuře." *Umělecký měsíčník* 1, no. 3 (1911–1912): 78–80, 105–107.

Janák, 1912
Janák, P. "Užitečnost uměleckého průmyslu." *Umělecký měsíčník* 5 (1912): 147–149.

Janák, 1912–1913
Janák, P. "Obnova průčelí." *Umělecký měsíčník* 2 (1912–1913): 85–95.

Janák, 1912–1913a
Janák, P. "O nábytku a jiném." *Umělecký měsíčník* 2 (1912–1913): 21–29.

Janák, 1912–1913b
Janák, P. "Hranol a pyramida." *Umělecký měsíčník* 2 (1912–1913): 162–170.

Janák, 1919
Janák, P. "Deset let Artělu." *Umění* 1, nos. 2–3 (1919): 253–254.

Jessen, 1915
Jessen, P. "Die deutsche Werkbund Ausstellung Köln 1914." In *Jahrbuch des Deutschen Werkbundes*, 1915, pp. 1–42.

Jiránek, 1909
Jiránek, M. "O českém malířství moderním." *Volné směry* 13 (1909): 199–210, 251–263.

Kabelka, 1913
Kabelka, J. "Ideové vztahy novodobé filosofie a moderních umění." *Volné směry* 17 (1913): 131–151.

Kratochvíl, 1917
Kratochvíl, Z. "Vzpomínky na Osmu a Skupinu." *Kmen* 1 (1917), no. 21: 1–2; no. 22: 1–4; no. 23: 3–5; no. 29: 6–7.

Kroha, 1920
Kroha, J. "O prostoru architektonickém a jeho mezích." *Veraikon* 6 (1920).

Kroutvor, 1987
Kroutvor, J. "Fenomén 1910." *Umění a řemesla* 4 (1987): 23–32.

Kubišta, 1909
Kubišta, B. "Émile Bernard." *Volné směry* 13 (1909): 80.

Lahoda, 1984
Lahoda, V., and K. Srp. "Příspěvek k rané teorii kubismu." *Umění* 5 (1984): 48–434.

Lamač, 1963
Lamač, M. "L'école cubiste tchèque." In *Lettres françaises*, 1963.

Lamač, 1965
Lamač, M. "Il cubismo ceco 1907–1917." *La Biennale di Venezia* 15, no. 159 (1965): 13–17.

Lamač, 1966–1967
Lamač, M. "Die tschechische kubistische Schule." *Die Kunst* 65 (1966–1967): 691–694.

Lamač, 1981
Lamač, M. "Kubismus." *Výtvarná kultura* 5, no. 4 (1981): 15–22.

Lamarová, 1978
Lamarová, M. "Cubismo ed espressionismo nell architettura e nel design." *Lotus International* (Milan), no. 20 (1978).

Lamarová, 1980
Lamarová, M. "Poznámky k vazbám kubismu a expresionismu v české kubistické architektuře a užitém umění." *Acta UPM XV, C2. Commentationes* (1980): 182–195.

Lamarová, 1982
Lamarová, M. "The Bohemian Cubist Avant-Garde—the Cubist Phenomenon in Architecture and Design." *Architectural Association Quarterly* 13, no. 2–3 (1982).

Lamarová, 1985
Lamarová, M. "Kubistické poučení v díle J.Krohy." *Umění a řemesla*, no. 2 (1985): 23–25.

Lipps, 1913a
Lipps, T. "Estetika prostorová." *Styl* 1, no. 5 (1913): 98–117.

Lipps, 1913b
Lipps, T. "Stylisace." *Styl* 1, no. 5 (1913): 127–139.

Lukeš, 1984
Lukeš, Z., and J. Svoboda. "Architekt Emil Králíček—zapomenutý zjev české secese a kubismu." *Umění* (1984): 441–449.

Matějček, 1910
Matějček, A. "Podzimní pařížský Salon." *Volné směry* 14 (1910): 34–40.

Nešlehová, 1975
Nešlehová, M. "K vrcholnému dílu Bohumila Kubišty." *Umění* 23, no. 4 (1975): 325–346.

Novotný, 1909–1910
Novotný, O. "Interieur, architekt a obecenstvo." *Styl* 2 (1909–1910): 67–70.

Novotný, 1912
Novotný, O. "Tvoření formy v architektuře." *Styl* 4 (1912): 3–14.

Novotný, 1914a
Novotný, O. "Shody a rozpory." *Volné směry* 18 (1914): 27–40.

Novotný, 1914b
Novotný, O. "Architektura symbolická, pomník a Žižkův pomník." *Volné směry* 18 (1914): 84–85.

Pistorius, 1969
Pistorius, M. "Kubistická architektura v Praze." *Staletá Praha* 4 (1969): 139–153.

Šalda, 1903
Šalda, F. X. "Etika dnešní obrody aplikovaného umění." *Volné směry* 7 (1903): 137.

Šalda, 1905
Šalda, F. X. "Boj o uměleckou kulturu." *Volné směry* 9, nos. 11–12 (1905): 291–306.

Šalda, 1907
Šalda, F. X. "Impresionism: jeho rozvoj, resultáty i dědictví." *Revue* 4 (1907): 70–159.

Šlapeta, 1986
Šlapeta, V. "Cubismo bohemia." *Quadernus* (Barcelona), nos. 169–170 (1986): 48–55.

Šlapeta, 1991
Šlapeta, V. "Der Prager Kubismus." *Daidalos* 3 (1991).

Švácha, 1980
Švácha, R. "Josef Chochol 1880–1980." *Umění* 28, no. 6 (1980): 545–552.

Taut, 1914
Taut, B. "Eine Notwendigkeit." *Der Sturm* (Berlin) 4, nos. 196–197 (1914): 174.

Teige, 1922
Teige, K. "Kubismus, orfismus, purismus e neokubismus v dnesní Paříži." *Veraikon* 8, nos. 3–4 (1922): 98.

Tschumi, 1975
Tschumi, B. "Questions of Space. The Pyramid and the Labyrinth (or Architectural Paradox)." *Studio International* 190, no. 977 (1975): 136–142.

van de Velde, 1913
van de Velde, H. "Amo-Credo." *Styl* 5, no. 1 (1913): 141–143.

Vokoun, 1966a
Vokoun, J. "Česky architektonický kubismus 1911–1914." *Domov*, no. 3 (1966): 24–30.

Vokoun, 1966b
Vokoun, J. "Bohemian Cubism." *The Architectural Review* 139, no. 829 (1966): 229-233.

Vondráčková, 1968
Vondráčková, S. "Artěl." *Tvar* 19, no. 3 (1968): 65–89.

Wirth, 1908
Wirth, Z. "Barokní gotika v Čechách z XVIII a 1. polovice XIX. století." *Památky archeologické a místopisné* 23 (1908): 128.

Wirth, 1929–1930
Wirth, Z. "Josef Gočár." *Volné směry* 17 (1929–1930): 252–256.

Worringer, 1912
Worringer, W. "Architektura a plastika z hlediska vcítění." *Styl* 4 (1912): 77–100.

List of Exhibitions

Prague, 1912a
Art Exhibition at the Municipal Hall near the Prasna vez. 1st hall—The Union of Plastic Artists; 2nd hall—Mánes Association of Plastic Artists; 3rd hall—the Group of Plastic Artists. Prague, 1912.

Prague, 1912b
2nd Exhibition of the Group of Plastic Artists. Intro. by V. V. Štech. Prague, Municipal Hall, 1912.

Prague, 1913
3rd Exhibition of the Group of Plastic Artists. Picasso, Braque, Derain, modern graphics, old graphics, folk and exotic art. Intro. by V. Beneš. Prague, Municipal Hall, 1913.

Cologne, 1914
Deutsche Werkbundausstellung. Catalogue published by the directorate of the exhibition. Cologne, Berlin, 1914.

Prague, 1914
4th Exhibition of the Group of Plastic Artists. Members and guests, drawings by Z. Kratochvil. Prague, Municipal Hall, 1914.

Prague, 1921–1922
First Exhibition of the Czechoslovak Artistic Industry. Intro. by P. Janák. Prague, Museum of Decorative Arts, 1921–1922.

Prague, 1926
Jan Kotěra 1871–1923. Intro. by Z. Wirth, Mánes Association of Plastic Artists. Prague, Municipal Hall, 1926.

Prague, 1935
Vlastislav Hofman—lifetime retrospective. Intro. by Josef Čapek. Prague, Umělecká beseda, 1935.

Prague, 1940
Toward a New Architecture. Prague, Museum of Decorative Arts, 1940.

Prague, 1943–1944
Architectural drawings by Jan Kotěra. Intro. by Z. Wirth. Prague, Czech Technical Museum, 1943–1944.

Hradec Králové, 1947
Josef Gočár, lifetime retrospective. Intro. by Z. Wirth. Hradec Králové, Municipal Museum, 1947.

Prague, 1947
Josef Gočár, lifetime retrospective. Intro. by Z. Wirth. Prague, Mánes Association of Plastic Artists, 1947.

Prague, 1948
Vlastislav Hofman, lifetime retrospective 1–2. Texts by M. Kouril and O. Stefan. Prague, Umělecká beseda, Slovanský ostrov, 1948.

Prague, 1956
Bedřich Feuerstein 1892–1936. Selected Works. Intro. by J. E. Koula. Prague, National Technical Museum, 1956.

Prague, 1960
Vlastislav Hofman. 50 Years of Plastic Work. Intro. by L. Hlaváček. Prague, Municipal Hall, 1960.

Brno, 1963
Jiří Kroha—Entry into the Avant-garde of the Twenties. Selected Works 1914–1923. Intro. by J. Císařovský. Brno, Ethnographic Institute of the Moravian Museum, 1963.

Prague, 1963
Czech Cubism. Texts by Č. Berka and F. Doležal. Prague, V. Kramář Gallery, 1963.

Prague/Brno, 1964
Jiří Kroha. Lifetime Retrospective of Work. Intro. by J. Císařovský. Prague/Brno, 1964.

Milan, 1964
Vlastislav Hofman—Opere 1905–1951. Intro. by A. Martini. Milan, Stendhal Gallery, 1964.

Paris, 1966
Paris–Prague 1906–1930. Texts by A. Hoffmeister, M. Lamač, and J. Zemina. Paris, Musée national d'art moderne, 1966.

Brno, 1967
Antonín Procházka. Drawings 1910–1925. Brno, House of Arts, 1967.

Prague, 1967a
Czechoslovak Architecture 20th Century. For the 9th Congress of UIA. Prague, Mánes Association of Plastic Artists, 1967.

Prague, 1967b
Bedřich Feuerstein. Architecture, Scenic Designs, Paintings. Intro. by A. Masaryková. Prague, V. Kramář Gallery, 1967.

Prague 1969
Czech Cubism. Intro. by Č. Berka. Prague, V. Kramář Gallery, 1969.

London, 1970
Czechoslovak Architecture of the 20th Century. London, RIBA, 1970.

Prague, 1971a
Josef Gočár. Exhibition of Architectural Designs. Intro. by M. Benešová. Prague, Fragner's Gallery, 1971.

Prague, 1971b
Jan Kotěra. Intro. by M. Benešová. Prague, Fragner's Gallery, 1971.

Prague, 1971c
The Czech Poster 1890–1914. Intro. by T. Vlček. Prague, 1971.

Prague, 1976
Czech Cubist Interior. Texts by O. Herbenová and M. Lamarová. Prague, Museum of Decorative Arts, 1976.

Prague/Olomouc, 1980
Otakar Novotný 1880–1959. Intro. by V. Šlapeta. Prague, Mánes, 1980. Olomouc, Gallery of the Plastic Arts, 1980.

Olomouc, 1981
The Beginnings of Modern Art in Moravia and Silesia. Intro. by P. Zatloukal. Olomouc, The Graphics Room, District Gallery of the Plastic Arts, 1981.

Prague, Vienna, Helsinki, 1982–1987
Pavel Janák 1882–1956—Architektur und Kunstgewerbe. Texts by A. Schweighofer, O. Herbenová, P. Janák, and V. Šlapeta. Prague, Emauzy, 1982; Vienna, Semper-Depot, 1984; Helsinki, Museum of Applied Arts, 1987.

Berlin, 1982
Vlastislav Hofman—Architektur des böhmischen Kubismus. Text by F. Burkhardt. Berlin, IDZ, 1982.

Brno, 1982
Antonín Procházka. Intro. by J. Hockeová. Brno, Moravian Gallery, 1982.

Malmö, 1982–1983
Filla, Gutfreund, Kubka och tjeckisk kubism. Texts by E. Högestatt, J. Kotalík, and M. Lamarová. Malmö, Konsthall, 1982/1983.

Jaroměř, 1983
Josef Gočár—The Cubism Interior. Text by O. Herbenová. Jaroměř, Municipal Museum, 1983.

Darmstadt, 1984
Tschechische Kunst 1878–1914. Auf dem Weg in die Moderne. Texts by J. Kotalík, et al. Darmstadt, Mathildenhöhe, 1984.

Prague, 1984
Modern Czech Poster 1918–1945. Intro. by J. Kroutvor. Prague, Museum of Decorative Arts, 1984.

Tokyo, 1984
Czechoslovakian Cubism—the World of Architecture, Furniture, and Craft. Texts by V. Čiháková-Noshiro, D. Hejdová, O. Herbenová, M. Lamarová, and J. Rous. Tokyo, Parco, 1984.

Innsbruck, 1985
Die Brünner Funktionalisten. Moderne Architektur in Brünn. Text by V. Šlapeta. Innsbruck, Institut für Raum-gestaltung, Technische Fakultät der Universität, 1985.

Prague, 1988
Prague Corners 1890–1940. Intro. by J. Kroutvor. Prague, Museum of Decorative Arts, 1988.

Darmstadt, 1988–1989
Tschechische Kunst der 20er + 30er Jahre. Avantgarde und Tradition. Texts by B. Krimmel, J. Kotalík, and collective. Darmstadt, Mathildenhöhe, 1988–1989.

Pardubice, 1990
The Glory of Cabarets in the History of the Poster. Pardubice, Gallery of Eastern Bohemia, 1990.

Index of Names

Photographic Credits

Antonín Alexander 135
Gerd von Bassewitz 120
François Burkhardt 99
Linda Burkhardt 99, 101, 105
Roland Engerisser 178, 179, 184, 185, 187, 190–194, 196–199, 201–205, 208–211, 214, 215, 221–226, 230–235, 242–247, 249–251, 253–261, 267, 268, 272, 275, 279, 282, 283, 288–294, 300–322
Jaroslav Franta 114, 138
Štěpán Grygar 85, 86, 87
Tibor Honty 84, 88, 89
Oldřich Karásek 118
Věra Kodetová 137
Miloš Pistorius 145
Chris Reinewald 115, 118
Jan Svoboda 53, 68, 69, 185, 192, 196, 198, 202, 222–224, 231, 235, 246, 248, 250, 251
Miloslav Šebek 16, 43, 123, 127, 128, 130, 132, 142, 144, 146, 148–177, 181, 182, 187, 190, 199, 200, 204, 206, 207, 213, 216–219, 225, 227–229, 234, 236, 237–241, 262, 263, 266, 268, 269, 271–281, 283–287, 295–299, 302
Pavel Štecha 10, 14, 20, 36, 55, 97, 114–119, 127, 128, 131, 133
Gabriel Urbánek 212, 215
Alena Urbánková 252, 294
Gerald Zugmann 107
Photographic Services, NG (Vladimír Fyman, Zdeněk Matyásko, Oto Palán, Milan Posselt, Čestmír Šíla) 25–33, 84–89
NTM Archive 34–37, 40–51, 59–61, 64, 73, 76, 77, 79, 91–94, 104, 116, 118–124, 126–135, 137–145, 180, 183, 276
Centre Pompidou Archive 103
Photographic Services, UPM 59, 103, 104, 248
Private archive 32, 39, 55, 98, 101, 103, 105, 106, 108, 144, 146, 244, 270
SÚPPOP Archive (Štenc Collection) 56–58, 62–67, 70, 71, 74, 75, 124–126, 130, 145–147, 184, 186, 188, 189, 191–193, 195, 200, 214, 220, 228, 280, 284, 297
Photographic Services of the Západočeská Gallery, Plzeň 27

Abbreviations and Explanatory Notes

MG	Moravian Gallery, Brno
NG	National Gallery, Prague
NTM	National Technical Museum, Prague
PUD	Prague Artistic Workshops
SÚPPOP	National Institute for the Protection of Heritage and the Environment
S.V.U.	Mánes Association of Plastic Artists
UPM	Museum of Decorative Arts, Prague

The dimensions of the exhibits are given in centimetres, beginning with height. The abbreviation "repr." identifies exhibits reproduced in the catalogue of the particular exhibition. No numbers of districts are given for buildings in Prague, due to the anticipated administrative redistribution.

Map Supplements

Existing Buildings

Bohemia and Moravia

Bohuslav Fuchs and Josef Štěpánek

6. Plhák brothers' hydro-electric power station, 1921
Háj near Mohelnice
7. Plhák brothers' villa, 1921
Háj near Mohelnice

Josef Gočár

9. Bohdaneč spa, 1911–1912
Spa grounds, Bohdaneč, Pardubice County
11. Family home for Mr. Bauer, 1912–1913
Libodřice, Kolín County
14. Anglo-Czechoslovak Bank, 1922–1923
Branch office in Hradec Králové, Masaryk Square, Čelakovský Street no. 642, Hradec Králové

Pavel Janák

16. Family home for Mr. Jakubec, 1911–1912
Marshal Koněv Street no. 157, Jičín
17. Family residence, 1912
Strachovská Street no. 331, Pelhřimov
18. Reconstruction of Dr. Fára's house
Masaryk Square no. 13, Pelhřimov 1913
19. Villa for Dr. Pick, veterinarian
Jaroměřice 1920–1921
20. Crematorium, 1921–1923
Pod břízkami Street no. 990, Pardubice

Otakar Novotný

23.
Managers' and workers' residences for the "Domovina" (Homeland) building co-operative, 1920
U Domoviny Street no. 1, General Jaroš Avenue, nos. 18, 20, 22, 24, 26, Znojmo

Rudolf Stockar

25. Reconstruction of and addition to Mrs. Lipčík's house, 1918–1919
Zelená Street no. 80, Olomouc–Nová ulice

Hradec Králové 14
Bohdaneč 9
Pardubice 20
Háj u Mohelnice 6.7
OSTRAVA
Olomouc 25
BRNO
Jaroměřice 19
Znojmo 23
BRATISLAVA

Existing Buildings

Prague

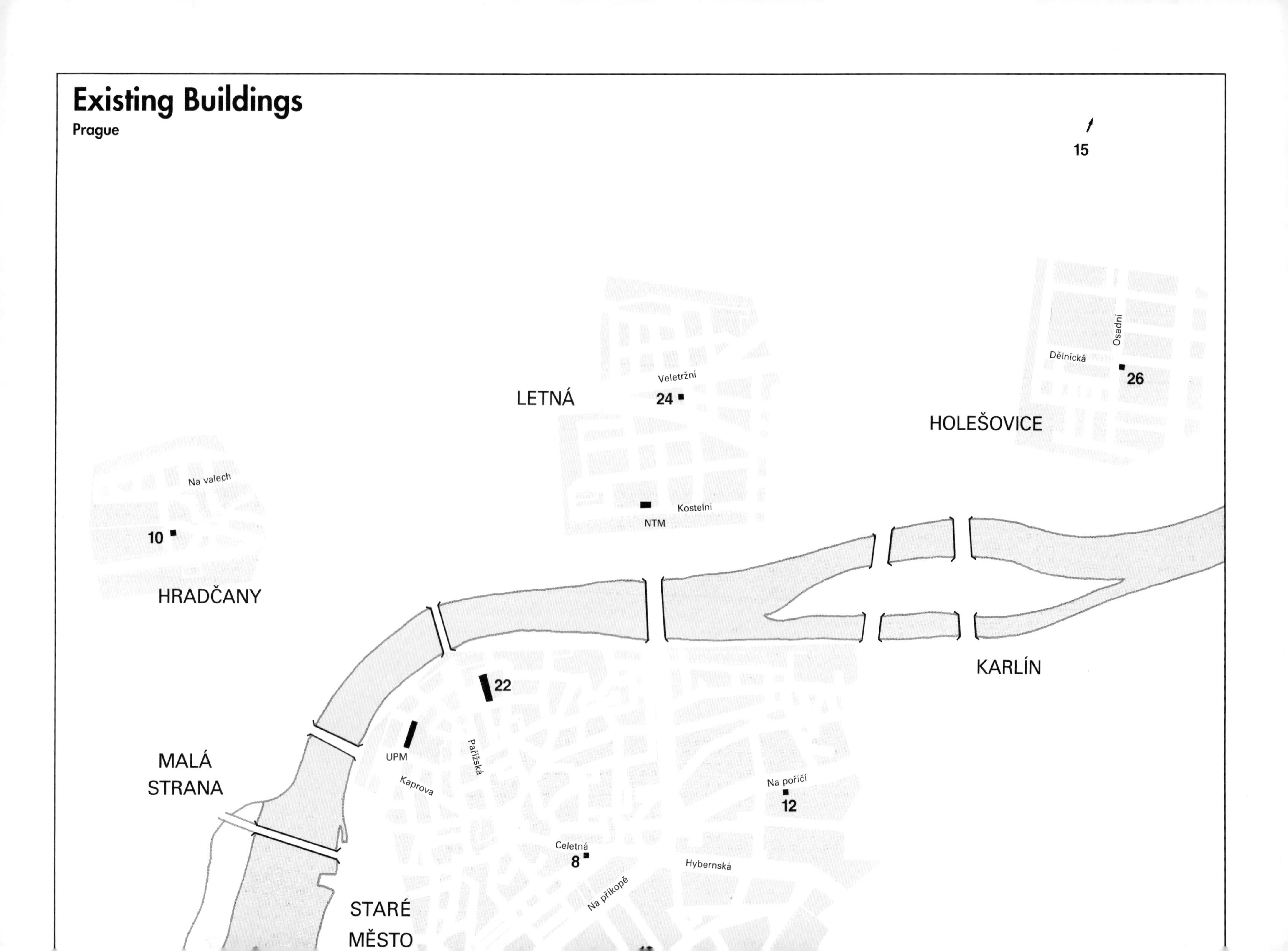

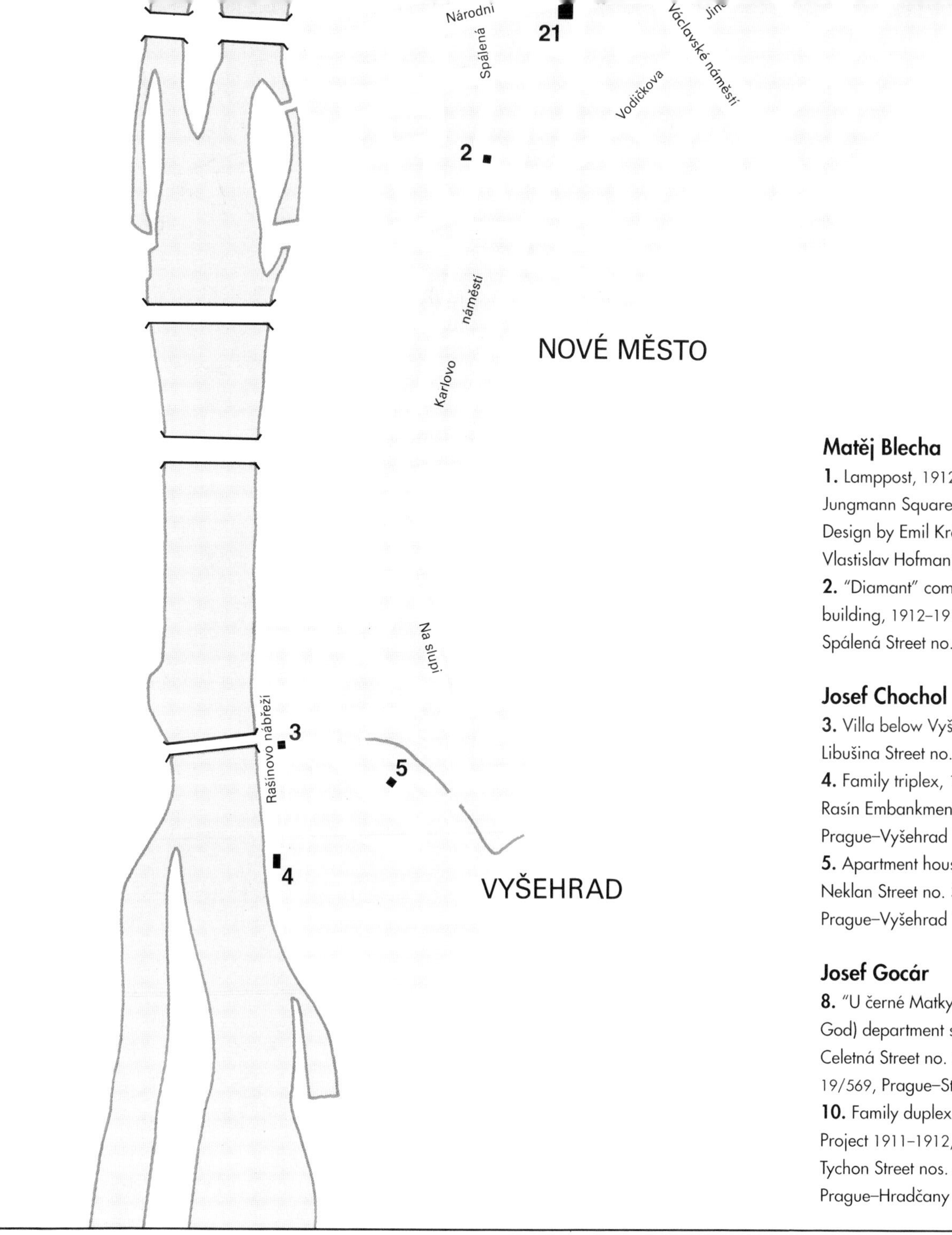

Matěj Blecha

1. Lamppost, 1912
Jungmann Square, Prague–Nové Město
Design by Emil Králíček (formerly attributed to Vlastislav Hofman)
2. "Diamant" commercial and apartment building, 1912–1913
Spálená Street no. 4/82, Prague–Nové Město

Josef Chochol

3. Villa below Vyšehrad, 1911–1912
Libušina Street no. 3/49, Prague–Vyšehrad
4. Family triplex, 1912–1913
Rasín Embankment nos. 6/42, 8/47, and 10/71 Prague–Vyšehrad
5. Apartment house
Neklan Street no. 30/98, Přemysl Street no. 11, Prague–Vyšehrad 1913

Josef Gocár

8. "U černé Matky Boží" (At the Black Mother of God) department store, 1911–1912
Celetná Street no. 34, Ovocný trh Street no. 19/569, Prague–Staré Město
10. Family duplex
Project 1911–1912, realized 1912–1913
Tychon Street nos. 4/268 and 6/269, Prague–Hradčany

12. Bank of the Czechoslovak Legion
Design 1921, realized 1922–1923
Na poříčí Street no. 24/1046, Prague–Nové Město
Collaboration with sculptors Jan Štursa and Otto Gutfreund
13. The Bank of Brno
Project 1921, realized 1922–1923
Panská Street no. 9, Jindřišská Street no. 15/1308, Prague–Nové Město
Collaboration with sculptor Karel Dvořák

Vlastislav Hofman

15. Cemetery Entrance with Gate and Kiosks, 1912–1913
Ďáblická Street, Prague 8—Ďáblice

Pavel Janák

21. "Riunione Adriatica di Sicurtá" commercial and department-store building, 1922–1924
Jungmann Street no. 31/36, Prague–Nové Město
Collaboration with Josef Zasche

Otakar Novotný

22. Apartment buildings for the Teachers' Housing Co-operative, 1917–1919
Elišky Krásnohorské Street nos. 10, 12, 14/123, 1021, 1037, Prague–Staré Město
24. Teachers' Co-operative apartment building, 13923
Kamenická Street no. 35/811, Prague–Holešovice

Rudolf Stockar

26. Office building for F. J. Materna's factory, 1920
Ďelnická Street no. 20, Osadní Street no. 10/313, Prague–Holešovice
27. Reconstruction of a commercial and apartment building, 1920–1921
October 28th Street no. 8, Jungmann Square no. 4/764, Prague–Nové Město